Prisons and Prison Life

Prisons and Prison Life

Costs and Consequences

JOYCELYN M. POLLOCK
Texas State University—San Marcos

SECOND EDITION

New York   Oxford

OXFORD UNIVERSITY PRESS

Oxford University Press is a department of the University of Oxford. It furthers the University's
objective of excellence in research, scholarship, and education by publishing worldwide.

Oxford   New York
Auckland   Cape Town   Dar es Salaam   Hong Kong   Karachi
Kuala Lumpur   Madrid   Melbourne   Mexico City   Nairobi
New Delhi   Shanghai   Taipei   Toronto

With offices in
Argentina   Austria   Brazil   Chile   Czech Republic   France   Greece
Guatemala   Hungary   Italy   Japan   Poland   Portugal   Singapore
South Korea   Switzerland   Thailand   Turkey   Ukraine   Vietnam

For titles covered by Section 112 of the US Higher Education Opportunity Act,
please visit www.oup.com/us/he for the latest information about pricing
and alternate formats.

Published by Oxford University Press.
198 Madison Avenue, New York, New York 10016
http://www.oup.com

Oxford is a registered trademark of Oxford University Press.

Library of Congress Cataloging-in-Publication Data
Pollock, Joycelyn M., 1956-
Prisons and prison life : costs and consequences / by Joycelyn M. Pollock.—2nd ed.
    p. cm.
Includes bibliographical references.
ISBN 978–0–19–978325–0 (alk. paper)
1. Prisons—United States.   2. Imprisonment—United States.   I. Title.
HV9471.P648 2013
365'.973—dc23
2012012543

9 8 7 6 5 4 3 2 1
Printed in the United States of America
on acid-free paper

To Eric and Greg, as always,

and

To John Irwin, RIP

BRIEF CONTENTS

CONTENTS

PREFACE

꧁

I want to thank Oxford University Press for the opportunity of updating my 2004 book. In the intervening seven years, some things have changed and some things remain the same. What has changed is that the country's use of incarceration is now being scrutinized more closely by politicians, policy makers, and the public at large. Just as the dot-com meltdown and consequent state budget cutting in the early 2000s spurred a focus on alternatives to imprisonment, the more recent economic catastrophe has also created efforts to reduce prison populations. This has resulted in some states actually reducing their prison admissions for the first time in 30 years. Some other things remain the same. Prisons still harbor individuals who should not be there. Programming is still at lower levels than what the public believes occurs and recidivism is still high.

NEW TO THIS EDITION

- Expanded discussion of the rapid expansion of incarceration over the last few decades
- Prison population numbers, recidivism findings, and all other statistics have been fully updated
- Each chapter now includes online resources for further reading
- Latest findings on prison sexual assault have been included.

In this edition, I have left the basic structure of the book the same. I have chosen to keep the book at 10 chapters. I have done this because the chapters did not seem to logically break apart in any other way. Some chapters are a bit longer than others and I leave it to the instructor as to how to divide them for 14 week classroom coverage. The major structural change has been to drop the drugs chapter and replace it with a more expansive discussion of the reasons behind the increased use of incarceration in the last several decades. While drug prosecution policies have certainly played a major role, there are other contributing elements that have been given more attention in this edition. The new chapter is organized to discuss, in turn, all of the suggested reasons why this country uses imprisonment six times more than our "sister countries" in Europe. Some of the information in the old chapter has been moved to a more logical location, for instance, the section on drug treatment programs is now in the chapter on prison programs (Ch. 5). There has been some minor reordering of chapters to improve the flow, for instance, prison programs (Ch. 5) now comes after the chapter on prisoners (Ch. 4), but before the chapter on the prison subculture (Ch. 6). The chapter on prisoners' rights (Ch. 8) now comes after the chapter on women's prisons (Ch. 7).

I have updated prison population numbers, recidivism findings, and all other statistics whenever possible. I have also included information on current federal initiatives, such as Crimesolutions.gov which offers the best research on correctional programming. In fact, in response to reviewers' comments, each chapter offers some relevant websites for instructors and/or students to browse for other information. More recent evaluations of private prisons and prison programming have been included. Current prisoner rights cases have been included, such as *Brown v. Plata*, a Supreme Court case decided in May of 2011.

Since the 2004 edition of this book, the Prisoner Rape Elimination Act (PREA) has resulted in large scale prisoner surveys on prison sexual assault. Findings from the latest survey are provided, along with a number of other findings from other studies. The author has been involved in a PREA research study funded by NIJ and awarded to Dr. Barbara Owen. This study, available through NIJ, explored the gendered nature of prison violence and prison sexual violence. Some of the results of this study have been incorporated in the chapter on women's prisons.

The final chapter covers not only reentry and parole, but also reiterates some of the initiatives taking place around the country that seek to reduce the reliance on prison, including the Justice Reinvestment strategies. This book maintains an approach characterized as a critical analysis of this country's use of imprisonment; however, there is a concerted effort to illustrate both sides of all issues. For instance, conflicting research exists as to how much, or even whether, imprisonment has contributed to the crime drop. Both sides of this debate are represented with a resolution that emphasizes the most unbiased research. Throughout the book, every effort has been made to provide the most current information possible.

ACKNOWLEDGMENTS

Once again, I want to thank Sarah Calabi and Oxford University Press for allowing me the opportunity to update and revise this book. I appreciate the comments I have received over the years from those who have used the book in courses, and am grateful that I can now respond to the requests for a more current book. I would also like to acknowledge Barbara Owen, who gave me the opportunity to get back into prison through her NIJ funded research project on gendered violence. Our many hours in the prisons, talking to female prisoners and correctional staff were extremely rewarding and I am proud of the work we have done in the NIJ report *Gendered Violence and Safety in Women's Prisons*. It was obviously beneficial to this current edition to have had this recent research experience. It was also a great pleasure working with her, James Wells, Bernadette Muscat, and Stephanie Torres. I want to thank Matthew Herrera, my very able graduate assistant who helped me track down sources and suggested appropriate websites. I also must thank Quint Thurman for his able administration of the Criminal Justice Department here at Texas State University—San Marcos. He makes the difficulties of combining research/writing and teaching a bit easier.

Every book revision is partially influenced by comments from reviewers. The reviewers for this edition provided some very helpful comments and I hope that I have responded adequately to their suggestions for improvement. They are Valerie J. Callanan, University of Akron; Janet T. Davidson, Chaminade University of Honolulu; Dawna Komorosky, California State University—East Bay; Shelley Johnson Listwan, Kent State University; Jody L. Sundt, Portland State University; Robert Swan, University of South Dakota; and others.

CHAPTER 1

⤳

Prisons: Then and Now

According to the Bureau of Justice Statistics, in 2010, there were 1,605,127 individuals incarcerated in state and federal prisons in the United States (Guerino, Harrison, and Sabol 2011). The incarceration rate today is 497 per 100,000, which is almost five times what the rate was in 1980 (139 per 100,000). The United States also incarcerates five to eight times more of its citizens per capita than does any Western European nation (Abramsky 2002). How did we get here? What has occurred in the last 30 years to make incarceration the preferred punishment for offenders?

We will take a closer look at the incredible increase in the use of prison in this country and examine some reasons behind this phenomenon in chapter 2. In this chapter, however, we will briefly revisit the history of prisons in the United States. By understanding the philosophy behind imprisonment and the goals assigned to prisons since the birth of this country, we may better understand why, today, we have become labeled by some as the "Gulag Nation."

THE PURPOSE AND FUNCTIONS OF PRISONS

Why do we punish individuals who commit a crime? "Because they deserve it" is one answer (retribution), as is, "so they won't do it again" (specific deterrence) or "so others won't do as they did" (general deterrence). The connection between these rationales and the infliction of punishment was quite clear when punishments were public and corporal (meaning they were physical). With the rise of imprisonment, however, the rationale for punishment is less clear. Prison is unlike earlier forms of punishment in that the offender is hidden from public view, and the pain inflicted is unknown to and unseen by all except those immediately connected with the prisoner himself. Further, in addition to the earlier rationales of retribution and deterrence, the rationale of reform or rehabilitation emerged; it was proposed that prison, or at least prison programs, were "helping" rather than "hurting" those within. This evolution in the philosophy behind the use of prison has, arguably, led to the overuse of prisons. It has certainly led to confusion over the goals of imprisonment. Can we punish and "help" the offender at the same time? If prisons rehabilitate, how can they be a deterrent? Further, how do we measure out the amount of punishment offenders deserve when everyone experiences prison differently? The only thing we know for sure is that today's prisons incapacitate; in fact, the number of people incapacitated is unprecedented.

The use of imprisonment as punishment is a relatively recent occurrence, although there were instances even in ancient times when individuals were imprisoned as punishment (Johnston 2009). Historically, communities punished offenders through the use of corporal punishment, fines, or banishment. Before the mid-1700s, people in this country were held in jail typically only until a debt or fines could be paid, or until some form of corporal punishment could be carried out. Imprisonment *as* punishment was not widely utilized until late in the 18th century.

In the colonial era, communities were small and close-knit. Offenders were usually dealt with through some form of public humiliation. The stocks and pillory, whipping, the ducking stool, and other public punishments were used to inflict injury and humiliate the offender. If this shame did not deter him or her, the individual was banished. Even though most felonies could be punishable by death, execution was usually reserved for repeat or serious offenders. Generally, communities defended themselves against violent offenders by banishment or execution and against property offenders by banishment, fines, or corporal punishment. The offender might be incarcerated in a gaol (jail), but only until some other form of punishment was carried out, or until the individual, or his relatives, paid the fine imposed (Barnes 1987). The purpose of punishment during this time was simply general deterrence and incapacitation.

In the late 1700s, older forms of punishment, which depended on public humiliation, became less effective. Cities were too big, communities were less cohesive, and populations were mobile—new forms of social control were necessary. The congregate care facility was created to control and provide services to larger numbers of people (Rothman 1971/1990). Orphanages were used to house orphaned or abandoned youngsters; hospitals were created to house the sick and infirm; and mental institutions were opened to take care of those who were unable to function. Workhouses or poorhouses ("almshouses" in England) were used to control and house indigents who had no work or means of making a living. Houses of correction were created to "correct" poor vagrants by teaching them a trade to change their life of idleness to one of productive work (Rothman 1971/1990).

One important principle of this period is known as the "principle of less eligibility." Jeremy Bentham (1748-1832) is credited with this utilitarian concept that in order to make sure men worked, paupers must be treated in a way that made their life more miserable than the lowest paid worker (Sieh 1989). Applied to the concept of the poorhouse (or workhouse), it is understandable that the poor who found themselves within were treated almost as if they were criminal because to do otherwise was to risk all workers deciding that living in a poorhouse was preferable to working. We see this principle still operating today in the public's belief that prisoners have it "too easy," for if they are too comfortable in prison, there is no incentive to stay out. The public is usually averse to college education or anything other than basic medical care for prisoners, again, owing to the idea that their lives should be worse than the poorest person on the outside.

The workhouse, house of correction, and jail housed a similar and overlapping population: the poor who might also be minor criminals. Communities controlled vagrants by forcing them to go to workhouses. Workhouses were run with a rigorous system of discipline in place, and inmates were sent there at times against their will. Alternatively, a poor vagrant who had committed minor crimes to survive would be sent either to a house of correction or a gaol. In many cases, there was not much difference between these institutions. Houses of correction were modeled after Bridewell Palace (1556), which was used to house minor offenders. In time, any house of correction came to be known as a "bridewell." Inmates were petty offenders, but also might be lepers, disobedient children, orphans, or the mentally ill. Houses of correction were established in Massachusetts (1632), Pennsylvania (1682), and New York (1736) among other locations (Johnston 2009).

Philadelphia's original Walnut Street Jail, built in 1773, adhered to the architecture of the time; it included large rooms where all prisoners were housed together. Quaker reformers, including Benjamin Rush and others, were appalled at the debauchery and inhumane conditions they found in Walnut Street and other jails. The group formed the Philadelphia Society for Alleviating the Miseries of Public Prisons (now called the Pennsylvania Prison Society). This group was successful in having their ideas adopted when an addition to the jail was built in 1790. This new building had small individual cells instead of large common rooms in order for inmates to contemplate their sins in silence. The name of the institution was changed from jail to penitentiary to reflect the new goals of religious penitence and redemption. The reformers championed such concepts as classification and reformation through penitence (Garland 1990; Hirsch 1992). Women and men were separated, children were kept separate from adults, and the sick were isolated so they did not infect the healthy. Also, the Pennsylvania legislature passed a new criminal code that abolished the death penalty for all crimes except murder and imposed imprisonment instead of corporal punishment for many crimes (Barnes 1987).

Reformers in Pennsylvania were no doubt influenced by John Howard (1726-1790), who toured prisons and gaols and wrote about what he saw in the late 1700s. He advocated more enlightened treatment of prisoners, promoting two institutions: the Hospice of San Michele in Rome, which housed young male offenders under a strict regimen of work and penance, and the Maison de Force at Ghent, Belgium, where four sections separately housed male offenders, beggars, women, and unemployed laborers and abandoned children (Johnston 2009). Howard's views came to influence the development of penitentiaries in this country. Clergymen, politicians, and educators all believed that the penitentiary was the perfect place to instill the characteristics of sobriety, regularity, and piety. The only influence permitted was the Bible and a religious guide to aid in finding salvation. After a due period of "penitence," the individual was expected to emerge as a new person (Johnson 1997).

Unfortunately, overcrowding and corruption displaced the goals of the reformers within the space of a few years. Johnston (2009) notes that by 1817 it was not uncommon to have 30 to 40 men in one sleeping room in the Walnut Street Jail, and observers noted that alcohol, riots, and escapes were common. However, the ideals of the Walnut Street Jail were carried over to, and came to full fruition at, the Eastern State Penitentiary on the outskirts of Philadelphia. By then, however, there was a competing model of imprisonment, thus beginning the rivalry between the Philadelphia and Auburn models.

THE PHILADELPHIA AND AUBURN MODELS

The concepts of the Walnut Street Jail were carried over to the Eastern State Penitentiary, opened in 1829, but not completed until 1836. Each inmate lived in a separate cell with a separate exercise yard. The individual was kept completely separate from outside influences and from other inmates. Meanwhile, in 1816 the New York legislature approved funds to build Auburn Penitentiary, and it was completed in 1823 (Barnes 1987). This facility adopted some of the principles of the Pennsylvania model and rejected others. The biggest difference was that inmates worked, ate, and exercised together, and were only in individual cells at night. Thus, cells were much smaller. Industrial manufacturing replaced the individual handicrafts that inmates worked at in the Philadelphia penitentiary.

> Everything passes in the most profound silence, and nothing is heard in the whole prison but the steps of those who march, or sounds proceeding from the workshops…the silence within these vast walls…is that of death. We felt as if we traversed catacombs; there were a thousand living beings, and yet it was a desert solitude. (Alexis de Tocqueville and Gustave Auguste de Beaumont describing Auburn Prison in 1831, as cited in Rothman 1971: 575)

There were more similarities than differences between the "Philadelphia" (or "separate") system and the "New York" (or "congregate care") system. In both institutions, outside influences were kept to a minimum and silence was maintained to reduce "contamination" from other inmates. In Pennsylvania, this was done physically by isolating the prisoner's body; in Auburn, it was done through a harsh punishment system that deterred talking, even when inmates worked side by side. If inmates persisted, they were placed in solitary confinement. Critics of the use of solitary confinement noted that it seemed to drive men insane. Even the warden of Auburn had misgivings about the use of extended solitude.

> There is no doubt that uninterrupted solitude tends to...harden the heart, and induce men to cultivate a spirit of revenge, or drive them to despair....A degree of mental anguish and distress may be necessary to humble and reform the offender; but carry it too far, and he will become either a savage in his temper and feelings, or he will sink in despair. (Gray 1847: 41)

Rothman (1971/1990) describes the shared vision of the two penitentiaries as the "trinity" of separation, obedience, and order. The Pennsylvania model and the New York model were compared and contrasted, becoming the topic of editorials, debates, and public speeches. The subject held much interest for Europeans as well, and Beaumont and de Tocqueville's description of American penitentiaries (1833/1964), written for Europeans, has been a classic source of prison history. In the 1800s, for traveling Europeans, the two prisons were as much a part of the "American Grand Tour" as the buffalo, "wild" Indians, and the transcontinental railroad (Rothman 1971/1990).

The Civil War interrupted the ongoing controversy over which system was better at reforming inmates; however, after the war, newfound interest in the debate led to the National Prison Congress in 1870. Here reformers and practitioners met and created a Declaration of Principles that would be the agenda for corrections for the next 100 years.

> Could we all be put on prison fare, for the space of two or three generations, the world would ultimately be the better for it. Indeed, should society change places with the prisoners, so far as habits are concerned, taking to itself the regularity, and temperance, and sobriety of a good prison, then the grandiose goals of peace, right, and Christianity would be furthered. (Reverend James B. Finley, quoted in Rothman, 1971: 84–88)

Whether one system or the other was "better" at reforming inmates was not the factor that ended the debate—it was economics. The New York (Auburn) model was cheaper to build and cheaper to maintain. Further, it could actually be profitable, since the inmates could be put to work at something other than handicrafts. Some early prisons were income producers for the state. Most were at least self-sufficient in the early years. Interestingly, the Philadelphia model became the more common form of imprisonment in Europe while the Auburn system became the model for most prisons in this country.

At the 1870 Prison Congress, a new model for imprisonment was born—the reformatory (Reichel 1997; Walker 1980). Zebulon Brockway, an active participant in the Prison Congress, implemented the idea of classification, in which the inmates earned privileges of liberty, education, and training, at the Elmira Reformatory in Elmira, New York, in 1876 (Sullivan 1990). Young offenders, who could benefit from a strict regime of disciplined living and education, were targeted for the new reformatory. Discipline was harsh. Brockway believed in earning liberties, but he was known for inflicting harsh punishments as well (Sullivan 1990). Along with the idea of the reformatory came graduated release, what we know today as parole. In this way, inmates could be rewarded for good behavior, and the possibility of release encouraged them to reform their behavior.

The penitentiary and the reformatory are still with us today. Most prisons have been built following the Auburn congregate style, but the Philadelphia system can be seen in today's "super max" prisons, which will be described in more detail in chapter 3. While the penitentiary and reformatory became the models for prison architecture in the North, the southern states followed a different course. Because so much of the South's economy depended on agriculture, the prison "farm" emerged. Northern prisons were also built in rural areas with a great deal of cultivated acreage, but prison industry became the more important economic contribution as states built prisons throughout the 1800s and early 1900s. Northern states either produced goods for sale or leased the institution and/or prisoner labor to private industry. In the South, prisoners were much more likely to work in fields than in prison "factories."

After the Civil War, prisoners, in effect, took the place of slaves, as leased labor or, later, on prison farms (Johnson 1997). The "leased labor" system refers to the contracts between landowners and states whereby landowners fed and housed prisoners in return for their labor. As can be imagined, in some cases conditions were horrific, with landowners literally working the prisoners to death. In fact, the average life span of a prisoner during this time was no more than six or seven years (Johnson 2002: 44). Periodic exposés of the terrible conditions that these prisoners lived under spurred some oversight and change, but the system continued in some states well into the 1940s (Stone 1997). As state prison systems reacted to public antipathy toward the leased labor system, they stopped leasing prisoner labor and, instead, undertook agricultural enterprises themselves. Thus, at the turn of the century, we had a dual prison system in this country: northern prisons typically followed a "factory model" while those in the South continued to be largely agricultural "prison farms."

1900–1950s

During the early 1900s through the 1950s, prisons enjoyed some improvement in conditions, but virtually no public attention was directed to them throughout both World Wars. Typically, prison wardens were expected to keep the prisons out of the paper. If they managed to do that, they were considered successful.

Inside the prisons, nothing much was happening. According to Robert Johnson, "Big Houses," his term for this era's penitentiaries, were "a world populated by people seemingly more dead than alive, shuffling where they once marched, heading nowhere slowly." (Johnson 2002: 42).

The most important reform of the early 1900s was the abolishment of the lease labor system throughout the South (Gottschalk 2006; Zimmerman 1987). To keep inmates occupied, the states themselves undertook massive agricultural cultivation and, also, instituted chain gangs for road work. Not only were these tasks considered cost effective for states, the idea of convicts exercising in the fresh air was considered a progressive reform from idleness or the horrific conditions associated with the lease labor system. Southern reformers were also successful in convincing prison administrators to bring women and youth in from the fields and segregate them from male inmates. Women still worked, but they tended "kitchen gardens" and did the laundry rather than work alongside men in the cotton fields. Young people were also removed from the fields. In the early 1900s, offenders as young as nine were sent to prisons for adults. This gradually changed as states began building reformatories.

Another reform in the first half of the century was the gradual abolishment of some types of corporal punishment. Even though the lash continued to be used well into the 1960s, other forms of punishment, such as the "crucifix," "yoke," and shower bath, were abolished (Zimmerman 1987). One other reform was conditional release. By 1930, many states had some form of release for good behavior or commutation of sentence.

We have very few descriptions of the prisoner world in the early part of this century. Johnson (1997; 2002) provides some historical context, as does Rothman (1971/1990). Life for those in early penitentiaries was harsh. Conditions were, for the most part, abysmal, and there was pervasive brutality and racism. Inmates tended to be older, with long criminal careers. There was a large gulf between guards and inmates that neither side breached. Each knew their place and both sides valued predictability and order. A large difference between these early prisons and today was that the prisons were smaller and there were not many inmates incarcerated. Rarely was a prison population close to 1,000, as compared to today when many prisons are five times that in size.

In the 1950s, a rash of prison riots brought prisons to the front pages of newspapers. It was also during this time that the disciplines of sociology, psychology, and psychiatry began to influence prisons. The seeds of the "rehabilitative era" of the 1960s and 1970s were planted in the 1950s with the creation of prison sociologists and counselors. Eventually, the Big House of the 1940s was replaced by the "correctional institution" and psychology replaced religion as the agent of reform.

The agricultural model continued in the South well into the 1980s, at which time the winds of change finally began to reach "plantation prisons." Some argue that though there were abuses, there were also some good elements to farms such as Parchman in Mississippi, where inmates were housed in "camps" of less than 200 and were kept out in the fresh air rather than caged 23 hours a day. An ex-warden notes that the Parchman he came back to in the 1980s was very different from the one he left in the 1970s (and that had continued unchanged from the 1950s):

> The way the original camps were organized was a prison administrator's dream.... The smallness of the camps also permitted a sense of informality that simply did not exist in most correctional facilities. The camp sergeants knew their inmates, and they got to know their families as well.... The institution had truly been transformed in the last dozen years to just another prison.... Not only was Unit Twenty-Nine [a new building] a concrete monolith surrounded by double fences, razor ribbon, and motion detectors—it housed fifteen hundred inmates (Cabana 1996: 131–132).

Inmates as well remembered that the old days weren't all bad.

> Back then, you didn't have to go to chow hall, they let you go fishing instead. In the wintertime you could always catch a rabbit in the cotton field (an inmate describing an Arkansas prison, Nelson 2002: 1).

Descriptions from the 1940s through the early 1960s painted a somewhat idealized view of prison life, where "right guys" were looked up to and lived by an honor code that included such principles as "don't snitch" and "don't exploit other inmates." Other principles of the code included "be cool," "do your own time," "be tough," and, above all else, "never talk to a screw [guard]" (Sykes and Messinger 1960). Later researchers argued that most prisoners, when asked, knew very few right guys, the type of prisoner who upheld all the principles of the prisoner code. However, the descriptions are fairly consistent of a prison where convicts created their own world and prison administrators left inmates alone as long as things were quiet. Prisoners could fashion a life that was, if not comfortable, at least livable.

1960–1980s

The so-called "rehabilitative era" is a time period roughly from the mid-1960s to the late 1970s. It is characterized by a change in at least rhetoric whereby prisons became "correctional institutions" and the goal was reform rather than simply punishment. By the late 1960s and 1970s, prisoners in some states underwent rudimentary "diagnoses" and were classified according to their problems and their degree of security risk. In many states, inmates started their prison terms in "classification centers," where they took a multitude of educational, aptitude, and interest tests and had medical examinations. These tests were then used to determine what prison they would be sent to and the appropriate mix of educational, vocational, and treatment programs to which they would be assigned. By the 1970s, in addition to basic and advanced education, a prisoner might partake of group therapy, transactional analysis, or behavior modification; even transcendental meditation and yoga were offered in some prisons.

It should be noted that many prisons were much slower to change than others. The South was known for brutal prisons where rehabilitation was a foreign word, even well into the 1970s. For instance, a prisoner's petition from the notorious

Tucker and Cummins prison farms in Arkansas was the impetus for a federal district court to overturn the "hands-off" doctrine that had insulated prison authorities from court scrutiny for years. Court testimony documented individual cases of torture with the "Tucker telephone," an electrical apparatus that transmitted electric shocks to the inmates' genitals and other body parts. Inmates were made to work in the fields without coats or shoes in the winter, they had to pay for medical care, and some were kept in the "hole" without light despite damage to their retinas. The federal court, clearly shocked at the level of brutality, wrote a holding that included a stern warning—if a state chose to run a prison system, then it must run it in a way that met basic constitutional protections (*Holt v. Sarver* [1970]).

> They would make you lie down on your stomach and whip you with a bull hide.... It was like being backed up against a heating stove all day long. At night, you couldn't pull your shorts off. You had to take a shower and shake them loose. (an inmate describing the Arkansas prisons before court intervention, Nelson 2002: 1)

Glenn (2001), a retired prison warden, described the Texas prison system in the early 1960s as fair and just, arguing that the allegations of abuse by guards and building tenders was slander (2001: 24). He then describes the forms of punishment used. The "rail" was a two-by-four turned on its side. An inmate found guilty of a minor offense was required to stand on the rail for a period of four hours; if he fell off, the time would start again. If an inmate didn't pick enough cotton, he would be made to stand on a barrel for four or five hours. Up to four inmates might be placed on a single barrel, and if one fell off, the time would start again for them all. Other inmates would have their hands raised above their head and be handcuffed to the bars in the inmate mess hall; their feet would be handcuffed too (2001: 25–26). He also described a situation where an inmate tried to escape, was shot, and then was hung on the front gate, bleeding, for the field hoe squads to see as they came back in from the fields. This was described as an "effective...object lesson" (2001: 44). Glenn also described a prison captain who played a "game" with inmates who he believed weren't working hard enough on the hoe squad. He would have them tied and stripped, and then he would lower his pants and threaten to sodomize them (2001: 69).

Irwin (1980; also see Austin and Irwin 2001) explained that the changes that began in the 1960s fragmented the prison social world. By the 1960s, the code, even if idealized, was clearly changing with the entry of drug offenders and a younger prisoner population; furthermore, the old prison rules no longer seemed to apply and the established relationships between guards and inmates were in flux. Four elements converged to create a completely different prison world from any that had come before: (1) new expectations, (2) racial politics, (3) drugs, and (4) a massive influx of much younger criminals.

New Expectations

With the move toward rehabilitation, inmates were operating under new ground rules. To be a good prisoner not only meant staying out of trouble, or at least not getting caught; it also meant the person had to "program." The inmate subcultural rule to "never talk to a screw" was difficult to adhere to when a guard was running a group therapy session that the inmate had to attend. Officers, too, were confused, since their task was expanded to not only guard but also to be an influence on the offender. They greeted the changes with a considerable amount of cynicism. From their perspective, prisoners were gaining more freedom and that made their job more difficult and dangerous. A few inmates and a few guards welcomed the changes and embraced the correctional philosophy; others manipulated the system; and a few bemoaned the good old days when guards and inmates knew their place. Old norms against inmate-guard interaction broke down but have never entirely dissipated.

Court decisions arguably changed the balance of power in prisons by giving prisoners some early victories, leading to new expectations in what prisoners could or should expect from prison authorities. These changes sometimes led to violence as prisons accommodated change. For instance, between 1972 and 1975 there were 40 inmate murders and 360 stabbings in Angola Prison in Louisiana (Bergner 1998: 64).

Racial Politics

In the 1960s, political consciousness was growing among some prisoners, especially African-Americans. The number of African-Americans and other minorities in prisons was increasing. As they became a more powerful force in the prison world, and especially as some redefined themselves as political prisoners, racial strain developed. The racial strain often broke out in race riots or individual acts of violence. Prisoners alleged that officers incited and encouraged racial unrest in order to control prisoners, but, in truth, prisoners probably did not need much help to justify acts of aggression.

Groups that began as political entities with political agendas quickly turned to prison rackets (gambling, drugs and other contraband sold and bartered as a black market). Gangs were powerful competitors because of the number and loyalty of members. In states like California, gangs such as the Mexican Mafia, the Texas Syndicate, the La Nuestra Familia, and Black Guerrilla Family rapidly took over prison drug markets and forced inmates to join or be victimized by the gang. The Chicano gang now known as the Mexican Mafia began with a group of Los Angeles Chicanos locked up in juvenile institutions. As they graduated to Chino and other prisons, they preyed upon northern Chicanos. Eventually Chicanos from northern California formed their own gang for protection—this gang became known as La Nuestra Familia.

The Black Guerrilla Family started as a black nationalist group stemming from the Black Panthers. Today, the political agenda has been completely supplanted by criminal objectives. Two other African-American gangs—the Crips and the Bloods— are more closely tied to neighborhood allegiances and tend to engage in conflict with each other rather than other races (Hunt, Morales, and Waldorf 1993; Parenti 1999).

Whites responded to the threat of gang victimization by forming gangs of their own, usually with some neo-Nazi element, such as the Aryan Brotherhood and the Nazi Lowriders. Whites, however, are still less likely to belong to any gang than are minority prisoners, which leaves them more vulnerable to victimization (Parenti 1999; Pelz, Marquart, and Pelz 1991; Trout 1992). Even racism, however, takes a back seat to profit, and the Aryan Brotherhood has been known to partner with La Eme (Mexican Mafia) for profitable smuggling or distribution schemes.

Drugs

Drugs influenced the prison in a number of ways. First, drugs led to a breakdown of the so-called "inmate code." Often drug offenders did not have entrenched criminal identities, nor were they socialized through the criminal street culture. Also, the drug culture was an entity unto itself and principles such as "don't snitch" were replaced with more egocentric concerns. Drugs led to increased prison violence in several ways. Some drugs themselves may create irrationally violent behavior (e.g., PCP). Also, violence is sometimes used by drug dealers in prison to enforce a contract or punish a debtor. Finally, dealers will use violence or the threat of violence to coerce other inmates and their families to participate in drug smuggling. Today, drugs continue to be a management issue for prisons. Because most prisons are so large (many house over 5,000 prisoners), it is extremely difficult to control all contraband coming into the prison. In fact, a certain percentage of drugs are smuggled in by officers who are seduced by the large financial compensation or coerced by intimidation and blackmail to take the risk. Prisons have adapted to the presence of drugs by more stringent controls on both inmates and officers, including frequent and random drug testing on inmates and more entry security procedures that sometimes include random searches of officers.

Young Offenders

Another element that changed the prison was an increase in the number of young offenders sent to prison. Prisoners in the 1950s were usually older, and although certainly not upstanding citizens, they tended to be stable, taking care of their own problems and desiring little interaction with guards. Drug offenders tend to be younger, and this influx of younger offenders, beginning in the 1960s but reaching its zenith in the mid-1980s, led to increased disturbances and violent incidents. In an effort to control younger inmates, some systems mixed older and younger inmates together, but usually all this did was make prison life miserable for the old cons, who could not control and were not respected by the Young Turks. Housing all younger inmates in one facility created havoc for officers since the frequency of fighting and other incidents went up dramatically.

> They have nothing but younger guys in prison now. And...it has just
> changed...since there are so many children and kids in prison it is hard to
> do time now. It is not like it used to be where you can wake up one morn-
> ing and know what to expect. But now you wake up and...anything might
> happen....(an older inmate, cited in Hunt, et al. 1993: 407)

The Death of the Rehabilitative Era

The 1970s echoed the 1950s in the sense that there was both a wave of reform, but also, a spate of riots. There were 48 prison riots in 1972 (Gottschalk 2006: 178). The Attica riot in 1972 brought prisons into every living room during the evening news broadcasts. Citizens watched live footage of prisoners holding knives to the throats of hostages. The nation waited as negotiations continued over the course of many days until New York state police regained control after a bloody assault. Public opinion, which had been relatively supportive of rehabilitative programs and treatment, shifted to a less tolerant view of prisons and prisoners. It was hard to see prisoners wielding machetes and other crudely lethal weapons as a group that was amenable to education and other programs. Further, the politicalization of prisoners, especially African-American prisoners, made the treatment ethic (that the individual needed to be diagnosed and treated for his "problem") irrelevant. For many social reformers and prison activists, the concept that the individual needed to be changed was replaced with the belief that it was society that was the cause of crime, either because of poverty, racism, or capitalism.

Another blow to the rehabilitative trend was the Martinson Report of 1974 (Martinson 1974). This report, paid for and then suppressed by the New York State Department of Corrections, was a meta-analysis and evaluation of over 200 prison and correctional programs across the country. According to the first articles published from this study, no correctional program was successful in reducing recidivism. Actually, the findings were a little more complicated and Martinson attempted in later articles to modify his original harsh stance, but the damage had been done. Politicians interested in the bottom line of reducing the budget and/or wanting to appear "tough on crime" promoted the ethic of punishment first, and treatment not at all. Academics offered philosophical justification for retribution (e.g., von Hirsch 1976). Prisoner advocates also argued against the rehabilitation ethic, believing that it ignored society's role in crime. Further, indeterminate sentencing was criticized as lacking due process protections. The unusual alliance between conservatives who wanted more punish-ment and less treatment and liberals who wanted more transparency and clarity in sentencing and release decisions created the political environment whereby indeter-minate sentencing was discarded in some states and treatment eventually ceased to be the primary goal of the penitentiary. Garland (2001b) describes this period as the decline of penal welfarism and a retreat from the position that offenders' and society's needs could both be met by helping programs. The shift in view by the end of this time period was that inmates' interests, by definition, contrasted with the interests of the rest of us. The so-called rehabilitative era was pretty much over by the early 1980s.

1980–TODAY

A spike in crime rates in the 1980s and the burgeoning "War on Drugs" campaign on both the federal and state levels led to an unprecedented rise in incarceration rates in the 1980s and prison populations soared. Prisons met and exceeded their maximum capacity levels. State-sentenced prisoners were held back in jails awaiting space, and then jails filled to capacity and beyond. Prisoners were housed in cafeterias, gyms, and, in some cases, tents in the prison yard. State legislatures increased prison budgets, doubling, tripling, and then quadrupling the amounts allocated for departments of correction. States went on building binges to meet the ever-expanding numbers. In fact, the dizzying numbers led to an incredible surge of a profitable new industry—private prisons. Multitudes of small private companies were created to meet the need of states for quick construction and management agreements. The biggest companies, such as Wackenhut (now Geo Group) and Corrections Corporation of America, boasted exponential growth and even began trading on the New York Stock Exchange. Incarceration rates doubled and then tripled nationally.

The 1980s can be characterized as the time when prisons were "out of control." Changes that had occurred in the 1960s and 1970s in the prisoner subculture and guard-prisoner relationships continued to have effects, and in the 1980s, these instabilities were exacerbated by overcrowding. It might also be noted that the rhetoric and reality of rehabilitation was replaced with a more punitive philosophical rationale. Prison rhetoric no longer offered much hope that individual change was possible, much less that the inmate was valued as a human being. Huge numbers of convicts were coming into prison with long mandatory sentences for drugs, and they were angry. In some prisons, the explosive mix of changing norms and overcrowding led to violence.

In Texas, for instance, an inmate and legal aid attorney brought a case that eventually changed the Texas system completely. In *Ruiz v. Estelle* (1980), Judge Justice ruled on crowding, programs, sanitation, and a host of other subjects, but the biggest focus of the lawsuit was on brutality, especially by the inmate building tenders, who were said to terrorize other inmates to maintain order. Judge Justice eliminated the building tender system in a sweeping court order that barred the state from using inmates to guard or in any way provide custodial supervision or discipline over other prisoners.

The vacuum of power was soon taken over by gangs and cliques that exploited weaker inmates (Crouch and Marquart 1989). Killings were common. Prison homicides in Texas alone went from 16 in the period 1970–1978 to 52 in 1984–85 (and 641 nonfatal stabbings) (Glenn 2001: 125; Ralph and Marquart 1991). Officer-on-inmate violence escalated also. In 1984, for instance, 200 disciplinary actions were taken against officers who had used excessive force (Martin and Eckland-Olson 1987: 38).

Change was afoot in other prisons as well. In Massachusetts, Walpole Prison was described as a hellhole where excrement littered the hallways and officers rarely ventured into inmate living areas (Kauffman 1988). In Rhode Island, a very similar transformation took place, although quite a bit earlier, when officers, who felt betrayed by the courts and management, in effect gave up guarding. Carroll tracked the changes that occurred during the 1970s in Rhode Island and described how the events there were quite similar to those of Texas in the 1980s and of other states when court decisions upset the balance of power (Carroll 1998).

> Assaults and stabbings became almost everyday events. On just one weekend near the end of May 1973 two officers were assaulted with a pipe, and another suffered a fractured foot when he was pushed down a flight of stairs; two inmates were likewise assaulted with pipes, and two others were stabbed, all requiring hospitalization. And on Saturday afternoon of the following weekend, an inmate was stabbed over 100 times, his body stuffed in a trash can and set on fire. (Carroll 1998: 82)

Hassine (1999) provides a firsthand account of his experience in Pennsylvania's Graterford prison during turbulent times.

> These were violent and deadly times at Graterford; times of random violence, murders, cell fires, paranoia, and knife carrying. According to the Department of Corrections' Monthly Morbidity Report in 1986–87, Graterford accounted for the highest rate of assaults out of Pennsylvania's 12 state prisons: 392 assaults by inmates against inmates and 47 by inmates against staff.... While it seemed like total anarchy, it really wasn't. This was mob rule with a purpose, a throwback to a time long before civilized man developed modern social institutions. By now I began to realize how fragile civilization was and how easily modern man could be reduced to the savagery of his prehistoric ancestors. (Hassine 1999: 28)

It is interesting that prison violence may have reached its peak at the same time as did criminal violence on the street. By some accounts, it has also followed the downward trend of violent street crime, but prison has never been, and probably will never be, a place free of fear.

> If you clearly didn't care, if you could convince inmates and guards that you had absolutely nothing to lose and that your countermeasures to even the most trivial provocation would be totally unrestrained and pursued to the utmost of your abilities—then you were given respect and a wide berth, and people looked to you for leadership and advice. "He's crazy," they'd say admiringly, even longingly, when the name came up. "He's just totally, completely insane." (Early 1992: 12)

PRISONS AND POLITICS

Prisons have always been a political issue, but it was not until the 20th century that crime and punishment were elevated to a political platform issue. Some identify Richard Nixon in the 1970s as the first political figure to make crime a prominent issue in his campaign and presidency (Abramsky 2002). Others have identified Barry Goldwater (Gottschalk 2006: 33). The so-called War on Drugs began in earnest during President Reagan's term of office in the 1980s.

Although obviously controversial, an argument is made that the social issues of crime and drugs have a subtext of race. Alexander (2010) and others, such as Loic Wacquant, provide a historical chronicle linking the rise of prison populations in the South to the emancipation of blacks, an observation made previously by those who noted that as many as 75 percent of the prisoners in southern prisons after the Civil War were black (cited in Johnston 2009: 143). Alexander argues that the emergence of Jim Crow laws served as a method of social control of blacks after Reconstruction, and then that the rapid dismantling of such laws during the Civil Rights Era of the 1960s led to a new form of social control of blacks— the drug war and massive imprisonment. There is evidence to show that whites and blacks use drugs in roughly equal numbers, but blacks are more likely to be arrested and prosecuted for drug crimes, and even more likely to be convicted. About 13 percent of drug users are African-American, roughly the same percentage as their proportion in the population (Schemo 2001), yet over 60 percent of all narcotics convictions are of African-Americans. More telling, 84 percent of crack defendants in 2000 were African-American (Fields 2001: 3). In fact, according to some studies, African-Americans make up about 13 percent of all monthly drug users but 35 percent of all drug arrests, 55 percent of all drug convictions, and 74 percent of all drug prisoners (Parenti 1999: 239). Four of every five drug prisoners are African-American (56 percent) or Hispanic (23 percent) (King and Mauer 2002a: 2). More recent numbers indicate that 35 percent of those arrested for drugs and 44 percent of all those in prison for drug offenses were black in 2006 (Justice Policy Institute 2010: 2).

The most extreme example of race-based disparity in our approach to drugs was seen in the Anti-Drug Abuse Act of 1986, which included a mandatory sentence of five years in prison for five grams of crack and the same sentence for 500 grams of powder cocaine. This disparity was fueled by the belief that crack was more addictive and was associated with more crime, but critics noted that it was probably not a coincidence that crack was also more likely to be used by blacks. Since the chemical composition of crack and powder are the same, critics argued that the 100:1 ratio was incredibly unfair. Despite decades of criticism the guidelines were not changed until 2010 when President Obama signed a law that reduced the disparity to a ratio of 18:1 and eliminated the mandatory nature of the prison term called for by sentencing guidelines.

The 1988 presidential campaign has been presented as a classic case of how politics utilizes the "race and crime card." The infamous "Willie Horton" advertisement blamed Michael Dukakis for Horton's release on Massachusetts's prison furlough program and subsequent rape and murder of a white woman. The Horton case destroyed any hope Dukakis had of winning the election, despite the fact that hundreds of inmates had been furloughed without risk to the public and that Dukakis had virtually nothing to do with the decision anyway. Observers opined that Horton was chosen specifically because he was black and the campaign capitalized on voters' fears (Alexander 2010).

Even if one discounts the racial elements of the drug war, there is no doubt that the drug war itself was political and led directly to the dramatic increase in prison populations. The beginning of the modern drug war might be assigned to the Harrison Act of 1914. In the early part of the 20th century, a wide variety of patent medicines were marketed with no oversight or control by government. Many of these elixirs, which contained derivatives of morphine, cocaine, and/or alcohol, were touted as cures for everything from depression to bunions. Marijuana, cocaine, and heroin were also in use, although for the most part restricted to small segments of the population. For a variety of reasons, some obscured by the passage of time, instead of merely requiring documentation of prescriptions, the Act led to a prohibition of all uses of drugs. The Supreme Court upheld the absolute prohibition, and drug prescriptions of narcotics were ruled illegal even if they were being prescribed as part of withdrawal treatment (Inciardi 2002).

In the 1930s, federal attention shifted away from cocaine and heroin to marijuana, which was used by fringe groups and minorities. There seemed to be a clear racial tone in the campaign against marijuana. Evidence of this, for instance, is a *New York Times* article from 1927 that warned against the "devil weed" used by "blacks and wetbacks" (cited in Inciardi 2002: 32). Harry Anslinger, appointed commissioner of the Treasury Department's Bureau of Narcotics in 1930, took up the campaign and Congress passed the Marijuana Tax Act of 1937, which placed marijuana on the same list as heroin and cocaine and defined it as a controlled substance.

In the 1940s, the drug problem was not perceived as pervasive. Hollywood offered a few movies illustrating the evils of narcotics addiction, e.g., *To the Ends of the Earth* (1948), *The Man with the Golden Arm* (1955), and *The Pusher* (1959). Most explanations of drug use were psychological, in that users and addicts were seen as having weak ego functioning or other individual traits that caused their addiction.

In the 1950s, drug penalties continued to be severe, but drug use was, for the most part, confined to small fringe groups. Federal penalties for marijuana ranged from two to 20 years, depending on whether it was a first, second, or third offense. Then in the 1960s, white middle class kids began using marijuana in greater numbers and many were convicted and sentenced under these laws. Suddenly public views changed—almost every state reduced criminal penalties between 1969 and 1972. For instance, by 1973 simple possession was a misdemeanor in all but eight states. Some states decriminalized small amounts completely (Cole 1999:153).

Of course, the pendulum swung again to a more aggressively punitive stance, led by Richard Nixon's White House. In 1970, the Comprehensive Drug Abuse Prevention and Control Act was passed. It provided $189 million for various forms of treatment programs and $220 million for enforcement. The Bureau of Narcotics and Dangerous Drugs (later known as the Drug Enforcement Agency [DEA]) hired 300 new agents. The Law Enforcement Assistance Administration received $3.55 billion to be distributed to local and state law enforcement (Parenti 1999: 28).

President Gerald Ford's federal drug strategy emphasized addressing causes of addiction, such as poverty and hopelessness, and even called for the "serious" study of decriminalizing marijuana. President Jimmy Carter continued the tolerant trend, and during his tenure 12 states decriminalized marijuana (Parenti 1999: 28). In fact, from 1976 to 1992, marijuana could be legally prescribed to a small number of patients for research and treatment of impending blindness and reduction of pain in cancer and AIDs patients (Bianculli 1997: 173).

President Ronald Reagan's White House reversed this trend and took an aggressive stance on drugs. The Comprehensive Crime Control Act was passed in 1984. Part of this legislation was the Sentencing Reform Act, which abolished federal parole and created a Sentencing Commission to set guidelines for federal crimes. This Act also allowed federal preventative detention and expanded the possibilities of asset forfeiture. After 1984, state and local police could have drug cases tried in federal courts and still keep as much as 90 percent of the drug-related property. These forfeitures could take place in civil courts, with lower burdens of proof (Parenti 1999: 51).

It seems that 1986 was a watershed in the war on drugs. There was what can only be described as a media frenzy in pursuit of drug stories; for instance, the *New York Times* increased its coverage from 43 drug stories in the last half of 1985 to 220 in the last half of 1986. Len Bias, a Boston Celtics basketball star, died from a cocaine overdose. The "crack epidemic" and its related epidemics of abandoned "crack babies" in public hospitals, drug wars between dealers, and related crime gripped the nation. The public believed we were in the middle of a "plague," "epidemic," or, more appropriately, a "war." In 1986 Congress passed the Anti-Drug Abuse Act. This Act imposed 29 new mandatory minimum sentences in addition to the 100:1 mandatory term for crack and cocaine discussed earlier. "Liberal state" holdouts that had resisted the drug war's monolithic approach to all drugs finally succumbed to federal pressure to take a harsher stance. Oregon recriminalized small amounts of marijuana in 1986, followed by Alaska in 1990 (Inciardi 2002: 58).

President George Bush signed the Anti-Drug Abuse Act of 1988. This Act created a federal death penalty for participation in "continuing criminal enterprises" or any drug-related felony that related to the killing of another. The bill also created a "drug czar" position to coordinate the "anti-drug" policy of the White House. Over $2 million was given to the Department of Defense to train police and $3.5 million to equip police with military gear. Over $1 billion was given to state and local law enforcement. Millions went to the DEA, FBI, U.S. Marshals, Customs, and federal prosecutors. Forfeiture laws were expanded in order for government to recoup some of its money (Parenti 1999: 61).

By the 1990s, politicians outdid each other in their anti-crime platforms. Democrats co-opted the traditionally Republican mantra of "toughness" and President Bill Clinton signed the Violent Crime Control Law Enforcement Act in 1994. As a Democrat, Clinton had been perceived by some to be a new diplomat in this war who would soften the stance and put treatment ahead of interdiction and enforcement. Instead, he pledged to put 100,000 more police officers on the street and in signing the 1994 crime bill provided for 16 more federal death penalty crimes and overhauled the federal appeals process, making it harder for defendants to appeal capital cases. The Act also provided for $7.9 billion in grants for states to build prisons, directed the Sentencing Commission to eliminate parole for those who sold drugs near schools (even if the dealers were often close to being children themselves), created a three strikes provision, and paved the way for waiver provisions that would allow juveniles as young as 13 to be tried in adult courts. New federal laws also prohibited drug offenders from living in public housing, forcing some families to choose between eviction and having to turn away recently released relatives who needed a place to stay. This eviction policy has affected countless families of drug users as well as the users themselves, and was upheld by the Supreme Court in *Department of Housing and Urban Development v. Rucker* (2002). Further, the Violent Crime Control Act required "truth in sentencing" on the part of states. If states wanted federal money, they had to limit the amount of "good time" an inmate could receive (Rich 2002).

Some argue that the drug "problem" was largely created by the federal government offering money to states and communities if they agreed to aggressively arrest and prosecute drug users. Since financial resources are rarely refused, a drug war was created. This argument is bolstered by the fact that public concern about drugs came *after* the drug war had been declared by politicians (Alexander 2010). On the other hand, the argument fails to recognize the chaos and destruction of some families and communities due to the emergence and diffusion of crack; although separating the negative effects of the drug itself from the effects created by the criminal justice system would be impossible.

It is clear that the federal government was instrumental in the exponential increase in incarceration due to federal incentives to build prisons. Latter-day analysts now opine that if President Clinton had shown a scintilla of leadership in reducing and reversing the incredible trend of incarceration, especially of minority men, the Democrats would not have lost the election to George W. Bush in 2000 (Alexander 2010; Robinson 2000). Federal funding for the drug war rose from $1.5 billion in 1981 to $6.6 billion in 1989. It continued its astronomical rise to $17 billion in 1999 (Mauer 2001: 6). In 2003, it was estimated to be over $19 billion, but the federal government revised the method of calculating the cost, eliminating a major portion of the cost of prosecuting and incarcerating federal drug offenders, so that the reported figure appears to be a decrease from prior years (Common Sense for Drug Policy 2003). In more recent years, the stated federal budget for the drug war continues to be in the area of $15.5 billion. It is estimated that about 60 percent of this figure goes to interdiction and enforcement. (Office of National Drug Control Policy 2010). These numbers do not include state and local costs, and some estimates put the total annual cost of fighting the drug war at around $50 billion (Miron 2010)!

It now appears that the recent economic meltdown has spurred serious scrutiny of the costs associated with the drug war and whether or not it is money well spent. Even some staunch conservatives have proposed that our current policies of interdiction and punishment make no sense. Some have always opposed them. The leading voices from the resistance have been the Drug Policy Foundation (created in 1987) and the Lindesmith Center (started in 1994 by Alfred Lindesmith). These merged in 2000 and are now known as the Drug Policy Alliance. The goals and objectives of this organization are to move the country toward a "harm reduction" policy, which would include decriminalization of some drugs to some degree, reducing penalties, and emphasizing treatment. The billionaire George Soros has supported decriminalization efforts in Arizona and a number of other states. He funds the Open Society Institute, whose mission is to promote democracy and social programs and alleviate poverty. The choices made concerning how to allocate spending between interdiction and enforcement versus treatment are political choices. Drug possession and delivery, perhaps more than any other crimes, have contributed to the massive size of the prison population. How this country chooses to deal with the "drug problem" is largely a political issue and one that is tremendously important for the future of prisons in this country.

CONCLUSION

The birth of the prison was linked to a zeal for reform. Quakers believed that prisoners could find redemption and better their lives. Indeed, they believed that prisons could better society by extolling the virtues of sobriety and order. This optimism was followed by overcrowding and corruption, and the cycle was repeated after the Civil War. In the first part of the 20th century, prisons barely registered in the public's consciousness, but in the 1960s, prisons once again emerged from their obscurity with a newfound zeal for reform, albeit fueled by psychology rather than religion. The rehabilitative era was short-lived, however, and in the early 1980s, it was all but forgotten. In the early 1980s, the prison population literally exploded. Partly as a response to rising crime, and partly as an effect of the drug war, states began to double and even quadruple their prison populations. As the prison populations exploded, prison management became crisis management.

The cycle of reform and overcrowding continues to be repeated. Prisons again have become warehouses. Of course, there are differences between the prisons of earlier centuries and today—there is not the pervasive brutality and racism that occurred in earlier years, basic education now exists in almost all prisons, legal rights give prisoners some modicum of due process and protection against arbitrary actions of administrators, and the facilities themselves are often newer and cleaner. It is also true, however, that a prison is always a prison and when over 1.5 million people are incarcerated in them, it is important to understand why.

WEBSITES

For more information on the Bureau of Justice Statistics, visit:
  http://bjs.ojp.usdoj.gov/
For more information about the Walnut Street Jail, visit:
  http://www.prisonsociety.org/about/history.shtml
For more information on the Drug Enforcement Administration, visit:
  http://www.justice.gov/dea/
For more information on the Office of National Drug Control Policy, visit:
  http://www.whitehouse.gov/ondcp

STUDY QUESTIONS

1. Briefly describe three reasons for the use of prisons.
2. What type of punishment was typically used before the creation of prisons? Why did this work? Why does it not work now?
3. What is the "principle of less eligibility?" Why is it important?
4. Describe the origin and differences of the Philadelphia and Auburn models.
5. What was the goal of the "rehabilitative era" of the mid-1960s to 1970s?
6. List and briefly describe the four elements that created a different prison environment in the 1980s.
7. What caused the downfall of the "rehabilitative era"?
8. What are some of the issues that brought race into the politics of punishment?
9. What effects did the "War on Drugs" have on minorities?
10. What are the elements of the Sentencing Reform Act?

CHAPTER 2

꙳

Explaining Incarceration

In 2010 (the most current year available), there were 1,605,127 prisoners in state and federal prisons with another 748,728 in local jails. We incarcerate about a million more people than we did in the 1970s. It is true that the 2010 prison population represented a decrease from the year before, the first decrease since 1972 (Guerino, Harrison, and Sabol 2011: 1). The annual increases had already slowed substantially in recent years compared to the 1980s when the annual rate of increase averaged eight percent per year (Snell and Morton 1992: 1), and the 1990s when there was a 6.5 percent average increase (Sabol, West, and Cooper 2009: 1). In contrast, the average rate of increase for the 2000s was about 1.5 percent (Glaze 2010: 1). In fact, some states have reduced their prison population, but prison populations in other states and, especially, in the federal system continue to increase. The federal system has experienced a four percent increase in population through the 2000s, counteracting the decrease in the state prisoner population (West, Sabol, and Greenman 2010: 2). The rate of increase in federal prisoners between 2008 and 2009 was around 3.4 percent (Glaze 2010: 3) but declined to a 0.8 percent increase between 2009 and 2010 (Guerino, Harrison, and Sabol 2011: 14). Even with the more recent slowdown in the rate of imprisonment, our incarceration patterns remain incredibly disproportional to those of Western countries, and the thirty-year period from 1980 to 2010 has shown itself to be a historical anomaly.

THE RISE OF IMPRISONMENT

Between 1925 and 1973 the increase in the number of prisoners tracked the increase in the population of the country. Beginning in 1973, however, the imprisonment rate began its climb. In less than four decades (between 1973 and 2008), the prisoner population increased 705 percent (Pew Center on the States 2011: 1).

About 30 years ago, some academics and some policymakers warned against the increasing prison rates. In 1982, the Edna McConnell Clark Foundation published a monograph entitled "Overcrowded Time: Why Prisons are so Crowded and What Can Be Done" that described how inmates were sleeping in tents and cafeterias. The author explained that the incarceration of a half million people in prisons and jails at the time was due to harsher sentencing policies (mandatory minimums and habitual sentencing laws) (Schoen 1982). Those critics in the 1980s had no idea that their concerns would be completely ignored and incarceration rates would double and then double again before the century came to a close. Instead of seeking alternatives to prison, states went on a building binge to accommodate the increasing prisoner population. The number of prisons in this country increased 70 percent, from 600 in the mid-1970s to over 1,000 by 2000 (Lawrence and Travis 2004: 1). Today, there are 1,719 prisons (BJS [key facts] 2011).

In order to track patterns of incarceration, we utilize rates per 100,000. The *incarceration rate* is a function of the number of offenders sentenced to prison, the length of time they serve, and the number of probationers or parolees who are revoked and sent to (or back to) prison. Changes in any of these will affect the number of people in prison relative to the population outside of prison. In 1972, the incarceration rate was 93, meaning that for every 100,000 people, 93 were incarcerated in state or federal prisons. In 2009, the rate was 502 per 100,000 (Beck, Karberg, and Harrison 2002: 3; West, Sabol, and Greenman 2010: 1), but dropped to 497 per 100,000 in 2010 (Guerino, Harrison, and Sabol, 2011: 1). Thus, we incarcerate almost five times as many people as we did in 1972. It should be noted that the trend in the last couple of years has been a declining incarceration rate; for instance, the rate in 2007 was 506. As Figure 2.1 shows, the increases in the rates of imprisonment in the last 30 years have been unprecedented.

While the most dramatic increases in rates of imprisonment occurred in the 1980s, the building boom in prison construction occurred in the late 1980s and early 1990s. In 1978, about $5 billion was spent on prison and jail incarceration. In 1990, correctional costs rose to $12 billion. They jumped to $22 billion in 1996. By 2000, the cost of incarceration for states and the federal government had ballooned to $40 billion, and in 2002 estimates put the figure at $46 billion (Butterfield 2002: A15; Kaplan 1999; Greene and Schiraldi 2002: 2; Cernetig 2002: A9). By 2006, the total cost for prisons and jails was estimated to be $60 billion (Commission on Safety and Abuse in America's Prisons 2006). In 2011, the Bureau of Justice Statistics estimated that the total federal, state, and local expenditures on corrections was $74 billion (BJS [key facts] 2011). It is estimated that states spend seven percent of their budgets on prisons; some spend more on prisons than they do on

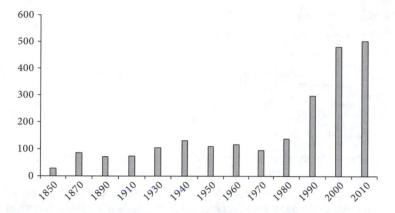

Figure 2.1 Incarceration Rates (prisoners per 100,000 of population)
Source: M. Cahalan. 1986. *Historical Corrections Statistics in the United States, 1850–1984* (Rockville, MD: Westat, Inc.); B.J.S. 1997. *Sourcebook of Criminal Justice Statistics* (Washington D.C.: Dept. of Justice). B.J.S. 1998. *State and Federal Prisoners, June 30, 1998.* (Washington D.C.: Dept. of Justice). P. Harrison and J. Karberg. 2003. *Prison and Jail Inmates at Midyear 2002* (Washington D.C.: Dept. of Justice). West, H., W. Sabol & S. Greenman, 2010. *Prisoners in 2009* (Washington D.C.: Dept. of Justice).

colleges and universities (Gottschalk 2006: 20). While states' spending on corrections rose 303 percent between 1987 and 2008, spending on education rose only 125 percent over the same time period (Clement, Schwarzfeld, and Thompson 2011: 3)

The average per inmate cost is around $78,000 per year (Pew Center on the States 2011: 6). With about 2.2 million incarcerated, it is easy to see why corrections budgets are eclipsing other governmental priorities. So-called *opportunity costs* refer to the fact that states must capture correctional dollars from other state services. In Ohio, for instance, state spending on prisons in 2002 grew at six times the rate of state spending on higher education between 1985 and 2000 (Collins 2002). Today, states spend $1 out of every $14 on corrections and one in six state employees are in corrections (Pew Center on the States 2011: 6).

THE UNITED STATES COMPARED TO THE WORLD

Figure 2.2 compares the United States with other countries (the rate is higher than that discussed in the previous section because this rate also includes the number sentenced to jail as well as state and federal prisons). No Western nation approaches the United States in its rate of imprisonment. The United States incarcerates in a pattern more similar to that of Russia and Cuba than to Australia, Canada, or any of the Western European nations.

Why our incarceration patterns are so high relative to our sister-countries cannot be explained by crime rates. While it is true that the United States has a much higher violent crime rate than other nations, the vast majority of crimes

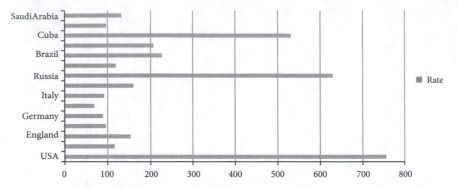

Figure 2.2 Incarceration Rates (Selected Countries) (per 100,000 of population)
Source: International Centre for Prison Studies. (2010). *World prison population list* (8th ed.). London: International Centre for Prison Studies. Accessed 7/21/2011 from http://www.kcl. ac.uk/depsta/law/research/icps/downloads/wppl-8th_41.pdf.

involve property and public order (drugs). These offenders are more likely to end up in prison in the United States and/or to receive longer sentences than in other countries that use alternative means of punishment, such as day-fines, community supervision, or, for drug offenders, mandatory treatment programs. We will discuss the reasons for our high incarceration rate in a later section.

COMPARING STATES' RATES OF INCARCERATION

One of the interesting things about prison rates is the tremendous variability in states' rates. It is important to compare states by rates since there is such a tremendous difference in state populations and the number of prisoners. While Texas had 173,649 prisoners in 2010, Maine had only 2,154. Obviously, Maine is a much smaller state so you would expect a smaller prison population; however, Maine's rate of incarceration was 148 compared to 648 in Texas. This indicates that Texas incarcerates about five times as many of its citizens as does Maine (Guerino, Harrison, and Sabol 2011: 14, 22). There are tremendous regional differences in incarceration patterns. Southern states (551 per 100,000) have almost double the incarceration rate of northern states (302 per 100,000). Patterns of crime do not seem to explain these differences. Observers attribute the differences to sentencing practices and other factors. One correlate of incarceration rates is the percentage of minorities in the state population (Irwin and Austin 1994; Sorensen and Stemen 2002).

In Table 2.1, the highest and lowest rates are presented, using the years 2001 and 2010. The table also shows that some states have been able to reduce their incarceration rate. In fact, half of the states reduced their prison population from 2009 to 2010 (Guerino, Harrison, and Sabol 2011: 1). More discussion of these states and the methods by which they have been able to reduce their rate of incarceration will be presented in the last chapter.

Table 2.1 Incarceration Rates of Selected States: 2001/2009

HIGHEST		LOWEST	
STATE	RATE PER 100,000	STATE	RATE PER 100,000
	2001/2010		2001/2010
Louisiana	795/867	Maine	126/148
Texas	731/648	Minnesota	131/185
Mississippi	689/686	North Dakota	158/226
Oklahoma	669/654	Rhode Island	179/197
Alabama	592/648	New Hampshire	184/209
Georgia	540/479	Vermont	221/265
South Carolina	526/495	Nebraska	225/247
Delaware	505/443	West Virginia	225/363
Missouri	500/508	Utah	235/238
Nevada	485/472	Massachusetts	247/200

Beck, A., J. Karberg & P. Harrison, 2002. *Prison and Jail Inmates at Midyear 2001.* (Washington, DC: Dept. of Justice), p. 6. Guerino, P., P. Harrison & W. Sabol, 2011. *Prisoners in 2010.* (Washington, DC: Dept. of Justice), p. 22.

INCARCERATION AND RACE/ETHNICITY

One cannot discuss imprisonment without mentioning the disproportional number of minorities in the prison population. The incarceration rate for blacks is six times that for whites and the rate for Hispanics is about double that of whites (Mauer and King 2007: 3). Figure 2.3 a&b shows the relative incarceration rates of white, Hispanic, and black men and women. It is difficult to construct this table for earlier years because Hispanics have not been (and, in some sources, are still not) separated from whites. Counting Hispanics with whites has masked the true nature of incarceration patterns; whites are overcounted because Hispanics are included in the count. Holman (2001: 3) found that whites were overcounted by 22 percent in 1985 with reports indicating they comprised 52 percent of the prison population, when, in reality, they comprised only 43 percent; and in 1997, the 41 percent figure for whites was really only 35 percent after recognizing Hispanics as a separate category. Today, true numbers are more accessible, but there are still gaps where it is difficult to find accurate rates of whites separated from Hispanics. Further, it is almost impossible to obtain accurate numbers of Native Americans, and they are probably underrepresented in state figures because of reporting practices (Archambeault 2003).

As seen in Figure 2.3 a&b, the dramatic surge in imprisonment that began in the 1980s impacted minorities far more than whites. These tables do not capture the greatest increase of imprisonment, which occurred in the 1980s. Between 1980 and 1999, the incarceration rate for blacks (both men and women) increased from 551 to 1,789, compared to whites (85 to 217) and Hispanics (163 to 719) (Austin, et al. 2000: 7). Blacks' and Hispanics' rates of increase were much more dramatic than the rate of increase for whites, and this becomes even more clear when Hispanics are separated out from the counts of white prisoners.

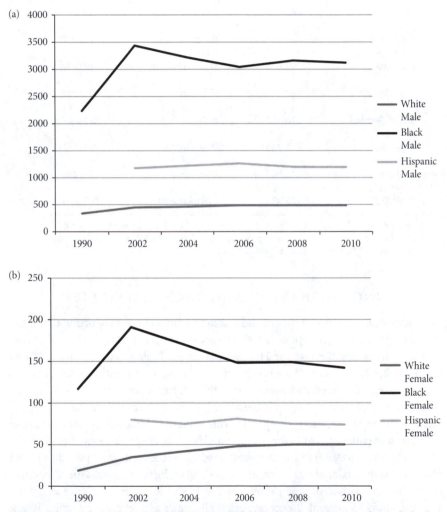

Figure 2.3 Incarceration Rate Trends By Race/Ethnicity/Sex (per 100,000 of population)
Source: A.J. Beck and C.J. Mumola. 1999. *Prisoners in 1998* (Washington D.C.: Dept. of Justice) p. 9 (Table 12). H.C. West, W.J. Sabol, and S.J. Greenman. 2010. *Prisoners in 2009* (Washington D.C.: Dept. of Justice), p. 28 (Table 14).

Table 2.2 shows the relative rates of imprisonment (including jails) between black men and other demographic groups. The rate for black men (3,119) is about six times that for white men (487).

A review by Chiricos and Crawford (1995) of 38 studies published since 1975 revealed that while race did not have a direct effect on sentence length, convicted black offenders were more likely to be incarcerated than whites even after controlling for crime seriousness and prior record. They also showed that blacks are significantly more disadvantaged than whites in the South, where incarceration is high. Large numbers of unemployed blacks in a jurisdiction, they theorize, may be perceived as such a social and political threat as to increase the probability of incarceration. Spohn and Holleran (2000) examined sentencing decisions in three different cities to explore the impact of race and ethnicity on sentencing. They found that blacks and Hispanics were 10 to 15 percent more likely than whites to be sentenced to prison, although race/ethnicity did not seem to affect the length of the sentence. Race/ethnicity was more influential in sentencing decisions for young offenders than older offenders, and young black males received the most severe sentences of any demographic group, especially when they were unemployed.

Imprisonment has taken a tremendous toll on the black community. About 7.5 percent of all black children have a parent in prison and 1 in 40 Hispanic children have a parent in prison (Gottschalk 2006: 248). One in six black men were incarcerated in 2001 (Mauer and King 2007: 2) and 12 percent of black men 25–29 were in prison in 2004 (Western 2006: 3).

Statistics from specific states are even more troubling. The Justice Policy Institute reports that nearly four in 10 black men in their twenties are under some form of criminal justice control in California. While blacks constitute about 20 percent of all felony arrests, they make up 43 percent of third-strike defendants. In New York, more than 90 percent of the people doing time for drug offenses are black or Hispanic. It is reported that there are more blacks and Hispanics locked

Table 2.2 Incarceration Rates By Race/Ethnicity and Sex

	MALES	FEMALES
Total	938	67
White	456	47
Black	3,059	133
Hispanic	1,242	77

SOURCE: Guerino, P., P. Harrison, & W. Sabol. 2011. *Prisoners in 2010*, BJS Bulletin. (Washington, DC: Dept. of Justice), p. 27.

up in prison in New York than attending colleges and universities. In Maryland, since 1990, nine out of every 10 new inmates imprisoned are black (Kaplan, Schiraldi, and Ziedenberg 2000: 1). In Texas, one out of three young black men is in prison, jail, or under some form of community supervision. Blacks are incarcerated at a rate seven times higher than that of whites in Texas (Kaplan, Schiraldi, and Ziedenberg 2000: 3).

More recent data indicate that the rate of imprisonment for blacks varies from a high of 4,710 per 100,000 in South Dakota to a low of 851 in Hawaii, but the lowest rate for blacks was still higher than the highest rate for whites (740 in Oklahoma). Hispanics' rates of incarceration range from a high of 1,714 in Pennsylvania to 185 in Hawaii (Mauer and King 2007: 7). The tremendous variation in states echoes the general incarceration rate variability but raises troubling questions concerning why there are such differences in incarceration patterns.

As discussed in chapter 1, some argue that these figures are evidence of a pervasive racism that permeates not only the criminal justice system but the entire socioeconomic system, relegating minorities to second-class citizenship. In this view, consciously or unconsciously, prisons are used as a tool for controlling excess and disenfranchised groups (Alexander 2010; Foucoult 1977; Mauer 1999; Parenti 1999; Rusche and Kirchheimer 1939; Wacquant 2001).

EXPLAINING THE INCREASE

What is the explanation for our dramatically increased use of prison? The simple answer might be crime—we have more people in prison because we have more criminals today than in years past. This is demonstrably not true. In fact the United States has enjoyed a declining crime rate since the mid-1990s even while the incarceration rate continued to increase. Other explanations that have been offered include sentencing changes (mandatory sentences, three strikes, and presumptive sentencing), the increased punitiveness of citizenry, increased revocation rates of parolees, the so-called War on Drugs, the deinstitutionalization of the mentally ill, and the privatization of corrections. We will examine each of these explanations.

As stated earlier, the incarceration rate is influenced by the number of people sent to prison, the length of time they stay in prison, and the number of people returned to prison on some form of revocation. The number of people admitted to prison as new court commitments has declined since 2007, but the number of those returned because of parole revocations has increased (Pew Center on the States 2011; West, Sabol, and Greenman 2010: 2). Raphael and Stoll (2008) found that while average sentence lengths looked to be about the same between 1980 and 2002, when individual crimes were examined an offender would be spending more time in prison for any given offense in 2002 than he did in 1980. For instance, a robbery prison term was 20 percent longer and a rape prison term was 75 percent longer. The average length of sentence for the prison population as a whole was about the same because there were many more offenders sentenced for less serious crimes in prison in 2002, a large portion of these were drug offenders. Western (2007) also noted that the likelihood of receiving a prison term for all crimes doubled between 1980 and 2001, and both violent and property offenders experienced an increase in average sentence lengths.

Crime

There are actually two questions to consider in evaluating the connection between imprisonment and crime. The first is: Did prison populations increase because more people commited crimes? The second is: Has increased imprisonment contributed to the decline of crime? As for the first question, it does not seem so. Although some argue that increased crime explains up to 44 percent of the increase in prison population (Spelman 2009), others argue that crime explains only 17 percent of the increase (Raphael 2009).

According to the Uniform Crime Reports (UCR), crime has been steadily declining since the mid-1990s. Property crime has been declining for 30 years. During this same time period, we've seen incarceration rates continue to rise. In Figure 2.4, a visual comparison is presented between incarceration rates and crime rates. We see that the rate of incarceration continues to rise even though crime rates have been declining.

The second question of whether or how much incarceration has affected the crime decline is a complex research undertaking. Many researchers have addressed the question and there is controversy in methodology, assumptions, and

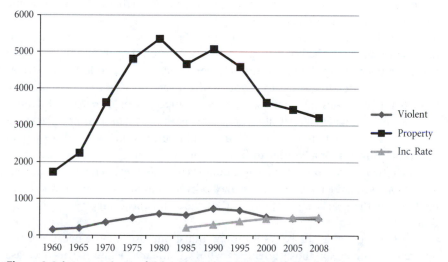

Figure 2.4 Incarceration and Crime Rates (per 100,000 of population)
Source: UCR, Table 1. *Crime in the United States*. By Volume and Rate, 1986-2005. Retrieved from: www.fbi.gov/ucr/05cius/data/table/_.01/html and *Crime in the United States*, 2008, By Volume and Rate, 1989-2008, www.fbi.gov/ucr/cius2008/data/table_01.html. Bureau of Justice Statistics, (multiple years). *Prisoners in 1998, 2000, 2003, 2008* (Washington, DC: Department of Justice).

interpretation of data. Mauer (2001: 7) points out that in the 1980s, incarceration rates climbed quite dramatically, but so did crime rates. More tellingly, he points out there is no correlation between the rate of the crime decline and the imprisonment or enforcement patterns of states. For instance, the prison population of Texas increased five times faster than New York's prison population during the 1990s, but New York experienced a 26 percent greater decline in crime for the same period (Greene and Schiraldi 2002: 3). The prison population of Texas increased 224 percent between 1990 and 2002 while New York's prison population increased only 22 percent (Jacobsen 2005: 33).

More sophisticated analyses have been undertaken and estimates range from some who say that two to five percent of the decline in crime occurred because of the increase in imprisonment, to others who put the figure at closer to 33 percent (Pratt 2009; Western 2006: 185). There are major issues, however, over the methodology of such studies. Durlauf and Nagin (2011), for instance, question what conclusions one can draw from such studies because they do not control for other policies that may also affect incarceration rates and/or crime. It is hard, according to these authors, to separate out causality from mere correlation.

Sentencing Changes

Prison administrators, when asked what accounted for the population increases in prison, responded that four factors contributed to the phenomenon: increased sentence length, the "drug problem," legislative response to the drug problem, and the public's desire to "get tough" on crime (Vaughn 1993: 15–16). Actually, these issues are all interrelated and involve sentencing practices that have become harsher over the last several decades.

In addition to an increase in the number of people sentenced to prison, what has also occurred in the last 30 years is that sentences are getting longer and/or there is a decrease in the use of discretionary release and parole. Three strikes laws sentence offenders, sometimes young offenders, to 25-year or life sentences. Over half of all states now have some type of three strikes or habitual offender laws (King and Mauer 2001). California's law is perhaps the best known. Passed in 1994 as a direct reaction to the horrifying killing of Polly Klaas, the three strikes provision provides for a 25-year-to-life sentence for a third felony. Less known is the law's "two strikes" provision, which doubles the offender's sentence upon conviction of a second felony. The two strikes provision impacts many more offenders than the three strikes punishment (Clark, Austin, and Henry 1997; King and Mauer 2001).

Critics argue that the law is not only unjust but also unwise because it ties up state resources for those offenders who are already beginning to decrease their criminal activity. The so-called *maturation effect* refers to the fact that all offenders drastically curtail criminal activity after age 35. It was estimated that by 2026 there will be 30,000 inmates serving sentences of 25 years to life in California prisons at an annual cost of $750 million (Zimring, Hawkins, and Kamin 2001: 71).

The first thing a convict feels when he receives an inconceivably long sentence is shock. The shock usually wears off after about two years, when all his appeals have been denied. He then enters a period of self-hatred because of what he's done to himself and his family. If he survives that emotion—and some don't—he begins to swim the rapids of rage, frustration, and alienation. When he passes through the rapids, he finds himself in the calm waters of impotence, futility, and resignation. It's not a life one can look forward to living. The future is totally devoid of hope, and people without any hope are dangerous—either to themselves or others. (an ex-inmate, Martin and Sussman 1993: 259)

These laws are not necessarily reserved only for violent offenders. In fact, large numbers of offenders sentenced under habitual felon laws have committed nonviolent felonies. A California report indicated that 85 percent of those imprisoned under the law committed a nonviolent third felony (Butterfield 1996: A14). A study of those convicted under Florida's habitual felon law found that in 87 percent of the cases there was no injury to the victim (Austin and Irwin 2001: 42). In Clark, Austin, and Henry's (1997) review of the three strikes laws of California and Washington in 1997, they noted that 98 percent of those sentenced under Washington's law had committed a "crime against a person," while only 25.5 percent of California offenders sentenced under its three strikes law had committed such a crime. In fact, close to three-quarters had committed either a property or a drug crime. Examples of third felonies that resulted in life sentences include theft of a pair of sneakers, attempted breaking and entering, and theft of a jar of instant coffee (King and Mauer 2001: 10). While many offenders sentenced are violent, the three strikes law, which promised to keep violent offenders off the streets, has actually cast a much broader net than perhaps many voters intended. Another troubling aspect of California's three strikes law is that blacks tend to be disproportionately affected by such laws. In California, blacks make up seven percent of the population but 43 percent of those sentenced to prison under the three strikes law in 1996 (Cole 1999: 148).

Similar to the research on incarceration in general, researchers argue over whether California's three strikes sentences have reduced crime, with most agreeing that three strikes sentencing does little to reduce crime (Pratt 2009; Western 2006). King and Mauer (2001) examined 50,000 California inmates sentenced under the law and found no link to the drop in crime California had experienced along with the rest of the country. California legislators disagree, arguing that their 41 percent drop in crime was twice the national average (Sherman 2001). Austin and Irwin (2001: 212) compared three strikes states (California, Georgia, and Washington) with states without three strikes laws but with similar crime rates before such laws were passed (Massachusetts, Michigan, and Texas). They found that there was little difference between states with three strikes and those without in their levels of crime decline. All states experienced a crime decline between 1991 and 1996. Further, they looked at counties within California and found that those that pursued three strikes prosecutions vigorously experienced no greater decline than other counties that used three strikes convictions more sparingly. More troubling, Kovandzic, Sloan, and Vieraitis (2004) found that there was a positive relationship between the use of three strikes and the incidence of homicide— and no correlation between such laws and a reduction in crime.

Such laws have also seen challenges in court. However, the U.S. Supreme Court, in a five-to-four decision, upheld California's three strikes law. Ruling that the long sentences were not disproportional, even for minor property offenders, the Court's opinion seems to have forestalled any other challenges to habitual felon laws (*Ewing v. California* [2003] and *Lockyer v. Andrade* [2003]). A California ballot initiative that would have restricted the use of three strikes to violent or serious felonies failed in 2004. There is another initiative that voters will be asked to consider in November 2012. Public opinion polls indicate that about three-fourths of Californians are in favor of eliminating three strikes sentences for nonviolent felons (Gabrielson 2011).

Increased "Punitiveness"

Others note that the use of imprisonment in this country has risen to unprecedented levels and is part of a trend of "getting tough" toward marginalized groups (Abramsky 2002). This trend started with the Reagan White House and has continued fairly unabated since. Beckett and Western (2001) note that, since the Reagan administration, there has been a shift from public spending on human services to social control, including justice and corrections. They argue that reduced welfare benefits and increased incarceration rates are not mere coincidence; this inverse correlation illustrates the government's philosophical shift in how those at the fringes of economic self-sufficiency are treated. While welfare benefits have been drastically reduced over the last 25 years, government spending has not. Instead tax dollars have been absorbed by prisons and the entire criminal justice system. In fact, Beckett and Western found that states' welfare spending was negatively associated with the incarceration rate. In other words, states with generous welfare benefits had lower incarceration rates, and states that had very low welfare spending had the highest incarceration rates. They also found that the percentage of blacks in a state's population was positively associated with the state's incarceration rate (2001: 45). Others have also noted that the punitiveness expressed by politicians and the public seems to be differentially assigned to the poor (Herivel and Wright 2003).

Western (2006) argues that the collapse of urban labor markets for unskilled men in the 1970s led to large increases in unemployment that were, in effect, masked by the concomitant increase in imprisonment of the same demographic group. In fact, imprisoning this group diminishes by as much as 24 percent national unemployment figures (Western 2006: 92). Similar to the discussion presented in chapter 1, he argues that the increased imprisonment was a thinly disguised solution to large-scale unemployment of urban black men. He notes that in 1980 black male dropouts were four times more likely than the college-educated to be in prison, but in 2000 these men were eight times more likely to be in prison and the rate of imprisonment for black male drop outs was nearly 50 times the national average (Western 2006: 18). In an analysis of state sentencing, he found that the percentage of unskilled young men affected imprisonment more than did race alone.

In a sentencing study conducted in conjunction with the Vera Institute of Justice, it was found that crime rates, the proportion of blacks in the population, and the *ideologies favored by a state's citizens* were the most influential factors affecting incarceration rates. Having a sentencing guideline system (a method of guiding a judge's sentencing decisions) was also an influential factor. It was found that a presumptive sentencing guideline system lowered a state's incarceration rate by 72 per 100,000 (Sorensen and Stemen 2002). Other variables, although less influential, included the percentage of the population in the age group 18–34 and the poverty level. On the other hand, determinate sentencing, mandatory sentencing policies, and truth-in-sentencing legislation did not seem to have much effect on prison admission rates, contrary to what many believe (Sorensen and Stemen 2002). Note, however, that prison *admission* rates are different from *incarceration* rates (which factor all those in prison against a base population figure). Laws that increase sentences will eventually affect imprisonment rates because more people will serve longer sentences.

Some polls indicate that the public is more in favor of rehabilitation and less likely to support increased spending for prisons than has commonly been believed (Greene and Schiraldi 2002: 6). Even though a substantial number still believe in punishing nonviolent offenders, there is also support for rehabilitation, a growing belief that long mandatory prison sentences are not fair, and an unwillingness to take state monies from education to devote to corrections (Greene and Schiraldi 2002: 6). About 65 percent of those responding to a public opinion survey supported addressing the root of crime compared to 32 percent who favored strict sentencing. Further, survey respondents were more willing to cut prison budgets than child care, terrorism protection measures, education and job training, or health care. About 63 percent agreed that drug addiction should be dealt with by counseling and treatment rather than punitive measures, and 70 percent believed that the current approach is a failure. In fact, the majority of respondents believed that prisons were only "warehouses" that provided little or no rehabilitation (Open Society Institute 2002).

The Open Society study also found that Americans were losing confidence in mandatory sentencing policies. Over half favored the elimination of three strikes laws, and most saw prevention as the most important function of the criminal justice system (Open Society Institute 2002). The prevention program perceived to be most effective was teaching young people personal responsibility and moral values. Over three-quarters (77 percent) believed that expanding after-school programs would save money by reducing the need for prisons (Open Society Institute 2002).

More recently, public opinion polls show strong support for treatment over punitive approaches (Gottschalk 2011). A 2007 poll in Texas indicated that 71 percent of voters preferred a mandatory intensive treatment program over a prison sentence and 83 percent supported diverting lower-level offenders from prison (Pew Center on the States 2011: 6).

Increased Parole Revocations

Between 1990 and 1998 there was a 54 percent increase in the number of parolees returned to prison. In California, nearly 70 percent of parolees returned to prison in the early 2000s (Virella 2003: 101). In 2009, prisons admissions in California showed that there were twice as many (84,779) parole violators returned to prison as there were new court commitments (44,926). Nationally, parole violators represent about 35 percent of prison admissions. Though the number of parole violators returned to prison had been increasing, in the last couple of years it has declined slightly (West, Sabol, and Greenman 2010: 5, 26). Even so, the numbers are still much higher than they had been in earlier decades.

The "War on Drugs"

The war on drugs and the concomitant sentencing of drug offenders has been perhaps the largest contributor to rising incarceration rates. Western (2006: 47), for instance, estimates that about 45 percent of the increase in prison populations has been due to drug offenders. Only about seven percent of all new court commitments to prison were for drug offenses in 1980, but by 1992, almost 31 percent of all new prison commitments were for drug offenses (Gilliard and Beck 1994: 7). In 1998, 59 percent of all federal prisoners and 21 percent of all state inmates were there for drug offenses (Zimring and Hawkins 1995: 162). In 2009, 51 percent of federal prisoners and 18 percent of state prisoners were incarcerated for drugs (West, Sabol, and Greenman 2010: 33).

There is no question that more people are being sent to prison for drug crimes than 30 years ago (even though the number has been declining in more recent years). There are unresolved questions, however, as to whether or not drug use has increased or whether the increase is due to policy choices in how to deal with drug users and those who provide drugs to others. While some individuals attributed a rapid rise in the number of drug offenders to the explosion of crack in urban ghettos in the mid-1980s, and also attributed a spike in violence to the crack drug markets, others dispute whether this activity had any appreciable impact on prison populations. Raphael and Stoll (2008) argue that the numbers were small compared to the total prison population and prison populations continued to rise even after crack markets fell apart in the late 1980s.

The Office of National Drug Control Policy (ONDCP) provides drug use trends. According to the national surveys it has conducted for many decades, Americans' drug use patterns have only slightly increased from 31 percent who indicated they had ever used an illicit drug in 1979 to 41 percent in 2001. When asked if they had used an illicit drug in the last 30 days, 14 percent admitted such use in 1979, but that number declined to 5.9 percent in 1993. Then the number began to climb again and it is now at about 8.7 percent (ONDCP 2004: 1; SAMSHSA 2010).

By most accounts, marijuana use reached an all-time high in 1979, with about 60 percent of high school seniors reporting at least one use incident. In 1992, only about 33 percent of seniors reported ever having used marijuana and only about two percent reported daily use, but by 1999 about 50 percent of seniors reported ever using and about eight percent reported daily use (cited from information in the National Household Survey on Drug Abuse, 1998, in Inciardi 2002: 295). In the 2000 study of high school seniors, 21.6 percent reported using within the last month, but in 2009 the number had declined to 11 percent (youth 12-17) (SAMHSA 2010). For adults, the "ever used" numbers were 52 percent for marijuana and 15 percent for cocaine (SAMHSA 2010: 96). Heroin and other drugs show even lower use figures. Generally, incarceration figures don't seem to be correlated with use figures at all. Incarceration numbers began their climb in the early 1980s and have continued to rise upward ever since while use figures seem to go up and down.

Increasing numbers of Americans believe that the nation's war on drugs has been ill conceived and wasteful of public dollars. In one poll, 77 percent of respondents agreed with the statement "Many people in prison today are nonviolent drug addicts who need drug treatment, not a prison sentence" (Greene and Schiraldi 2002: 6). Further, there are declining numbers of Americans who believe that criminal justice policies are the most effective responses to drug use, decreasing from 41 percent of respondents in 1990 to 31 percent in 1995 (Lock, Timberlake, and Rasinki 2002: 384). Still another survey found that 76 percent of respondents favored mandatory drug treatment rather than prison for those convicted of possession and 71 percent favored mandatory treatment and community service for those convicted of sales of small amounts (reported in King and Mauer 2001: 1).

In the early 2000s, states responded to these trends by eliminating mandatory minimums, instituting drug courts to divert first time drug offenders from prison, and used other means to reduce the numbers of drug offenders who cycled in and out of prison without treatment. Even after diverting substantial numbers of offenders, these states did not appear to experience any negative effects such as increased crime rates (Greene and Schiraldi 2002, 19).

The Deinstitutionalizaton of the Mentally Ill

It is a little-known fact that the rate of institutionalization of the mentally ill was about the same as the current incarceration rate before a massive deinstitutionalization effort occurred in the 1970s. In 1955 there were about 559,000 people in mental hospitals and this was, per capita, similar to the number in prison today (Gottschalk 2009). In the 1950s, the institutionalization rate was about three times the incarceration rate; today, the incarceration rate is, of course, dramatically higher. Raphael and Stoll (2008) present research from other countries that indicate there is a negative relationship between a country's incarceration rate and the institutionalization rate of the mentally ill. In the 1970s a host of factors, including a newfound recognition of due process rights, the discovery of anti-psychotic drugs, and a belief that treatment was more effective in the community led to the dismantling of a huge number of mental hospitals in this country. The possibility that this led to individuals with mental problems being sentenced to prison cannot be overlooked, especially when about 10 percent of the incarcerated population is believed to have mental health issues.

Raphael and Stoll (2008) discount the possibility that deinstitutionalization of the mentally ill has led to the growth of the prison population due to the different demographics of those who are in prison versus those who were in mental hospitals; mental patients tended to be older, white, and female as compared to prison populations. Gottschalk (2009) offers the possibility that, just as politicians, policy makers and the American public made a concerted effort to deinstitutionalize large numbers of the mentally ill in the 1970s, the same could occur today with prisoners.

The Privatization of Prisons

There are some who argue that part of the reason that prison populations rose in the 1980s and remain stubbornly high is because it has become a profitable industry (Gottschalk 2006). In this section we will examine the increase in the use of privatization, leaving to chapter 3 a review of evaluations that analyze whether private prisons are more effective than public prisons. During the building boom in the 1980s, states could not build prisons fast enough to accommodate the rising numbers, so many contracts were signed with private prison providers. Even counties got into the prison business. Many counties built huge new jails with the expectation of filling them with state prisoners and paying for them with state "per diems" (cost per day to house inmates). Many of these county jails sat empty in the 2000s because states had, by then, built their own prisons. Some states continued to pay private providers or counties to house prisoners even though they had extra beds because of contract or political reasons (Ward, M. 2002a: A13).

In 2001, 31 states, the District of Columbia, and the Federal Bureau of Prisons (FBOP) held 94,948 prisoners in private prisons (Beck, Karberg, and Harrison 2002: 4). In 2009, there were 129,336, representing about a five percent annual increase (West, Sabol, and Greenman 2010: 33). Texas purchases the most private prison beds of any of the states. In 2001, 17,746 prisoners were housed in 43 private prisons. In 2002, the state substantially reduced its reliance on private vendors, and the number of prisoners in private prisons dropped to 10,764. But by 2009, the number was back up to 19,207. The federal government is, by far, the best customer of private prison companies, with 34,087 private beds in the federal system in 2009, which is double the number in 2000 (15,524) (Beck, Karberg, and Harrison 2002: 4; Harrison and Karberg 2003: 6; West, Sabol, and Greenman 2010: 33, 34).

Immigrant prisoners, a rapidly growing group, are increasingly housed in private facilities. Critics argue that these prisoners have virtually no voice. They often do not speak English and have no legal representation or family to stand up for their rights. They languish in detention facilities for years without knowing what is happening to them or when they will get out (Greene 2001). Welch (2002) provides an exhaustive study of the incredible growth of federal immigration detainees and the number detained in county jails and private facilities under contract with the federal government. Advocates for detainees point out that these are not criminals in the typical sense, yet they are being housed in prisons. Allegations of brutality, sexual assault, lack of programs, and inhumane conditions are frequent and consistent.

Privatization is certainly not a new concept in corrections. Some of the very earliest places of confinement were run by private individuals who contracted with the state to operate the facility. In the South, lease labor systems were contractual arrangements between the state and landowners whereby landowners fed and clothed inmates and paid the state a certain amount of money in return for the prisoners' labor. Many states continue to contract with private groups to provide treatment, medical, or other services; and private–public partnerships in prison industries are gaining momentum. What is capturing the attention of some critics, however, is the increasing prevalence of private corporations that contract with a state to build and/or run a correctional facility. Corporations such as Corrections Corporation of America and Geo Group (formerly Wackenhut) have their stock traded on the New York Stock Exchange, spurring critics who question the legitimacy of prisons for profit.

> Sorry to be late clueing you to this great new money-making opportunity, but there may still be time to get in on the seminar that will show you how to imprison people for fun and profit.... If you're looking for something really reliable, what better to invest in than human misbehavior? It has been a sure thing since Cain and Abel. (columnist Tom Teepen 1996)

The pattern for new construction has been for prisons to be built in small towns that have lost their manufacturing base. These small towns in rural areas have offered land and other benefits to have companies build prisons there in the hope for jobs and a boost to the local economy (Lawrence and Travis 2004). For the most part the jobs have failed to materialize and, at least in one study, rural communities with prisons show lower economic growth than those without (King, Mauer, and Huling 2003). Despite these findings, when states try to close down prisons there is a fierce outcry and a strong political pushback (Gottschalk 2011).

Another aspect of this growth has been a shift of population to rural districts since prisoners are counted in the census as residents of the county where the prison is located. While only five percent of the national population resides in "non-metro" counties, 23 percent of the prisoner population does (Lawrence and Travis 2004: 16). The result has been that federal dollars are directed to these rural communities through grants based on population. Federal aid for Medicaid, social services, road construction, and public housing are all driven by population counts. Some argue that these federal and state dollars, desperately needed in the largely urban, poor neighborhoods where prisoners come from, have been unfairly transferred to rural communities that do not need the infrastructure support since prisoners are taken care of by the state. Lawrence and Travis (2004) point out, however, that there has been a greater increase in the number of prisoners housed in metro counties than the increase of prisoners in non-metro counties, and the pattern of prisoners being housed in non-metro counties goes back to the origin of prisons. Their analysis does show, however, that there is very little overlap in the counties that sentence offenders to prison and the counties where these offenders are housed (2004: 33).

Even apart from private prison corporations, prisons are big business. The expenditure of $70 billion annually goes to prison guards, telephone service providers, construction workers, food service companies, textile manufacturers, and a host of other goods and services that rely on contracts from private and public prisons. The contractors constitute a strong force of resistance to reducing prison populations.

REVERSING THE TREND

Recent figures indicate that in 2010 there were 9,228 fewer prisoners than there were in 2009; the first time since 1972 that the total prison population decreased (Guerino, Harrison, and Sabol 2011: 1). In the early 2000s the rate of increase slowed, probably spurred by an economic recession that stressed states' budgets. Ohio, Illinois, Florida, and Missouri closed one or more prisons in the early 2000s because of declining numbers of prisoners and budget shortfalls (Greene and Schiraldi 2002: 4). A number of states passed legislation that revised sentencing laws or mandated reviews of sentences in order to reduce the number of nonviolent and/or drug offenders spending long periods of time in prison (Greene and Schiraldi 2002: 11). Yet, even though the rate of increase slowed, prison populations continued to increase and the federal prisoner population grew dramatically. The federal prisoner population was 25,000 in 1980, 145,416 in 2000, and 208,118 in 2009, with an average annual increase between 2000 and 2009 of about four percent. State prisoner populations in comparison showed only a 1.5 percent annual increase and between 2008 and 2009 actually declined (Harrison and Karberg 2003: 1; West, Sabol, and Greenman 2010: 2). Between 2009 and 2010, the number of state prisoners continued to decline and the rate of increase of federal prisoners slowed to only 0.8 percent, resulting in a net decline of prisoners from the year before. The federal increase has been due almost entirely to drug laws that require mandatory terms of imprisonment and long sentences. Other contributors are the growing number of noncitizen offenders and immigration violators.

In 2011 it was reported that New York, Texas, Colorado, Connecticut, Georgia, Michigan, Florida, Nevada, North Carolina, Oregon, Rhode Island, Washington, and Wisconsin had closed or planned to close prisons. Four states (Kansas, Michigan, New Jersey, and New York) reduced their prison populations between five and 20 percent (Sentencing Project 2011). Other states have also reduced their prison populations, sometimes under court order to do so. Even though California had reduced its prison population in the last couple of years, the U.S. Supreme Court upheld a circuit court's opinion in 2011 that required the state to release close to 50,000 inmates because the overcrowding in the state's prisons created unconstitutional conditions (*Brown v. Plata*, May 2011). According to reports, cells designed to hold one inmate house three and gymnasiums and clinics have been converted into makeshift dormitories. A suicide occurs every eight days, and the medical care or lack of it contributes to frequent deaths (Mears 2011).

Just as the recession in the early 2000s led to prison closures, the fiscal crisis of today seems to have spurred states to reevaluate incarceration practices. It should also be noted, however, that some observers predict the tide will turn once again and economic stress may lead to greater punitiveness (Gottschalk 2011).

CONCLUSION

We have seen that prisons are a relatively new weapon in our arsenal against offenders. In a short 200-year history, they have risen to become the "first-choice" option for judges sentencing offenders. So much so, that now we are having difficulty paying for all the prisoners we have incarcerated. In a careful review, Raphael and Stoll (2008) analyze a number of factors said to contribute to the rise of imprisonment. While they note small effects from the 1980s crack market, the deinstitutionalization of the mentally ill, demographic changes, and the loss of employment markets for the unskilled, they attribute most of the increase to policy decisions. Basically, the argument is that we have dramatically increased our prison population because we chose to do so. This is actually good news because it means that we could undertake different policy choices that could dramatically reduce the prison population given the political will to do so. One thing that all the numbers and charts cannot do is describe the effect these sentences have on families. Two million people is hard to imagine; harder still are the many more millions affected outside of prison.

> Let me describe what prison is like for me. Prison is deep emotional pain with no release from the hurt.... Prison is the picture, etched in my memory, of my wife breaking down in convulsive wracking sobs for what I did. Prison is watching the tears run down my mother's face every day. My daughter was in high school and we used to enjoy working through her homework in the evenings. She was an A and B student. Prison is her report cards that came after I was locked up—with Ds and Fs because she was hurting so for what I did. I have these memories with me every day.... How do I show them that I do love them? I am in prison. That is prison. It is pain, deep, frequent, and daily. (an inmate in Johnson and Toch 2000: 68)

WEBSITES

For more information on prison populations, visit the Bureau of Justice Statistics: http://bjs.ojp.usdoj.gov/

For more information on the Office of the National Drug Control Policy, visit:
http://www.whitehouse.gov/ondcp.

For more information on the Substance Abuse and Mental Health Services
Administration (SAMSHA), visit:
http://www.samhsa.gov/

For more information about the Open Society Institute, visit:
http://www.soros.org/.

For more information on the Federal Bureau of Prisons, visit:
http://www.bop.gov/

STUDY QUESTIONS

1. How many people are incarcerated in the United States? How does this compare with other countries? What are the regional differences in rates of incarceration?
2. What is the trend in incarceration rates? Are we incarcerating more or fewer people than in years past?
3. What are the reasons proposed for our patterns of incarceration?
4. What do the incarceration rates look like by race? What is the issue concerning grouping Hispanics with whites when looking at incarceration rates?
5. Is the increase in use of prisons due to increase in crime? If not, what are the reasons for the increase in use of prisons and number of imprisoned?
6. What are the three strikes laws? How do they affect incarceration rates?
7. Is there a difference between admission and incarceration rates? If so, explain.
8. How did the "War on Drugs" affect the incarceration rates? What views did the public have of drug offenders?
9. What do public opinion polls show regarding their support for rehabilitation versus imprisonment?
10. How have some states tried to reverse the trend of increased prisoner populations?

CHAPTER 3

ᴧ

The New Bastille

> Prisons are hellholes. They are nothing but human warehouses for society's misfits, outcasts, and transgressors. For the prisoners, the loss of freedom is devastating. Everything they have taken for granted is gone. They have no control over their lives, no choices. Others decide when and where they wake, eat, work, and sleep. Their lives are fastened to rules and regulations that discourage and disregard normal impulses. They accept the rules and adjust to them, just as they do to the overcrowded conditions, body odors, lack of privacy, standing in lines, and the like. They have no choice. (an inmate, in Johnson and Toch 2000: 141)

In this chapter we will take a closer look at some of today's prisons. In discussions of prisons, it bears repeating that there is a wide variation in the types of prisons in existence, the types of living situations inmates are exposed to, and regional and statewide differences in philosophies and policies. It is, in fact, misleading to have any discussion that assumes prisons are all alike, because they are most definitely not.

THE NUMBER AND TYPES OF PRISONS

There were over 1,500 prisons in this country in 2001; today, there are 1,719 prisons (Austin and Irwin 2001: 65; BJS [key facts] 2011). About five percent of them are private, and the rest are state or federal institutions. Some prisons look, smell, and sound like their predecessors of 100 or even 200 years ago. Other prisons are the ultimate in modern technology. Steel and cement, cameras and computers have replaced stone walls and guard towers. Some minimum and even medium security prisons are surprisingly unintimidating, but ask any prisoner, and they will tell you that a prison, no matter how benign it appears, is still a prison.

Prison systems have different custody levels, from minimum security to maximum security. Minimum-security institutions might be work camps, forestry camps, or urban work release centers. Maximum-security institutions are the epitome of the big house prisons, with high walls, razor wire, and guard towers. A few are considered "super-max" prisons, the most secure facilities in the world, where inmates spend the majority of their sentence completely alone in a way that is very similar to the old Pennsylvania system described in chapter 1.

FEDERAL AND STATE SYSTEMS

Keve (1991) chronicles the history of the Federal Bureau of Prisons, beginning with the Congressional act in 1891 that provided the legal authority to build Leavenworth (Kansas), Atlanta (Georgia), and MacNeil Island (Washington), the first federal penitentiaries. Today, the federal system has a system of over 100 penitentiaries, medium-level, and low-level security correctional facilities, satellite facilities, and camps. The growth in the size of the federal prison system has been phenomenal, prompting federal officials to rely increasingly on private vendors to house federal prisoners and detainees. In recent years, state prison populations have been declining while the federal prisoner population continues to increase. In 2000 there were 145,416 federal prisoners and in 2009 there were 208,118 (West, Sabol, and Greenman 2010: 16). About 34,087 of federal prisoners are in private prisons (16 percent) (West, Sabol, and Greenman 2010: 34).

Historically, there were very few federal prisoners because there were few federal crimes. In the 1980s the number of federal crimes, largely drug-related, exploded, leading to a huge increase in federal prisoners and, also, leading to a different demographic. Federal prisoners today are more likely to be drug offenders than white-collar offenders, and they often have long mandatory sentences. In 2009, almost 52 percent of the federal prison population was composed of drug offenders, 15 percent were incarcerated for weapons, explosives and arson, and 11 percent for immigration crimes. In that same year about 42 percent were serving sentences of 10 years to life (Bureau of Prisons [BOP] 2010: 2). The federal system also runs immigration detention facilities, and the number of these facilities has increased in recent years as well; many are privately run. The inmate population in the federal system is about 58 percent white, 39 percent black, 33 percent Hispanic. The average inmate age is 38. About three-quarters of the prisoners are citizens. About 94 percent are men (BOP 2010: 2).

Similar to state prison systems, federal prisons are sometimes clustered in one community. Florence, Colorado, has four federal prisons with over 3,000 inmates.

The super-max federal prison in Florence has housed federal prisoners such as John Gotti, Ted Kaczynski, and Oklahoma City bombers Tim McVeigh and Terry Nichols. The facility is built almost entirely underground and is described in the quote below.

> You enter ADX Florence by descending a 50 foot staircase. The prison cellblocks are located below ground level. The facility has 550 permanently locked down one-man cells....Prisoners eat all their meals in their concrete "boxcar" cells, leaving only to exercise in a private room an hour per day....The prison staff can use four-point spread-eagle restraints, forced feedings, cell extractions (forceful removal), mind control medications, and non-lethal chemical weapons to incapacitate resistant prisoners. (Ross and Richards 2002: 39)

State Prisons

In 1923 there were 61 state prisons in the United States; by 1950 there were 127. In 1974 that number had risen to 592 and more than doubled to 1,023 by 2000 (Lawrence and Travis, 2004: 8). In the next 10 years, the number increased to 1,719 (BJS [key facts] 2011). As mentioned in the last chapter, an unprecedented increase in prison admissions occurred in the 1980s. In the 1990s, states built their way out of their overcrowding problem—temporarily at least. However, the number of prisons continues to grow. In Texas, for instance, between 1979 and 2000, the state built 124 prisons (Lawrence and Travis 2004: 9).

Some prisons today are over 100 years old, and visiting them is like returning to the past. Most are newer, having been built in the "boom" of prison construction in the last 15 years or so. The towering brick or stone structures of the 1800s with massive high walls and small cells arranged down long tiers are the exception today. Newly built prisons are modular, "cookie cutter" buildings constructed in the same way as self-storage buildings—an appropriate analogy, actually, since some argue that they are no better than human storage facilities. "High tech" has replaced high walls as security, with remote cameras and chain link and razor wire serving as perimeter security.

In the South, many prisons may still be considered prison farms with thousands of acres of crops, often cotton. Guards on horseback carrying rifles still watch over inmates who are taken out to the fields each morning in wagons pulled by tractors. In Texas and other southern states, a familiar sight along some highways is a long unbroken line of white-uniformed prisoners swinging their hoes in unison as they move down the rows of cotton. Chain gangs are also still a reality in many states. Prison work crews might clear trash from roadways, dig ditches, clean rivers, or perform other labor for the state or local communities.

A prison, especially a minimum security facility, might also be a high-rise in a city. Inmates may check themselves in and out to go to work or job interviews during the day. It is possible that the passersby may not even know they are looking at a prison unless they happen to read the sign near every entrance that warns individuals they are entering a prison facility and are subject to search. Although the movie version of prison usually includes cells, prisoners today are more often housed in dormitories. They are no doubt cheaper to build and maintain, but not safer. Further, the spread of contagious disease in dormitory settings is said to be twice that of cells. (Cox, Paulson, and McCain 1984: 1154)

> Upon entering one of these makeshift dorms, I am struck first by the noise level, including constant shouting, security officers barking orders or calling out inmates' names, and the flushing of the ten or twelve toilets that have been installed along one wall of the gymnasium. The inmates report that the noise never dies down, and there is always someone hassling you. The lights are usually left on all night, presumably for security reasons, and inmates tell me that they have a hard time sleeping. The men bring food to their bunks, so there are roaches and mice. Tempers flare, fights erupt, victimization is rampant. (Kupers, describing a gym made into a dormitory, 1999: 48)

OVERCROWDING

Since the very earliest history of the prison, cycles of reform and optimism have given way to overcrowding and a deterioration of conditions. The overcrowding in the 1980s led to a massive construction phase in which hundreds of prisons were built. Today, these prisons are still overcrowded, with at least one state (California) facing a court order to drastically reduce its prisoner population. Prisons designed for 500 inmates may hold double that number or more, and inmates are double- or even triple-celled in cells designed for one. Overcrowding is difficult for both inmates and officers. Research indicates that overcrowding can lead to a number of pathologies, including a rise in suicides, deaths from contagious diseases, disciplinary infractions, increases in mental health admissions, and disciplinary infractions (Cox, Paulus, and McCain 1984).

California and Texas run the largest prison systems in the country, but they are very different. California's system is the third largest prison system in the world, eclipsing the size of the systems of entire countries. In 2010, California held 165,062 prisoners, which was actually a decrease from 2009 (171,275) and 2008 (173,670). Texas held 173,649 prisoners in 2010, which was an increase from 2009 (171,249) and 2008 (172,506) (West, Sabol, and Greenman 2010: 16; Guerino, Harrison, and Sabol 2011: 14). In 2007, Texas undertook an initiative to direct funds toward community sentencing alternatives (probation and community drug treatment) with the expectation that this approach would reduce the number of offenders sent to prison. It was a successful approach and, contrary to projections that Texas would have to build four new prisons in the coming years, what happened instead was that Texas reduced the size of its prison population. In fact, in some years it led the nation in the percentage decrease of prisoners. Unfortunately, more recently, the state fiscal crisis has led to budget cuts and observers note that cutting programs may be penny-wise and pound-foolish since it may lead to the need for more prison beds, which are much more expensive than community treatment alternatives (Grissom 2011).

California, by contrast, has been mandated by the courts to reduce its prison population. In *Brown v. Plata* (2011) the U.S. Supreme Court held that the state must reduce its population by 40,000 prisoners because the conditions in the prison were intolerable and violated the Eighth Amendment of the Constitution. In 2010, the state was 200 percent over its stated prison capacity (Dominack 2010). Earlier, in *Madrid v. Gomez* (1995), a federal appellate court had placed California on notice that the system needed to change. Even though the state had built dozens of new prisons, prisoners were still being housed in gyms, chapels, and recreation areas. Medical care was compromised. It was reported that there was one doctor for every 6,000 inmates in the system. Inmates died because of lack of medical care and many more suffered because medical care was either nonexistent or came too late. Since *Madrid v. Gomez*, California has attempted to alleviate overcrowding, but it was still over 200 percent capacity at the time of the 2011 decision.

The California prison system already takes eight percent of the general state fund ($10.6 billion annually) (Dominack 2010). The size of the system is due partially to three strikes and two strikes sentencing, but also to high parole revocations. California prisoners have a recidivism (return to prison) rate of 67 percent (Dominack 2010: 1). The state cannot seem to build its way out of the overcrowding crisis and has been unable to reduce the costs of the prison system by utilizing alternatives to prison. One of the reasons that it has been difficult to trim the prison system is the political power of the California Correctional Peace Officers Association (CCPOA). Under former governor Gray Davis, the correctional officer union was successful in securing a 34 percent pay raise to officers when the state was facing a $27.5 billion budget deficit and all other state employees' salaries were frozen. Observers noted that Governor Davis had received $2.2 million from the union for his reelection campaign. The union opposed legislation that would have limited three strikes sentencing to violent offenders and it has blocked attempts to reduce the prison population by utilizing community sentencing alternatives. It now appears, however, that the U.S. Supreme Court will force the state to either build many more prisons (a political and fiscal impossibility) or release inmates.

Despite first-person accounts of how prison overcrowding affects prisoners (Carceral 2005), the link between crowding and violence has not been consistently found in studies. Steiner and Woolredge (2009) discuss the difficulties of using rates to evaluate whether crowding affects the likelihood of assaults. Instead of looking at the total population as the denominator, they suggest design capacity should be used in calculations of whether assault rates are related to overcrowding; they also suggest program participation figures should be utilized. These authors also note that crowding may affect different locations of a facility differently; for instance, it may be that crowding may lead to more assaults in dormitories or in locations that are unsupervised. Pooling all populations, especially across studies, may mask crowding effects because they incorporate many different living situations.

In the last couple of years, prison populations have declined in many states, and this may be the beginning of a new era where prison overcrowding will be alleviated by a combination of sentencing reform and reentry efforts that will help reduce recidivism.

THE SUPER-MAX

Institutions like Alcatraz, California, and MacNeil Island, Washington, were built to house the "worst of the worst"—prisoners whose violent tendencies or organized crime connections made it impossible to house them in "normal" prisons. The federal system closed Alcatraz in the 1960s but Marion, Illinois, opened in the early 1980s, replicated the features of Alcatraz with solitary cells and highly restricted privileges for the inmates, including 23-hour cell confinement and a lack of programming.

In the 1980s and 1990s, states began to build their own "Alcatraz-type" prison called the super-max. The original impetus for such facilities was to isolate gang leaders and inmates who were chronically violent toward other inmates and officers. Correctional officials argued that they were needed despite the huge price tag associated with them, and they generally were able to convince state legislatures of their need. In 1997, 36 states and the Federal Bureau of Prisons operated 57 super-maximum units (Corrections Alert 1997: 8). In 2008, 44 states had opened super-max prisons which housed around 25,000 inmates (Mears and Bales 2009: 1132, 1134). It should be noted that there is less than unanimous agreement on what facilities should be considered super-max facilities and this disagreement has led to confusion and difficulty when researching the facilities (Naday, Freilich, and Mellow 2008). As criticism of super-maxes have increased in the last several years, states have redefined some prisons as maximum security instead of super-max, although inmates are still in their cell 23 hours a day with no programming. Thus, there is no general agreement on even the number of such facilities, much less their relative need or worth.

There are also major differences between states in how they are used. In some states, less than one percent of the prisoner population is housed in the super-max, in some there are no super-max prisons at all, but in other states more than 10 percent are housed in a super-max (Pizarro and Narag 2008: 26). Some states have hearings and transfer inmates only after some form of due process, while in others the transfer is a classification decision and a suspected gang member may go directly to the super-max upon entry into the system. Only six states have any type of transitional program whereby super-max prisoners are transitioned back into the general population and never are released directly from the super-max into the community (Pizarro and Narag 2008: 27).

The most notorious of the super-max prisons is Pelican Bay, California. This facility was built in 1989 in a remote northern region of California to house 2,080 prisoners. It quickly became overcrowded, with over 3,250 prisoners. Prisoners were housed two to a cell designed for one (Austin and Irwin 2001: 127). Pelican Bay has been the target of court action, television and newspaper journalistic investigations, and American Civil Liberties Union action. In *Madrid v. Gomez* (1995), it was ruled that there was an insufficient number of medical and mental health professionals, excessive force had been used, and policies regarding the use of force were inadequate. Pelican Bay, like most super-max prisons, confines inmates in their cell 23 or 24 hours a day. That alone is enough to generate some concern, since cell confinement has been found to be detrimental to mental and physical health. Beyond confinement, however, is the practice of limiting and greatly restricting any human contact. In these modern-day Alcatrazes, sophisticated technology is used to open and close cell doors and service the inmates inside the cells. They literally may never touch a human hand for months.

> ...Pelican Bay's low, windowless, slate-gray exterior gives no hint to outsiders that this is a place where human beings live....On each visit to this prison I have been struck by the harsh, visual sameness and monotony of the physical design and the layout of these units...you search in vain for humanizing touches or physical traces that human activity takes place here....Prisoners at Pelican Bay are not even permitted to see grass, trees, or shrubbery....(Haney 2002: 162)

Such practices are regrettable but understandable when used for those inmates who are so violent that it is impossible to trust them not to attack anyone who comes near them, and any contact without a full contingent of specially trained and outfitted officers would be foolish. However, there have been allegations that inmates are sent to such facilities not because of a prediction of extreme violence, but rather because they are being punished for demanding rights or for being troublemakers (Haney 2008; Parenti 1999: 209). Prisoners in California allege that they are sent to Pelican Bay if they are perceived to be gang affiliated and then told that they can be released back to general population only if they "give up" other gang members or provide other information to the gang investigators. In protest of this practice and the inhuman conditions, prisoners organized and held a hunger strike during the summer of 2011 with a second one in the fall of 2011. If these allegations are true, there are serious questions as to the right of the state to subject such individuals to such draconian measures.

Mears and Bales (2010), in their study of a Florida super-max, found that those in the super-max were about four times as likely to have committed violence in prison as the non-super-max inmates, but they were about seven times more likely than non-super-max prisoners to have exhibited "defiant behavior." They also found that in the Florida system, super-max inmates have an average of four stays in the super-max with an average stay of about 13 months, but about a third of the inmates spent up to a third of their entire prison stay in the super-max (2010: 549).

Wisconsin opened its super-max facility in 1999 at a cost of $47.5 million for 509 beds. The annual operating budget for each bed is twice that of a general population bed (Kaplan 1999: 1). The cell measures 6 feet by 12 feet. There is a combined stainless steel sink and toilet and a shower in one corner (with a drain in the floor). A 6 foot x 6 foot window, high up on the wall, is fogged to prevent any view of the outside. No clock, radio, or television is allowed in the cells. Video cameras can be kept on 24 hours a day. One-hour-a-day exercise is allowed, but the inmate is shackled and guarded by two guards and led to a room not much bigger than the cell itself. Technology includes a "biometric" system that scans hands for security identification, a video visitation system (in place of face-to-face visits), motion detectors and surveillance cameras, and a central command post that uses computers to control movement through every door. Prison officials estimate that inmates may spend one to three years at the facility before being able to return to general population prisons. Critics argue that after such a length of time, the inmates may not be fit to return to any type of freedom, no matter how limited (Jones 1999).

> [He] has broken down from the stress of his isolation. He has difficulty sleeping and eating and suffers from shakes or tremors…he falls into fits of weeping. He's written letters to the judge begging for some form of human contact.…The kind of mind it would take to create a place like that is beyond me. (a lawyer talking about his client in the federal super-max in Florence, Colorado; quoted in Annin 1998: 13)

In Virginia, twin super-max facilities, opened in 1998 and 1999, have had several outside investigations stemming from allegations of abuse and inhumane conditions. These facilities were built at a cost of $147 million, and some legislators argue that Virginia does not even have the 2,400 "worst of the worst" inmates to fill the beds. In fact, some of the beds were "rented" to New Mexico until the attorney general of New Mexico asked for an FBI investigation of conditions and pulled out all New Mexico inmates. Allegations included the charge that inmates were shocked with stun guns even when shackled and were fired upon by guards (Hammack 2000).

Haney (2003) and others point out that the super-max prison is different from traditional solitary confinement in the length of time prisoners live in the conditions of total isolation. There are also differences in that greater technology is used, including being under observation by camera 24 hours a day, there is almost complete idleness for long periods of time, many never see the outside because there are no windows, and many who are transferred to super-maxes have not been accused or found guilty of committing any prison infractions.

These facilities concern prisoners' rights' groups and those who believe that the United States already lags behind most of Western Europe in meeting standards for humane treatment of prisoners. There are also those who believe that the super-max violates the 1994 UN Convention Against Torture and Other Cruel, Inhuman or Degrading Treatment or Punishment. Advocates for prisoners have filed lawsuits alleging that the super-max violates the Eighth Amendment prohibition against cruel and unusual punishment, while others argue that prisoners deserve due process before being transferred to a super-max. Generally, courts have not found the conditions of the super-max prison to constitute cruel and unusual punishment, except for the mentally ill. Some courts have required states to have policies clearly identifying which inmates can be sent to the super-max and such policies are required to exclude the mentally ill. The court cases below are a sample of those concerning the super-max prison:

- *Madrid v. Gomez*, 889 F. Supp. 1146 (1995) (California)
- *Taifa v. Bayhm*, 846 F. Supp. 723 (1994) (Indiana)
- *Wilkinson v. Austin*, 544 U.S. 74 (2005) (Ohio)
- *Joslyn v. Armstrong*, No. 3:01-cv-00198-CFD, slip op. at 1 (D. Conn., October 17, 2001)
- *Jones'El v. Berge*, 374 F.3d 541 (2004) (Wisconsin).

Critics argue that the super-max prison is psychologically harmful. It is especially so for those who have psychological problems to begin with, and many contend that those who are sent to a super-max for violent acting out are often diagnosed with psychological problems. Symptoms noted include massive free-floating anxiety, hyper-responsiveness to external stimuli, perceptual distortions and hallucinations, a feeling of unreality, difficulty with concentration and memory, acute confusional states, emergence of primitive aggressive fantasies, persecutory ideation, motor excitement, and/or violent destructive or self-mutilatory outbursts (Kupers 1999: 57). Also noted have been appetite disruptions, panic, rage, lethargy, paranoia, and loss of control (Haney 2003).

> This isn't making the community safe … you're just making them the most sickest, most impulse-ridden, most enraged, paranoid, impaired human beings. And then you're just putting them right back into the community. (Dr. Grassian, a psychiatrist opposed to the use of super-max prisons, quoted in Jones 1999: 3)

Inmates deprived of any measure of control over their behavior become unnaturally docile and dependent on others, or they irrationally act out to express their own existence, injuring themselves or others in the process. Deprived of any social contact, they may become even more socially withdrawn, avoiding interaction and finding it increasingly difficult to maintain the simplest interchanges with others. Living in a reality that holds nothing but pain, they may retreat into fantasy and lose touch entirely (Haney 2002).

Those who do receive counseling get what is called "cell front therapy" whereby the psychologist or counselor stands outside the cell and the individual, if he wants to communicate, must talk loudly enough for anyone to hear the conversation. Haney (2003) also describes a surreal group therapy session at which the group members sit in their own personal cages.

Haney (2008) has argued that the super-max does damage to the guard as well as the prisoners. He writes that there is an "ecology of cruelty" in the super-max where guards are socialized to be even more punitive and harsh toward prisoners than in regular prisons. This leads to extreme behavior on the part of inmates, which then spurs more harsh reaction from the guards. In these escalating cycles, the abnormal levels of violence and inhumanity become normal—a unique product of the environment of the super-max. It becomes figuratively a "zoo" where men are treated worse than animals. Toch (2001) has also described the effects of the guards in a super-max and the idea that guards go into the prison with the expectation that the prisoners within are the "worst of the worst," treat them that way, and then create the very behavior they expected. Another element of the super-max is that because inmates are locked in 23 hours a day, they depend on the guards for their very survival. This dependency creates an oppositional reaction in the inmates and the opportunity for guards to abuse their power.

> Even the cells are eerie. There are no mirrors. The only time you can see yourself is on the little knob in the shower. You shave on your knees looking at the one-inch reflection. There is very little for you to control in your cell. The light switch is a silver bump and no one seems to know how it works....Though the cells are more than 80 square feet, with or without a "cellie" (cellmate), they quickly shrink when you are inside them for 22 hours a day. (Morris 2002: 183)

It should be noted that some studies have not supported such negative conclusions about super-max facilities. For instance, King (2005) noted that some super-max prisoners said they had benefited from the experience in that they had time to think and control themselves and not be influenced by negative peers. At least one study, in research involving states that used super-max facilities compared with those that did not, found that the use of a super-max prison did not always result in reduced violence among inmates, but there did seem to be a decrease in violence against officers (Briggs, Sundt, and Castellano 2003; Sundt, Castellano, and Briggs 2008). However, others have noted that neither this study, nor any study, could control for system-wide changes that might influence the assault levels instead of, or in addition to, the presence of the super-max (Mears 2008).

Critics who argue against super-max prisons maintain that the experience is so debilitating that super-max releasees should prove more likely to recidivate than other prisoners. A study matched Washington state prisoners who spent time in a super-max facility to those who had served their time in regular prisons. They attempted to create matched pairs based on factors that might be correlated with recidivism. They found that, although prisoners who spent time in a super-max had no statistically significant difference in recidivism (53 percent to 46 percent), those who were released into the community directly from a super-max facility did have a significantly higher recidivism rate (69 percent) (Lovall, Johnson, and Cain 2007). Mears and Bales (2009), in a similar study with Florida inmates, found that there was no difference in recidivism between a super-max group and a matched group (59 percent compared to 58 percent), although there was a difference in those who committed violent crimes after release (24 percent compared to 20 percent). They also found that the amount of time spent in super-max was not correlated with recidivism. Finally, they did not find that inmates released directly from a super-max facility were more likely to recidivate than those who were released from the general population of other prisons.

In other evaluations, researchers have found that wardens express generally positive attitudes toward the super-max and its ability to reduce violence, but over half also believed that alternatives to super-maxes could be effectively used. Such alternatives included staff training, segregation cells, and the "transfer and trade" of troublesome inmates (Mears 2008). In a review of all the evaluations and research concerning the super-max, Mears (2008) concluded that there was little evidence the super-max prison was needed to address the violence that was the stated reason for its existence, there is no strong theoretical support for its deterrence effectiveness, there are troubling vagaries in the administration of super-maxes, especially concerning who is transferred there, and there is minimal evidence of their effectiveness on any measure.

PRIVATE PRISONS

Private sector involvement in prisons is nothing new. There has been privatization since the beginning of prisons in this country. In the 1800s, some states contracted with private firms to create and manage the first prison in the state (Schneider 1999). In chapter 2 the lease labor system was described; in this system, inmates were leased to private landowners for their labor. The landowners fed and clothed prisoners and paid the state for their services. The lease labor system gradually was abandoned by states as periodic exposés of horrible conditions and mistreatment led to public antipathy toward the practice.

There were also lease labor arrangements in the industrial prisons of the North where factory owners would pay the state for prisoner labor. In fact, in the early days of prisons, some states saw prisons as revenue generators. Opposition from labor groups toward private companies utilizing inmate labor eventually led to federal legislation. In 1935, the Hawes-Cooper Act allowed states to bar prison-made goods from being transported across state lines to compete with private businesses and in 1940 the Sumners-Ashurst Act made it a federal offense to take prison-made goods across state lines. This legislation, in effect, destroyed private-public partnerships in prison industry until the 1980s.

In the 1980s, as states were experiencing massive increases in prison populations without the prison beds to accommodate the new prisoners, several private companies emerged that offered to build prisons for the state and/or manage prisons for a per diem prisoner cost. Schneider (1999) points out that this emergence of privatization was different because, instead of local companies or individuals doing business with the prison, as was the case in the earlier models, private prison companies of today have developed into national and even international corporations. Earlier privatization generally involved the private company paying the state for the labor of the prisoners instead of, as today, the state paying the private provider to build and/or run the prison. The other major difference is that, today, prisoners are sometimes transported and housed great distances from their home state.

The capacity of private prisons has grown from a couple of thousand in the early days to 129,336 in 2009. Texas had 19,207 inmates in private prisons; this is far more than Florida's 9,812, and no other state comes close to these numbers (West, Sabol, and Greenman 2010: 33). As states have backed away from their use of private corrections, the federal government has stepped in to offer contracts. The number of private prison beds utilized by the Federal Bureau of Prisons increased from 20,293 in 2001 to 34,087 in 2009 (Beck, Karberg, and Harrison 2002: 4; West, Sabol, and Greenman 2010: 33).

Issues regarding the propriety of private prisons include the following:

- Should the government (whether it be county, state, or federal) delegate its responsibility to incarcerate?
- Do these private institutions cost less, as promised?
- Even if they cost less than public facilities, is it at the expense of quality, either in security or service?
- Does the profit motive encourage more imprisonment?
- Does the private sector respond more quickly and flexibly to changing needs?
- Does the private sector have the legal authority to ensure security?
- Who is liable—the state or the private vendor or both—over issues of violation of rights of prisoners or victimization if there is an escape?
- Is the private sector better or less able to control corruption (Logan 1987)?

Proponents and Opponents of Privatization

Proponents of privatization argue that the private sector can build prisons quicker and faster than state agencies or the federal government, can lower operational costs, and can provide a better quality of service to the inmates. Libertarian and conservative groups that seek to reduce government favor privatization, believing that private enterprise is inherently more efficient than government agencies. The strongest argument for privatization has always been a projected cost savings.

Proponents argue that private corporations are more efficient, they can build faster with less cost and less red tape, and they have economies of scale (i.e., they can obtain savings because of their size). It may be true that private prisons can be built faster because private corporations are not bound by restrictions placed on government. For instance, a state would most likely have to go to voters to pass a bond in order to build new prisons; however, the state can contract with a private provider without voter approval. Also, unlike private corporations, state and local governments are bound by a myriad of bidding and siting restrictions.

The greater flexibility of private prisons is considered an issue as well since legislators do not need to seek public approval before committing the state to multiyear, multimillion-dollar contracts with private vendors. Instead of voters agreeing to take on the debt of new prison construction, legislators can simply approve a contract that commits the state to pay a certain per diem rate for a certain number of prisoners for a given number of years. Or they can approve build-and-lease agreements in which the private vendor agrees to build a prison in exchange for a contract to run it for a certain number of years, after which the state is obligated to purchase the facility. Although the money involved can be as much in the long run as a prison construction project, voters do not need to be consulted.

> ...it's as if the prison expansion is now being funded by way of a credit card issued by the prison-industrial complex—a high-interest credit card that the tax payers have no control over when it comes to spending, but are nonetheless still being required to pay for at the end of the month. (Dyer 2000: 5)

It is also no coincidence that private prisons are more prevalent in southern states where unions are not as strong or are nonexistent. Unions oppose privatization largely because private prisons pay much less than state prisons. Since personnel costs are the largest single portion of correctional costs, this difference is the main reason why private prisons can offer lower per diem rates.

Opponents of privatization argue that there is something philosophically wrong with making a profit from incarcerating human beings. The major argument against privatization is that government should not delegate what should be a uniquely state function—that is, confining individuals and holding them against their will (Reisig and Pratt 2000). Legal questions of authority and liability have been hammered out for the most part, creating a delegation of authority, but not of liability, so that the state shares responsibility with the private corporation. For instance, prisoners in private facilities are still able to utilize protections against unconstitutional treatment on the part of state officials under Section 1983 of Title 42 of the U.S. Code—protections which guard against abuses by state actors. However, most state contracts with private providers also include an indemnification clause which requires the provider to be responsible for any liability incurred by its actions. To oversee private institutions, states use monitoring practices similar to those used for state-contracted nursing homes, but opponents argue that monitoring is nonexistent or lax and point to a string of scandals involving private facilities.

Scandals have included escapes, abusive conduct by officers, and poor management practices that contributed to high rates of violence. For instance, in one medium security facility, in 15 months of operation, there were 44 assaults, 16 stabbings, and two murders. The culmination was an escape by six inmates. When inspectors arrived to investigate the situation, evidently they were turned away at the front gate (cited in Parenti 1999: 222). The litigation that resulted ended with a $1.6 million settlement offer from the private company to affected inmates (Perez 2001). Other reports document escapes, beatings, and corrupt practices in private facilities (Greene 2001: 23–24). Proponents of privatization argue that these events occur in public prisons as well.

A more abstract and subtle criticism of private corrections is that if someone is making money from incarcerating offenders, where is the incentive to correct them? If recidivism were to somehow mysteriously plummet, corporations would show reduced profits and stockholders would lose money. Private corrections officials point out that their piece of the "corrections pie" is quite small in comparison to the states' share, that they are closely monitored by state officials who are unhappy with sharing any amount of resources with them, and that there is plenty of opportunity to expand in other states and even in other countries without somehow conspiring to keep offenders in prison solely for some profit motive.

Yet, critics point out that private prison corporations contribute to political campaigns and political parties and engage in lobbying (Justice Policy Institute 2011). Their political goals are not only to acquire contracts with states and the federal government for the provision of services. They have also been active in lobbying for legislation that has the effect of creating more prisoners, such as blocking alternative sentencing legislation or the revision of three strikes legislation.

Corrections Corporation of America and GEO Group

Corrections Corporation of America (CCA) has, until recently, been the largest player in the private prison industry, holding a little more than half of all private prison beds (over 60,000 beds in the United States alone). CCA has built prisons in 27 different states and in many foreign countries. Started in Tennessee in the mid-1980s, its owners were well connected politically and proposed taking over the whole Tennessee correction system. They were unsuccessful in that effort, but they did obtain a more modest contract and, thus, began the new wave of privatization in prisons. Texas was an early client of CCA and, more importantly, passed legislation in 1987 that allowed local entities to contract with private providers without voter approval (Schneider 1999).

After their first public offering of stock in 1995, the value of the stock increased by over 400 percent in the first year. After this incredible growth, the stock declined and by 2001, CCA's stock had lost 93 percent of its 2000 value (Greene 2001: 26). This financial meltdown was partly caused by a decline in crime and prisoners and partly by a rash of scandals that plagued CCA's prison facilities. Stock prices have increased since then, from $6 a share in the early 2000s to $22 a share in 2011 (*New York Times* 2011).

The GEO Group, formerly called Wackenhut, changed its name in 2003. The prison division is a spin-off of the older company's private security business. Holding over 25,000 beds at several dozen facilities across the country, it has come in as number two among the private prison providers, but with a recent purchase of another company, may be the largest private prison company today. In the early

2000s it held 11,000 prison beds internationally (57 percent of the international market of private prisons) (Austin and Irwin 2001: 66; Perez 2001). Today, according to their website, they own/manage 116 facilities with 80,000 beds internationally. The company also runs mental health facilities and addiction treatment centers. Since going public in 1994, the GEO Group's stock price has increased by 800 percent. This private prison company has also had a series of incidents reported in its facilities that have affected its reputation and financial standing (Greene 2001). In New Mexico, Governor Gary Johnson threatened to move all state prisoners out of Wackenhut-run facilities because of four murders that occurred between 1998 and 1999 (compared to only two since 1986 in state-run facilities) (Fecteau 1999). Lawsuits and investigations in other states concern the use of tear gas (Louisiana), failing to prevent sexual abuse (Texas), and paying $3 million to a member of the state's prison policy panel (Florida) (Solomon 1999).

Critics question the close ties between these companies and federal officials. Michael J. Quinlan and Harley Lappin hold positions with Corrections Corporation of American after having served as directors of the Federal Bureau of Prisons. Norman Carlson, also a former director of the Federal Bureau of Prisons, is on GEO Group's Board of Directors. Further, both companies have contributed to political campaigns. These two companies plus Cornell Company (the third largest private prison company, which was recently purchased by the GEO Group) have contributed $835,514 to federal politicians since 2000, and in 2010 they contributed $2,223,941 to state politicians (Justice Policy Institute 2011: 16). They have contributed almost twice as much to Republicans as Democrats and concentrate in states where they are seeking or have contracts (Justice Policy Institute 2011: 19). They also employ lobbying efforts targeting legislation that concerns sentencing and prisons. From 2003 to 2010, CCA registered 179 lobbyists in 32 states and the GEO Group registered 63 in 16 states (Justice Policy Institute 2011: 25). Because of their size and financial resources (CCA and GEO Group had a combined revenue of $2.9 billion in 2010), they are influential when state legislators decide on issues concerning privatization. (Justice Policy Institute 2011). This power concerns opponents of private prisons.

In addition to the big two, there are over a dozen smaller companies across the nation that compete for the private prison bids put out by the states. Replete with allegations of bribes, sweetheart deals, and other forms of corruption, the private prison industry has been the subject of a consistent string of investigations and exposés across the country.

Evaluations of Private Prisons

There have now been several evaluations of private prisons, but the evaluations are less than clear in their results because most have been funded by groups that philosophically or financially benefit from the findings that were reported. This does not mean that the results have been manipulated, but it does call into question whether a conflict of interest may color the interpretation of results in some way.

Groups opposed to privatization typically report findings showing that there is no cost savings with private prisons and that there are many more operational problems in the private prison evaluated than state prisons, including program deficiencies, classification problems, and lack of trained personnel (e.g. Greene 2001). Greene further reports that other evaluations found 49 percent more inmate-on-staff assaults and 65 percent more inmate-on-inmate assaults in private facilities, 41 percent higher officer turnover, and 37 escapes (compared to eight in a state system of a size similar to all the private prisons in the country) (Greene 2001).

Other evaluations show substantial cost savings, but they were either funded or conducted by proponents of privatization. Bourge (2002) describes Segal and Moore's study that examined 28 governmental and institutional studies comparing public and private facilities and found that 22 of the private prisons showed cost savings of 5 to 15 percent. They concluded that there is "significant evidence" that private facilities can provide comparable quality to state institutions. However, the evaluation by Segal and Moore was funded by a libertarian think tank that arguably would promote private enterprise over government involvement (Bourge 2002).

The biggest scandal in private prison evaluation research concerned Charles Thomas, a University of Florida professor who has published many evaluations of private prisons. Thomas testified before Congress and state legislatures considering private prison contracts. He consistently promoted the effectiveness and efficiency of private prisons; however, his objectivity was called into question when it was discovered that he was a highly paid consultant to CCA and owned over $500,000 worth of CCA stock. He was sanctioned by the state of Florida for violating their conflict of interest laws in 1999, yet he continued to write articles on private prisons and provide evaluations that tout their effectiveness (e.g., Lanza-Kaduce, Parker, and Thomas 1999; for discussion, see Geis, Mobley, and Shichor 1999).

A second issue with evaluations has been that there is no consistent or agreed upon definition of how to measure costs. The measurement of cost, while seemingly simple, is actually very complex, and how cost is measured determines whether there is a cost savings found or not. The difference in how to measure costs was the reason why a study by Abt Associates (a public policy research company) and a Bureau of Prison study showed inconsistent findings (Gaes 2010). A sampling of the kinds of issues that must be resolved when determining cost is offered below:

- How should indirect costs (state-level administration) be apportioned between private and public prisons?
- Should costs be based on actual average daily population or capacity? How should costs be counted if a prison is over capacity?
- How should contract costs and monitoring be allocated?
- Should in-kind services provided to the state agency be counted?

- Should services provided to the public prison, such as escape pursuits or prosecutions, be counted equally to the private prison?
- Should the taxes paid by private prisons be counted or credited? (Schneider 1999)

In a Government Accounting Office meta-analysis, it was concluded that private and public institutions cost about the same (GAO 1996). Any profits realized by a private entity being "leaner and meaner" is offset by the profit margin private companies maintain and a regulatory system the state must put in place to make sure contract specifications are adhered to. Another meta-analysis of 33 evaluations concluded that the per diem cost of the prison has more to do with the security level and size of the prison than whether it is public or private. This study did not support the idea that private prisons were cost effective (Pratt and Maahs 1999).

Another issue is whether or not private prisons show reduced recidivism. There have only been a few studies that have compared private and public prisons on recidivism. For the most part, except for female inmates, no differences were found, although the studies had some methodological difficulties. However, in a large evaluation of Florida inmates, Bales, Bedard, Quinn, Ensley, and Holley (2005) found no difference in recidivism between private prisons and public prisons. The data set included 81,737 inmates and a 60-month follow up period. Researchers measured "time of exposure" to private prisons and also collected information and controlled for a range of variables that might affect recidivism. There were no statistically significant differences in recidivism between private and public facilities for adult males, youthful offenders, or female prisoners. The most favorable conclusion one can reach after a survey of available evaluations is that private prisons may be comparable to state institutions with low-risk inmates but do not compare favorably to state institutions in cost or security in housing maximum security populations (Bourge 2002). Further, the cost savings is largely because of reduced salaries for correctional personnel, which may be something that is perceived as a benefit or a negative aspect of privatization depending on one's point of view.

Interstate Transfer
One element of privatization is that contracts often involve a prison in one state (often a southern state) housing prisoners from another state. Shichor and Sechrest (2002) discuss the widespread practice of interstate transfer. The Interstate Corrections Compact creates the mechanism by which an inmate can be legally incarcerated in a state different from that in which he or she was convicted. Private prisons have substantially increased the number of prisoners who serve time in other states. Viewed as a commodity, prisoners are, in some ways, marketed and moved around as products. More accurately, empty beds are the products and they are brokered by businesses created specifically to locate and/or sell prison bed space.

> Once inside the receiving building, I was stripped, processed, and placed on a converted bus like livestock. I was a commodity that had been contracted for payment. I was a product in the free enterprise system. I was on my way to a newly built private prison—Enterprise Correctional Facility—that was owned and operated by the Venture Correctional Corporation. (Carceral 2005: 5)

The fact is that large numbers of prisoners now spend at least part of their sentence far away from their home state. In past years, there were incidents where privately run correctional facilities contracted with faraway states to house offenders without ever informing the host state of the arrangement. Or, in other cases, a host state might be misled concerning the type of inmates held in a private facility. For instance, Texas officials were surprised when they were told by private prison officials that a facility would be for illegal alien detainees, but then 244 sex offenders were brought in from Oregon. The type of prisoners that were being "imported" was discovered only when two multiple rapists escaped and state officials were called in to help recapture them (Shichor and Sechrest 2002: 397). When disturbances occur in privately run facilities, state corrections staff are asked to intervene, even when none of the prisoners are from the host state. Some states have started to charge for their services, presenting a bill to the private corporation after the disturbance has been quelled.

Another problem of this aspect of the prison industry is that when prisoners are far away from their home, it makes it difficult or impossible for family members to visit them. It also makes it more difficult for state officials to monitor the conditions under which the prisoners are being housed. In 1998, officers in a privately run jail in Brazoria County, Texas, were videotaped kicking and setting dogs on nonaggressive Missouri inmates (Parenti 1999: 224). It was later discovered that one of the guards participating in the brutality had been fired from the Texas Department of Criminal Justice and had served some time in a federal facility for beating a Texas prisoner. Evidently, the private company running the facility, Capital Correctional Resources, either did not do a background check or did not care (Parenti 1999: 224). When the videotape hit the airwaves, Missouri pulled all its prisoners from the facility, but questions remain as to how states can monitor treatment from thousands of miles away and what is the responsibility of the home state in such a situation.

In 2001, 11,800 prisoners served their sentences in other states (Beck, Karberg, and Harrison 2002: 5). Not all these prisoners are sent to private prisons. Some states also rent out beds. Among the states that sent the most prisoners to other states were Wisconsin (4,526), Hawaii (1,225), Alaska (777), and Connecticut (657) (Beck, Karberg, and Harrison 2002: 5). In some ways, this practice makes sense. If a state is experiencing a temporary increase in prisoners, contracting with another state saves money because there is no need to build a new prison. In other ways, however, it is an ominous trend. Prisoners are cut off from their families, they often have less program opportunities than similar prisoners who are housed in home-state prisons, they have difficulty pursuing legal issues, and, most important, states have a harder time monitoring conditions from far away. These prisoners, to some extent, have no voice at all unless there is a major scandal—and there have been several.

CONCLUSION

Prisons come in all shapes and sizes; they can be state, federal or privately owned. What should a prison be like? A new Dutch prison is described as a model for the future. In this prison, inmates live in six-person cells. Each cell is furnished with three bunk beds and each bed has a touch screen. On this touch screen, the inmate can watch television, schedule his daily activity, and do his shopping. Every cell has two toilets, a shower, a washing machine and drier, a range and cookware, and a dining table with six chairs. There is a range of vocational, educational, and recreational programs for the inmate to choose from. Two guards supervise and interact with each group of six prisoners. Prisoners can earn money for their account by obeying rules, and they can also earn extra telephone privileges, television time, longer visiting hours, or transfer to another cell. Prisoners wear electronic bracelets to aid in tracking and controlling the population (Kenis, et al. 2010). The Dutch prison will never be a common prison model in this country. Primarily because of cost, but also because the principle of least eligibility ensures that prisons, at least in this country, will always be balanced between making sure inmates are uncomfortable enough for prisons to be considered punishment, while stopping short of inhumane conditions. The future of prisons in this country seems to be firmly tied to their past.

There is a range of different types of prisons, from forestry camps for minimum security inmates to the super-max. The super-max prison has been the subject of strong opposition and lawsuits because of perceived cruel and unusual conditions and transfers of troublesome inmates rather than violent inmates to the extremely punitive facilities. Overcrowding has been and continues to be a problem in some state systems. At least one state (California) has been directed by the Supreme Court to reduce the number of prisoners because of overcrowding. There has been a decline in the rate of imprisonment and the number of prisoners in many states (but not all).

One of the ways states have dealt with their overcrowding problem has been to utilize private prison companies to build and/or manage prisons. These companies have come under scrutiny for activities appearing to influence legislation that would increase the number of prisoners. Just as critics argued, it appears that the profit goal of such companies necessitates a steady stream of prisoners, even if crime rates decline, and thus it may be inevitable that the companies will attempt to ensure that we do not reduce prison populations. That may be good for the stockholders of such companies, but not for taxpayers, and certainly not for the men and women who may have been no danger to the community and successful on alternative community sentences.

WEBSITES

For more information on the Corrections Corporations of America, visit:
  http://www.cca.com/
For more information on the GEO Group, visit:
  http://www.geogroup.com/
For more information on the Federal Bureau of Prisons, visit:
  http://www.bop.gov/
For more information on the Interstate Corrections Compact, visit:
  http://www.interstatecompact.org/
For more information on super-max prisons, visit:
  http://www.supermaxed.com/Federal-SM-Page.htm

STUDY QUESTIONS

1. What is the most common offense of federal prisoners? What percentage of the federal prison population does that group make up?
2. How did California and Texas differ in their attempts to deal with overcrowding?
3. What contributed to California's overcrowding and difficulty in dealing with it?
4. What is Pelican Bay? Why did it receive so much attention from the courts, TV, newspapers, and the ACLU? What have prisoners alleged about placement in Pelican Bay?
5. Briefly list some of the supervision methods used in a super-max. What methods are used to deprive prisoners of stimulation? How is a super-max different from solitary confinement?
6. Describe the harmful effects of super-max prisons on its prisoners. What effects does the super-max have on the guards?
7. What did Mears conclude regarding evaluation and research concerning super-max prisons?
8. What is the difference between the privatization of prisons in the 1980s compared to before the 1980s?
9. Briefly discuss the arguments for and against the privatization of prisons.
10. Briefly discuss the evaluations of private prisons. What are the concerns regarding these evaluations?

CHAPTER 4

Prisoners

> We have our rapos [rapists], serial killers, con men, factory workers, pimps, whores, religious groups, wine shops, grocery stores, lenders, laundries, artists, musicians, intellectuals, and people of all political persuasions. You name it, we've got it. We've got the whole world in our can. (an inmate, in Martin and Sussman 1993: 73)

Who ends up in prison? Prisoners are likely to be poor blacks with juvenile records and/or multiple crimes, and have histories of drug use. The vast majority of prisoners in the United States are men—about 93 percent. Despite larger "percentage increases" in prison commitments of women in the last 10 years, women still constitute only about seven percent of all prisoners (West, Sabol, and Greenman, 2010, 1). Women's prisons are so different from men's that we must discuss their issues separately in chapter 7.

One of the first things to understand about prisoners is that they are not all alike. They are not all violent, although many are, and some are forced to be. They are not all drug addicts, although many are. Officers find many inmates to be relatively easy to supervise and even decent human beings. Their crimes may be an aberration. They may have seen the error of their ways and reformed. Many hold the social norms of us or our neighbors. In fact, some were our neighbors and will be again. Placed in the prison environment, however, they do act differently—they must to survive.

THE DEMOGRAPHICS OF PRISONERS

In 2001, almost 49 percent of prisoners were convicted of violent crimes, 20 percent of the prison population committed property crimes, and 31 percent committed drug or public order crimes (Harrison and Beck 2002: 12). In 2010, the respective percentages were 53 percent committed violent crimes, 19 percent committed property crimes and almost 18 percent committed drug crimes, with the remaining prisoners convicted of public order and other crimes (Guerino, Harrison, and Sabol 2011: 29). This does not necessarily mean that there are more violent offenders today. One should be aware of the difference between prisoner *population* demographics and prison *admission* demographics. In any prison population, the number of prisoners incarcerated for violent crimes is not the same as the number of those admitted to prison in that year for violent crimes. Violent crimes receive much longer sentences and these prisoners are less likely to receive parole, so they "stack up," comprising more of the total prisoner population as sentences become longer even if there are no more or even fewer people sent to prison for violent crime. It is difficult to acquire offense information about prison admissions (as opposed to prison populations). In 2008 (the most recent year this information is available), 27 percent of prison admittees were convicted of violent crimes and this percentage was the same as that in 2000. About 30 percent of prison admittees were convicted of property offenses and 29 percent for drug offenses (West, Sabol, and Greenman 2010: 9). Felony processing information is also available, and the Bureau of Justice Statistics shows that in 2006 (the most recent year available), 18 percent of all felony commitments in state courts were for violent offenses, 28 percent were for property offenses, and 33 percent were for drug offenses (Bureau of Justice Statistics 2011: Table 1.1).

The largest increases in prison admissions in the last several decades have occurred in nonviolent crime categories, especially drug offenses (Greene and Schiraldi 2002: 4). Some argue that there are at least one million people incarcerated in this country who, because of the nonviolent nature of their crimes, might be punished by other methods with no increased risk to public safety (Greene and Schiraldi 2002: 5). It appears, however, that the pervasive criticism of our sentencing and imprisonment practices toward drug offenders has resulted in some change because between 2008 and 2009 there were 12,400 fewer drug offenders in prisons. In 2000, 33 percent of new prison admissions were for drug convictions, but in 2008 this percentage had declined to 29 percent (West, Sabol, and Greenman 2010: 9).

Contrary to public opinion that our system is "soft on crime," many offenders receive prison sentences for first offenses. For instance, about 95 percent of those convicted of homicide receive a prison sentence; but so do about 73 percent of all drug offenders and 71 percent of all burglars (cited in Austin and Irwin 2001: 21). In fact, about 70 percent of all felony sentences are for incarceration (Bureau of Justice Statistics, 2011). The average sentence length for violent offenders was 44 months, and for property and drug offenders 15 months, in 2009; this average length was lower than it had been in recent years (Gilliard and Beck 1998: 12; West, Sabol, and Greenman 2010: 7).

The number of prisoners who are recidivists (returning to prison on a new charge or parole violation) is depressingly high. In a large national study of prisoners released in 1994 and followed for three years, it was reported that 68 percent were rearrested sometime during that three-year period. Further, about 47 percent were reconvicted and 52 percent were sent back to prison, although only about one-quarter on new charges. Those most likely to be rearrested included those who had been in prison for robbery, burglary, larceny, motor vehicle theft, or possessing/selling stolen property (Langan and Levin 2002).

About 17 percent of new admissions in 1980 were returned to prison for parole violations; this increased to almost 30.7 percent of all admissions in 1997 (Harrison 1999: 6). In 2009, parole violators comprised 35 percent of all prison admissions (West, Sabol, and Greenman 2010: 5). Parole violations may occur because of failed drug tests, even if no other crime has been committed. In one state (Texas), it was reported that nearly two out of every three prisoners are being returned on parole or probation violations (Kaplan, Schiraldi, and Ziedenberg 2000). We will revisit the issue of recidivism in chapter 10.

While the public may have the perception that prison houses only violent and recidivistic criminals, the reality is that many thousands of individuals in prison have committed relatively minor crimes. The following profile is taken from a representative sample described by Austin and Irwin (2001: 27): Edmond was a 50-year-old white carpenter who worked in Florida in the winter and Seattle in the summer. He had been arrested once 22 years before for receiving stolen property. He was passing through Las Vegas on his way to Seattle and said he found a billfold with $100 on a bar where he was drinking and gambling. The owner, who suspected him of taking it, turned him in. He was charged with grand larceny and received a three-year prison sentence. When proponents of prison use argue that we need to lock up criminals for our safety, one suspects they are not thinking of people like Edmond.

Prisoners are most likely to be male and under 35. Table 4.1 offers some demographic information about prisoners. In the following paragraphs a more detailed picture emerges.

Race

As discussed in chapter 2, the huge spike in incarceration that occurred in the 1980s and 1990s impacted minority men more severely than white men. In 1990, about 50 percent of the male prisoner population was white, but by 2002 that percentage had dropped to 34 percent (Harrison and Karberg 2003: 11), and today is 33 percent (West, Sabol, and Greenman 2010: 27). The incarceration rate for black men was 2,234 per 100,000 in 1990 but rose to 3,437 in 2002 (compared to 338 and 450, respectively, for white men). In 2009, the rate had declined somewhat to 3,119 for black men and was 487 for white men. Hispanic men were incarcerated at a rate of 1,016 in 1990, 1,176 in 2002, and 1,193 in 2009 (Harrison and Karberg

Table 4.1 Characteristics of Prisoners

Male				Female			
Total	**White**	**Black**	**Hispanic**	**Total**	**White**	**Black**	**Hispanic**
1,443,500	33%	39%	21%	105,200	49%	27%	17%

Male					Female				
Total	**<24**	**25–35**	**35–45**	**45+**	**Total**	**<24**	**25–35**	**35–45**	**45+**
1,443,500	16%	34%	30%	20%	105,200	12%	33%	37%	19%

SOURCE: West, H., W. Sabol, & S. Greenman. 2010. *Prisoners in 2009*. (Washington, DC: Bureau of Justice Statistics, U.S. Dept. of Justice), p. 27.

2003, 11; West, Sabol, and Greenman 2010: 28). What bears repeating is that in the space of less than 100 years, the percentage of prison inmates who were minorities increased from 30 percent of the prison population to about 70 percent.

Prisons are disproportionately populated by young minority men. It is an inescapable fact that can only be partially explained by crime rates, seriousness of crime, or other factors. In Ohio, for instance, in 2002 there were about 23,200 young black men in prison, but only 20,074 were enrolled in colleges and universities (Collins 2002). In the 18-to-24 age group the ratio of college to prison attendees is 2.6:1; for white men in this age group the ratio is 28:1 (Hocker 2002: 1). Arguably, in some communities, young black men grow up expecting that they are likely to end up in prison. Rap music and movies glorify or endorse the cultural legend of the black male criminal.

Kupers (1999) describes how whites are disproportionately represented in the mental health units of prisons, while blacks are overrepresented in the solitary confinement and secure housing units. What may be interpreted as a mental health problem with a white inmate will more likely be viewed as a behavior problem with an African-American inmate. He also noted that whites are more likely to fill drug treatment beds even though 70 percent of all those sent to California prisons for drug crimes were black at the time of his study.

To what extent does disproportional crime have to do with the disproportional incarceration of black men? Mauer (1999: 127) reports on several studies by Alfred Blumstein that show that arrest rates explain about three-quarters of the race differential. However, that leaves one-quarter to be explained by racial discrimination or other factors. Further, arrest figures are themselves the product of the system and cannot necessarily be used as a purely objective measure of criminality. It is true, however, that blacks tend to be more involved in street crimes, such as robbery and auto theft, and these crimes are more likely to receive prison sentences than white-collar crimes. What research also shows is that drug sentencing has a greater amount of difference unexplained by any factor related to the crime itself. It seems clear that it is in this area that a great deal of racial disparity exists (Mauer 1999: 127).

Age

In 2010, there were 2,295 inmates under age 18 in state prisons; a reduction from the 2,779 incarcerated in 2009 (Guerino, Harrison, and Sabol 2011: 1). The problem of juveniles in prison is a troubling one. Waivers to adult court and subsequent incarceration in adult facilities are a fate awaiting some juveniles who commit serious crimes such as murder. These young people are highly vulnerable in prison, where weakness is exploited and there are precious few altruistic defenders of children. Not all youthful offenders who end up in prison commit murder. A significant number (about 40 percent) have committed only property or drug crimes (Austin and Irwin 2001: 56).

Even though prisons are largely populated by young men, the average age of prisoners seems to be increasing. In fact, the number of inmates 55 and older is increasing at twice the rate of younger prisoners (Kempker 2003: 1). One effect of longer sentences and a higher incarceration rate has been the increasing number of elderly prisoners. The strange reality is that in most prison systems there is now a geriatric wing. Here walkers and wheelchairs are as much a part of prison life as bars and uniformed guards. These prisoners are highly vulnerable and must be protected from other prisoners. Kerbs and Jolley (2007) noted in a literature review that, while older inmates were reportedly less likely to be injured because of involvement in gambling or "games" (referring to the prisoner subculture), geriatric prisoners were vulnerable as victims of extortion and theft. In their study with 65 older inmates, they found that 17 percent had been threatened in the past year with a weapon and a quarter had been threatened with being hit. About 10 percent had been hit, punched, or shoved. While these are not large percentages, 84.6 percent of their sample reported having had other inmates cut in front of them in line—a sign of disrespect and potentially a precursor to more serious victimization (2007: 199). Older inmates reportedly did not fight back against these actions as they would have in their younger years. The insults and intimidation were usually in relation to the use of resources (television, recreational facilities, food). Since many geriatric prisoners are there for sex crimes, the dual elements of being a "baby raper" and an elderly inmate set the individual up for severe risk of victimization. Most of their respondents agreed that a segregated institution or unit for older inmates would prevent many of the problems of victimization.

Elderly prisoners experience failing eyesight, decreased mobility, loss of mental acuity, loneliness, and disorientation; unique to prisoners, however, is the fear of release, which often holds nothing for them, since family and friends all may be dead and the inmate has nowhere to go. Such inmates have even been known to refuse parole, preferring the familiar world of the prison to the unfamiliar world outside.

> Everything had gone fast-forward with me....I didn't know how to use
> computers or cell phones or the Internet. (an ex-prisoner who served 26 years
> in prison, was released to San Antonio, Texas, and set fire to an abandoned
> house so that he could be sent back to prison, reported in Associated Press,
> 2011: B1)

Related to the issue of geriatric prisoners is that of prisoners with extremely long sentences. Most of them will be in the geriatric population before they have served their sentences. The prisoners who face 10, 20, or 30 years or more in prison pose different programming needs and security issues than young offenders, who usually have shorter sentences. Custodial staff will usually describe long-termers as better behaved than short-termers, but that is after a period of adjustment in which they are likely to experience rage and frustration over their fate. Further, they can be uncontrollable because they know that the prison staff cannot do much to affect the sentence length—losing a year of good time does not mean much when the prisoner is facing 30 years before being eligible for release (Flanagan 1995).

One study indicates that at least 52 percent of elderly prisoners are incarcerated for nonviolent crimes (National Center on Institutions and Alternatives 1998). At least one state (Virginia) has passed legislation allowing compassionate release for geriatric prisoners (Greene and Schiraldi 2002: 15). One of the most consistent findings in criminology is called the *maturation effect*. This is the pattern whereby criminals older than 35 years of age seem to substantially lower their criminal activity. Unfortunately, by that time, many have accumulated enough convictions so that they are facing 25-year sentences and won't leave prison until retirement age.

Medical/Physical Characteristics

Individuals in prison have, on average, more physical infirmities and medical problems than the general population. Maruschak and Beck (2001) reported from a national prisoner sample that, even after controlling for age, prisoners reported more chronic medical problems, physical impairments, and learning disabilities than what would be found in the general population. About 11 percent of both state and federal inmates reported some medical problem, such as circulatory, respiratory, kidney/liver conditions, HIV/AIDS, or diabetes. About a quarter reported being injured in prison. Medical problems were more common among inmates who had been homeless or unemployed, were older, and among female inmates. Inmates who reported injecting drugs were also more likely to report medical problems. In comparing the self-reports to official reports for federal prisoners, it was found that the inmate reports were lower than official reports; for instance official reports indicated that 7.8 percent of inmates experienced high blood pressure, while only 1.7 inmates reported the medical condition (Maruschak and Beck 2001: 1).

Inmates have been five times as likely as the general population to develop AIDS; however, the number of active cases has been shrinking and is now around twice that of the general population (Marushak 2007: 3). They are also prone to other infectious diseases such as Hepatitis C, called the "silent killer" because people can carry the virus asymptomatically for years but can infect others. Some develop liver problems and die from the virus. Some reports estimate rates of infection as high as 40 percent while the general population's rate of infection is around two percent (Herivel and Wright 2007: 184).

While there are no statistics that indicate how many people contract AIDS in prison, prisoners have complained that they should be protected from those who have the virus. Court cases are not consistent, with some courts upholding mandatory testing, and other courts supporting states which refuse to do mandatory testing (Belbot and del Carmen 1991). Because of budget problems, there is probably less mandatory testing today than in the past, and it remains to be seen whether that will have some effect on HIV/AIDS rates.

Education and Employment Histories

Most prisoners are young and have less than a high school education; therefore, high school and basic literacy education is extremely important. Although there are vociferous critics who oppose providing a college education to prisoners, the number of prisoners who can take advantage of such programs, even if they exist, is very small. The majority of inmates are either functionally illiterate or have yet to achieve a high school diploma or its equivalent. Thus, the largest education programs in prison are basic education (literacy) and GED certification.

According to most studies, about two-thirds of prisoners were working prior to their imprisonment (Lin 2000: 147). The idea that criminals commit crime full-time is a myth; most offenders commit crime sporadically and often have legitimate jobs, pay rent, and support families. Drug offenders, especially, may be surprisingly "middle class." Of course, their jobs may be unskilled and pay very little.

Family

Prisoners are very likely to have parents or other relatives who have spent time in prison. Justice Department figures indicate that 47 percent of inmates in state prisons have a parent or other close relative who has been previously incarcerated. Half of all juveniles in custody have a father, mother, or other close relative in jail or prison (Butterfield 2002b). This intergenerational history of incarceration is expensive. An Oregon prison staff person estimated that five members of the same family who were currently incarcerated were costing the state $5 million a year. That estimate did not even count the expenses of court costs or community supervision—just prison (Butterfield 2002b). It is not unusual to have multiple generations within the same prison; for instance, a grandmother, mother, and daughter in the same prison.

> My family keeps telling me, "You're just going to end up like your father," and they're right. I didn't have anyone teach me to be a man. All the men in my family, they're either dead, locked up in jail, or on their way, but I'm trying to be the first to make it to graduation. (an inner-city youth whose father is in prison, quoted in Kleiner 2002: 48)

The other commonality among prisoners is domestic violence. To recognize the fact that many people in prison come from abusive and/or neglectful backgrounds does not excuse the fact that they victimized others or violated the law. However, it does help to explain why they commit such crimes. There are large differences between male and female inmates in their reporting of abuse. Whereas 57 percent of state female prisoners reported "ever" having been abused, 16 percent of male prisoners did. About 38 percent of the women said they had been abused before the age of 18, whereas 14 percent of male prisoners reported early abuse. About a quarter of women reported both physical abuse and sexual abuse, while about 12 percent of men reported physical abuse and only 5 percent reported sexual abuse. Of course, it is possible that men might be more likely than women to underreport their abuse. These numbers also do not tell us what percentage of men lived in families where they saw either parent being abused (Harlow 1999).

> Understanding that some thieving, conniving son-of-a-bitch behaves the way he does because he's black and his mother was a whore and he never knew his father and he had to steal to eat—understanding that—is important, but it don't alter the fact the son-of-a-bitch is still a son-of-a-bitch. (a guard, quoted in Webb and Morris 2002, 77)

Family members were more likely the perpetrators of abuse of men, whereas abuse of women was likely to be by intimates as well as family members. Those who reported abuse were more likely to have been raised in foster care if their parents or caregivers were heavy users of drugs or alcohol and/or if either parent or caregiver spent time in prison. Further, abuse seemed to be linked to violent crime, especially for men. Those who reported abuse were more likely to be abusers of drugs (Harlow 1999). The tragedy is that prisoners are also parents, and if they do not understand the forces that influenced them, they will have a difficult time helping their children avoid the same path.

When more and more people are incarcerated, more and more children are affected. Sometimes, it is a good thing that an abusive or drug-abusing parent is out of their lives. More often, it is psychologically traumatizing. The sad reality is that children with a parent in prison are six times more likely to end up in jail themselves. In 2000, more than 1.5 million children had a parent in prison; by 2007, the figure had risen to 1.7 million (Glaze and Maruschak 2008). These children are at higher risk for emotional problems, school difficulties, and delinquency.

In a Bureau of Justice Statistics study of parents with children under 18 in prison, it was found that the number of children with parents in prison increased 80 percent from 1991 to 2007. The number of children with a mother in prison increased 131 percent in the same time period. Black children were 7.5 times more likely and Hispanic children were 2.5 times more likely to have a parent in prison than white children. Prisoner-parents are most likely to be between 25 and 34 years old and married. Parents in prison were more likely than nonparents to have a criminal history. Mothers in prison were three times more likely than fathers in prison (42 percent compared to 14 percent) to report living as a single parent before incarceration. They were also three times more likely (77 percent compared to 26 percent) to report being the primary caregiver of the child. Prisoner mothers were also twice as likely as fathers to report homelessness, four times as likely to report physical or sexual victimization, and 1.5 times as likely to report medical or mental problems. While 88 percent of fathers said that the children were being cared for by the mother while he was in prison, only 37 percent of female prisoners reported that their children were being cared for by the other parent. The most common placement for children of incarcerated women was with a grandparent (44 percent). Only 2.2 percent of fathers' children were in foster care compared to 10.9 percent of mothers' children. Men and women were equally likely to report being the principle financial support of their children before incarceration (52 percent of women compared to 54 percent of men). Women were more likely to report weekly or more frequent contact with children while in prison (56 percent compared to 39 percent). Only 12 percent of all parents reported having participated in any parenting program (Glaze and Maruschak 2008).

Many prisoners want to be good parents, but the distance between the prison and family and restrictions on visitation and telephoning make keeping in touch difficult. There are programs, especially in women's prisons, that help the prisoner improve parenting skills, but these programs are not found in every prison and often they cannot do much to improve the visitation opportunities.

PRISONERS: YESTERDAY AND TODAY

One of the early pieces of research on prisons developed a prisoner typology. In fact, there were several, but one of the earliest and best-known typologies describes the "con politician," the "outlaw," the "square john," and the "right guy." The con politician was an inmate who was articulate and interacted with the administration. Although he might participate in prison programs, he was, at heart, a con and furthered his own interests. The outlaw was a prisoner who would use violence to get what he wanted. The square john was the middle-class guy who committed a crime but did not have a criminal outlook or lifestyle. He was vulnerable in prison and was not trusted. The right guy was the king of kings in prison. He was respected for his toughness but also for his strict adherence to the inmate code, which included the precept "don't exploit inmates." He was likely to be in prison for a serious crime like mob activity or bank robbery; but he was perceived as honest. He was the hero of the prison subculture (Schrag 1961).

Although this typology was developed 40 years ago, it still has some validity today. Of course, there are differences. Irwin and Cressey (1962) added some
additional types connected with the drug culture. Also, many inmates never fit
neatly into a type at all. Still, the idea of the right guy continues in prison today,
if only by prisoners noting that none exist. Winfree, Newbold, and Tubb (2002)
described inmates in New Mexico and New Zealand penitentiaries. They found
that inmates, when asked what qualities they respect in other inmates, listed most
frequently the qualities of honesty, how they treat others, intelligence, attitude, and
reservedness (2002: 223). These characteristics closely represent the right guy role
of years past.

If the right guy has the highest status in prisons, the child molester and rapist are on the lowest rungs of the ladder. The highest status criminals are robbers,
drug offenders, murderers, burglars, assaultive offenders, and thieves; the lowest
are murderer-rapists, rapists, incest offenders, and pedophiles (Winfree, Newbold,
and Tubb 2002).

Recently there have been other descriptions of prison typologies. Richards
(2003) describes some types of prisoners found in federal prisons, including
smugglers, pilots and boat crew members, Latino and Hispanic drug soldiers,
members of the Mafia, bikers, and white supremacists. Sabo, Kupers, and London
(2001: 9) also describe types of prisoners and rank them in order of status in the
prison: the highest ranking prisoners are the "tough guys" (Mafia members) and
prisoners with resources (gang members, merchants). Then there are marginalized prisoners who do not truly belong to the subculture (college kids, program
participants, prisoners who do their own time). Finally, there are the weak and
victimized (snitches, homosexuals, child abusers, and "punks").

It is impossible to fully describe the variety of individuals one might encoun-
ter in prison. In segregation, one is likely to find a "cutter." This is an inmate covered in self-inflicted scars. She might slice with razor blades, but if she cannot get
a blade, she will use broken glass, scissors, a pen or pencil, the edge of an electrical
plate, or a piece of a metal bed. Her ingenuity is matched only by her pain. Cutters
inflict injury on themselves evidently as a way to feel. Their mental trauma is so
great and so protracted that their minds often retreat into numbness where the
world and the people around them do not seem real. Cutting is a way to recon-
nect to the living. The physical pain and the attention assuage, at least for a time,
the utter loneliness and despair that they feel. In the outside world, this behavior
would clearly be seen as a cry for help and a need for immediate mental health
intervention. In prison, it is viewed quite often as a disciplinary issue. It is against
the rules.

One might also find individuals who exhibit their mental health problems in
other ways. Throwing urine and feces on guards and other inmates has long been
a way of showing contempt and one of the only ways inmates locked in isolation
cells can get revenge. Other inmates smear feces on themselves. They may be in
segregation because of an incidence of violence—either against another inmate or
a guard. Once they are locked up in an isolation cell for 23 hours a day, their mental

health deteriorates so much that they may be in active psychosis most of the time. They literally may not know who they are or where they are. Often, if some attention is paid to them, it takes the form of Thorazine or other antipsychotic drugs.

In southern prisons, prisoners used to act as "dog boys." These prisoners would help train the tracking dogs used to find escaping inmates. Tracking dogs, in order to train, must receive the scent of and chase a human. So these inmates would be given a running start and then the dogs would be released. In most cases, the handlers reached the dogs before they attacked the dog boys; but not always. Today, although inmates are still used to help train, the dogs do not attack; most of the time (Bergner 1998).

Another inmate may be a "programmer." Many inmates take full advantage of correctional programs. A typical day for one of these inmates might be: Rise at 5:30 to work in the kitchen until 10; go to school from 10 until 4; back in the cell for count, dinner at 5; evening programs might be group therapy, Jaycees, or a volunteer group that makes toys for kids; lights out at 11. The inmate might also be working on a correspondence course or filing an appeal *pro se;* these inmates are usually able to avoid the darker elements of prison living by keeping themselves busy and out of harm's way.

Another inmate may be on a prison work crew. He may have worked with the same correctional officer (CO) for years. Usually on these work crews, the guard is chosen partly for his knowledge of carpentry or plumbing skills. The relationship between guard and prisoner is more boss-to-worker than CO-to-inmate. Although it is always clear who is in charge, the CO may give the prisoner a great deal of latitude in his schedule, or how he plans to prioritize jobs, or even the right way to do the job. When an inmate finds this niche, it is unusual for him to disrupt it by becoming involved in activities that could get him disciplined.

Bergner (1998) described a tattoo artist in prison. Tattoos are sometimes extremely crude in prison, but not always. Some prisoners take tattooing to fine-art status. One particular artist created his tattoos by completing the following steps: He burned plastic and caught the burning colored soot on paper. He then mixed the soot with toothpaste and water to make an ink. He had threaded a steel guitar string through an empty pen shaft and attached it to a tiny motor from a cassette player. With this handmade instrument, the steel string was jabbed thousands and thousands of time into the skin to deposit the ink according to the design the tattoo artist had sketched on the skin (Bergner 1998: 109).

There are many other prisoner profiles that can be drawn from the 1.5 million individuals incarcerated in prisons and jails in this country. The point is that prisoners are not a monolithic group composed of violent, antisocial characters, although those people do exist. There are also those for whom the prison experience has been the trigger to a mental breakdown, and they descend to active psychosis or extreme personality disorder, sometimes resulting in violence to themselves and others. There are others who are far more victimized in prison than the injury they inflicted on their victim—if indeed there even was a victim, on the outside. There are those, too, who actually use the prison experience to improve themselves—earning a college degree or at least credit hours, learning to control their anger, and/or overcoming their addictions. Some ex-addicts, in fact, say "If it wasn't for prison, I'd be dead now."

Prisons are emotional zoos filled with paranoids, manic-depressives, aggressive homosexuals, schizophrenics, and assorted fruits and vegetables without labels that explode at various times. (an inmate, in Johnson and Toch 2000, 141)

SPECIAL POPULATIONS

In this section we focus on the mentally ill, mentally handicapped, and drug offenders. These are obviously somewhat overlapping groups. The mentally ill often attempt to self-medicate by illegal substances when they cannot or will not access legal medications. According to a Bureau of Justice Statistics study, an estimated 49 percent of inmates in state prisons were found to have both a mental health problem and a drug dependency (James and Glaze 2006: 5). Female offenders especially are perceived to use drugs more often to address anxiety and depression than for social or stimulus reasons.

Mentally Ill

Some estimate that between 10 and 20 percent of the prison population suffer from either mental illness or some form of mental handicap (Johnson 1999: 107). One government report from 1997, using self-reports by inmates, estimated that 10 percent of state and four percent of federal prisoners had some form of mental condition that required care (Maruschak and Beck 2001: 1). A more recent report from the Bureau of Justice Statistics (BJS) indicates that 56 percent of all state prison inmates had a mental health problem, defined as either a diagnosis or symptoms that met the criteria of a mental disease or disorder; 15 percent met the criteria for a psychotic disorder (James and Glaze 2006). The rate of prisoners with mental health problems is considered to be two to four times the rate in the general public (Human Rights Watch 2003: 1). The BJS study indicated that 56 percent of prisoners compared to about 11 percent of the general public could be categorized as having a mental health problem (James and Glaze 2006).

Female inmates evidently are more likely to have mental health issues than male inmates. The BJS survey reported that while 55 percent of male inmates had a mental health issue, 73 percent of female inmates did. About 23 percent of women had been diagnosed by a mental health professional in the last year—this rate was three times that of male prisoners (James and Glaze 2006: 4). Another report stated that 37 percent of the Pennsylvania female prisoner population was on the mental health caseload (Human Rights Watch 2003: 38), and a Department of Justice report noted that 23 percent of female inmates had been diagnosed with a mental health problem (Lord 2008: 934).

It has been reported that twice as many mentally ill are in our nation's prisons and jails as are in mental facilities, and others put the figure at three times those in mental health facilities (Human Rights Watch 2003: 1). Recall from an earlier chapter that the number of mentally ill in prisons has risen since the deinstitution-alization of mental hospitals in the 1970s. In 1955 the rate per 100,000 of persons in mental hospitals was 339; in 1998 it was 29 (Human Rights Watch 2003: 6). What happens to the mentally ill who in past decades would have been institution-alized? Unfortunately, jails and prisons are the largest providers of mental health services in the nation. These institutions also have the least trained staff, are the least equipped, and are the most under-resourced of facilities with mentally ill residents. Only 60 percent of those diagnosed as mentally ill reported that they had ever had any treatment (Ditton 1999). In the BJS study, only one in three state prisoners had received treatment (James and Glaze 2006: 1).

> We are literally drowning in patients, running around trying to put our fingers in the bursting dikes, while hundreds of men continue to deteriorate psychia-trically before our eyes into serious psychosis. (a psychiatrist, in Human Rights Watch 2003: 16)

Inmates may be especially vulnerable to mental illness because of their past lives. A large percentage of inmates have been exposed to violence, sometimes starting very early in their childhood. Estimates are that they are three times as likely as the general population to have experienced traumatic events such as death of a loved one, homelessness, victimization, and so on (Hochstetler, Murphy, and Simons 2004). It is not uncommon at all for inmates to relate experiences in which they have seen people die violently, sometimes loved ones, when they were quite young. It is probable that many individuals who grow up in poverty-stricken, high-crime areas and experienced violence suffer from untreated post-traumatic stress disorder. In the BJS study, it was found that state prisoners with mental health problems were over twice as likely as those without to have been sexually or physi-cally abused. They were also more likely to have had family members who abuse drugs, alcohol, or both, and to have had a family member incarcerated (James and Glaze 2006: 5).

As stated above, those with mental health problems are likely to abuse drugs as well. Over 50 percent of state prisoners with mental health problems also abused drugs. Over a third of them had used drugs at the time of their offense. Almost a quarter had used cocaine or crack cocaine in the month before their offense, but marijuana was the more frequent drug (James and Glaze 2006: 6). These individu-als may then become involved in the criminal justice system and undergo even more extreme stress and sometimes abuse. Rape is all too common in prison, and the mentally ill are especially vulnerable to victimization. Overcrowding stresses even the most even-tempered and mentally healthy inmate. For those who suffer from mental illness, extreme overcrowding, as it occurs in some of this nation's prisons and jails, may be the trigger for a psychotic breakdown (Kupers 1999).

> …he ate dirt, dust balls, pieces of trash, with the voraciousness of a billy goat. We knew that Dirt Man understood what he was doing wasn't right because he would do it on the sly. His favorites were the old mop strings that got caught and broke off beneath the legs of the tables in the chow hall.…(Stratton 1999: 84)

The most common diagnosis for prisoners with mental problems is antisocial personality disorder and borderline personality disorder. Behavioral indices include a pervasive pattern of disregard for the rights of others, being manipulative, volatile, disruptive, and aggressive. Also, self-mutilation and suicide attempts characterize these individuals. The diagnosis has been criticized as being vague and misused as a catch-all diagnosis for too many individuals (Human Rights Watch 2003: 32). Other common diagnoses include depression, schizophrenia, bipolar disorder, or co-occurring disorders (Adams and Ferrandino 2007).

The mentally ill are not an easy group to manage and are more likely than others to be involved in assaultive incidents in prison (Adams and Ferrandino 2007: 918). They are more likely to be violent offenders (53 percent versus 46 percent of other inmates) and recidivists (about 75 percent have already been in prison or on probation). Those with diagnosed mental problems are seven and one-half times more likely to get disciplinary reports than the greater population (Ditton 1999). Another study noted that 80 percent of unusual incident reports in one prison for women involved women who were on mental health caseloads (Human Rights Watch 2003: 39). The BJS study reported that almost 58 percent of those with mental health problems had rule violations compared to 43 percent of prisoners without mental problems. The difference was more extreme when looking only at violent infractions. Twenty-four percent of those involved had mental problems compared to only 14 percent who did not (James and Glaze 2006: 10). In fact, it is probably true that the greatest majority of officer assaults and repetitive acting-out behavior is performed by those who have chronic mental health problems.

Toch and Adams (1989) explored and analyzed breakdowns in prison by sampling prisoners with disciplinary records. Those whose mental illness manifests itself in assaultive or acting-out behavior are obviously difficult to handle— correctional staff want them transferred to mental facilities because they are irrational; mental health staff don't want them in such settings because they are violent. Adams and Ferrandino (2007: 924) reported, however, that after training for correctional officers that helped them recognize and manage the mentally ill, the number of use of force incidents and the number of assaults declined.

> ...it's kind of like kicking and beating a dog and keeping it in a cage until it gets as crazy and vicious and wild as it can possibly get, and then one day you take it out into the middle of the streets of San Francisco or Boston and you open the cage and you run away. (a prison doctor, cited in Weinstein 2002: 121)

Evidence indicates that those who have been victimized in the past are more likely than others to be victimized in subsequent years. This seems to be true for both female and male victims (Hochstetler, Murphy, Simons 2004). Victimization in prison results in mental stress and depression just as it does on the outside. Some victims experience post-traumatic stress syndrome symptoms. Inmates in these groups are especially vulnerable to victimization and manipulation. The prison experience, stressful as it is, may serve to exacerbate mental problems. Some inmates taunt and torment those with mental illnesses. Officers may be unable to differentiate between an inmate who is unwilling to follow an order from an inmate who is experiencing a psychotic episode or may be psychologically unable to conform his behavior to what is ordered. Management is concerned that sometimes these inmates are irrationally violent (for instance, an inmate with paranoid delusions may suddenly and unpredictably attack another standing behind him in line because of some delusion). Those who are mentally handicapped may be manipulated and intimidated by other inmates.

Court cases have established these inmates' rights to some form of treatment if not doing so constitutes "deliberate indifference;" however, more often than not, they are housed with the general population and get minimal special attention unless they commit some act that attracts the attention of custodial officials. Treatment consists of stabilizing the inmate through the use of anti-psychotic drugs and then sending the person back into the general population. Psychiatric counseling is widely considered to be ineffective (Johnson 2002, 252; Martin and Sussman 1993). The most common form of treatment seems to be medication.

> It was common practice for a third of a unit's inmate population to be walking around under the influence of Thorazine or some equally powerful psychotropic drug....After taking the drug for a while, convicts tended to get a yellow, jaundiced look about them. The blank stare and the short, stuttering steps referred to as "the Thorazine shuffle," made them look like zombies as they slowly marched down the hallway. Their speech became slurred and their mental reactions slowed; a previously loud, disruptive convict would adopt a meek and mild manner. (a retired Warden, Glenn 2001, 271–272)

In one study, it was found that nine percent of a sample of men in prison and 16 percent of females were receiving psychotropic medication (Morash, Har, and Rucker 1994: 200). Some object to the use of psychotropic medications because they can be easily abused. They may be used simply as behavior controls, they may not be accompanied by any professional therapy, and they may be given to an inmate for long periods of time, leading to a range of side effects. Perhaps the most troubling element of the use of psychotropics is that inmates may have their medications stopped abruptly upon release.

In one review of the treatment of the mentally ill in prison, Hartstone, Steadman, Robbins, and Monahan (1999) concluded with these findings:

1. Department of Corrections staff perceive about six percent of offenders as suffering from a serious psychotic mental disorder and another 38 percent as requiring some type of psychological treatment.
2. Different states operate with different philosophies regarding who should provide mental health treatment: i.e., the prison system or the mental health system.
3. Almost always, a transfer recommendation by the prison psychiatrist is followed.
4. Usually it is behavioral management concerns that instigate identification of an inmate as needing psychiatric care; thus, many who "suffer in silence" are missed.
5. A sizable number of staff feel more inmates should be transferred to mental health facilities.
6. Most staff members felt the transfer procedures worked well; but prison staff were less satisfied than those in central office positions or in the mental health units.

> You didn't have to work the galleries long to realize that a large proportion of inmates were mentally ill. The symptoms ranged from the fairly mild—talking to oneself, neglecting to bathe—to the severe: men who didn't know where they were, men who set fire to their own cells, men so depressed they slashed their wrists or tried to hang themselves. (Conover 2000: 138)

Suicide. Suicide happens with depressing regularity in jails and prisons, despite mandated suicide diagnosis and watch programs. Suicide ranks behind only natural causes and AIDS as the cause of death in prisons. Rates of suicide vary depending on the study, ranging from 18 per 100,000 inmates to 53 (Hayes 1996: 88). In more recent years, the rate has declined to 16 per 100,000 (BJS [key facts] 2011).

Suicide accounts for at least half of all deaths in prison. The suicide rate in prison is about twice that of the general population, but it varies dramatically from state to state. For instance, rates in Florida and Georgia have been reported to be less than half those of Texas and California. (Kupers 1999: 177). Suicide in jails is even more commonplace than in prison (Bonner and Rich 1990; Haycock 1991; Kennedy and Homant 1988).

Reasons for suicide include finding out one has AIDS, despair over long sentences, anxiety about release, being denied parole, being raped, missing loved ones, finding out that loved ones have divorced or disowned the inmate, fear over being in prison, and a number of other triggers. In a truly bizarre example of our "corrections" system, Kupers (1999) reports that sometimes prisoners who fail in a suicide attempt are punished for it because it is considered a prison infraction, and they are put in solitary confinement, where their precarious mental health decomposes even more rapidly.

A report was issued in Maine prompted by the deaths of 17 inmates in five years. The deaths were at least partially attributable to the dearth of mental health services. The recommendations included adding forensic beds to the new state mental health hospital, training judges in how to divert the mentally ill from the corrections system, requiring treatment of those who act out in prison because of mental illness, and conducting independent reviews of all mental health services in prisons and jails (Hench 2002). In *Ruiz v. Estelle* (1980), Judge Justice enumerated the minimal necessary elements for a mental health system in prison:

1. A systematic screening procedure;
2. Treatment that entails more than segregation and supervision;
3. Treatment that involves a sufficient number of mental health profession- als to adequately provide services to all prisoners suffering from serious mental disorders;
4. Maintenance of adequate and confidential clinical records;
5. A program for identifying and treating suicidal inmates; and
6. A ban on prescribing potentially dangerous medications without adequate monitoring.

There is no doubt that the massive deinstitutionalization of the mentally ill in the 1970s, the closing of mental health facilities, and underfunding of community health centers has led to large numbers of the mentally ill being in jails and prisons. Most receive virtually no care other than medication. Many are victimized in prison and/or they victimize others through unpredictable violence. If medicated, they shuffle through their prison sentence, and, upon release, for the most part are left to fend for themselves. It is no surprise that so many of them come back, and it is tragic that some ensure that they do not by killing themselves.

Mentally Handicapped
The mentally handicapped have an IQ of 70 or below. They are characterized as being childlike in their lack of understanding and gullibility. There are estimates that one to two percent of the general population is developmentally disabled, and up to 10 percent of prison populations can be defined as having developmental issues (although most studies put the figure at around four percent). These indi- viduals are disproportionately low income and minority. They are easily convicted of their crimes and receive longer sentences. At times justice personnel are not even aware of the individual's mental status. In prison, they are unlikely to receive special treatment (Petersilia 1997).

Similar to the mentally ill, the mentally disabled are targeted and victimized by inmate predators. They are easily manipulated, so inmates will use them to conduct rule violations. They are also easily victimized. Unless such individuals request protective custody, there is little protection offered by correctional authorities. There are no special housing units for the developmentally disabled and it is inappropriate to house them with the mentally ill.

Petersilia (1997) notes that the American Disabilities Act (ADA) applies to corrections and it requires that accommodations be made for the developmentally disabled if their condition prevents them from benefiting from prison programs. Authorities are obligated to identify, classify, and offer appropriate educational programs for this group of inmates.

Drug Dependent Offenders

Being a drug offender and having a drug dependency do not necessarily go together. Drug sales and possession are obviously a crime, but drug dependency is a medical issue. Drug dependent offenders may be in prison for drug offenses, but they might have been convicted of property or violent crimes instead of, or in addition to, a drug crime. From a variety of studies, it appears that although drug use may not cause an individual to begin a life of crime, those who engage in crime do so more frequently while using drugs and their criminality decreases or is eliminated altogether when they stop using drugs. These findings obviously lend support to those who plead for more treatment dollars (Inciardi 2002, 188).

Estimates indicate that two-thirds of prisoners meet the medical criteria for a substance use disorder (National Center on Addiction and Substance Abuse 2010). The United States Office of National Drug Control Policy reports that up to 85 percent of prisoners need drug treatment but only about 13 percent ever receive it. Drug offenders report high levels of drug use. For instance, two-thirds of state drug offenders in prison reported using drugs the month before their arrest and 41 percent were under the influence at the time of their offense. About 28 percent admitted they committed the offense to get money to buy drugs (King and Mauer 2002b: 9). However, it would be a mistake to imagine that the drug abusers in prison are necessarily dangerous. In a study of drug offenders in prison, it was found that 58 percent of incarcerated drug offenders have no history of violence or even a high level of drug sales. Almost a third were convicted of simple possession. Further, three-quarters had been convicted only of drug and/or nonviolent offenses (King and Mauer 2002, 2).

This same study found that only about a third of inmates who were sentenced for drug crimes have attended any treatment. Probationers were even less likely to have had access to treatment programs; only about 20 percent reported that they had been through treatment (King and Mauer 2002: 9). Obviously, not all offenders who are sentenced for drug crimes are addicts or even users; however, as noted above, a large percentage of drug offenders do need treatment, as do many offenders sentenced for other crimes.

CLASSIFICATION

Each prisoner, upon entry to the prison, goes through classification by which prison staff members attempt to predict the likelihood that the individual will commit prison infractions, especially violence against other inmates or staff. In decades past, classification involved a battery of educational and psychological assessments designed to identify the most effective treatment programs and job assignments. Today, classification has more to do with security. Inmates are classified into maximum, medium, or minimum security level prisons, and within the prison, to different levels of supervision from close custody to trustee. There is some attempt still to meet serious medical needs upon entry to the prison, and so some states still have inmates go through rudimentary medical and dental exams. We will discuss medical care in the next section. Inmates are also assigned to programs, jobs, and housing units during classification, although the criteria is often wherever there are empty slots. Educational testing is done in order to determine what jobs the inmate is suited for, for example, clerk positions would require basic literacy skills. The major emphasis of classification, however, is on custody.

Two types of approaches to classification are the clinical and the actuarial. Clinical classification assumes that professionals can predict risk based on interviewing the offender while actuarial classification systems look for correlations between violence and factors such as age at first arrest. Berk, Ladd, Grazaiano, and Baek (2006) note that it is difficult to predict serious violence because it is rare, even for prison samples. While 15 percent of the inmates in their state sample engaged in some kind of misconduct, less than 3 percent engaged in violent incidents. They could accurately predict only about half the time, even with the best predictive classification measures.

Berk, Ladd, and Graziano (2003), in a study using 20,000 inmates, found that while marital status, pre-prison employment, military service, and education played almost no role in predicting violent infractions; gang involvement, mental illness, age when first arrested, prior incarceration and age correlated with prison violence. In a later examination using the same data set, Berk, Kriegler, and Baek (2006) discovered that sentence length, age at first arrest, age at first reception, and gang activity had the most predictive power. Berk et al. (2006) found that prisoners who are very young but have already developed extensive criminal histories, are active in gangs, and are serving long sentences are the most likely to commit violent offenses while in prison.

Cunningham and Sorensen (2007) found that the Risk Assessment Scale for Prison (RASP) was modestly successful in predicting which inmates would commit violent disciplinary infractions. The two strongest predictors are age (e.g., younger offenders are more likely to engage in violence) and education (e.g., those educated higher than the 9th grade level are *less* likely to engage in violence). Having a conviction for a violent crime was not found to be predictive of violent infractions, but having a short sentence was. Both of these factors run counter to typical prison classification systems. The authors admit, however, that the classification system itself may be the reason why these inmates did not commit more violent infractions; that is, those with violent crimes would be classified into maximum security institutions with less chance to commit violent infractions in prison. According to the researchers, the scale predicted violence better for female prisoners than for male prisoners (Cunningham and Sorensen 2007: 261).

Drury and DeLisi (2010) reviewed prior research on prison misconduct and analyzed misconduct reports in a sample of Arizona inmates. They noted that the correlates of prison misconduct have been identified as: age (younger inmates), sex (male), race/ethnicity (nonwhite), education (less), lacking a social support network, criminal histories, and a history of violent behavior. In several previous studies the most consistent individual-level predictor of prison misconduct was prior institutional misconduct. In their study, they also found that prior institutionalizations were not as predictive as prior prison sentences *with* misconduct reports which explained 10-20 percent of the variance (2010: 343). Camp, Gaes, Langan, and Saylor (2003) also found that the strongest predictor of misconduct was prior misconduct and age. In their study of 120,000 federal prisoners, race was not a predictor of misconduct. It should be noted that these studies that use official reports of misconduct do not capture all violent incidents or all episodes of misconduct, only those that come to the attention of the authorities.

The so-called *third generation* of assessment involves looking at static (called first generation assessment) and dynamic (second generation) factors. Static factors include demographics and historical information (e.g., age at first arrest) and dynamic factors involve personality tests and interviews. Three instruments that are considered third generation are the Wisconsin Risk and Needs Assessment Instrument, the Community Risk-Needs Management Scale, and the Level of Service Inventory-Revised (LSI-R) (Van Voorhis 2004).

The Level of Service Inventory-Revised (LSI-R) was developed and first used with probation samples to predict recidivism, but it has also been employed in prisons to predict prison misconduct and found to be somewhat helpful. When used with prison samples, the items in the inventory apply to the year before prison. The LSI-R has also found moderate success in predicting recidivism for prison inmates (Manchak, Skeem, and Douglas 2008).

MEDICAL SERVICES

Medical budgets for state prison systems are expanding exponentially, partially due to lawsuits, partially because of the increasing number of geriatric prisoners and the continuing plague of AIDS. Because of sexual practices, intravenous drug use, and the widespread practice of tattooing, inmates who enter prison without the disease may contract it there. Some prisons have gone so far as to defy public opinion and offer condoms to stem the contagion. Almost all prisons offer counseling and education on AIDS.

> Back in the early days of "The Game, [homosexuality]" nobody gave a damn about AIDS. Hell, we weren't exactly sure what it was. We knew from reading the newspapers or watching television that a whole lot of people were afraid of whatever it was. We might have been, too, if we thought that it had something to do with us. Back then, only gays got AIDS. I never considered myself gay until some years later. (an inmate, in Gilbreath and Rogers 2000: 188)

Offenders, because of their sexual practices and drug use, are already a high-risk group. Court decisions have made it difficult but not impossible for institutions to segregate HIV positive inmates. Inmates argue that segregation exposes them to stigma and harassment by other prisoners and staff (Welch 2000). On the other hand, a lack of segregation and confidentiality creates the situation where an infected prisoner may spread the disease to his sex partners or drug partners without their knowledge. If a prisoner develops a full-blown case of AIDS, the medical costs are astronomical, and this expense is multiplied by the number of prisoners suffering from HIV/AIDS.

Some states have tried to resolve the issue by releasing sick offenders, but this practice is legally questionable and arguably does not remove the state's responsibility in providing care. In reality, most prisoners with AIDS do not receive state-of-the-art care. In fact, there are allegations that AZT and other drugs are withheld from prisoners as punishment or through incompetence. Not receiving the drug according to its required dosage is obviously less effective, so correctional officers and medical care providers can literally kill an inmate by neglect (Hemmons and Marquart 1998; Welch 2000).

Other diseases also pose problems in prison. In the early 1990s, several dozen prison inmates died of a strain of tuberculosis resistant to all available medications. One correctional officer died as well (May 2001: 133). Overcrowding probably hastened the spread of this disease, as did poor ventilation and the practice of moving prisoners from one facility to a central medical facility without proper precautions taken for infectious diseases. Outbreaks of pneumococcal pneumonia and meningitis have occurred in jails and prisons around the country.

Obviously, the costs involved in meeting the needs of the elderly in prison are not insubstantial. One estimate is that they cost about three times as much to house as a younger prisoner because of increased health needs—$69,000 per year compared to $22,000 (National Center on Institutions and Alternatives 1998). Brown (2002) reported that a Pennsylvania study estimated that an average inmate's health care cost $3,809 per year, but that figure rises to $11,427 for older inmates. Because of the increasing use of three strikes laws and life without parole sentences, the number of geriatrics in prison will only increase. This will mean that prison management will increasingly have to consider issues regarding housing the elderly, including expanded health care and special diets. Several states have established hospice units for terminally ill patients.

There are widespread allegations of medical neglect. It can be argued that inmates may misuse and manipulate the medical treatment system for special privileges or drugs. Further, the state could not possibly undo years of living in which the inmate himself or herself did not care for their health and abused drugs, practiced poor nutrition, smoked, abused alcohol, did not take care of their teeth, and/or did not seek medical care when sick. However, the extent and consistency of allegations in some state systems are evidence that the medical care system is often inadequate, either because of a lack of resources or because of staff who do not care. After years in the system, staff burnout is understandable, but medical personnel who do not listen to inmates' complaints or overlook serious conditions create a type of torture for truly sick individuals because obviously they are unable to seek assistance elsewhere. In addition to serious illness, inmates require medical treatment for injuries that occur either through assaults or on a prison work assignment. Inadequate care may result in an inmate needlessly losing a limb or even dying.

There is a truism in corrections that female inmates demand much more medical attention than men. In a national survey of incarcerated men and women, about 25 percent of women and 20 percent of men reported some type of medical condition, but the percentages reversed when asked about injury, where 29 percent of the men and 21 percent of women reported being injured (Maruschak and Beck 2001).

> The medical staff is the worst of the lot. If they weren't taking away the meds or changing and mixing them, they were overdosing us....Drug withdrawals were tough to see, but we had all witnessed them. Women couldn't breathe because inhalers had been taken away from them. Seizures would grab a girl at any unexpected moment; then she was told she was faking it or that they had given her her drugs wrong or that they didn't know. A girl died earlier this year because the medical staff didn't know what they were doing. She wasn't the only death this year....(an inmate, Redifer 2000: 145)

Vaughn and Smith (1999) document cases of medical abuse in jails, but many of the same issues apply to prisons as well. Their list of abuses include using medical care to humiliate inmates, withholding medical care from AIDS patients and other patients with problems as severe as broken bones or miscarriages, exposing prisoners to extremes in temperature and sleep deprivation, using dental care as an instrument of ill treatment or withholding dental care, and falsifying medical records. The authors looked at inmate letters that described abuses. One inmate was a Vietnam veteran who suffered from post-traumatic stress disorder and was prevented from continuing his free-world prescribed Xanax; he thereupon suffered hallucinations and anxiety. Also described was a woman who went through DTs with no medical care and suffered delusions and psychotic behavior, a woman who experienced a miscarriage and bled for several hours before receiving any medical attention, a male inmate who had a broken jaw swollen to several times its normal size and was denied medical assistance, and so on. Their findings indicated widespread mistreatment through the denial or misuse of medical care.

In California, the state agreed to spend $21 million in 2002 and $122 million a year in subsequent years to settle a lawsuit filed on behalf of inmates. The lawsuit alleged that the prison system was primarily responsible for the deaths of several inmates because of inadequate or delayed medical care. Included in the deaths was a young man with a two-year drug sentence who died from tongue cancer diagnosed three months before he had any treatment. Eight women's deaths were chronicled in the lawsuit, including one who died after having an asthma attack. Inmates testified that medical care did not come for three hours after they alerted officers that the woman had collapsed in her cell. Along with extra money for more doctors and medical staff, new procedures were also part of the settlement agreement. Inmates who are transferred now must have their medical charts transferred with them to ensure continuity of treatment. Further, inmates must be seen, when feasible, by a primary care physician rather than by rotating doctors or nurses. Also, a team of auditors and a panel of outside medical experts review the medical care for prisoners (Warren 2001: 2002).

> My son was a drug addict, but he was not a bad person. I never dreamed something like this could happen in American prisons. Unless you have a loved one in the system, you have no idea what goes on. (a mother whose son died in prison of a curable form of cancer, Warren 2001: 3)

In other states there are also allegations of poor medical care. An investigation in Texas chronicled the same type of allegations that led to the California class action suit, including interruption of prescribed medicines, neglect of diagnosed conditions, and nonmedical staff making "gateway" decisions (deciding who was sick enough to see the doctor). The series of newspaper articles that chronicled the investigative findings spurred some legislators to call for a special inquiry (Ward, M. 2002b).

CONCLUSION

John Conrad (1981) has argued that prisoners have several fundamental rights as a function of having their liberty taken away. In other words, society has a right to incarcerate, but if we do, then prisoners deserve:

1. The right to personal safety;
2. The right to [appropriate] care;
3. The right to personal dignity;
4. The right to work;
5. The right to self-improvement; and,
6. The right to a future.

These are rights that every person deserves regardless of what he or she has done. They are rights that prisoners may not enjoy in some prisons, or at least to the extent that Conrad intended. According to Conrad, to do less denies prisoners basic humanity and degrades our own.

One of the most important realizations learned by visiting prisons is that they are full of people who are not monsters. Visitors to prisons inevitably rue-fully, sheepishly, or innocently say, "They are not like I thought they'd be." Even those men who are covered with prison tattoos and talk the talk of the prison yard might be studying sociology in a college class or learning computer programming. Women in prison will show visitors pictures of their children and proudly display their artwork on the walls of their cells. Clearly, there are dangerous, violent peo-ple locked up, but there are also many who are not dangerous. In the next chapter, we will see how prisoners learn to live in the prison subculture.

WEBSITES

For more information on the National Center on Institutions and Alternatives, visit:
http://www.ncianet.org/
For more information on Jaycees, visit:
http://www.usjaycees.org/
For more information on the American Psychiatric Association, visit:
http://www.psych.org/
For more information on the American Disabilities Act, visit:
http://www.ada.gov/
For more information on the National Center on Addiction and Substance Abuse, visit:
http://www.casacolumbia.org/templates/Home.aspx?articleid=287&zoneid=32
For more information on the Office of National Drug Control Policy, visit:
http://www.whitehouse.gov/ondcp

STUDY QUESTIONS

1. Describe the demographic profile of prisoners, both men and women.
2. What are the figures regarding minority representation in prisons.
3. Discuss the growing problem of the elderly in prisons.
4. Explain the role of childhood abuse for men and women in prison.
5. Provide a typology of prisoners.
6. Briefly describe the status hierarchy assigned to criminals. Who is at the top? At the bottom?
7. How many prisoners suffer from a mental health problem according to the Bureau of Justice Statistics? Who are more likely to have a mental health issue, men or women? What are the two most common diagnoses?

8. Do drug dependency and being a drug offender always go together? How many prisoners meet medical criteria for a substance use disorder? According to the Office of National Drug Control Policy, how many prisoners need drug treatment? How many receive it?

9. List the correlates of prison misconduct. Which two are the strongest correlates?

10. According to Conrad, what rights do prisoners deserve? (List the six).

CHAPTER 5

&

Rehabilitation Revisited

> …with few and isolated exceptions, the rehabilitative efforts that have been reported so far have had no appreciable effect on recidivism. (Martinson, 1974, 25)

As noted in the first chapter, penitentiaries began as institutions of reform. Originally, penitentiaries were places where a religious transformation was to take place—the sinner would be transformed when he sought repentance. Later, in the reformatory era, secular views of change supplanted religion and young, amenable offenders were educated and given vocational skills along with a strong dose of discipline. Constant monitoring, discipline, and education were believed to be the way to reform offenders. Then in the 1970s, the so-called rehabilitative era was a time when the vision of the penitentiary as a correctional institution was at its strongest. Prison systems had "diagnostic centers" and the medical model or treatment ethic was the philosophy of change—specifically, that crime was a result of an underlying pathology that could be treated. At the height of the rehabilitative era a variety of treatment programs—including behavior modification, transcendental meditation, and even psychodrama therapy—could be found in some prisons. Most of these types of programs have been abandoned as irrelevant, ineffective, or inconsistent with the mission of the prison, which changed to retribution and punishment rather than rehabilitation and correction. Other program offerings evidently were victims of disinterest or the changing fads of treatment professionals.

THE LEGACY OF THE REHABILITATIVE ERA

The end of the modern rehabilitative era was said to be hastened by Robert Martinson's famous finding that "nothing worked." This conclusion and the premise upon which it is based are somewhat overstated. Martinson and his colleagues reviewed the effectiveness of 231 offender rehabilitation programs from the prior 30 years. When examined in a meta-analysis, an evaluation that collapses many studies into one data set, they could find no statistically significant improvement in recidivism figures for those who participated, but their larger (ignored) message was that the major problem was that the program evaluations were poorly designed with poor measures. A later examination of the findings, including some studies that had, at first, been excluded, found "pockets of success" (Farrabee 2002).

Pearson and Lipton's (1999) meta-analysis found that, while some treatment programs are not effective, some are, and some are for some people. Recently the National Institute of Justice has led the way in promoting effective programs by stringent requirements for evaluation and creating a user-friendly interface on their website (http://www.CrimeSolutions.gov.) in order for policy makers and correctional practitioners to access information about effective programs. "Evidence-based corrections" is most definitely a current "buzz word," but it can restore legitimacy to the field of corrections. More discussion of this concept will be provided in a later section.

WHAT IS TREATMENT?

Prison management is often divided into the "custody" side and the "treatment" side. The custody side always has the upper hand in any policy decisions. The treatment staff includes teachers, counselors, vocational training instructors, psychologists, medical staff, and others who are not involved in custody. An expansive definition of treatment can be anything that has, as its goal, to meet the needs of offenders. In this definition, visitation, religion, and even medical/dental professionals are included. A more restricted definition of treatment would only include those programs designed to reduce recidivism. Because of budget shortfalls, pure treatment programs have been cut back in recent years and treatment staff laid off. While treatment staff members are viewed as expendable in tough economic times, custody staff members never are.

It is an overstatement to declare that prisoners today receive no education, training, mental health treatment, or personal improvement programs. Virtually every prison offers some type of basic education and at least a few vocational programs. The problem is that there are more prisoners than program slots and services available. For instance, although most prison administrators will profess that their prisoners all have work assignments, many of these assignments are make-work, such as sweeping one hallway for four hours. In reality, many prisoners are idle not because they choose to be, but because there are not enough program slots or work assignments for everyone. The same is true for treatment slots; many inmates wait months or even years to get into a program.

Treatment programs include psychotherapy, behavior modification, group therapy, family therapy, therapeutic communities, AA, and a wide range of eclectic programs. There are also some rehabilitative programs that have a religious base. Charles Colson, of Watergate fame, has promoted the use of one particular religion-based program, Prison Fellowship Ministries, and several states have implemented the program. This is an ironic return to the early years of the penitentiary when the prisoner was encouraged to seek forgiveness and expiation through religious reformation. At least for these programs, religion has once again replaced psychology (Marks 2001). The issue of whether or not such programs violate the First Amendment's separation of church and state clause will be considered in a later chapter.

Recently, there has been news coverage of meditation programs in prisons. Reports indicate that the inmates who successfully graduate from voluntary courses are calmer and deal with their emotions better. In a maximum security Alabama prison, Vipassana meditation has been offered in courses for many years. Inmates say that it helps them deal with prison life. A study by the prison indicated that successful graduates had 25 percent fewer disciplinary infractions than other inmates. In Texas, meditation classes have also been offered for eight years. While such programs may have beneficial effects for prisoners, whether or not they reduce recidivism remains to be seen since no one has conducted such an evaluation.

> Physically, I've changed: I've gotten older. Mentally, I've changed: I've gained knowledge. Emotionally, I'll always be the same. The thoughts will always be there. You talk about the thoughts of doing harm, violence, anger—they're going to be there, but by putting space around those thoughts, you can look at them before you react. That's my biggest change: I'm much less reactive, much less impulsive. (a Texas inmate discussing meditation, Turner 2011: B5)

Recreation

Perhaps no issue of prison life receives more negative publicity than recreation programs. Prisoners lifting weights or playing ball are inevitably the topic of those who argue against making prisons "hotels" instead of "hard labor camps." Yet, prison officials are sometimes the biggest supporters of such programs. Why? Officials largely support recreation because it is, usually, a proactive use of time, and it tends to direct energy away from more deviant pursuits. To be sure, at times recreation programs can be the impetus for violence. Fights will break out on the basketball court or on the softball field. Betting takes place over games that can then lead to violence when losers must pay. Further, many states have banned weightlifting equipment in prison because it is felt that the state should not be paying for equipment that will assist in creating a stronger prisoner who may assault officers.

In general, male prisoners tend to be more active participants in recreation than female prisoners. Virtually every prison has a yard and, in some part of the yard, there is probably a basketball court and an area to play softball. In some states, prisoner teams play against community teams or even guard teams. Some prisons also have a gymnasium although many of these were converted to dormitories during the 1980s in reaction to overcrowding. It is also true that many prisons today are in lock down so much of the time that inmates have less opportunity for yard time or exercise than in past years.

Other avenues for recreation exist in hobbies. Most prisons have arts and crafts opportunities for inmates although they must pay for their own supplies. Prisoners may create beautiful artwork that is sold to the public in the prison administration building or, perhaps, given to friends or relatives as gifts. Prisoners also participate in charitable works, such as taping books for the blind, sewing stuffed animals to be distributed by charitable programs on the outside, and so on. When asked why they participate in such activities they answer much as anyone would—usually some version of wanting to help others or giving back to the community. Club meetings and activities take place in the evening when all prisoners are allowed to go to the yard.

While there is no evidence that recreation programs in prison have any effect on recidivism, it may be that they at least have the potential to improve behavior in prison. Any type of sport is a healthy addition to one's life and can help the inmate avoid, perhaps, some temptation to use drugs or engage in less positive pursuits. Other types of recreation keep inmates busy if nothing else, and some activities are clearly helpful to the community.

EDUCATION, VOCATIONAL TRAINING, AND INDUSTRY

Virtually all prisons have some type of basic education. Most prisons also have at least a couple of vocational programs, even though most programs have a waiting list.

Education

Education in prison is dominated by ABE (Adult Basic Education), which is primarily literacy training or programs of study that lead to either a GED or high school diploma. It is reported that one in three inmates score at the lowest level of literacy (Jenkins 1999). In 1997, about 68 percent of prisoners had not received a high school diploma in 1997. About 40 percent had not received either a high school diploma or a GED, compared to only 18 percent of the general population (Harlow 2003). Harlow's (2003) national study found that only about 11 percent of state prisoners and 24 percent of federal prisoners had some college (compared to 48 percent of the general population). While over half of the sample reported that they participated in educational programs in prison, only about 10 percent of prisoners participated in college programs, a decline from 14 percent in 1991. More recent statistics indicate that only about a quarter of inmates participate in an educational program (reported in Cullen and Jonson 2011: 307).

In Harlow's national study, it was found that women in prison were more likely than men to have graduated from high school (30 percent compared to 25 percent) and to have had some college. The author reported that white, black, and Hispanic men in prison were "markedly" less educated than their counterparts in the general population (Harlow 2003: 6). Another important finding was that those inmates without a high school diploma or a GED were more likely to be recidivists (Harlow 2003: 10).

Some state systems have quite large educational systems and offer a range of educational programs from basic literacy to college classes. There is some controversy over whether or not education is correlated with a reduction in recidivism; however, no one can argue that education can help to make the inmates' time in prison productive and improve their lives upon release. Welsh (2002) and Messemer (2003) report on studies that show that a college education does reduce recidivism among prisoners. Other studies have also found education to be positively related to success after release. For instance, the Texas Criminal Justice Policy Council released a report in 2000 that tracked almost 26,000 inmates who had been released from prison in 1997 and 1998. They found that young property criminals were 37 percent less likely to recidivate if they learned to read while in prison. It was also found in this study that education seemed to have a greater impact on younger inmates than older inmates (Susswein 2000); however, Uggen (2000) found that older inmates who received education in prison were *more* likely to show reduced recidivism.

Just because there is an education program on paper does not necessarily mean that the program is helpful. Inappropriate resources, lethargic teachers, and hostile or unaccommodating security staff can sabotage a program. This makes large-scale evaluations of education problematic; it may be that recidivism is not affected because no real education takes place.

> ...about twenty functionally illiterate men sit facing their teacher. The men range in age from 20 to 55....Six or seven of the men are sitting, heads in hands, staring at workbooks; the rest are sleeping, talking, or doodling. The teacher reads a newspaper at her desk in front, looking up once in a while to restore order or answer a question when someone approaches her. Given the amount of sleeping and staring in the classroom, the occasions requiring her intervention are few. (Lin 2000: 15)

Lin (2000) describes prisons where educational programs were vibrant and inmates and teachers were invested in the process, but, also, others where the program existed but nothing much happened in the classrooms. In general, she found that any evaluations of rehabilitation programs were problematic because some on paper did not have any commitment on the part of the institutional staff, and, since they were merely "walking through the motions," the evaluation of such a program would be misleading.

In 1994, federal Pell grants, which had been used to fund prisoners' college, were taken away by an amendment to the 1994 crime bill. The Pell program contributed to 43 states offering Associate degrees and 31 states offering Baccalaureate degrees. Nine states even offered Master's degrees. In a 1997 survey, most states reported that the elimination of Pell grants resulted in a drastic curtailment or elimination of their college education program (Welsh 2002). Parenti (1999: 181) reported that degree granting programs in over 30 prisons ended and by 1998, only eight states still offered any degree granting at all. However, several years later, another study reported that 25 states offered college classes, with 15 offering Bachelor degree programs (Messemer 2003). The discrepancy may be that only nine states have a program in which the prisoner is able to complete a degree, or perhaps more states were able to revive their college programs. Alternative funding comes from other grants or private sources.

"Spector grants" (otherwise known as Youthful Offender Grants) were added to a crime bill as an amendment and provide up to $1,500 for inmates under 25, convicted of a nonviolent crime, and with less than five years remaining on their sentence until release. It is reported, however, that the program is woefully underfunded and not used at all for its intended purpose by some states (Treaga 2003).

Welsh (2002) looked at the effect of eliminating the Pell grants by surveying directors of education in prison systems across the country. She found that they perceived a significant decrease in the access, quality, and success of college programs after the Pell Grants were discontinued. Messemer (2003) found that some states were able to use other grant-making programs, such as the Carl Perkins Vocational and Applied Technology Education Act of 1998, to fund college classes, many educational programs appealed to private funding sources, and in many cases, the prisoner was obligated to pay for the college class either directly or reimburse the state at some future time.

The complaint that prisoners get college educations while honest people have to pay for them seems to be, by and large, an empty one since very few inmates are in college programs, and those few that are, are most likely paying for the privilege. Arguing against basic education for prisoners makes no sense at all since if prisoners are to obtain and retain a job upon release, they are going to have to have the skills to do so. Whether it is possible in today's prisons for prisoners to access these skills is less clear.

Vocational Training and Industry

Vocational training programs should be distinguished from prison labor. While "hard labor" has been associated with confinement facilities since their inception, vocational training programs have a shorter history. In the 1960s and 1970s, prisons were able to access federal money from several sources to provide vocational training programs, such as typewriter repair, auto-mechanics, data-processing, electricians' apprentice programs, and commercial cleaning, among many others. By the 1980s, overcrowding and budget shortfalls threatened the existence of many programs. Despite the numbers that indicate all prisons have one or more vocational programs, nationally only about nine percent of inmates were enrolled in the early 1990s (National Institute of Justice 1993). More recent statistics indicate that only about half of all prisons have some form of vocational apprenticeship program although more have some form of job readiness program (reported in Cullen and Jonson 2011: 308).

Austin and Irwin (2001: 104) reported that only 24 percent of inmates were officially "idle," but they also report that only seven percent are employed in prison industries, five percent on prison farms, and nine percent in prison vocational training or education. That leaves about half of inmates "employed," but such employment may be sweeping the tier or being on a yard detail. A more recent national survey also estimated that about half of all prisoners had some form of work assignment (reported in Cullen and Jonson 2011).

As mentioned, in 1994, the new federal Crime Bill prohibited inmates from receiving Pell grants. This legislation blocked the opportunity for many inmates who were or wanted to pursue a college degree, but it also closed many vocational programs dependent on these federal funds. Still, one might find programs such as computer repair, simple programming, carpentry, commercial cleaning, heavy equipment operation, and food service in prison. Some are more likely to lead to jobs upon release than others.

The best vocational model might be one that combines prison labor with job training. In this way, a product is produced that can offset the cost of the training. Private businesses have set up industries in prison and use prisoner labor to produce goods sold on the open market, although the business must meet certain federal guidelines. While this type of partnership has the potential to provide salaries and training to prisoners, the issue of prison labor competing with other labor has always been contentious. During the depression, several federal laws were passed that restricted prison-made goods from competing with the private market, including the Hawes-Cooper Act (1929) that made it illegal to sell prison-made goods in another state that did not allow such sales, and then the Ashurst-Sumners Act (1935) that made it illegal to knowingly transport prison-made goods across state lines at all. Other laws protected civilian workers by limiting prison-made goods to use by states only. The result was that it was not economically feasible for private companies to use inmate labor.

This situation changed with the passage of the Federal Prison Industries Enhancement Act of 1979 (PIE). This law allowed prison-made goods to be sold on the open market with certain restrictions. The prison must certify that the prison industry pays the same wages, consults with representatives of private industry, does not displace civilian workers, collects funds for a victim assistance program, provides inmates with benefits in the event of injury, ensures that inmate participation is voluntary, and provides a substantial role for the private sector. The inmate is allowed to keep up to 20 percent of his or her wages, but the rest can be taken to meet legal judgments, pay restitution, child support, and room and board. If all these conditions are met, then the goods can compete on the open market.

As of 2000, there were only 3,826 inmates involved in PIE-certified prison industries (cited in Johnson 2002: 304), and as of 2011, still only 4,700 (Sloan 2011: 4). This is a very small number considering that the number incarcerated in state and federal prisons is 1.5 million. Despite the small numbers, companies as diverse as Walmart and Boeing have begun prison industry programs and there are currently 42 participating state or county entities with PIE-certified programs. Critics of the private enterprise partnerships with prisons argue that companies circumvent the restrictions of PIE and do not pay prevailing wages, do not have adequate work environments, or do not consult with outside labor before beginning a prison industry.

Sloan (2011) writes that the Bureau of Justice Assistance outsourced the regulation of PIE programs to a nonprofit group, the National Correctional Industries Association (NCIA) that is composed of the very people it is supposed to monitor. Consequently, when asked to investigate abuses and violations of the PIE regulations, the group rarely sanctions any program. Some programs, for instance, avoid paying prevailing wages by very long training periods in which inmates are paid less because they are in "training," yet the training lasts several years. Other programs hire lifers even though these programs are supposed to be vocational programs to aid in release and reentry, take more deductions from the prisoners' wages than allowed by law, and begin programs without conferring with local labor. PIE-certified prison industry programs are not supposed to displace civilian job holders, yet this is evidently what happened in Texas when Lockheed opened a prison program and promptly laid off 150 workers in a nearby city (Sloan 2011).

UNICOR is the prison industry program in the Federal Bureau of Prisons. It employed about 27 percent of all federal prisoners in the late 1990s (Stone 1997: 123). UNICOR makes over 150 different products—from safety goggles to road signs. Selling only to governmental agencies, UNICOR is criticized by some as producing an inferior product for an inflated price (Parenti 1999: 232), but others tout it as an unqualified success. Studies indicate that federal prisoners involved in UNICOR or other vocational training were less likely to break prison rules, more likely to get jobs upon release, and were less likely to recidivate (Saylor and Gaes 1994: 538). The sales report available on UNICOR's website posted $362,136,266 sales in the first six months of 2011.

Despite the PIE program and governmental markets, only five percent of all inmates are employed in any prison industry at all, and proportionally fewer prisoners work today than in 1980 (Parenti 1999: 231). A 2005 survey of 44 states indicated that 54,000 inmates were involved in prison industry, but that is out of the 320,000 inmates eligible, and it was unclear whether these were PIE-certified programs or internal industry programs (Corrections Compendium 2002). Why do outside industries avoid prison partnerships? One reason is certification under the PIE program is difficult; it is hard to show how civilian labor is not displaced if there is any amount of unemployment in the area of the prison. Second, prisons are simply not built with the needs of private industry in mind. There is a lack of space and, often, an inability to accommodate the requirements of a private industry. Third, stringent prison rules and regulations clearly show that custody concerns will always eclipse profit concerns. Fourth, the prison labor force is largely unskilled and uneducated. Even apprentice programs require at least a high school reading level and many prisoners do not have such skills. Finally, prison laborers, while they may be there on time, are not necessarily the most committed and energetic group of employees. Parenti (1999: 234) also mentions that some employers are afraid of negative publicity if the public found out they use convict labor. They also fear lawsuits. These are some of the reasons industries have not formed prison partnerships.

Evaluations. What is the effect of vocational training on recidivism? Gerber and Fritsch (1995) provided findings from their study that indicated education and vocational programming can reduce recidivism and increase the likelihood of post-prison employment. Lawrence, Mears, Dubin, and Travis (2002) found, in their meta-analysis, that educational and vocational training did reduce recidivism, but Brewster and Sharp (2002), in their examination of such programs in Oklahoma, found no effect. Studies seem to show that the training is less important than what happens to the offender after release. A Texas study, for instance, found that those inmates who completed a vocational training program but did not get a job upon release were not significantly less likely to recidivate than controls. Further, those inmates who got a job that paid less than $10,000 a year were also no more likely than controls to stay out of trouble. It is clear from this study that education or vocational training must lead to employment upon release in order for recidivism to be affected (Susswein 2000).

Generally, however, the research on education and vocational training and its impact on recidivism is not as strong as it could be. Reviewers note that the weight of evidence seems to support the idea that such programs reduce disciplinary infractions in prison and there is also evidence that the programs do reduce recidivism. The problem with most evaluations of such programs, however, is that they do not control for selection bias. What this means is that even if they show that inmates who obtain a GED or college education while in prison, or successfully complete a vocational training program, have reduced recidivism rates, it is impossible to conclude that the program is the reason, as opposed to the personal characteristics of the individuals who had the discipline and fortitude to complete the programs (Cullen and Jonson 2011). Only random assignment would solve this methodological problem, but it is unlikely that we will withhold education from prisoners who want it and need it for the sake of research.

DRUG TREATMENT

One report estimates that drug addiction costs state governments $81 billion in any given year. Most of the money goes to welfare, law enforcement, corrections and the courts, health care, and so on. Only a small fraction, $3.4 billion, is spent on prevention or treatment (Nagy 2001). The report, conducted by the National Center on Addiction and Substance Abuse at Columbia University, noted state spending related to drug use and abuse in several areas. The comparison between what states spend "cleaning up after" drug abuse versus treatment and prevention is astounding. For instance, North Dakota and Colorado spend about six cents for treatment for every $100 spent on responding to drug abuse (CASA 2001). A Rand study reported that for heavy users of cocaine, treatment costs one-seventh as much as the traditional punitive approach (Rydell, Caulkins, and Everingham 1996).

Recent estimates indicate that two-thirds of prisoners meet the medical criteria for a substance use disorder (National Center on Addiction and Substance Abuse 2010). This would include alcohol as well as other forms of drugs. Other sources indicate that 40 percent of prisoners who used drugs the month before their current offense received treatment in prison (Mumola and Karberg 2006).

Austin and Irwin (2001: 162) and Lock, Timberlake, and Rasinki (2002: 380) report that while there were 158,000 drug treatment slots in 1984 and 201,000 in 1993, there were only 99,000 in 1998. Since the early 1980s, the percentage of federal dollars spent on drug treatment efforts as part of the total budget of the war on drugs has decreased from 31 percent to 18 percent (Rydell, Caulkins, and Everingham 1996). A news report from Minnesota in May of 2011 reported that despite statistics that indicated drug treatment cuts recidivism by 25 percent and $1 spent on treatment is worth $12 of enforcement, legislators would be cutting from the prison drug treatment budget. Due to be cut were the equivalent of 200 treatment beds and 12 counselors (*Star Tribune* 2011). In Texas, a similar scenario is unfolding as the state corrections department explores ways to cut its budget, including one plan that would close three drug treatment facilities. Unfortunately, such stories have been repeated across the country as states face major budget shortfalls. It seems that while few disagree with the proposition that treatment is more effective than punishment in combating drug addiction, there is no political will to fund treatment over interdiction and punishment efforts.

Drug treatment intervention has always been politicized; or, rather, there are competing approaches taken regarding the causation of drug addiction/dependency. For some, addiction is seen as a disease, perhaps inherited, certainly unintentional, with those who suffer from it needing both medical and behavioral intervention in order to live a drug-free life. Like the disease model of alcoholism, this approach holds that no one is cured, they are just "in remission." On the other end of the spectrum are those who see drug addiction/abuse solely as a reflection of a weak will. In this view, those who abuse chemical substances could stop if they wanted to; they just don't want to. In the middle are a range of positions and approaches. For instance, a psychological predisposition to chemical addiction: a poor self-image, a dependent personality, or an addictive personality, all have been offered as "explaining" addiction. Others see drug addiction/abuse as more of a biological predisposition: because of brain chemistry, some individuals simply cannot use alcohol or drugs to any great extent without becoming physically and/or psychologically addicted to them. They could stop, but it is harder for them than someone who is not predisposed. The analogy might be of someone whose body type is predisposed to create fat cells. They may escape obesity, but it is harder for them to do so than someone who is genetically predisposed to be thin.

Given these different approaches, it is no wonder that drug treatment programs have a wide range of approaches also. Modalities include drug education, "shock" group therapy, behavioral modification, and "talking" therapy, among others. Methadone and antabuse are not therapies per se, but they help control use. Therapeutic communities (TC) are probably the most common treatment approach. These self-contained communities allow treatment staff to isolate, to some extent, participants from negative influences present in the general population of the prison and also to reduce the temptation and opportunity for acquiring drugs. Therapeutic communities typically employ some type of graduated structure whereby new participants must earn privileges by good behavior. They have daily group meetings during which a participant's behavior in the community is utilized in the treatment process, which typically involves improving personal responsibility and increasing self-esteem. Treatment is eclectic, utilizing a variety of methods and techniques.

> The answer is not imprisonment and legal attack. The answer lies in sentencing reform, treatment, harm reduction and education.... The days of the "Drug War" waged against our people should come to an end. (Governor Gary Johnson of New Mexico, cited in Nagy 2001: 2)

Evaluating Drug Treatment

Programs that combine cognitive-behavioral components and life skill training (vocational training or education) seem to be the most successful treatment modalities (Sung 2001). Yet others strike a more cautionary note. Austin and Irwin (2001), for instance, conclude that there are many issues to consider before committing appreciably more money to drug programs. They question the conclusion that drug treatment would reduce much crime and point out that there are troublesome issues in the delivery of drug treatment. Since most of the model drug treatment programs are based on the therapeutic community (TC) model, they point out that TC programs can, by their nature, provide only a small number of treatment slots. Further, such programs have high in-program failure rates; sometimes as many as 60 percent drop out. These authors argue that equal or greater efforts should be placed on improving service delivery of education, employment training, and job placement.

Terry (2003) discusses drug treatment and addicts who have managed to remain sober for many years. What is important, according to Terry, is a new self-concept that includes a healthy dose of self-respect. This is an important point because our current approach to drug offenders is designed to make them feel like bad people and criminals. We may, in fact, be providing exactly the opposite setting of one that might help users and addicts reclaim their lives.

Cullen and Jonson (2011) note that the many evaluations and reviews of drug treatment indicate that such programs are more likely to be successful if they are intensive, long term, structured, backed by penalties for nonparticipation, multimodal, and include aftercare services. The National Institute on Drug Abuse has published some principles of effective treatment which include the following:

- Recognize drug addiction as a brain disease
- Recovery requires treatment and management
- Treatment must last long enough to produce stable change
- Assessment is the first step
- Tailoring services to the individual is important
- Continuity of care (into the community) is important
- Offenders with co-occurring disorders require an integrated treatment approach (Fletcher and Chandler 2007).

REHABILITATIVE PROGRAMS AND THE WILL TO CHANGE

Treatment programs in prison may focus on anger management, life skills, or group therapy for incest/rape survivors. Sex offender treatment programs are present in a few prisons. According to some ex-inmates, "programmers" in prison are looked down upon by those who actively participate in the subculture. That may be, but there are many inmates who do take advantage of programs and who may even obtain some measure of enlightenment by going through the experience. The all-important question, of course, is whether or not any of the programs lead to a reduction in recidivism.

> I am not a vicious dog or any other type of violent animal. I am a prisoner. I live in a world many of you believe I deserve…a prisoner's world is beyond a non-prisoner's comprehension. Any human can become an animal in prison. (an ex-prisoner, Arriens 1991: 46)

A common type of program found in prison is called the therapeutic community. As discussed above, a therapeutic community is a self-enclosed community within a prison that attempts to shield the prisoner from the negative effects of the general population. Inmates are separated as much as possible from the general population and learn to live together in their community. Daily meetings and interactions form the basis of the therapy with an emphasis on personal responsibility and self-awareness (Toch 1980). In the living unit, inmates are given increasing responsibility concomitant with their exhibiting responsible behavior. Most of all, the pervasive message and culture of such communities is support and trust, which, in itself, is a much different living situation than what prisoners in general population are exposed to.

Singer (1996), a director of a therapeutic community describes important elements of a successful program. He includes the following:

- Isolation from the general population. As much as possible, treatment inmates should be removed and isolated from the negative subcultural elements of the general population.
- A healthy partnership between custodial and treatment staff. If custodial staff continually undercut and sabotage treatment initiatives, the program is doomed to failure. Custodial staff are an integral part of a therapeutic community and must be invested in the success of the program.
- A referral system that provides appropriate inmates for recruitment. There should be a careful screening and selection process as well.
- A program director who can work well within the correctional environment, mediate staff conflicts, and is sensitive to burnout.
- Substance abuse counselors who are committed and consistent, and who have good decision making skills. The presence of recovering addicts and/ or successful ex-inmates is helpful. Treatment staff should be diverse and reflect the population of clients.
- Clients should not have mental health problems and they should be motivated. They should have time to complete the program.
- An atmosphere where the client is free to trust, to take risks, and feels free to challenge him- or herself and others.

Some participants of such programs, especially women, eloquently describe how the program may have saved their life. They explain how they have never felt support or caring from anyone before, even their families, and so they never respected themselves. They are able to get the degree of positive reinforcement that they need in order to explore the reasons they abuse themselves and others and find the will to change. It is actually very sad to think that they are perfectly serious when they say that the best time of their lives has been in prison. Therapeutic communities, combined with cognitive-behavioral approaches, and practical skill acquisition (i.e., education or vocational training), probably offer the highest probability for success in prison programming. If nothing else, therapeutic communities tend to counteract some of the negativity of the prison experience.

> [Without the prison program] I think I would have been dead…I didn't go in there looking for a change. I went in there looking to get off the work crew…I probably would have been back out there and either dead or back on the streets doing what I do best….What this class gave me, you know, was not some magic potion that I could walk out those gates and that life was going to be okay, because it wasn't. What this class gave me was the desire and the willingness to make things okay. (an inmate, in Pollock 1998: 120)

Evaluations

Researchers have consistently found that prison treatment programs moderately reduce recidivism. Gendreau and Ross (1979, 1980) and Palmer (1994) have published numerous studies, as have others (Cullen 1982; Harland 1996), all showing some measure of success in prison programming. Andrews, Zinger, Hoge, Bonta, Gendreau, and Cullen (1990) pointed out in their meta-analysis of a number of evaluations that the impact of treatment upon recidivism was influenced by the extent to which service was appropriate to the risk of the offender, the need of the offender, and the responsiveness of the offender. They estimate that appropriate treatment may cut recidivism by as much as 50 percent.

Don Andrews, James Bonta, Paul Gendreau, and Robert Ross have been involved in the development and evaluation of correctional treatment for decades and the cognitive restructuring program that they are associated with incorporates what is most clearly supported by evidence; specifically, that the inmate's thinking and behavior patterns can be changed by a multi-modal program that utilizes rewards, modeling, and practice in improving communication and problem-solving skills. Correctional programs should concentrate on high-risk offenders and not focus on what have been identified as non-criminogenic needs of the offender. Finally, the "responsivity" of the offender should be taken into account and there should be some attempt to match program elements with offenders, although they do not believe that this requires individual treatment plans (Cullen and Jonson 2011).

Others list the following elements as important when weighing the effectiveness of correctional programming: the program should include the inmate in program planning; successful programs address strengthening prosocial behaviors rather than targeting antisocial behaviors; and, successful programs are able to neutralize the antisocial peer group or turn it to support prosocial values (cited in Johnson 2002: 298). Gendreau (1996) further describes successful programs as those that are intensive (occupying 40 to 70 percent of the inmate's time), utilizing behavioral strategies, with therapists matched to offenders. Wilson, Gallagher, Coggeshall, and MacKenzie (1999) conducted a meta-analysis of 33 evaluations of education, vocational, or other rehabilitative programs in prison. Their findings indicated modest improvements in recidivism existed across all program types.

Current research indicates that the most effective types of programs are those that utilize a cognitive-behavioral approach. For instance, Pearson, Lipton, Cleland, and Yee (2002) presented the findings of a meta-analysis of 69 research studies on prison programming between 1968 and 1999. Their review of the literature indicated that cognitive programs were often correlated with lowered recidivism. Cognitive-behavioral programs include behavioral programs that utilize token economies and other forms of behavior modification. One such program is "contingency contracting" which is when the inmate enters into a contract for desirable behaviors that then earn rewards. "Cognitive-behavioral" programs emphasize thought and emotional processes. Social skills training, role play, problem solving, rational emotive therapy, and cognitive skills programs are some of the types of programs categorized under the cognitive-behavioral label. Pearson and his colleagues found that cognitive-behavioral treatment approaches did reduce recidivism by "significant amounts" (Pearson, et al. 2002: 490). Further, the programs within the category that showed these effects were those that employed cognitive skills training and social skills development training, not the token economies or the standard behavior modification programs (Pearson, et al. 2002: 491). Cullen and Jonson (2011) review the many studies that support cognitive-behavioral programs. Cognitive restructuring focuses on changing the content of what offenders believe, specifically their pro-criminal attitudes and rationalization for crime, while cognitive skills programs attempt to change how the offender reasons, for instance, how to control anger or impulses.

Evaluations of prison programming have been bedeviled by difficulties. Follow-up time periods are usually short and attrition is high. Furthermore, despite program descriptions, the actual policies, procedures, and curriculum of each program are often very different, making comparison of similar types of programs impossible. Recidivism is not uniformly defined, so while one program may count an arrest as a failure, another program may define a return to prison as failure. Crow (2001: 46) also mentions that a return to prison is not necessarily due to re-offending after treatment; it may be due to legal retainers from prior offenses (holds placed on the offender for arrests or convictions from offenses committed prior to the current incarceration).

Crow (2001: 49) points out that a meta-analysis may present some problems. First, it may mix "apples and oranges;" different measures for different things may be collapsed into one meaning. Second, poor quality research may be included. Third, meta-analyses depends on published research and, so, misses some efforts. Fourth, because researchers are using one data set, multiple results may not be independent of each other. Despite these difficulties, meta-analyses, even Martinson's 1970 study, have found that some programs, most notably cognitive and behaviorally based programs, show some degree of success (Palmer 1994; Glaser 1994). But others insist that even cognitive programs won't rehabilitate without also offering the inmate some chance at learning a skill that can earn the individual a living wage (Austin 1999: 293).

As mentioned before, one of the problems of evaluation is that a program may not consistently contain the same content. Programs are heavily dependent on staff characteristics; thus, a fully participating, enthusiastic staff is probably going to show more program success than a bored or burned out staff, regardless of the modality in which they operate. Lin (2000) fully explores the problems of programs "on paper" that do not display anywhere near the type of experience as one would expect when reading the institutional description of offerings. Treatment staff that must constantly fight against a custodial staff may simply give up and become bureaucrats. Custodial officers often feel oppressed because treatment needs strain staffing resources. If there are not enough officers to patrol the living units, the need to have officers assigned to a recreation program, for instance, is resented (Lin 2000: 59).

> They don't like us helping the inmates. They think they should make an inmate's life as miserable as they can. Custody's attitude is, get out of my way because you got nothin' comin'.... When I was in custody, I guess I had the same feeling, but I had to change when I got to education because you can't degrade people if you're going to do this job.... (vo-tech instructor, quoted by Lin 2000: 67)

The most obvious problem of all evaluations of treatment programs in prison is that they cannot control for all the many influences that each offender experiences once he or she leaves prison. If two offenders participate in the same drug program and, also, a vocational training program, they may still end up differently because of situational elements upon release. Perhaps one individual is able to find work and start a new life with helpful friends, but the other may not be able to find work, has to live at home with drug using parents and siblings, and is drawn inexorably back into the drug world because of desperation and loneliness.

The Will to Change

Can prisoners change? There is no doubt that they can. How many do so is another question. It is a mistake to assume that there will ever be one prison program that will be the "cure all" for the myriad of reasons why offenders commit crime. What prison programs can do is provide opportunities and remove barriers to success. If an inmate can't get a job when he is released, he is that much more likely to commit another crime, but a prison program might provide skills in order to get a job. If a prisoner has abused drugs most of her adult life and, in prison, she is able to figure out how to avoid addiction upon release, then that is one less challenge to overcome in the quest to stay out of trouble.

It is true that not all inmates want to stay out of trouble. Some are so twisted and warped in their views of what they deserve, and so unable to feel empathy or care for others, that they should be locked up until they pose no danger to society because of age or incapacitation. It is very important to understand, though, that these are the minority in prison, not the majority. There are many weak people in prison. There are many who have had terrible lives and have not had any role model for a moral lifestyle. There are also those in prison that, with help, could control their behavior. Finally, whether the public believes it or not, there are many in prisons who are not necessarily bad people, they just made bad choices. Some of their choices are perhaps no worse than many individuals' choices on the outside who have had the fortune to escape detection and go on with productive lives.

What is very interesting and needs to be explored in much more detail is the "spontaneous remission" of some inmates. There are individuals who, without any prompting or outside influence, suddenly decide to completely change their lives.

They can quickly change from being a troublesome, recalcitrant prisoner to one who utilizes every opportunity open to him. They stop looking for trouble and begin to try to avoid it. Why this change of heart happens is a mystery, even to those who experience it. If we could identify the process, it would greatly assist in designing rehabilitative efforts. In the meantime, the goal of those involved in program services is to make sure that such opportunities are available for those individuals who decide to use them. It is clear that prison cannot make people "go straight." However, it can help them do so or make it harder for them to do so, depending on the programs available. What is truly ironic is that instead of using incarceration to improve oneself, many prisoners end up coming out of prison with more problems than when they went in. Some may have a drug addiction they did not have before. Some may be the victim of violence and bear psychic as well as physical scars. Some may have become violent themselves as a reaction to their environment. While some prisoners have experienced transformation in a good way, the all too often result of prison is not greater enlightenment and improvement of skills to survive in the "real" world; but, rather, greater bitterness, anger, and despair. It does not have to be this way.

> I'm sitting there…and it's like I had an out-of-body experience, man,…I'm watching myself, and I said, Man, that's a fucking shame, fucking disgusting animal savage that I've turned into.…From that day on I tried to enlighten myself. But I still went and did what I had to do. Because I don't want to be no fucking victim. (an inmate in Angola Prison who described himself preparing a "feces cocktail" to throw at another inmate, in Bergner 1998: 6)

EVIDENCE-BASED CORRECTIONS

It does not make sense to spend public monies on programs that do not work. Especially in the current economic crisis, no state or public entity can afford to waste money. Latessa, Cullen, and Gendreau (2002) discussed "correctional quackery" even before the current economic downturn and identified numerous programs that had no theoretical or empirical support, such as boot camps, "Scared Straight" programs, drama therapy, acupuncture, confrontational therapy, and others. These authors argue that we have a fairly good grasp of why offenders commit crimes: antisocial values, antisocial peers, poor self-control and problem-solving skills, family dysfunction, and past criminality. These factors must be addressed in any therapeutic intervention.

There has also been growing consensus on the principles of a successful program. These include:

- The organizational culture has well-defined goals, ethical principles, staff cohesion, and utilizes self-evaluation.
- The program is based on empirically defined needs, with professionally trained staff, and uses risk assessment.

- The program targets criminogenic needs, using empirically valid behavioral, social learning, or cognitive behavioral therapies targeting high-risk offenders.
- The program uses therapeutic practices including anticriminal modeling, reinforcement and disapproval, problem-solving techniques, structured learning, cognitive self-change, and relationship practices.
- The program utilizes referrals and incorporates continuation of services in the community.
- The program incorporates evaluation practices (Latessa, Cullen, and Gendreau 2002).

The move toward evidence-based corrections has led to an emphasis on evaluation and national dissemination of findings so that unsuccessful programs are not replicated in various parts of the country. The Department of Justice, specifically the National Institute of Justice and the Bureau of Justice Assistance, has been instrumental in funding evaluations of correctional interventions and supporting efforts to share findings. The latest and most ambitious of these projects is Crimesolutions.gov (http://www.crimesolutions.gov.), a website that lists and describes effective programs as well as those that are graded as "promising" and those that show no effects. As of October 2011, there were 155 programs listed on the website categorized into juvenile programs, corrections and reentry, drugs and substance abuse, and several other descriptors. The national reviewers have a rigorous approach to evaluating whether or not the program meets the description of "effective." For instance, in the Corrections and Reentry category, only one program appears as effective, although there are 28 programs that are defined as "promising." A program that is promising can reach the definition of "effective" if subsequent rigorous evaluations show more significant results.

One program on the website was "Forever Free," a drug abuse program for women. The evaluation showed that about half of the graduates were convicted after release compared to 71 percent of a comparison group. The reason this program was listed as "promising" rather than "effective" was that there has been only one study. If the evaluation's findings can be replicated, then the program will be moved to the effective category. Programs can submit their evaluations to the website or anyone can nominate a program. There must be evaluations of the program in order for it to appear since reviewers do not conduct original evaluations.

A similar project was undertaken by the Washington State Institute for Public Policy. The 2009 Washington legislature ordered the Institute to calculate cost benefits of prevention and intervention programs, and provide a list of programs and policies that were successful and cost-efficient. The result was a report that calculated the cost to taxpayers of a variety of programs, what the projected benefit of such a program was, and the total net benefit. Almost all programs showed a net benefit to taxpayers. For instance, in the section where programs for juveniles were evaluated, "Aggression Replacement Training," an institutional program, showed a net benefit of $65,481 to taxpayers. Other probation and prison-based programs showed net benefits ranging from about $3,000 to $57,000. On the other hand,

"Scared Straight" cost taxpayers $6,095 because it was unsuccessful in reducing recidivism. Programs for adult offenders included programs for the incarcerated mentally ill, drug offenders, and others. Net benefits to taxpayers ranged from about $4,500 to $71,000, but there were also programs that resulted in no benefit, only cost to the taxpayer (Washington State Institute for Public Policy 2011: 4).

Crimesolutions.gov and the Washington State project have the potential to save time and money for jurisdictions that will not have to "reinvent the wheel" or spend a great deal of time researching what types of programs are effective. Treatment staff may be disappointed and discouraged when their program is not shown to be effective, but it is important to utilize the scant funds available for rehabilitative treatment only on programs that are proven successful.

CONCLUSION

In this chapter the range of programs in prison was described. Prisons today do have more programs than they did 50 years ago, but fewer than they did 30 years ago. Prisoners who desire to change themselves have the opportunity to do so to a point. The biggest barrier to change is that there are not enough program slots for all the people in prison, and the number of programs that are "on paper" only. Prisoners today can at least take advantage of education programs and some type of life-skills program. They may have access to a vocational program or even accumulate some savings from a prison-industry partnership. The problem is that there are never enough of these programs to meet the large numbers of prisoners in prison, nor are many programs able to counteract the incredibly negative stigma of a prison sentence, so that, upon release, prisoners have almost insurmountable barriers to a productive and law-abiding life.

WEBSITES

For more information on the National Institute of Justice, visit:
    http://nij.gov/
For more information on Crimesolutions.gov, visit:
    http://www.CrimeSolutions.gov
For more information on the Prison Fellowship Ministries, visit:
    http://www.prisonfellowship.org/prison-fellowship-home
For more information on the Carl Perkins Vocational and Applied Technology Education Act, visit:
    http://www2.ed.gov/offices/OVAE/CTE/perkins.html
For more information on the Federal Prison Industries Enhancement Act, visit:
    http://www.ojp.usdoj.gov/BJA/grant/piecp.html
For more information on the National Correctional Industries Association, visit:
    http://www.ojp.usdoj.gov/BJA/grant/piecp.html
For more information on the Washington State Institute for Public Policy, visit:
    http://www.wsipp.wa.gov/.

STUDY QUESTIONS

1. How did Robert Martinson's findings hasten the end of the modern rehabilitative era?
2. List some of the treatment programs available to inmates.
3. What does research show regarding prison education and recidivism?
4. What are Pell grants and what has happened to them and college programs in prison?
5. What types of vocational programs do prisons have? What percentage of inmates are enrolled?
6. Why do outside industries avoid partnerships with prisons?
7. How does vocational training affect recidivism? Are there other related factors that affect recidivism?
8. What types of treatment programs are there in prison? What are the principles of a successful program?
9. What seems to be the most effective type of treatment program in prison?
10. Briefly describe some of the varying views on drug addiction/dependency that affect the way drug treatment programs are evaluated. Are drug treatment programs effective?

CHAPTER 6

Living in Prison

> Secretly, we all like it here. This place welcomes a man who is full of rage and violence. Here he is not abnormal or perceived as different. Here rage is nothing new, and for men scarred by child abuse and violent lives, the prison is an extension of inner life. (Masters 2001: 205)

What is it like to live in a prison? Descriptions of prison life have been offered by screenwriters in movies such as *The Shawshank Redemption*, television series such as the HBO series *Oz*, and even reality series that film inside prisons. Academic researchers have also given us book-length descriptions, such as James Jacob's *Statesville* (1977) and Gresham Sykes's, *Society of Captives* (1958). Other books, written by convicts or ex-convicts, provide a firsthand account of prison life, including Jack Abbot's *In the Belly of the Beast* (1981), Vic Hassine's *Life Without Parole: Living in Prison*, Dannie Martin's *Committing Journalism* (1993), and K. Carceral's *Prison, Inc.* (2005). Some correctional professionals present their views in books as well. One thing that all these sources have in common is that they paint a prison world that is very different from the outside. There is more violence, more tension, and more hate. Especially for men, an individual who successfully navigates the treacherous waters of the prison world is that much less able to reintegrate successfully to the outside world. He has learned, if he didn't before, how to ignore human suffering, preemptively strike so that he is not victimized, mind his own business when he sees others victimized, submerge any perceived weaknesses such as kindness or tolerance, and, more than anything else, has probably become an expert at anger.

PRISONER SUBCULTURE RESEARCH

Some of the earliest studies of prison were by early sociologists who worked in prisons. These researchers started to sketch out the parameters of the social world of prisoners. Their work included typologies (types of prisoners differentiated by behaviors, values, and pre-prison experiences) and the "inmate code." Some of the earliest prison research portrayed the prison as a world complete with its own culture. Inmates were socialized to that culture; in other words, they were "prisonized," which meant that they behaved differently and even believed differently in an accommodation to their new world. The earliest documented descriptions of this culture included Hans Reimer's (1937) observation of a Kansas penitentiary and Hayner and Ash's (1940) study of Washington State Reformatory. Donald Clemmer (1940) more fully described the inmate code, which included such tenets as: Be cool. Don't interfere with inmate interests. Don't weaken. Be sharp. And, do your own time (cited in Sykes and Messinger 1960: 6–9).

Sykes (1958) explained that the culture one found in a prison was a direct result of the deprivations of the prison world. Thus, homosexuality occurred because of the deprivation of the opposite sex; the black market developed because of the deprivation of autonomy and goods and services; and so on. Later research tested and enlarged these original ideas. For instance, it was hypothesized and proven that maximum security institutions had a stronger prison culture because these prisons were less permeable, and had more deprivations. This was the deprivation theory of prisoner subculture.

Irwin and Cressey (1962), Schrag (1961), and Irwin (1970) all presented evidence that the prison culture was not purely a creation of deprivation. Rather, many aspects of the culture came from the street. Irwin, especially, pointed out how the newly emerging drug culture was finding its way into prison, both in types of prisoners and in changing values. This was the importation theory of prisoner subculture. Thus was born the long-standing debate—whether the deprivations of prison created the subculture or whether the subculture was simply imported from street culture. The literature on this question is quite extensive.

Later researchers came to the common sense conclusion that both theories helped explain the subculture one found in prison. The theories are still being tested today and used to study a range of issues, including cross-cultural comparisons, the impact of crowding, homophobia, predictions of violence, rule violations, high-risk behaviors for HIV transmission, and the like (for a review, see Krebs 2002; Pollock 1997; or Winfree, Newbold, & Tubb 2002). Most studies find that a combination of both theories has the greatest explanatory power (e.g., Akers, Hayner, & Grunninger 1977). It is obvious that a minimum-security camp is not going to have the same type of prison culture as a maximum-security institution. At the same time, pre-prison factors such as crime of conviction and prior criminal history do influence whether or not the inmate is involved in the prisoner subculture, the black market, and violence.

ELEMENTS OF THE SUBCULTURE

A culture is composed of language (argot), roles, and norms or mores (known as the "inmate code"). The prisoner subculture is no different. In this section we will discuss these elements of the prisoner subculture.

Prison Argot

Prison argot refers to the unique terms used by prisoners. Actually, prison argot is dynamic and as words find their way into the lexicon of the larger society, prisoners continue to reinvent their own vocabulary. Words such as snitch, hack, con, and others originated in the prison. The importance of a concept, a type of person, or object in the subculture is reflected by the number of words used to define it; for instance, the prison snitch, the prison guard, and, especially, drugs have many words to describe them.

Einat and Einat (2000), although describing an Israeli prison, accurately describe the idea that the use of prison argot expresses loyalty and adherence to the subculture. Individuals who are "square johns" are not familiar with the terms and not comfortable, at least not initially with their use. Unique to the prison sub-culture are terms that refer to the black market, prison sex, prison scams, and types of food (Hensley, Wright, Tewksbury, & Castle 2003). Women in prison use similar terms, but also have some unique to their environment, such as these from Texas prisoners: "spit boxing" (arguing), RPGs ("rape prevention goggles," refer-ring to the black-framed, state-issued eyeglasses), and "ho bath" (washing in the sink rather than a shower) (Johnson, Bina, Cornelius, Holder, Kennerer, & Larson 2010). Interestingly, some slang terms are the same across many states, and even are similar in different nation's prisons, while other terms are unique to a particu-lar state or a particular prison.

Lerner (2002) described the prison from the perspective of a prison "fish." Once in prison, he became a "lawdog," since he had a college education and could help other inmates interpret court papers. Soon his vocabulary absorbed the prison slang, including descriptions of prisoners such as "dawgs" (friends, associates, acquaintances), "queens" (homosexual men who dress like women), "punks" (the sexually victimized or anyone who is taken advantage of), "fish" (new inmates), "woods" (from "peckerwoods," a name for whites), "toads" (also a derogatory name for whites), "shotcallers" (prisoners who had some power), "wig-gers" (whites who associated with blacks), "fishcops" (new COs), and "old heads" (older cons who liked to talk about the old days in prison). Queens in prison were obvious. They wore the state-issued denims cut off about two inches below their crotch, with the prison shirt cut short to show the midriff. Mascara was blue pool-cue chalk and cherry Kool-Aid served as lipstick. Much of the violence revolved around sex and relationships. Shotcallers could "fix" anything, including securing a cell assignment, obtaining drugs, and ordering a hit on another prisoner. Although their power might come from gang affiliation, it was not necessarily mandatory. Individuals who were affiliated with the mob also would be shotcallers in the prison.

> The code I was taught isn't really followed anymore but consists of, basically,...don't gamble, do drugs, and don't mess with queens. Mind your business and don't trust anyone. (Hassine 2004: 202)

Inmate Code

The inmate code that Sykes and Messinger (1960) described is now believed to be idealized; it probably represented the ideal values of inmates, even though most did not uphold them in their daily behavior. Inmates were supposed to be tough and avoid guards, and mind their own business, but not exploit other prisoners. The changes in the prison population in the 1970s led to a clash between the "old-timers" and younger inmates. Many old-time cons saw that younger prisoners did not respect them and cared nothing for their values.

> To the Old Heads, prison life today lacked the honor, quiet solitude, and routine that had once made incarceration more noble. Now the greatest threat to an inmate had become other inmates, particularly the "young bucks" who had infested the general population. (Hassine 1999: 31)

Hassine (1999) provides a fascinating account of one inmate's experience through the 1980s and, if it is representative at all, it illustrates how the prison culture itself adapted and stabilized, gaining control over roving predators and the violence of the drug trade. The inmate code he describes is quite different from the one the earliest researchers provided. Today, the inmate code includes the following principles:

Don't snitch, don't borrow, don't mess with homosexual; don't "see", don't "hear", don't "say" (don't be a witness); don't gossip, watch who you walk with, don't debate PRS (politics, religion, sports)...(Hassine 2004: 203).

Carceral (2005), another prisoner-author also described the difference between the ideal convict code and the "real rules" that govern prisons today. The driving motivation behind these rules, according to Carceral, is selfishness. He explained that today, instead of an "us against them" world between inmates and guards, it is more of every prisoner for himself.

Real Rule #1: Snitching must have a purpose. It is okay to tell to further your own purpose. For example, if you tell on an enemy, it's okay. Real Rule #2: Manipulate. Taking advantage of staff and other prisoners is normal. Real Rule #3: If you can get away with it, don't pay your debt. This is an aspect of the manipulation in Real Rule #2. Real Rule #4: Gossip. This rule runs counter to the Con Rule of "do your own time." In reality, gossips flourish in prison. This is the actual rule that governs the reality in prison. Real Rule #5: Steal whatever you can. This rule makes theft open to anyone at any time. (Carceral 2005: 124)

Lerner (2002) described other aspects of prison life. He learned that every newcomer to prison would face a "heartcheck" and must show a willingness to fight; otherwise, he would become a punk or a "yard trick" (one who carried contraband and did menial labor for others). He discovered that there was a daily yard toll, a cell or bunk rental fee, and if the fish had resources he might end up paying a life insurance policy of $500 a week. If an inmate did not fight, have friends, or could not pay, he would be victimized. Other newcomers were greeted warmly. He explains that those with "full sleeves" (many tattoos) were not vulnerable to extortion, especially if they sported a swastika or a teardrop (said to denote someone who has murdered a police officer).

He also explained why the requests prisoners fill out to see a counselor or go to sick call are called kites: "clear to anyone who has ever been advised to go fly a fucking kite" (Lerner 2002: 67). Lerner's description paints a prison world where the guards, in a sense, become prisonized and even adopt the prisoner language. *You've Got Nothing Coming* was the title of his book and the mantra of the prison staff, according to Lerner. Cruelty by guards wasn't necessarily extreme; rather, it was banal and pointless.

Richards (2003), Ross and Richards (2002, 2003), Sabo, Kupers, and London (2001), and Carceral (2005) have also provided more current descriptions of prison life. For instance, Ross and Richards (2002) note that convicts are extremely polite because to bump someone without apologizing is risking serious retribution. They observe that "mind your own business" is still the best advice one can give a prison fish. In a book written for new inmates, they caution prison "fish" to never accept favors, stay away from groups, and watch what they say. The prison world is, in some ways, different from 30 years ago and, in some ways, very much the same. For instance, the black market has always characterized prison life.

The Black Market

One of the most enduring elements of the prisoner subculture is the black market one can find in any prison of any size. Inmates are truly ingenious in acquiring and utilizing contraband. One can literally "buy" anything in prison. Prisoners operate fairly freely with some degree of tolerance by prison officials, except for drugs, weapons, and violence.

Prisoners have always sought mind-altering substances. "Pruno," a substance more valued for its intoxication qualities than its taste or robust "bouquet," has been and continues to be made in prison from smuggled fruit and some form of yeast (usually bread). As drug offenders constituted greater and greater numbers of prisoner populations, drugs replaced alcohol because they were easier to conceal. Drugs are smuggled in by visitors, staff, and correctional officers. There is the temptation of large amounts of money or the coercion of threats to make guards "pack." Inmates who were not affiliated with drugs on the outside and, therefore, are under less scrutiny by officials, are coerced to have their visitors bring them drugs. The drugs are then taken and sold on the prison black market. Interestingly, because prisons have now banned smoking, cigarettes have become the new drug of choice and are probably the most commonly sold commodity on the black market. A possible result, however, is that correctional officers may be more tempted to smuggle this type of contraband since it is seen as less harmful than other types of contraband.

Drugs cause management problems in a number of ways. Those prisoners who get high on some substances become belligerent or irrationally violent. Much more common, however, is the violence that exists in the drug trade itself. Competitors fight or kill each other; those who owe drug dealers money are either assaulted or hurt their creditors first. Drug stashes are stolen. Snitches are killed. Ironically, sometimes prisoners who did not use drugs on the outside begin their drug use in prison or change to a "harder" drug because it is available. Then the inmate is released with a drug addiction that virtually ensures future criminal activity undertaken to service the habit.

Today, while drugs have not been completely eliminated, some prisons have taken aggressive steps to curtail the drug trade, including random drug tests on prisoners and prosecuting guards who are caught smuggling. Mandatory, random drug testing has been helpful in identifying drug users. Some prisons employ a "patch" system for drug detection that is supposed to be more effective than urinalysis. The level of drug use varies quite a bit from prison to prison in relation to the preventative and enforcement steps taken by administrators.

The other elements of the black market are more resistant to enforcement, and there is some question as to whether or not prison officials even desire to curtail all aspects of it. Some guards may believe that a satisfied inmate (whether his needs are for alcohol, drugs, sex, or sandwiches at night) is less likely to cause trouble.

> I had at my disposal the eager services of swag men [contraband food], laundry men, ice men (for summer ice cubes), barbers (to cut my hair in my cell), and phone men (to make sure I got signed up for phone calls). I could even have a cell cleaner, though I felt there were certain things a man should do for himself. (Hassine 1999: 37)

RACE AND GANGS

Racial segregation in prison was (and is) practiced by the prisoners themselves. In some prisons, the day rooms have chairs allocated to Hispanics, African-Americans, and whites, and the person who accidentally sits in the wrong chair is in trouble. The yard is balkanized into racial groupings, and an inmate will rarely, if ever, sit with someone of another race in the dining hall if allowed to select a seat. Prison officials predicted a bloodbath if forced to integrate cell assignments, and there is some evidence that indicates at least some officials tried to instigate prisoner unrest (Trulson and Marquart 2002a).

According to some research, the predicted violence due to racial integration did not occur to the degree feared, at least in the Texas system after it began to integrate cell assignments in 1991. Trulson and Marquart (2002b; 2002c) compared violent altercations between cell partners (both integrated and nonintegrated). The official reason for an altercation was racial tension in only 4.7 percent of the cases. When comparing the rate of violent incidents, they determined that integrated cell partners were either equally likely or less likely to engage in violent altercations than same-race cell partners. At the end of 1999, more than twice as many prisoners were assigned integrated cells in Texas as in the rest of the nation (Trulson and Marquart 2002a, 515).

Trulson and Marquart (2002b) show that, at least in the Texas prison system, intraracial and interracial violence occur at about the same rate; however, there is still quite a bit of racial violence. Much of the violence in prison is related to racial gangs. The California Department of Corrections estimated that nearly 7,000 gang members reside in their state prisons (cited in Parenti 1999: 194). In addition to the older gangs described in chapter 1, new gangs have formed, including new forms of the split between northern and southern California Chicanos—the Nortenos and the Surenos, and the "border brothers" (Hunt, Riegel, Morales, & Waldorf 1993). The Crips and Bloods are now joined by the 415s (named for the 415 area code in San Francisco). Some argue that because there are many more gangs today than in the past, they are looser and do not have the power over prisoners they once did (Hunt, et al. 1993). However, it may also be true that the shifting allegiances and loyalties between these gangs make it more difficult to stay safe today in prisons. Also, inmates form less formal, semi-organized groups that utilize racial and geographic categories. These cliques draw individuals together for defense, support, and trade in the prison black market.

It should be understood that tension between racial gangs today has as much to do with financial interests as it does with racial prejudice. Since gangs control most, if not all, of the black market, violence between gangs is often attributed to business and gang members protecting their market.

Gang management policies are a mix of control (identifying and separating gang leaders), enriching program offerings (to keep inmates busy), and practicing good management (eliminating procedures and locations in a prison that are vulnerable to violence) (Fleisher and Rison 1999: 237). There are continuing allegations that guards encourage racial violence to keep inmates from organizing together against the guards (Hunt, et al. 1993). The most notorious stories came from Corcoran Prison in California. Numerous allegations of guards setting up gladiator fights and otherwise pitting racial gang members against each other have surfaced and have even been the object of litigation (*Madrid v. Gomez*, 1995). Overtly or covertly racial guard organizations exist (such as the "Society for the Prevention of Niggers Getting Everything" and the "European American Officers Association") and provide support to neo-Nazi inmate gangs (Parenti 1999: 206).

Gangs continue to be an issue in prison management. According to some studies, membership in gangs is increasing and prison authorities estimate that 19 percent of all prisoners belong to gangs (Winterdyk and Ruddell 2010: 731). According to some research, 80 percent of all homicides in prison are gang-related and 43 percent of all major infractions are gang related. Gang membership is highly correlated with recidivism (Winterdyk and Ruddell 2010).

PRISON VIOLENCE

More than anything else, the prison world is associated with violence. Violence takes the form of verbal intimidation and threats, assaults, homicide, and sexual violence. Rape and the threat of rape are used as a device of intimidation. Rapes, along with beatings, are used to humiliate, control, punish, and/or exploit. Riots and other disturbances are also a form of violence.

One author characterizes the types of violence occurring in prison as the following: intrapersonal (self-mutilation, suicide attempts, etc.), interpersonal (sexual, physical, or psychological), group (gang activity or loose associations), organized (riots or organized attacks on officers), and institutional (beatings or other physical or emotional harm inflicted by officers) (Braswell, Montgomery, & Lombardo 1994). Elements of the prison subculture contribute to the level of violence found in prisons. The culture of hypermasculinity, a pervasive black market that creates debts and the opportunities for extortion and theft, racial and ethnic gangs, crowded conditions that cause inmates to have to share space, boredom, and the importance of reputation and not being perceived as a victim all contribute to the likelihood of violent incidents.

In an early study, Wooldredge (1998) found that 48 percent of inmate-respondents reported victimization. Nancy Wolff and her colleagues conducted a single-state study, incorporating 12 prisons for men and one prison for women. There were 7,233 male inmates and 564 women in the sample; 83 percent of male prisoners were nonwhite and 69 percent of the female prisoners were nonwhite (Wolff and Shi 2009; Wolff, Blitz, Shi, Siegel, & Bachman 2007). The most common victimization was theft. More than three-quarters of male inmates and 80 percent of female inmates reported one or two types of victimizations (including theft) (Wolff and Shi 2009: 183, 184). About 20 percent of female inmates and 25 percent of male inmates reported being assaulted within their current sentence (Wolff, et al. 2007: 589) and a third of men and a quarter of women reported physical victimization within the previous six-month period (Wolff and Shi 2009: 186). Most inmates do not report these victimizations to prison officials (Wolff and Shi 2009: 186).

Correlates of Violence

Sorensen and Cunningham (2010) examined the disciplinary data on 51,527 Florida inmates. Gang members, female inmates, and death-sentenced inmates were excluded for the purpose of the study. These researchers found that potentially violent or violent infractions accounted for about 10 percent of the total number of prison infractions. These types of infractions constituted 12 percent of the total infractions of an admissions cohort, but about twice that (21.2 percent) of a close custody cohort (2010: 111) and involved 10.5 percent of the inmate population (2010: 11). Many of these infractions were verbal threats and did not involve actual violence. Serious bodily injury and assaults on staff were quite rare, although this study obviously utilized only officially reported misconducts/infractions. There are many more violent incidents, especially threats and intimidation but also assaults that do not appear in official statistics.

Age is the strongest correlate with prison misconduct and prison violence as well (Perez, Gover, Tennyson, & Santos 2010; Sorensen and Cunningham 2010; Wooldredge 1998). Interestingly, age is a predictor for being both a perpetrator and a victim of prison violence. Other predictors of victimization are sex (although results are mixed and depend on what type of victimization); race (results are also mixed); number of hours spent in education classes, and length of time incarcerated (with mixed results as well). In a study by Sorensen and Cunningham (2010: 118) male inmates were more likely than female inmates to be involved in violent infractions, gang membership positively predicted violence, and a prior prison experience increased the likelihood of violent infractions by almost 30 percent. Inmates with shorter sentences were more violence-prone and those who had been in prison longer periods of time were less likely to be involved.

Younger inmates were significantly more likely to report being victimized by assault in the Wolff study; this was true for both inmate-inmate and staff-inmate victimization (Wolff, et al. 2007). In this study, women were more likely to report an assault without a weapon while men were more likely to report an assault with a weapon. Overall, the six-month victimization prevalence rates of men and women were about the same (206/205 per 1,000). However, men were more likely to report having been assaulted by staff members. These victimization rates are 18 times higher than the national rates for the general population outside of prison for men and 27 times higher than the general population of women. They are also 10 times higher than the victimization rates reported by the urban poor, which is a more appropriate comparison to a prison population (Wolff, et al. 2007: 595).

In the Wolff study, smaller prisons seemed to be more correlated with inmate-on-inmate violence while larger prisons were associated with assaults by staff members (Wolff, et al. 2007: 594). Further, rates of reported assaults by staff varied quite a bit; in some prisons 30 percent of respondents reported being assaulted by staff members (2007). On average, male prisoners were twice as likely to report being assaulted by staff as by other inmates (8.9 percent versus 4.5 percent). In fact, only one-third of the male prisoners (compared to two-thirds of female prisoners) felt mostly or very safe from staff using physical force (Wolff and Shi 2009: 189).

In a study by Perez, et al. (2010), sexual and physical victimization but not economic victimization was examined. They found that 32 percent of their sample reported being victimized in the last year; 16 percent had been victimized by staff and 24 percent reported inmate perpetrators. In this study, individual demographics such as age, gender, and race were significantly related only to staff-inmate victimization, not inmate-inmate. The only correlate that predicted inmate-inmate victimization was being housed in maximum security.

Some studies combine individual and institutional level factors. Lahm (2008) found that age and past aggressive incidents were the strongest predictors of committing violent infractions. Inmates were also more likely to engage in aggressive infractions in prisons that were crowded and had a higher number of younger prisoners. Steiner (2009) compared violence rates in 512 prisons for men at two time periods (1995 and 2000). He found that the racial composition of inmates and staff, measures of administrative control, and state-level factors influenced the level of violent misconduct. Specifically, higher numbers of black inmates, maximum security, lower ratios of correctional officers to inmates, and the lack of structured inmate routines all were associated with higher levels of violent misconduct. Crowding seemed to have no effect on violence in this study.

> There, at two a.m. one night, Terry woke to see a man sliding a pair of sneakers from beneath another's cot. While the second inmate slept under the soft blue of the security lights, the man pulled the high-tops onto his feet, laced them snugly, tied them, and, fully dressed now, walked up the aisle to his own bed. He removed the padlock from his box. Holding it, he returned to the sleeping inmate, knelt on top of him, and pinned his head to the pillow with one hand. Terry guessed he was about to deal out a whipping with the padlock, then saw he carried a razor in addition.... Now he carved with the razor. He sliced deep from temple to jaw. Then he dealt out the lock-whipping. And then the guard's backup arrived. (Bergner 1998: 226)

Inmates protect themselves from violence by avoiding the yard and mess hall. Wolff et al. (2007) reported that 50 percent of men and 27 percent of women in their sample admitted carrying a weapon. Inmates also protect themselves by avoiding risky areas or staying in their cells (Wolff and Shi 2009).

Economic Violence

Much of the violence that occurs in prison has an economic motive, either directly or indirectly. In the Wolff et al. (2009: 183) study, theft was the most common victimization reported (48 percent of female inmates and 24 percent of male inmates reported theft). Many inmates do not have family members who send money to them for their inmate account and make very little or no money at a prison job. Most prison jobs will only earn the inmate $20 to $30 a month. In order to make life bearable, inmates buy from the commissary a multitude of items, including food, drinks, hygiene products, and other items. If an inmate does not have financial resources, he innovates by extortion, manipulation, or direct theft. Contrary to the phrase, there is no honor among thieves, and inmates' possessions are at constant risk of theft.

Depending on the institution and housing unit, theft can be pervasive or rare. Factors that affect theft include the ability to lock up items, whether there is surveillance of cell doors, whether it is a dormitory or not, and so on. Carceral (2005) described a private prison where he served time in which economic violence was rampant and out of control and involved physical intimidation in the form of "beat down crews" who used violence to rob inmates of their possessions.

> "Beat down crew? I'm starting to hear more and more people say that. What the fuck is a beat down crew?" "Yeah, it's the latest fad here. It isn't bad enough with all the fighting and cell robberies but now them GD boyees are getting really bold. They are getting together to straight up beat down dudes and steal whatever they can. Especially if they think you're holding weed or cash." (Carceral 2005: 54)

Sexual Violence

One of the ubiquitous elements of prison life is the threat of sexual assault. The risk is so well known it is used as a threat or even as a joke in media sources and common parlance. It is no joke, however, and victims of sexual assault in prison are traumatized by the experience, often suffering PTSD and other effects. One victim of sexual assault, Stephen Donaldson, was a Quaker peace activist. He was jailed when he refused to post a 10-dollar bond. He was raped over 50 times in a Washington, D.C. jail and died of AIDS, contracted from one of his assailants (Man and Cronan 2001: 127). It is difficult to see why, after reading such accounts of prison rape, that anyone would think the subject was humorous.

This type of prison violence has been chronicled since the early 1900s. Officers sometimes ignore it, pretend it does not exist, or even encourage sexual predation by the strong against the weak or inmates who are perceived as "needing a lesson." Gilligan (2002) reviewed the literature and utilized his own experiences as a prison doctor to conclude that officers benefit by allowing some inmates to brutalize others. Some believe that a predator becomes more manageable and calm if he has a "wife," a man forced into sexual submission.

> [Staff members] used to perform prison marriages in which the convict and his galboy-wife would leap over the broomstick together in a mock ceremony. (Wilbert Rideau, an inmate in Angola State Penitentiary in Louisiana, in Rideau and Wikberg 1992: 90)

A report by Human Rights Watch (2001) noted that staff members did little to try to stop rape, describing their reaction as "callous and irresponsible" (Human Rights Watch 2001: 151). One inmate reported why he believed guards ignored victimization:

> The guards believe that the tougher, colder, and more cruel and inhumane a place is, the less chance a person will return. This is not true. The more negative experiences a person goes through, the more he turns into a violent, cruel, mean, heartless individual (inmate reported in Human Rights Watch 2001: 121).

According to Eigenberg (2000), officers believe that rape is only defined as such if an inmate is physically overpowered. The many other incidents of sexual victimization that involve coercion, either through threats or implied threats, are not considered rape by officers, which partially explains why the response to sexual victimization is less than effective.

In the early 2000s a coalition of religious and human rights groups led by the Washington-based Hudson Institute and grassroots group called "Stop Prison Rape, Inc." began to put pressure on Congress to do something about prison rape. The result became the Prison Rape Elimination Act (Public Law 108-79), passed in 2003. The Act mandates states to keep records of prison rape allegations and address the problem or risk losing federal money. The other element of PREA was a mandate to conduct national surveys of prison rape. The Bureau of Justice Statistics (BJS) now has published several years' of annual surveys of men's prisons, women's prisons, and youth facilities.

Sexual victimization ranges from verbal harassment to rape. Generally the threat of rape and other forms of sexual victimization are more common than physical rape. According to Hassine (2004), a prisoner-author who committed suicide in 2008, sexual assault includes strong arm rape (physical force by one or several), extortion rape (the victim is coerced to trade sex for a debt owed), date rape (usually of a homosexual inmate who has had sex with others or the rapist but is unwilling at that time), confidence rape (heterosexuals are "groomed" by a prison wolf), and drug rape (the victim is drugged before sex). Research on nonconsensual sex in men's prisons confirms that sexual predators used tricks, debt, and threats in addition to physical violence to gain compliance by the victim (Hensley, Struckman-Johnson, & Eigenberg 2000; Hensley 2002). In fact, Keys (2002) noted that "turning out a punk" was more common in the inmate culture than physical rape. Submitting to sex was described by Keys's inmate-respondents as "accommodation," "a favor," "fulfillment of an obligation," or "solidifying alliances" (Keys 2002: 268). Trammell's (2006) respondents also described the participation of "wives" or "punks" as something less than consensual, but short of being physically coerced. They struggled to find an accurate term and settled on "business arrangement."

One of the advantages of PREA has been that more researchers use standardized definitions of sexual victimization rather than a variety of different terms or uses of terms which made studies difficult to compare. The Bureau of Justice

Statistics uses the following definition for *sexual victimization*: all types of sexual activity, e.g., oral, anal, or vaginal penetration; hand jobs; touching of the inmate's buttocks, thighs, penis, breasts, or vagina in a sexual way; abusive sexual contacts; both willing and unwilling sexual activity with staff. Sexual victimization includes nonconsensual sex acts and/or abusive sexual contacts. Sexual victimization includes *nonconsensual sex acts*, defined as unwanted contacts with an inmate or any contacts with staff that involved oral, anal, vaginal penetration, hand jobs, and other sexual acts; and, a*busive sexual contacts*, defined as unwanted contacts with another inmate or any contacts with staff that involved touching of the inmate's buttocks, thigh, penis, breasts, or vagina in a sexual way (Beck, Harrison, Berzofsky, Caspar, & Krebs 2010: 31–32).

Prevalence. One of the earliest studies in the late 1960s reported that about three percent of those in the Philadelphia jail system reported sexual assault in a 26-month period. Estimates of prison rape in past studies have included: 1 percent, 1.3 percent, 3 percent, 12 percent, and 14 percent (Hensley, Struckman-Johnson, & Eigenberg 2000: 365). Other studies have reported rates of rape between 1 and 25 percent (Krebs 2002: 21). Fleisher and Krienert (2006), in their study of the prison culture surrounding rape, which was not a prevalence study, found that very few individuals had been victimized, but their study was criticized because it was through interviews and critics argued that prisoners were not likely to admit sexual victimization to an interviewer. All research shows that estimates of sexual coercion or harassment are higher than physical rape, including estimates of victimization that have been 14 percent, 22 percent, and 28 percent (Hensley, Struckman-Johnson, & Eigenberg, 2000: 366).

In the Wolff study described above, researchers found that female inmates were more than four times more likely to report sexual victimization than male prisoners (Wolff, Shi, Blitz, & Siegel 2007). The six-month prevalence rates for sexual acts were 3.2 percent for women and 1.5 percent for men. Staff-on-inmate sexual victimization was reported at 1.7 percent for women and 1.9 percent for men. Abusive sexual contacts (touching only) were much more likely to be reported than nonconsensual sex acts (21.2 percent of women and 4.3 percent of men). About the same rates of men and women reported staff abusive sexual contacts (7.6 percent). These rates are much higher than sexual assault rates for the general population (0.2 to 0.9 percent compared to prison rates of 2 percent) (Wolff, et al. 2007: 535-538).

The latest published BJS report presents findings from 2008-2009 (Beck, et al. 2010). This national survey was taken between October 2008 and December 2009 in 167 state and federal prisons. The survey was also taken in jails and youth facilities, but findings from adult prisons are the only ones included in Table 6.1. About 4.4 percent of prisoners reported one or more incidents of sexual victimization. An unexpected finding was that male inmates reported more staff sexual misconduct than female inmates. Also contrary to perceptions was the finding that female inmates are more likely to report victimization by other inmates than male inmates. As with other surveys, more inmates reported abusive sexual touching

Table 6.1 Findings from the National Inmate Survey, 2008-2009

VICTIMIZATION	PERCENT	PERCENT/MALE	PERCENT/FEMALE
Total	4.4	4.3	6.0
Inmate-Inmate	2.1	1.9	4.8
–Non-consent sex	1.0		
–Abusive sexual contact	1.0		
Staff sexual misconduct	2.8	2.9	2.2
–Unwilling activity	1.7		
–Excluding touching	1.3		
–Touching only	.4		
Willing activity	1.8		
–Excluding touching	1.5		
–Touching only	.3		

SOURCE: Beck, Harrison, Berzofsky, Caspar, & Krebs. 2010. Sexual Victimization in Prisons and Jails Reported by Inmates, 2008-2009. Washington, D.C.: Bureau of Justice Statistics, U.S. Dept. of Justice.

as opposed to nonconsensual sex acts. About half of the sexual contacts with staff were "willing." Prior research has also indicated that about half of all staff sexual misconduct is between female correctional officers and male inmates (Marquart, Barnhill, & Balshaw-Biddle 2001). These relationships are more likely to be "willing"; however, inmate consent is not a legal defense in those states that have passed laws making such contacts crimes.

One of the findings of this study is that facilities vary greatly in the percentage of inmates who report victimization. High-rate facilities had rates on inmate-inmate sexual victimization as high as 8.6 percent in the prisons for men and 11.9 in a prison for women. Sexual misconduct by staff members was also much higher in some facilities (8.2 in one prison for men and 11.5 in a prison for women) (Beck, et al. 2010: 7-8). Prisoners in other institutions reported very low rates and in some facilities prisoners reported no incidents of sexual victimization at all. Inmate-inmate victimization was more likely to be reported by women, white or multi-racial, college-degreed, and never married. Staff sexual misconduct was more likely to be reported by men, blacks, and younger inmates. Inmates with a same-sex orientation were significantly more likely to report sexual victimization by inmates (11.2 percent compared to 1.3 percent) and staff (6.6 percent compared to 2.5 percent) (Beck, et al. 2010: 14).

Characteristics of Perpetrators. Morash, Jeong, and Zang (2010) compared 121 perpetrators of sexual assault to nonassaulters. They found that sexual aggressors were more likely to have been sexually abused as a child, have a life sentence, and have had adult sexual assault convictions and juvenile robbery. A review of the literature on sexual assault revealed that these characteristics were fairly consistent in past studies of sexual assault in prison. In contrast, race/ethnicity as a correlate of sexual aggression received mixed findings.

Characteristics of Victims. Research indicates that victims in men's prisons tend to be younger prisoners, who are physically smaller and weaker than the average inmate. They are more often white, first time offenders, middle class, and convicted of nonviolent crimes (Donaldson 2001; Hensley 2002). Other research shows that the most likely victims are prison "fish," inmates with a "weak" public image, and/or who are attractive. Other predictors include being a known homosexual, being convicted of a sexual offense against a child, having had a prior victimization (before 18), possessing a mental disorder, having higher levels of education, and, finally, a perceived high level of gang activity in the facility (Wolff, et al. 2007: 538).

Rape is devastating and victims suffer a range of medical and psychological effects. There is virtually no professional intervention for victims of rape within a prison. Men who suffer rape are released bearing psychic scars that last a lifetime and that may lead to the victim becoming a sexual offender (Dumond 2000). Human Rights Watch (2001) reports that victims (both male and female) commonly report nightmares, depression, shame, loss of self-esteem, self-hatred, and suicidal thoughts.

Sexual Violence in Men's Prisons. There is more coerced sex than physical rape in both men's and women's prisons. The differences between men's and women's prisons are great enough that we will concentrate solely on men's prisons in this section and discuss sexual violence in women's prisons in the next chapter.

It is reported that inmates may enter into sexual relationships in order to forestall a rape incident or because they owe the aggressor a debt and do not want to be seriously injured for nonpayment. Aggressors do not consider themselves to be homosexual. While it does not impact one's masculinity to be the aggressor (in fact, in a way, it enhances it), the "catcher" or "receiver" is considered less than a man. Once made into a punk, whore, or sex slave, the man is emasculated. Sex slaves are bartered, traded, and sold in prison. They are forced to do service labor, including laundry, cleaning, and food preparation for their husbands or whoever their husbands sell them to. The punk may act as wife in all senses of the word in some relationships, providing emotional support as well as services. In most relationships, however, the "man's" relationship with the punk does not stop him from lending him out for sexual services. Observers note that prisoners engaged in homosexual dyads, just as heterosexual couples, have varied relationships: "The men tend to treat their catchers much as they habitually did their female companions, so a wide range of relationships, ranging from ruthless exploitation to romantic love, exists" (Donaldson 2001, 121).

Research also indicated that only about a third of male victims reported their rape to authorities (Struckman-Johnson, Rucker, Bumby, & Donaldson 1996). Another researcher notes that the nonreport figures would be higher if one counted those who consent to sex after being threatened with homosexual rape (Kupers 2001). Human Rights Watch (2001), reporting on the problem, also concludes that it occurs much more often than reported figures indicate.

> The sexual activity is rampant and encouraged by guards. Guards believe that the sex will provide release for sexual tension; this is faulty logic though, as more tension is produced from the dislike of homosexuals, the bartering of homosexuals, and the protection of gays by other prisoners. I sincerely believe that the promiscuous sexual activity here is encouraged to alleviate the tension here. The authorities it is my belief don't give a damn if we kill each other; so what, they say, he is a fag or they are just inmates. (an inmate responding to a questionnaire, quoted by Krebs 2002: 38)

Inmates rape each other partly as an outlet for sex but also as a means of ensuring their masculinity. In a prison world, to be a man is reduced down to the very basic element of power. For some, power is experienced as the power to abuse and enslave another. It is instructive to note that most men in prison feel powerless in their lives; in fact, quite a bit of the incentive for crime includes the feeling of power that comes with taking control of a victim, even if it is only over property.

> It's fixed where if you're raped, the only way you [can escape further abuse is if] you rape someone else. Yes I know that's fully screwed, but that's how your head is twisted. After it's over you may be disgusted with yourself, but you realize you're not powerless and that you can deliver as well as receive pain. Then it's up to you to decide whether you enjoy it or not. Most do, I don't. (an inmate, cited in Mariner 2001: 128)

If inmate victims sue the prison system, the test used by the court to determine whether or not officers or administrators are liable is the "deliberate indifference" test. Basically, this means that the inmate victim has to prove that the prison officials knew there was a risk and consciously disregarded it and that their disregard was instrumental in the victimization. This test is a difficult one to meet since the argument could be that there is no way to prevent all rapes in prison (Man and Cronan 2001).

It should be noted that not all sex in men's prisons is obtained through rape or even coercion. In Hensley, et al.'s (2000) review, they note that most of the research has focused on prison rape and coerced sex and, therefore, we know very little about noncoercive sex in men's prisons. Although consensual sex is believed to be more common in women's institutions while forced sex is more common in men's institutions, some research indicated that 30–65 percent of men had engaged in consensual homosexual sex in prison (Hensley, et al. 2000: 365).

Riots and Collective Violence

Prison disturbances occur with some regularity. In fact, it is reported that there have been over 1,300 prison riots in the 20th century (Montgomery and Crews 1998: 1). Two well-known prison riots in this country are the Attica (1971) and the Santa Fe riots (1980). They are interesting in their differences and tell us something about the changing nature of prisons and prisoners. The Attica rioters took over the prison in an attempt to force the governor and prison commissioner to concede to a list of demands. Their "manifesto" was a composite of demands that had been used by California inmates in earlier disturbances and called for such things as better food, more exercise, and programs. By some accounts, after a short period of chaos, organizers (especially Black Muslims) controlled the prison, protected the guard-hostages, and prevented inmate-on-inmate violence.

After several days of negotiations, some of which were televised, state police stormed the prison and regained control but in the process killed many of the hostages. The total count was 43 killed—39 of whom were killed by state police. Abuses occurred after the riot, including making naked prisoners run a gauntlet of officers who beat them with sticks, clubs, and guns. It was years before all court actions against inmates were complete. No officials, despite photographs and eyewitness accounts, were ever convicted of abuse of power. A lawsuit by inmates who had been beaten and tortured after the violent retaking of the facility was finally settled in February of 2000, after 30 years, for $8 million dollars to be divided among all injured inmates—at least those that were still alive (Chen 2000).

> When you explain to your kids and your grandkids what the whole essence of Attica was, you'll be able to tell them that it was to be treated as human beings....(Frank Smith, an ex-Attica inmate testifying at the settlement hearing between New York State and ex-inmates, quoted in Chen 2000)

In contrast to the relative self-control of prisoners at Attica, the Santa Fe riot was a display of horrific violence by inmates against other inmates. Specifically, protective custody inmates were targeted and subjected to various types of torture before being killed, including being set on fire, hung on cell bars and literally filleted, and thrown off tiers. Other killings took place as roving bands of prisoners took advantage of the chaos. Over 200 inmates were severely injured. Guards were beaten, stabbed, and sodomized. There was no agenda, no political consciousness, and no control. It was a wild killing spree, ending in the death of 33 inmates. While some inmates represented the depth of depravity to which men can descend, others found and protected injured officers, risking their own lives in doing so. They also found and took injured inmates to the front gate to be evacuated for medical treatment (Colvin 1992; Useem and Kimball 1983; Rolland 1997).

Rolland (1997), an inmate who took part in the riot, provides his firsthand description of what happened. According to his account, the riot occurred because of the harassment and abuse inmates experienced at the hands of the guards and the practice of using and taunting inmates with the use of informants. What is especially chilling from his account, and others, is how violence is cyclical and related to revenge and counter-revenge. Some offenders were sent to prison because they hurt someone, where some guards felt justified in humiliating and brutalizing them because of what they'd done; then inmates felt justified in horrifically brutalizing guards when the tables were turned and they briefly had power over them; and finally, after retaking the prison, some guards felt justified in inflicting their revenge on the inmates. These inmates eventually served their sentences and got out, and in all likelihood, felt it was their turn again, and so it goes. The story of the New Mexico riot was an ancient passion play in which blood vengeance solved nothing and resulted in nothing but continued violence.

> [the author describes how a group of inmates hunted down and killed another who had been randomly hacking to death anybody he happened upon]...I stepped down off the fence to get a better look at this dead madman. The blood from his body had puddled around him from numerous holes and rips. Everything was deathly quiet...."How many did he kill?" Another voice said, "At least eight or ten."...[the author then describes how the man is decapitated and his head is put on a shovel handle]....(Rolland 1997: 89)

Those who study riots and prison disturbances destroy the myth that they occur most often in the summer months. According to one study, the months with the most riots and disturbances in descending order of frequency were December, November, August, and July, indicating that Christmas and the holiday season were more powerful triggers than the heat of summer. These same researchers identified a long list of causes and triggering events for riots, including food, racial tension, rules, regulations and policies, mass escape attempts, gangs and other special groups, rumors, security issues, conflict with other inmates, conflict with correctional staff, and alcohol and other drug usage (Montgomery and Crews 1998: 88).

Theories of riots include the powder keg theory, which presumes that the prison is full of violent individuals and that when incidents accumulate, there is an explosion. Another theory is the relative deprivation/rising expectation theory that presumes that when conditions improve, but don't improve fast enough, there is a higher likelihood of a disturbance. Another theory (power vacuum) assumes riots take place when there is no strong authority in control (Montgomery and Crews 1998, 88).

Goldstone and Useem (1990) identified five causal factors to riots: (1) new and increased demands on prison administrators from external sources without an increase in resources; (2) internal pressures from correctional staff along with dissension and alienation; (3) internal pressure from prisoners regarding conditions; (4) riotous prisoner ideologies; and, (5) internal actions perceived as unjust. Useem and Reisig (1999) evaluated which factor was more predictive of collective violence in prison: a lack of administrative control or "oppressive" administrative control that allowed for no input from prisoners. They concluded that the latter factor was more predictive; specifically, the "inmate balance" theory proposes that inmates need to feel some participation in the running of the prison. If they feel totally oppressed, anger and frustration will result in collective violence. Along with these elements, however, there seems to be an additional element of institutional breakdown or disorganization that leads to a lack of essential services and procedures, that is, food service, recreation, commissary operating effectively in the prison (Rynne, Harding and Wortley 2008). According to some sources, the number of riots and collective disturbances in prison are declining (Rynne, et al. 2008), but it seems safe to say as long as there are prisons, there will be prison riots.

Changes in Prison Violence

The explosion of violence in prisons in the mid-1980s was said to be related to court decisions that gave prisoners greater freedom of movement within the prison. Prison officials allege that their control was reduced by court actions and the result was an increase in assaults and killings by inmates. It is argued, for instance, that eliminating the "building tenders," inmates who helped keep order in Texas prisons, created a vacuum of power that was soon filled by warring gangs. There was an unprecedented number of killings that took place in 1984–1985 after the building tenders (BTs) were abolished by the court order in *Ruiz v. Estelle* (1980). No less than 52 killings took place, along with 600 stabbings, compared to the 16 killings recorded in eight years between 1970 and 1978 (Ekland-Olson 1986).

It should also be noted, however, that Crouch and Marquart (1990) point out that in a survey of inmates, Texas prisoners reported feeling less secure in prisons before the ruling than after, and in fact in the early 1980s, when there were high rates of homicides recorded, prisoners did not report elevated levels of fear. This could be due to the fact that the violence was centralized at certain parts of the prison and restricted to certain groups. After 1985 there was a dramatic shift and prisoners reported feeling substantially safer than ever before. This period was marked by a reduction in gang wars and prison system officials who had given up fighting Judge Justice's orders in *Ruiz v. Estelle* and had begun to comply. They also discovered through their survey that African-Americans felt less safe than whites in the 1970s and early 1980s, but that after court-mandated reforms, whites felt less secure than African-Americans.

> Getting rid of the BTs, turnkeys, and countboys was a very good thing because in the old days it was a simple matter for them to "cross out" somebody they didn't like. They did that shit all the time....Most people were tense all the time. (a Texas inmate quoted in Crouch and Marquart 1990: 119)

While some observers perceive an increase in violence, official records indicate that dramatic reductions have occurred. According to the Bureau of Justice Statistics, the in-custody homicide rate declined from 54 per 100,000 in 1980 to 4 per 100,000 in 2003. Suicide rates have also declined from 34 per 100,000 to 16 per 100,000 (BJS [key facts] 2011).

COPING IN THE PRISON WORLD

Prison is home to inmates. For some, it is home for decades. Many "rip and roar" and engage heavily in the inmate subculture; others try to find some semblance of safety by choosing job assignments that take them away from the mainstream and avoid the mess hall and yard and any other place where they may get involved in trouble. Zamble and Porporino (1988) described long-termers who sought a structured, safe, and orderly life. These inmates stayed in their cells during free time, they developed only a few relationships with other prisoners, and they avoided commerce in the black market. They, in effect, created a world within a world, moving through the chaotic and trouble-plagued social world of the prison, but they were not a part of it.

Others also describe inmates, perhaps a growing number of inmates, who try to avoid the prison subculture. Owen (1998) describes how most of the women she talked to avoided the yard and stayed away from "the mix" (the term for the homosexual and drug subculture in prison). Irwin (1980) describes how many prisoners minimize their interactions with the black market and avoid the violent gangs and cliques, spending most of their time either at work or in their cell. Johnson (2002) describes how prisoners seek "niches" that provide safety and psychological support. Sheehan (1978) describes in detail the life of one prisoner, George Malinow, who seems atypically comfortable because he constructed his day-to-day activities in a way that reduced his exposure to danger or trouble. For these inmates, successful living in prison is dreary boredom.

> So I'll get up this morning, like every other morning, and I'll go through the routine, because the routine is what saves me. The days are all the same...and looking back a year ago when I got this jolt, it seems like only yesterday because yesterday was just like it was a year ago. (Manocchio and Dunn 1982: 188)

Hans Toch is one of the best-known contributors to the "prison ecology" literature. With a number of student-colleagues, he has studied the patterns of coping and the adaptation of prisoners for several decades. His contributions include the "ecological dimensions" of coping: activity, privacy, safety, emotional feedback, support, structure, and freedom. His research indicates that different ethnic groups and men and women experience prison differently, due to their different needs along these dimensions. For instance, Hispanics and women more acutely feel the absence of "support" and "emotional feedback"; freedom resonates more strongly in samples of African-American men. Certain groups of prisoners have such high needs for certain dimensions that the prison pushes them into crisis— this research is helpful for understanding mental breakdowns in prison (Johnson and Toch 1982; Toch and Adams 1989). Prisoners react to the prison world differently. Some exalt in it, others are destroyed. Prison staff should care to know how to recognize and respond to prisoners' differential needs, if only to prevent violence (Toch 1975, 1977, 1980a, 1982).

CONCLUSION

One of the first things to note in summarizing the changes that have taken place in the prison world is that we have less ethnographic research today than we did in previous decades. We get glimpses of the prison world through the eyes of prisoner writers, and try to put together what is happening with survey results; but the rich, detailed work of the early ethnographers are decades out of date. That being said, it seems clear that prisons today are more heterogeneous and therefore the subculture is not as monolithic. Many competing groups and gangs struggle for power. In the mid-1980s this evidently resulted in spikes of violence in some state systems. Also, the increasing presence of drugs led to violence. Today, the violence seems to have abated, partly because of prison officials controlling gangs and reducing the prevalence of drugs by testing and tighter security. However, given the constant stream of new prisoners, the increasing numbers of prisoners facing very long sentences, and the increasingly laissez-faire attitudes of courts toward official abuses of prisoners, one assumes that the level of violence may begin to climb again.

The subculture of prisons is a changing, dynamic entity partly formed by the elements of prison living and partly by those we send there. There are interesting similarities between prisoners of today and those of years past. For one thing, prisoners still yearn for right guys—even though outlaws seem to have taken over.

WEBSITES

For more information on the Human Rights Watch, visit:
    http://www.hrw.org/
For more information on the PREA legislation, visit:
    http://www.nicic.org/library/020137
    http://community.nicic.gov/blogs/prea/default.aspx
    http://www.nprec.us
    http://www.spr.org
For more information on the Bureau of Justice Statistics, visit:
    http://bjs.ojp.usdoj.gov/

For more information on prison sexual victimization statistics, visit:
  http://bjs.ojp.usdoj.gov/index.cfm?ty=pbdetail&iid=2202
For more information on the group Stop Prison Rape, Inc., visit:
  http://www.justdetention.org/en/spr_history.asp
For more information on the Attica prison riot, visit:
  http://www.history.com/this-day-in-history/attica-prison-riot-ends
For more information on the Santa Fe prison riot, visit:
  http://www.time.com/time/magazine/article/0,9171,924993,00.html

STUDY QUESTIONS

1. What are the two theories for the origin of prison subculture formation?
2. Describe the inmate code. How has it changed over time?
3. How does the black market operate in prison? What is sold? How are goods smuggled in?
4. Describe how drugs have affected the prisoner subculture.
5. How does race affect violence in prison? Which is more likely to cause racial violence when integrated: same race or mixed raced?
6. What types of violence exist in the prison?
7. What are some of the correlates of violence? Who is more likely to victimize? To be victimized? What conditions seem to create more victimization?
8. What percentage of prisoners have been sexually assaulted? Who commits sexual assault? Who are the victims? What are the effects of sexual assault on the victims? How does the subculture view prison rape?
9. What are some causes of prison riots?
10. What are ways that inmates try to cope with life in prison?

CHAPTER 7

≯

Prisons for Women

> We controlled every moment of the lives of the women we guarded. We told them when and where they could go, when they could eat, shower, sleep, when and with whom they could talk. We strip-searched them after an afternoon visit with their children. We made them work to acquire skills, but told them they were capable only of sewing, mopping floors, or preparing food. We confiscated their personal belongings. We read their mail....We were the ones who took away their dignity....[W]e were disempowering them and setting them up for failure once back on the street. (a prison guard, reported in Faith 1993: 162)

Only about seven percent of prisoners are women (Harrison and Karberg 2003). In previous decades, women comprised an even smaller percentage. This means that women's institutions have always been considered the stepchild of the corrections system. A typical statement of correctional managers is that there are prisons and then there are *women's prisons*. Historically, women's prisons had different staffing patterns and even a different mission from that of men's. About the mid-1980s, roughly corresponding with the spike in prison populations, there was a trend in correctional management to "straighten up" the management of women's prisons. This meant that women's prisons were to be brought into line with men's prisons. In some ways this has been a benefit, but in other ways the changes have hurt the prisons' abilities to meet the needs of women.

INCREASING NUMBERS

The rate of growth in women's prisons has been nothing short of phenomenal, although it has slowed in recent years and shows some signs that it may begin to decrease. In 2000 there were 85,044 women in prison and in 2009 there were 105,197 (West, Sabol, and Greenman 2010: 22). Although the total number of women incarcerated is dwarfed by the number of men in prison, the *percentage increase* of women sentenced to prison over the last three decades has been higher than the rate for men. Between 1990 and 2001, the average annual growth rate was 5.7 percent for men and 7.5 percent for women. Put another way, the number of men in prison increased by 80 percent, whereas the number of women in prison increased by 114 percent (Harrison and Beck 2002: 5). Between 2000 and 2008, the average annual growth rate for women was 2.8 percent, but between 2008 and 2009, there was a decrease of 1.1 percent (West, Sabol, and Greenman 2010: 23).In 2010, the female prisoner population decreased again by .6 percent (Guerino, Harrison, and Sabol 2011: 7).

In 2002, the national prison incarceration rate for women was 60 per 100,000, but the rate for men was 902 per 100,000 (Harrison and Karberg 2003: 5). In 2009, the incarceration rate for women was 67 compared to 949 for men. Of course this masks the importance of race and ethnicity. Interestingly, the rate of imprisonment for black women has been declining, even while the numbers for white and Hispanic women have been increasing. In 2000, the incarceration rate for white women was 34 compared to 205 for black women and 60 for Hispanic. In 2010, the rate for white women was 67, and for Hispanic women it was 77, but black women's rates had declined to 133. This is still over double that of white women, but it is significantly lower than it was 10 years ago (West, Sabol, and Greenman 2010: 28; Guerino, Harrison, and Sabol 2011: 27).

In 2001, Texas held the largest number of female prisoners (12,369), but in 2009, that number had declined to 11,620. The federal system held 10,973 women in 2001 and this number increased to 11,780. California came in third in 2001 with 9,921, and in 2009 held 10,735 (Harrison and Beck 2002: 6; West, Sabol, and Greenman 2010: 23). The states with the highest incarceration rates for women in 2001 were Oklahoma (130; 132 in 2009), Mississippi (113; 121 in 2009), and Louisiana (99; 109 in 209). The lowest incarceration rates for women were in Maine (8; 19 in 2009), Rhode Island (10; 19 in 2009), and Massachusetts (13; still 13 in 2009) (Harrison and Beck 2002: 6–7; West, Sabol, and Greenman 2010: 24). This pattern of increase is present in jail and community corrections populations as well. Ten years ago women constituted a little under 20 percent of the probation population, about 11 percent of the parole population, and 11 percent of jail inmates (Beck 1998); today, they are about 24 percent of the probation population, about 12 percent of the parole population, and about 12 percent of the jail population (Glaze and Bonczar 2009).

Are we sentencing more women to prison because they are committing more crime? Yes and no. While women's contribution to violent crime has not risen substantially, except for assault categories, there is no doubt they have increased their participation in property crimes (Belknap 2000; Pollock 2002; Pollock and Davis 2005). Even the increase in assaults is questionable and may have more to do with a greater tendency to use a formal system response today (Steffensmeier, et al. 2006). One possible explanation is that mandatory arrest policies for domestic violence have led to police officers arresting both parties, creating this increase in reported crime. While women's contribution to various property crimes is increasing the rapid rate of increase that appeared in the 1990s has slowed.

The increasing numbers of women in prison and other correctional populations is most probably due to a combination of increased participation in criminal activities and changing patterns of sentencing. Determinate sentencing systems, drug laws, and a more punitive sentencing culture all account for the increased numbers of women in correctional facilities. Determinate sentencing and sentencing guidelines take away judicial discretion to some extent, and if judges had been more likely to sentence women leniently in the past, they are no longer able to do so. Further, they may choose not to do so today in an effort to "equalize" sentencing between men and women, even if they have discretion. For whatever reason, the prison population explosion has reverberated in women's prisons as well, and the effect has been a mini-building boom, with states adding to their capacity either by constructing new buildings or by adding on to existing facilities. When a state exceeds its own capacity for housing female offenders, women (like men) are transferred far away to other state systems. This has extremely troubling consequences for women because they may already be struggling to maintain their role as mother.

HISTORY OF WOMEN'S PRISONS

Originally women were housed with men, and terrible conditions and sexual exploitation were prevalent. Even after they were segregated into their own wings or buildings, they usually had no exercise or opportunity to get fresh air. Part of the reason for their ill treatment was the fact that there were so few of them. Only women who committed crimes that shocked or enraged the public or those women who were chronic offenders were placed in confinement. Prisons were reserved for those females who were considered to be evil and irredeemable. Courts managed to find other solutions for most women who committed crimes.

In the 1800s, the number of female prisoners increased and some prison administrators began hiring female wardens to run the women's wing or section. There was also a growing perception that women were not evil, but misguided, and could benefit from the influence of proper "ladies" who could teach them how to be good housewives and mothers. This involved teaching them to read, cook, clean, and sew. Even music and art were added to the curriculum of some prisons.

In 1873, the first completely separate prison for women was built in Indiana. Several states followed in short order. Most women's prisons built in the late 1800s and early 1900s utilized a reformatory model (Freedman 1986; Rafter 1990). These institutions housed young women who were thought to be amenable to treatment. Many were not what we would consider even criminal today. Because of extremely flexible and broad sentencing authority, the "criminals" might have been young girls whose parents thought they were promiscuous, women who lived in "sin," or wives who ran away from their husbands (Rafter 1990). Even those states that opened separate reformatories usually kept open the wing or building at the prison for men for chronic or older female offenders. Minority offenders were also usually sent to custodial institutions (Rafter 1990).

In the South, incarceration followed a different path. Because the South followed an agricultural model, most prisoners were either leased to landowners or performed agricultural labor for the state. The few women who were incarcerated in these southern prison farms, usually minority women, worked in small garden plots for the prison staff's use or did domestic labor in the warden's and other staff members' homes (Rafter 1990).

It was not until the mid- to late 1970s that all states had separate institutions for women. Even as late as the 1950s, many states had only a wing or a building on the grounds of a prison for men. Some states transferred the handful of female prisoners they felt needed secure facilities to neighboring states. Rafter (1990) reported that between 1930 and 1950, only three or four women's prisons were built in each decade; however, in the 1980s, 34 prisons were built for women.

Prisons for women have always been different from prisons for men. Until the 1980s, female wardens had restricted career paths; their experience running a facility for women seldom helped them move up the administrative ladder in a system dominated by men's institutions. Also, wardens of prisons for women have had to fight for resources. Because women's institutions have never posed the threat of riots or major disturbances, their needs have been relegated to the end of the list.

Women's prisons gained greater attention in the 1980s because there were many more women sentenced and state systems had to find room for the burgeoning female prisoner population. There was also litigation in several states that forced them to equalize programming and improve medical care for women. For instance, *Glover v. Johnson* (1979) dealt with a challenge to the dearth of programs for women in the Michigan prison system. Sex-stereotyped programming in all women's prisons prevailed in past decades with female offenders having access only to cosmetology or food service as vocational choices. The state was under a federal monitor for years as it began to update and expand offerings for women. Medical care was the subject of *Todaro v. Ward* (1977). The court found that there were arbitrary procedures, failure to perform laboratory tests, long delays in diagnoses, a grossly inadequate recordkeeping system, and inappropriate screening in New York prisons for women. Unfortunately, the facts cited in this case over 35 years ago are still the subject of legal actions today, if not in New York, then certainly in other states. Women in prison suffer from a multitude of health problems, some of them self-induced. Drug addiction, alcoholism, smoking, promiscuity, untreated sexual diseases, inherited and untreated hypertension, diabetes, asthma, AIDS, and many other medical problems characterize the female prisoner population. One of the biggest concerns regarding female prisoners is their special need for gynecological care and prenatal care.

> I was...put on eyeball status, stripped of belongings, clothing, placed in a room with nothing but a plastic mattress on the floor. Watched 24 hours a day by a man or woman. I was hemorrhaging but because of my status not allowed to have tampons or underwear. I was very humiliated, degraded. Being on eyeball status with male officers, my depression intensified. I didn't want to be violated any more than I already was, so I put the mattress up against the window. When I did that I was in violation because they couldn't see me. The door was forced open, I was physically restrained in four point restraints—arms, legs spreadeagled, tied to the floor, naked, helmet on head, men and women in the room. (a woman who was considered a suicide risk in a Massachusetts prison; reported in Amnesty International 1999: 78)

Once separate institutions for women were built in the 1900s very few men supervised women in prison because of a belief that matrons could better supervise female offenders and a fear of sexual victimization. Beginning in the 1980s, more male correctional officers were assigned to prisons for women, and we have now come almost full circle back to a situation where the majority of officers in some women's prisons are men. Men who had been trained and worked in men's institutions and then transferred to women's prisons began to standardize visitation policies, contraband policies, and rules regarding movement, which were often different between the women's prison and the men's prisons in a state system. The homogenization of policies often led to women losing the few extra privileges they had in the women's prison, and, at times, prison administrators of women's prisons had to explain why some policies from men's prisons were not suited to prisons for women.

> Try explaining to a table full of men why female prisoners use three times as much toilet paper as the same size of prison housing men! It's obvious but I still need to justify it. (a female warden, private conversation 1993)

GENDERED PATHWAYS AND GENDERED PROGRAMMING

Female prisoners tend to be in their 30s, single, economically disadvantaged, and disproportionately minority. They are likely to be mothers. Women are sentenced to prison most often for drug offenses and/or property crimes—usually larceny. They are slightly older than male prisoners, and do not have criminal histories as extensive as do men in prison. They are also less likely to have been employed before incarceration. They are more likely to have come from dysfunctional families (with histories of sexual and physical abuse) and report more drug use (whereas men report more alcohol use). They are also more likely to have been custodial parents of children before incarceration and more likely to plan on being primary providers for their children upon release (Greenfield and Snell 1999; Pollock 2002). Women in prison share some characteristics with men in prison, but there are also differences: this has led to the idea of "gendered pathways," specifically, that women follow a different path to the crimes that led to their imprisonment. The gendered-pathways research has led to gender-informed classification and prediction systems, and to gender-specific programming.

Pathways Research

Gendered pathways research began with Daly (1992; 1994), and others, who noted that female offenders seemed to have different backgrounds, motivations, and patterns of criminality. Daly noted four major differences between female and male offenders: prior victimization, substance abuse, criminogenic familial and intimate relationships, and economic marginalization. Her typology of female offenders included: street women (these women fled abusive homes, became addicts, and engaged in survival crimes such as prostitution and drug dealing while living on the street); drug connected women (their crimes included using, manufacturing, or distributing drugs in the context of intimate partner or family relationships); harmed and harming women (whose early lives were marked by turbulence, abuse, and neglect and who developed a tough, bully-like demeanor with accompanying violent behavior); battered women (whose violence was confined to relationships with violent intimate partners); and a catch-all category of "other" (women who did not fit into the above categories, including those women who committed crimes from greed or economic necessity).

Other research has also pointed to differences between female and male offenders and prisoners. Covington (2001) and Bloom, Owen and Covington (2003; 2004) and many others have used the pathway approach to note certain sex-specific differences in the origin and pattern of criminality and, also, how these differences play out in prison environments. The differences most relevant involve the following: women are more likely to be caregivers, less likely to be convicted of violent crimes, have no stable work history, have experienced more psycho-social problems, are more likely to have dysfunctional and/or criminal parents, and are more likely to suffer from serious health problems. These characteristics affect not only women's crimes, but also their behavior in prison (Owen, et al. 2008).

In one national survey, female inmates were reported to have much higher rates of mental health problems than male inmates (73 percent compared to 55 percent). Looking more closely at these women, three-quarters of those with mental health problems also reported substance dependence or abuse. They were more likely than those women who did not report a mental health problem to have committed violent offenses (40 percent compared to 32 percent), to have been homeless (17 percent compared to 9 percent), to have been the victim of past physical or sexual abuse (68 percent compared to 44 percent), and to have had a parent who abused drugs or alcohol (47 percent compared to 29 percent). Once in prison, women with mental health problems were more likely to receive disciplinary charges (17 percent compared to 6 percent) (James and Glaze 2006: 1, 10).

Victimization

> I started using marijuana at age of eight, with my sisters and my cousin. I started drinking about that time too. Then I started cocaine binges. I started running away when I was eleven. It seems like I have always been in trouble. (a female offender quoted in Owen 1998: 46)

Needs assessment surveys of female prisoners conducted in California, Oklahoma, and Texas (Owen and Bloom 1994; Fletcher, Shave, and Moon 1993; Pollock 1998) were consistent with a national study of female prisoners (Snell 1994), which found that female prisoners were more likely than men in prison to have experienced both childhood and adult abuse—both physical and sexual. In most surveys, one-third to one-half of the women surveyed experienced sexual or physical abuse as children and even more as adults. The Bureau of Justice Statistics reported that 41 percent of female probationers, 48 percent of female jail inmates, and 57 percent of female prisoners reported either sexual or physical abuse (Greenfield and Snell 1999: 8). More specifically, 47 percent of female prisoners reported physical abuse and 39 percent reported sexual abuse at some point in their lives; 25 percent and 26 percent (respectively) reported such abuse before the age of 18 (Harlow 1999). In another study, half of the women interviewed for the study had experienced some form of sexual abuse in childhood or adolescence. Thirty-eight percent had been a victim of a violent assault, one-third had been a victim of a violent sexual assault, and 28 percent had been shot at or knifed (Browne, Miller, and Maguin 1999). These experiences are obviously traumatic and influence the women's lives in a variety of ways.

> When I was eight or nine, my mother's boyfriend molested me. I was afraid to say anything. He did it again and I told my mother; they got in a fight and she killed him with a knife. When she went away to prison, nobody talked to me. They acted like it was my fault. It was my fault, I should have stayed silent. I started to drink when I was eleven. A boy raped me on the roof when we were drinking. I was too afraid to tell anyone, even when I became pregnant. Everyone was shocked when I gave birth at thirteen years old. (a female prisoner, quoted in Bedell 1997, 28)

Childhood sexual victimization has been linked to personality disorders, depression, suicidal and self-destructive behaviors, poor self-esteem, poor interpersonal functioning, trust issues, substance abuse, sexual problems, and high-risk sexual behavior (Breitenbecher 2001). Furthermore, Maeve (2000) has linked childhood sexual abuse to post-traumatic stress syndrome symptoms, including "over remembering" (reacting with violence inappropriately), "under remembering" (disassociation leading to reacting with passivity to threats), and cyclical relationships marked by instability and violence.

> I knew that when my father was on the rampage, I just blacked out and I was just not there. And when I came here, I had terrible impending fear of the dark until my 20s. When I am in the presence of raw brutality, I just become not present. (an inmate, Owen, et al. 2008: 15)

While there seems to be a correlation between childhood abuse and violent crime with men, the same pattern does not hold for female offenders, except for juveniles (Holsinger and Holsinger 2005; Widom 1989a & b, 1996). Women evidently are much more likely to react to childhood abuse with self-destructive behavior (drugs, alcohol, suicide, mutilation) and depression. Victimization leads to drug use and then drug use has consistently been associated with sex work and high-risk sexual practices (Mullings, Marquart, and Brewer 2000; Mullings, Marquart, and Hartley 2003; Mullings, Pollock, and Crouch 2002; Pollock, Mullings, and Crouch 2006).

Drugs

Several authors have argued that the increase of women in prisons and correctional populations is largely due to the increased number of women arrested for drug crimes. Bloom and her colleagues reported that the percentage of women admitted to prison for drugs in California increased from 14.2 percent of total admissions in 1982 to 42.2 percent of total admissions in 1992 (Bloom and Steinhart 1993). About 34 percent of women in prison were serving time for a drug offense in 2002 and 28 percent were in 2009 (Greene and Schiraldi 2002: 12; West, Sabol, and Greenman 2010: 31). It does not seem to be true, however, that women are playing increasingly more powerful roles in drug distribution systems. Evidence indicates that women continue to have a fairly minor role in drug dealing, acting as "mules" or low-level dealers (Wellisch 1994). It is reported that drug use by women seems to be associated with prostitution, small-scale drug sales, and larceny/theft crimes (Webb, Katz, and Klosky 1995).

Female offenders are more likely to be drug dependent than male offenders. In 2004, 60 percent of female prisoners met the criteria for drug dependency (Mumola and Karberg 2006). The use of drugs or alcohol to "self-medicate" is a pervasive theme in research on female prisoners (Battle, et al. 2003; Maeve 2000;

Reed 1987). In a study by Batchelor (2005) the women had started drinking at an early age and had histories of self-injury, suicide attempts, and traumatic loss. Batchelor suggests that drugs and alcohol use can be seen as a way to cope with grief, and anger. Further, drug dependent women may be very different from drug dependent men in their needs and response to treatment. Female drug abusers may already have a great deal of shame and low self-esteem since there are cultural messages that stigmatize female drug users, especially if they are mothers. They may be more amenable to treatment and, in fact, may have sought treatment for depression and anxiety, and utilize both legal and illegal drugs as a way to cope (Reed 1987).

Importance of Relationships

Needs assessment surveys have found that more than half of women in prison have grown up in a household without both parents and are more likely than male prisoners to have relatives incarcerated and/or have relatives with drug or alcohol addiction. They also report domestic abuse (Fletcher, Shaver, and Moon 1993; Owen and Bloom 1994, 1995; Pollock 1998, 2002; Snell 1994).

As noted above, women who were abused as children often have cyclical patterns of abusive relationships. Female prisoners' crimes may relate to this pattern. For instance, they may have assaulted or killed their abusive partner. They may also be one of Daly's "harmed and harming" women who initiate abuse, for instance, against their children. In prison, women continue to enter into abusive relationships.

> But whether you come in here having been beat by a man or what, when you come in here, you look for the same kind of relationship, whether it is a woman or a man. In your subliminal mind, you are looking for the same thing, and before you know it, you are with an aggressor [in here] that is beating on you. Then you have become an aggressor: You find and go for a woman that you can control because you like being over her. (an inmate describing violent relationships in prison, Owen, et al. 2008: 15)

Pathways and Classification

Pathways research led to criticism that the standard classification instruments used to predict recidivism and/or violent infractions in prison were designed for and developed with male offenders and did not adapt well to female samples (Byrne and Taxman 2005). Classification systems, for instance, may over-classify women because a larger percentage of their violent crime is directed to intimate partners in the context of domestic abuse. They are unlikely to be involved in future violence as compared to male offenders who may have committed robbery or assault on a stranger as their violent crime (Hardyman and Van Voorhis 2004).

Some studies have found that the LSI-R, the classification and prediction instrument described in chapter 4, predicts equally well for men and women, but in one study of the LSI-R, it was found that it predicted recidivism for economically motivated women, but not for the other types in Daly's model. The instrument over-classified the harmed and harming women and under-classified drug-connected women (Reisig, Holtfreter, and Morash 2006). This research used the classification instrument to predict recidivism, not prison violence. In response to this criticism, a special addendum to the LSI-R that includes special factors identified by the pathways research was developed. Risk factors for women may include marital status, family structure, childhood abuse, depression, single parenting, dysfunctional relationships, and victimization (Van Voorhis 2005). Adding this special addendum to the LSI-R has improved its ability to predict prison misconduct (Wright, Salisbury, and Van Voorhis 2007; also see Salisbury, Van Voorhis, and Spiropoulos 2008).

Other efforts have been made to identify correlates of prison misconduct by women. Steiner and Wooldredge (2009b), for instance, conducted a comprehensive review of all the factors that have been previously identified as correlated with misconduct for men and analyzed a nationwide sample of more than 2,200 women in 40 facilities. They found that the following factors were significantly correlated in both a 1991 sample and a 1997 sample with assaultive infractions: age (younger), race/ethnicity (minority), marriage (not being married), prior incarceration, having been physically or sexually abused, having had at least one overnight mental health stay, and having been prescribed medication for mental health. The following factors were correlated with a violent infraction in *either* the 1991 or the 1997 sample, but not both: having children (negative correlation), incarcerated for a violent offense, incarcerated for a drug offense (negative correlation), sentence length, and having used drugs the month before arrest. They also looked at the correlations between these factors and nonviolent rule infractions. The only factors that were significant in both time periods were: age, having children (negative correlation), having had at least one overnight mental health stay, being prescribed medication for mental health, and the number of programs participated in (Steiner and Wooldredge 2009b). This last correlate was expected to be negative; its positive correlation led the researchers to speculate that because this research was cross-sectional and both factors were over the course of the inmates' sentences it may be that longitudinal research would be a better approach to see if program participation reduced infractions.

Gender-specific Programing

The idea that women need different programming from men seems obvious. Historically, women's prisons did have gender-specific programs, but they were based on sex stereotypes and not helpful to the needs of female prisoners. Women learned to cook, clean, sew, and behave like "ladies." No effort was made to provide them with a job skill because women were not expected to work. In later years, when some programs were developed in the 1960s and 1970s, they were usually secretarial, food service, or domestic programs (Young and Mattucii 2006).

In the 1980s, there were efforts across the nation to improve programming for women. Part of the impetus was that since there were more female prisoners vocational programs could be justified. There was also an attempt to move away from sex-stereotyped programs such as cosmetology and food service to computer repair and other neutral or non-traditional skills. Some states began vocational programs such as heavy machinery operation and automotive repair. However, rehabilitative programs and, especially, drug programming tended to be "men's programs with pink covers." Little attempt was made to adapt programming to female prisoners. Even the nontraditional programs came under criticism by female prisoners who thought that the prison system was simply transferring men's programs into the women's prison, not realizing that the programs were designed to help them achieve a wage much higher than they could ever make doing "women's work." Unfortunately, women who enter such programs sometimes do so unwillingly and report that they plan to ignore their training and get a job as a beautician or nurse's assistant upon release (Pollock 1998).

In the 1990s, the gendered pathways research led to "gender-specific programming" efforts. This approach involves designing programming that takes into account the special needs of women. The National Institute of Corrections supported the approach and Bloom, Owen and Covington (2003) developed guiding principles for gender responsive strategies:

- Acknowledge gender makes a difference.
- Create an environment based on safety, respect, and dignity.
- Promote healthy relationships with children, family, significant others, and the community.
- Address substance abuse, trauma, and mental health issues.
- Provide women with opportunities to improve their socioeconomic status.
- Establish a system of community supervision and reentry with comprehensive, collaborative services.

National studies indicate women's programming in prisons is improving but does not currently meet the many needs of female offenders (Morash and Bynum 1995; Pollock 2002). We know that women in prison are amenable to treatment. In needs assessments, women indicate that they appreciate all forms of programming and specifically ask for more programs that will help them overcome drug addiction, get a job upon release, and become better parents to their children (Pollock 1998). We also know, however, that many states do not even screen for such things as childhood abuse or battering. Further, many states do not know how the female offender has arranged for her children to be cared for during her imprisonment. Some states do not even collect information on whether or not incoming female inmates have children (Pollock 2000).

Drug treatment programs for women should recognize that many women have different motivations for drug use and incentives for change. Women have been found to have higher scores on the Addiction Severity Index and also to be more likely to report serious psychiatric problems such as depression and anxiety (reported in Peters and Steinberg 2000). Like men, women are likely to have co-occurring disorders, e.g., drug addiction and depression or drug addiction and personality disorder (Morash and Schram 2002).

Drug treatment programs designed for men do not necessarily work as well for women. For instance, while women tend to be more open and show less resistance to introspection, this advantage can be blunted by forcing them into treatment groups with men where they are more likely to be quiet and let men talk. Also, women may not need the confrontational tactics common in some group therapy programs directed to male offenders and may respond less well to them (Pollock 1998).

If it is true that female offenders are more likely than males to have dysfunctional family backgrounds, then it is important to create gender-specific programming that responds to this fact. Groups that deal with incest, sexual abuse, and the like are in demand when they are offered and often have waiting lists, despite the inmate subcultural prohibition against self-disclosure.

Evaluations of correctional programs have typically either ignored programs for women or included them in general findings where they have been eclipsed by the much larger samples of programs for men. It may be that certain characteristics of female offenders make them especially amenable to particular programs and not so amenable to others. There has been virtually no research that uses gender as an independent variable when evaluating correctional programming. It is important to isolate and evaluate programs for women separately from larger evaluation efforts. Only then will we be able to test whether programs impact men and women differently.

Morash and Bynum's (1995) survey of correctional programming for women is perhaps the only study available that specifically evaluates women's programming. In their study, they found that their sample of programs most often offered drug treatment (54.9 percent), but the programs sampled also offered "life skills" (40.3 percent), parenting skills (40 percent), information on relationships (30.6 percent), and basic education (29 percent). This study concludes that there are very few innovative programs for women across the country and those that might be described as innovative are gender-specific and individualized. Morash and Schram (2002) explain the need for programs that address co-occurring disorders, such as drug addiction and bipolar disorder or alcoholism and depression. Elements of good programs for female offenders should address a number of different but related issues. First, the program should address the woman's specific needs, including the cycles of poverty, violence, poor parenting, marital discord, parental psychopathology/mental illness/depression, lack of education, parenting issues, addictions, childhood incest or physical abuse, criminal behavior, and survival strategies (Bedell 1997; Pollock 1998).

Vocational programs should offer opportunities to acquire skills with the potential for use to earn a decent wage. If the programs are nontraditional, the staff may have to convince women that they are valuable. However, if women acquire nontraditional skills only to discover they cannot find work outside, then such programs are a waste of time and money. Brewster (2003) found, in an Oklahoma study, that educational programs for women resulting in a GED were successful in reducing recidivism but vocational-technical programs were not. What this means is unclear, but it could be that vo-tech programs may not lead to employment after release.

LIVING IN PRISON

> What bothers me most back here is these stinking ass women....(an inmate, quoted in Owen 1998: 116)

Women's prisons have a different atmosphere than prisons for men. There is less of the incipient threat of violence. There is more laughter. But there are also more tears. Officers say that women are more emotional than men (Pollock 1986). That may be true; at least women seem to feel free to express their emotions. Some women report that they feel that they have to put on a front, and some women are fearful, but overall there is less of the "jungle" atmosphere in women's prisons.

Women's social interactions and subcultural norms are somewhat different from male prisoner subcultures (Pollock 2002; Morash and Schram 2002; Sharp 2003). Men in prison are likely to form gang structures and have social/political organizations, while women tend to form small cliques and dyads (friendship pairs). If they do organize in larger groups, communication patterns tend to be less political and more familial. Women also tend to form pseudo-families, or play families. These social structures involve several or many women who take on familial roles such as mother, father, daughter, sister, and so on. The most common role is that of mother. However, roles can cross sexual identity lines. For instance, women will play male roles such as the authoritarian father or jealous husband. One can observe that these roles are played fairly stereotypically, but they seem to provide needed relationships for some women (Pollock 2002).

> I see it like maybe the reason they do that is 'cause they don't know who they[sic] father is, maybe they don't have any sisters or brothers, maybe their mother's passed away, maybe they don't have any kids and want kids, want a mother, want a father, want a brother, want a sister. I don't want none of it. It's not real, for one thing. (an inmate talking about make-believe families, quoted in Girshick 1999: 91)

Today, these roles seem to be changing somewhat. While Owen (1998) found that pseudo-families did exist, they were somewhat more diffuse than in past years. Fox (1990), Girshick (1999), and Greer (2000) argue that female prisoners do not bond in the way described in older research. Fox (1990), for instance, found that when he returned to the same women's prison about 10 years after his first visit, kinship systems were more fragmented. Greer (2000), utilizing a small sample, found that women reported less activity in kinship networks.

While earlier descriptions indicated that women's prisons did not have the same inmate code as the men's (for a review, see Pollock 2002), more current work describes norms that are more similar. For instance, prohibitions against snitching and the mandate to "do your own time" seem more similar now between men's and women's prisons. In a recent study, inmate code norms presented by respondents in women's prisons included: stay out of "the mix" (homosexuality, gambling, and drug use), don't tell others your business, don't get in the wrong group, avoid "messy" women (women who gossip), avoid drugs, don't let anyone see you cry, don't talk about your case, don't have an attitude, stand your ground, learn how to say no, and be clean (Owen, et al. 2008: 37).

Violence

There is not as much serious violence in prisons for women as in prisons for men, but there is always the threat of violence. Women have been known to rape (with an object) a prison "snitch," although the more common sanction is ostracism. There is fighting, usually caused by jealousy or hurt feelings. Since women do not have as organized a black market or as extensive a drug market as one finds in prisons for men, the fighting that ensues from business activities is relatively rare. Weapons are also not as prevalent in women's prisons (Pollock 2002). Some recent reports indicate that women's prisons may be becoming more violent than in past years (Girshick 1999; Greer 2000).

In the study by Wolff and her colleagues, female prisoners reported more theft victimization than men (48 percent compared to 24 percent), and the rate of physical violence was roughly the same (about 206 per 1,000) although men were three times as likely to report being victimized with a weapon (Wolff and Shi 2009: 183; Wolff, et al. 2007: 592). While 80 percent of the women in the study reported victimization in the previous six months, most victimization was theft. About 15 percent said they had been slapped, hit, kicked, or bit (compared to 10 percent of the men). Less than 5 percent reported physical victimization from staff members compared to 12 percent of the men, and about 10 percent said correctional staff members had stolen something from them, compared to 29 percent of men (Wolff and Shi 2009: 177).

While men in prison join racial gangs and a good proportion of violence is directly or indirectly attributed to racial tension and hostility, women do not seem to be as racially divided. In fact, many sexual dyads and pseudo-family structures are interracial. While there is some voluntary racial segregation while eating and in recreational activities, extreme patterns of segregation and hostility due to racial tension do not seem to be present in prisons for women (Pollock 2002).

In a study by Owen and colleagues, female prisoners reported violence or the threat of violence occurring because of jealousy within intimate partnerships, debts, and disrespect (Owen, et al. 2008). Some women were victims ("rabbits") because of personal characteristics and demeanor, while others were clearly predators who sought advantage through threats and intimidation. Much of the violence occurs within or because of sexual relationships.

SEXUAL RELATIONSHIPS AND SEXUAL VIOLENCE

Sexual relationships in men's and women's prisons include consensual sex within or without long-term relationships, and a continuum of coerced sexual behavior from implied threat to physical rape. In the study by Owen and colleagues (2008), a continuum of coercion in women's prisons was described that included: sexual comments and touching, sexual intimidation and pressure, "fatal attractions" (stalking), sexual aggressors, sexual violence within relationships, and sexual assault. None of these refer to what is probably most common in women's prisons—a consensual relationship between two women. As one lifer explained

> Look, those of us who have long sentences, there's three ways to deal with it: become involved with an officer, turn to homosexuality, or become a Christian. Nine out of ten, you fall into homosexuality. Some try all three. I've tried all three and I am most comfortable in a relationship. Look, we are just people (Owen, et al. 2008: 24).

Early studies of women's prisons described women's homosexuality in prison as largely consensual while in men's prisons, sex was more likely to be coerced or take the form of rape. Prevalence studies, however, indicated that this simplistic description was less than accurate (Hensley, Castle, and Tewksbury 2003).

> The homosexuality that is done in the male facilities is usually masked, and there is a percentage of rapes, but I think a lot more of it is permissive, it is sold and so forth. In the female facilities it's not sold, it's not rape, it's just an agreement between two people that they're going to participate and there is a lot of participation. (a correctional officer, quoted in Pollock 1986: 86)

Early reports indicated that three percent of female inmates had been sexually assaulted and 27 percent sexually harassed or coerced, with about half of the perpetrators being officers and the other half inmates (Struckman-Johnson, et al. 1996). In another study of three prisons for women, the prevalence rates for rape ranged from zero to five percent, and sexual assault (which included other forms of sexual touching) ranged from six percent to 19 percent. In this study 55 to 80 percent of the sexual victimization was perpetrated by inmates and the remainder by staff (Struckman-Johnson and Struckman-Johnson 2000, 2002). In a Texas study, about 17 percent of the female inmates reported sexual victimization in prison. The majority reported sexual abuse by touching or harassment, but three percent reported sexual assault and another 2.5 percent reported attempted sexual assault (Blackburn, Mullings, and Marquart 2008: 372).

Recall from the last chapter that Wolff and her colleagues found that six-month prevalence rates for any sexual victimization was four times higher for women than for men (212 per 1,000 compared to 43 per 1,000) (Wolff, et al. 2006: 842). In large part, the increased number of reports by women was accounted for by abusive sexual contacts, not sexual acts. The six month prevalence rates for sexual acts were 3.2 percent for women and 1.5 percent for men. Staff-on-inmate sexual victimization was reported at 1.7 percent for women and 1.9 percent for men. Abusive sexual contacts (touching only) were much more likely to be reported than nonconsensual sex acts (21.2 percent of women and 4.3 percent of men). About the same rates of men and women reported staff abusive sexual contacts (7.6 percent). These rates are much higher than sexual assault rates for the general population (0.2 to 0.9 percent compared to prison rates of 2 percent) (Wolff, et al. 2007: 535–538).

In the Bureau of Justice Statistics study of prison sexual victimization described in the last chapter, about six percent of female respondents reported some type of sexual victimization. Almost five percent reported an inmate perpetrator and a little over two percent reported a staff member perpetrator. There were fairly substantial differences between institutions, however, in that close to 12 percent of respondents reported inmate-inmate victimization in two prisons, but in most, the percentages were in the single digits; and, in one prison 12 percent reported staff sexual victimization, but in most facilities very few reported such victimization. As noted in the last chapter, men were more likely to report staff sexual contacts than female inmates, but female inmates were more likely than male inmates to report sexual victimization by other inmates. These findings are the opposite of expectations (Beck, et al. 2010).

Thus, the picture that emerges is that there are women in committed prison relationships who may have turned to same-sex relationships in prison as a way to cope with loneliness and sexual needs, but there are also coerced relationships. Women may be pressured into relationships in order to assuage their fear of prison. Women who pressure others to participate do so sometimes for economic reasons—some women describe how some inmates enter into relationships with those who have money in their inmate account in order to share in commissary. Sometimes women coerce someone to stay in a relationship simply to have some power over another.

Sexual Victimization by Staff Members

Most of these earlier studies on prison sexual violence were directed toward men's prisons; however, by the 1990s, increasing reports of sexual violence in women's prisons were noted in the popular media, and Human Rights Watch and Amnesty International began to publish reports documenting prison rape of female inmates by correctional officers, or other forms of sexual victimization including abuses during pat downs.

> It seems like every time you use the toilet or begin to undress for bed, he's standing there in front of your cell gawking at you. Sometimes he rubs his crotch and makes some crude comment about wanting to do something to you or have you do something to him. It's so disgusting, and there's nothing you can do about it because he's totally in charge. (a female inmate, quoted in Kupers 1999: 128)

Evidence of sexual exploitation and abuse has emerged in Hawaii, Texas, Michigan, New York, Georgia, and other states (Amnesty International 1999; Flesher 2007). In Georgia, inmates working with legal advocates came forward with stories of sexual extortion, sexual harassment, and assault. In this case, 17 staff members were indicted, although only one was convicted (Siegel 2002). Procedures in prisons such as strip searches, restraints, and isolation can traumatize women who have histories of abuse (Maeve 2000). The policy of utilizing male officers to supervise, pat down, and even sometimes strip search female inmates puts the United States in conflict with international treaties and the United Nations Standards for the Treatment of Prisoners (Flesher 2007).

One of the most shocking cases to date of prison rape occurred in Pleasanton, California, at FCI Dublin. This was a federal prison that inexplicably housed women prisoners in the segregation unit of the prison for men. In *Lucas v. White* (1999), the court found that three women were, in essence, sold to male prisoners by correctional officers who also opened the women's cells so the male prisoners could enter and rape them. Eight prison officials were forced to resign over the incident and the prisoners settled their civil lawsuit for $500,000 (Siegel 2002).

> The evidence revealed a level of sexual harassment which is so malicious that it violates contemporary standards of decency...Rape, coerced sodomy, unsolicited touching of women prisoners' vaginas, breasts and buttocks by prison employees are "simply not part of the penalty that criminal offenders pay for their offenses against society." (court holding in *Women Prisoners of D.C.*, 1995)

In the study by Owen and her colleagues, a continuum of sexual violence by correctional officers was constructed that included:

- Love and seduction (both parties at least facially consenting)
- Inappropriate comments and conversation
- Sexual requests (with no obvious coercion)
- "Flashing," voyeurism and touching
- Abuse of search authority
- Sexual exchange (some form of quid pro quo, often for soda or food)
- Sexual intimidation (prisoner consents only because of fear of what officer might do)

- Sex without physical violence (woman does not resist, perhaps because of PTSD)
- Sex with physical violence (Owen, et al. 2008).

All states now have legislation that criminalizes sexual abuse and/or any sexual contact with prisoners (Teichner 2008). But abuse still continues across the country in prisons and jails. More pervasive than sexual assault is a widespread sexual harassment or a "sexually charged" atmosphere that is created when men guard women. Observers and advocates relate instances where officers show off erections, make inappropriate sexual comments, needlessly touch and grope women, and remark on the appearance of female prisoners. These abuses are not restricted to correctional officers; medical professionals, groundskeepers, vocational and educational teachers, chaplains, and other civilian staff members have also been exposed as perpetrators.

> If I need Tylenol, all I need to do is ask him for a pelvic and he will give me whatever I want. (an inmate describing sexually inappropriate behavior by a prison doctor, cited in Siegel 2002: 137)

Some state officials, faced with such scandals, have responded with proposed policies that completely bar male officers from working with female inmates or bar them from searching female inmates. In some cases, courts have upheld states' regulations prohibiting supervision or searching by male officers. For instance, in *Jordan v. Gardner* (1993), the court held that because the women's prison population had a higher percentage of prior sexual victimization than did male prison populations, being searched, even patted down, by male officers might be "cruel and unusual punishment." This case has not been followed in other jurisdictions, however, and the law is not settled in this area.

It should also be noted that some female inmates actively pursue and engage in relationships with male officers (Trammell 2009). Women in prison have normal sexual drives and the presence of men in prison, just as the presence of female correctional officers in men's prisons, will inevitably lead some to ignore the rules against such relationships. The problem is that in a prison, with the inherent power-differential between officers and inmates, such relationships are unsafe, ill-advised, and illegal.

MOTHERS IN PRISON

Women in prison are very often mothers of small children (Enos 2001; Hungerford 1993; McGowan and Blumenthal 1978; Pollock 1998, 2002). Estimates of the number of women prisoners who have children under 18 range from 60 percent to about 85 percent (Bloom and Steinhart 1993; Henriques 1996; Hungerford 1993; McGowan and Blumenthal 1978; Pollock 1998, 2000). There seems to be consensus that about 70 percent of women in prison have at least one child under 18 and women have an average of two or three children (Pollock 1998; Greenfield and Snell 1999). A large number of these women were the primary caregivers of their children before their imprisonment. Mumola (2000) reports that while 64 percent of female prisoners were living with their children before incarceration, only 44 percent of men had been.

What happens to these children when their mother is imprisoned? Surprisingly, only about 10 percent enter foster care (Immarigeon 1994; Mumola 2000; Pollock 1998). Of those who retained custody during imprisonment, most placed their children with relatives, usually the maternal grandmother (Block and Potthast 1997; Pollock 2000). It is also true, however, that the children are moved around several times during the prison sentence. Placement and arrangements for guardianship of the children is often informal, ad hoc, and without resources. Women fear that state protection agencies will permanently take away their children, and so they don't involve the state. However, this means that there are no financial resources to help care for the children, necessitating already overburdened families with few resources to care for them. Most states do not keep records on children's placement in the community, so we have very little knowledge about what happens to these children.

Some women in prison never see their children (Bloom 1995; Courturier 1995). Bloom and Steinhart (1993) found that 54 percent of mothers in a national sample reported no visits. This compared to only two percent of those surveyed in a similar study in 1978 who reported no visits. The reason for such an increase in the number of women who never receive visits is attributed to a restriction of prison telephone privileges to collect calls only, the construction of new women's prisons in rural areas, and lack of financial support from social service agencies for travel (Bloom 1995). Bloom and Steinhart (1993) reported that visitation frequency was related to pre-prison factors. While 46 percent of those who lived with children prior to imprisonment received no visits, 72 percent of those who did not live with children prior to prison or jail received no visit.

Visits are difficult because of the long distances between the prison and home and the expense of traveling. Also, there may be hesitancy on the part of caregivers to take the children to the prison and/or anger at the mother for her actions that led to the situation. Many social workers may feel it is traumatic for the child to see their mother in prison and resist accommodating such visits. Finally, the mother herself may not want her children to see her in prison or subject them to the search and admission procedures required for visitation. She may feel guilty and ashamed over her imprisonment and refuse to let her children see her in such a setting. Furthermore, visits necessarily include saying good-bye—an experience that is so painful to both mother and child that many women in prison prefer to avoid it.

> I myself have a son who is 19 years old and he's sitting in a county jail…that's all he saw…motorcycles, drugs, guns, and his mom in and out of prison. His dad was never around. He left when he was a child. (a female inmate, reported in Pollock 1999: 108)

Some women may give birth during the time they are imprisoned. About six to 10 percent of women in prison on any given day are pregnant (Henriques 1996; Pollock 1998; 2000). This percentage may mean a few women a year in those states with small prison populations, but it could mean close to 100 women in larger states. These pregnancies are often high risk since women in prison may have been drug users, have avoided or neglected medical treatment, and/or have had difficult previous pregnancies. One report, for instance, indicated that 77 percent of imprisoned women had exposed their fetuses to drugs (Johnston 1995b). Some research indicates a higher than average rate of miscarriage for women in prison. Part of the reason for this is attributed to the fact that women must be transported to outside hospitals for delivery and for medical emergencies. In a report by Amnesty International (1999), cases were presented in which women giving birth were shackled to the hospital bed.

Shackling is commonly used when prisoners are taken out of the prison for any reason. It is a logical and reasonable precaution when escorting violent and/or escape-prone inmates. It does not make any sense at all when it is used for women who are in the hospital giving birth. There are reports of women being shackled to the hospital bed throughout labor and delivery. Advocates and medical personnel say it is unnecessary and dangerous. Women are unlikely to attempt escape during labor and being immobilized with leg chains prevents the woman from moving around to facilitate fetal heart monitors, epidurals, or simply changing positions to help ease labor pains. Only 14 states have legislation that prohibits shackling during childbirth and another four have policies; however, there is still room for interpretation even in those states. For instance, correctional officers are supposed to remove the shackles during labor, but labor might be interpreted as imminent to delivery, not hours earlier when labor pains first begin. In *Nelson v. Correctional Medical Services* (2009), an Arkansas female prisoner sued the state after she was shackled during her labor and immediately after giving birth. Her legs were shackled to opposite sides of the bed and medical professionals testified this position contributed to injuries she experienced during labor. The Eighth Circuit ruled that the practice of shackling was cruel and unusual and a violation of the Eighth Amendment.

Parenting programs should address the children's needs, including the provision of a safe, unintimidating location to visit the mother in prison, and preferably offer a long uninterrupted time for such a visit to take place. Also, there should be support for children outside of prison, either counseling or support groups. In the few published studies that evaluated parenting programs in women's prisons, a reduction of recidivism is rarely stated as a goal or objective. However, there is some evidence to indicate that family ties, and frequent visitation, are correlated with a reduction in recidivism (Block and Potthast 1997).

Martin (1997) examined mothers who were incarcerated in the Minnesota Correctional Facility at Shakopee in 1985 five years after their release. This study establishes the fact that frequent contact with children in a child-centered institution supports future reunification with children. Nearly two-thirds of the women studied who were imprisoned in Shakopee in 1985 emerged five years later as "primary, highly involved parents to at least one of their children." One-third of the women were no longer connected with their children. There was no relationship between seriousness of crime and ongoing connection with children. Mothers who were "connected" with their children were three times more likely than unconnected mothers to be drug-free and have no history of chemical abuse. Connected mothers were more likely to be married. Whereas 80 percent of connected mothers committed no new crimes, only 57 percent of unconnected mothers had not committed subsequent crimes (Martin 1997: 4–9).

Although it seems obvious that the children of incarcerated parents are at high risk for future incarceration themselves, there does not seem to be a national will to intervene. Programs for prison mothers are few and often paper-only programs that do not meet the needs of prisoner mothers (Pollock 2000; Sandifer and Kurth 2000). This is despite the fact that many female prisoners will leave prison to resume their caregiving duties. If prison does not provide them with any insight into what happened with their own lives, they will be unable to assist their children in avoiding the temptations they fell victim to.

The biggest challenge of release for women is attempting to reunite with their children. Some mothers have permanently lost their children to the state; some have to wrest them away from relatives. Some children don't want anything to do with their mother. For the mother who wants to regain custody, it is a struggle to make enough money to support herself and her children. Very few women return to homes with husbands and providers.

One of the added burdens placed upon them has been the federal law creating a lifetime ban on receiving federal aid from TANF (Temporary Assistance for Needy Families) if convicted of a drug offense. A state may opt out of this ban, but if it doesn't, women who would otherwise be eligible for financial assistance would be denied. Ironically, the law would bar assistance to a woman with a minor drug conviction, but an offender with a violent crime would be eligible. This law, combined with the federal law that prohibits those with felony drug convictions from living in public housing, makes it extremely difficult for any woman leaving prison with a drug conviction to make a new life for herself and her children. It is no wonder that so many retreat into the netherworld of drug abuse again.

CONCLUSION

It is clear that convictions for drug crimes account for many women's involvement in the criminal justice system. The criminalization of drug use has resulted in huge increases in the number of women we imprison and the number of children who are impacted by their mothers' imprisonment. Although these women admit that drugs have been a negative influence in their lives, prison is usually not the best answer for them, their families, or society in general. Women may benefit from treatment programs in prison, but, in general, prison is a negative world, and women benefit very little from putting their lives on hold. Further, their children suffer and the dislocation in some children's lives is severe. Because of the nonviolent nature of many women in prison, it would pose very little risk to the public to explore community alternatives to incarceration. Wherever they serve their sentence, they typically need assistance in learning how to take care of themselves and their children.

WEBSITES

For more information on the Women's Prison Association, visit:
   http://www.wpaonline.org/
For more information on Amnesty International, visit:
   http://www.amnesty.org/
For more information on the United Nations Standards for the Treatment of Prisoners, visit:
   http://www2.ohchr.org/english/law/treatmentprisoners.htm

STUDY QUESTIONS

1. Briefly describe the change in the number of women in prison.
2. What differences can be noted between prisons for men and for women historically and today?
3. Describe the demographic profile of female prisoners.
4. Explain the idea of gendered pathways to crime. What differences exist between male and female offenders?
5. What percentage of female inmates/prisoners experienced either physical or sexual abuse earlier in their lives? What kinds of issues arise from childhood sexual victimization? Is there a correlation between childhood abuse and violent crime?
6. Explain how the pathways approach has led to different classification instruments.
7. Explain what we know about women's programming in prisons.
8. Explain the prevalence and types of violence in women's institutions.
9. Explain the prevalence and types of sexual violence in women's institutions.
10. How many women in prison are mothers of children under 18 years old? What are some of the problems of inmate-mothers?

CHAPTER 8

Prisoners' Rights

> In essence, TDC [Texas Department of Corrections] has failed to furnish minimal safeguards for the personal safety of the inmates. Primarily because the civilian security force is insufficient in number and poorly deployed, inmates are constantly in danger of physical assaults from their fellow prisoners. . . . Simply put, inmates live in a climate of fear and apprehension by reason of the constant threat of violence. (*Ruiz v. Estelle* 1980: 26)

Once an individual has been found guilty and sentenced to prison, many people assume that he or she has (or should have) no rights. Up until the 1960s this was, to some extent, true. Federal and state courts refused to hear "prisoners' rights" cases or decided such cases in a way that made it clear that prisoners had few, if any, of the rights of free people. This era was called the "hands-off" era, meaning that the federal courts rarely became involved in prisoners' rights cases.

In *Ruffin v. Commonwealth* (1871), for example, the Virginia Supreme Court stated that the inmate was a "slave of the state," with only those rights given to him by the state. In contrast, in *Wolff v. McDonnell* (1974: 539), the U.S. Supreme Court held: "There is no iron curtain drawn between the Constitution and the prisons of this country." It should be noted that careful historical legal research by Wallace (2001) indicates that the "slave of the state" approach was never monolithic, and many early court decisions in the late 1800s and early 1900s condemned inhumane treatment, but there were no effective procedures to secure prisoners' rights. Tort remedies, habeas corpus relief, mandamus actions, and injunctive relief were not very effective means to enforce the courts' will.

During the so-called Warren Court era (1953–1969), named after Chief Justice Earl Warren, the Supreme Court published a number of opinions that expanded the civil rights of several groups of people, including students, the mentally ill, racial minorities, criminal defendants, and prisoners. This time period became known as the "activist era." The Court utilized the Fourteenth Amendment to expand the protections enumerated in the Bill of Rights. Most of the cases establishing prisoners' rights were first decided during this time period. For instance, some cases recognized a prisoner's right to practice religion as long as it did not interfere with the security of the institution. Other cases granted due process before prisoners were deprived of good time or placed in segregation. Still others granted the right to be free from corporal punishment.

In *Cooper v. Pate* (1964), the Supreme Court held that Muslims in prison did have standing to challenge religious discrimination on the part of prison officials under Section 1983 of the Civil Rights Act of 1871. This recognition was a trumpet call for prisoners to demand court intervention in a number of other areas where, before, prison administrators had operated with almost no oversight whatsoever. Many cases, most of which will be covered in this chapter, followed. Despite some people's belief that the courts still favor prisoners' rights, one could see increasingly restricted views of these rights as early as the 1970s. In *Meachum v. Fano* (1976), for example, the Supreme Court held that a prisoner had no due process rights before being transferred to a harsher prison. In their words, the prison administration could transfer for "good" reasons, "bad" reasons, or "no" reasons. In *Bell v. Wolfish* (1979), the Court held that pretrial detainees held in jails had no more rights than those convicted and that only those rights "consistent" with their confinement would be recognized. During the 1980s and 1990s, prisoners lost more cases than they won and the court took increasingly more restricted views regarding prisoners' rights.

Then, in 1996, Congress passed the Prisoner Litigation Reform Act (PLRA). This legislation was supposed to curtail "frivolous" lawsuits by prisoners, and was successful in dramatically reducing the number of prisoner rights cases heard in federal courts. One of the elements of the PLRA is that an inmate must exhaust all administrative remedies before filing a Section 1983 suit (a civil suit alleging that an agent of the state has violated one's constitutional rights). Further, the inmate must show physical injury; emotional or mental suffering is no longer sufficient to justify a claim. A $120 court filing fee was instituted, even for poor inmates, unless they show absolutely no income for a six-month period prior to filing. Another element of the act is that attorneys no longer are paid by the defendant state if they win. Their earnings must be taken out of the award to the plaintiff inmate. Such awards may not be very large, since often the victories are injunctive rather than financial. Finally, the act permanently bars an inmate from ever filing any other suit if he has had three suits declared frivolous or malicious. While this may seem fair, it should be understood that inmates may have legitimate cases thrown out as frivolous because they did not understand how to write the writ or present their evidence. In essence, this inmate is without recourse to the courts regardless of what happens to him.

> This sedulously crafted piece of legal language is so vicious, detailed, and sweeping that is has baffled journalists and academics into near-total silence. (Parenti 1999, 177)

The ire of the writers of the PLRA was also directed to activist judges who sought to reform the prison system. Elements of the Act prohibit judges from imposing indefinite consent decrees (the vehicle by which many state prisons were brought into compliance with humane standards) and limit a special master's (court monitor's) pay to $40 an hour (even if these masters are lawyers, whose pay is usually many times that amount). Obviously, this has meant that few highly skilled individuals are remaining in special master positions.

The Supreme Court has upheld the PLRA and, according to many, the rights of prisoners must be defended in state courts, using state constitutions, because the federal courts have been effectively silenced (Harding 1998; Roots 2002). Thus, the so-called "activist era" of the Warren Court ended long ago and we have been in the "due deference" era for around 30 years. Most prisoners' rights cases are decided in favor of prison administrators because courts give due deference to prison administrators' expertise in running the prison. In 2011, however, the Supreme Court indicated that their deference to prison administrators was not absolute and, in *Brown v. Plata* (2011), they held that the California prison system was so overcrowded that conditions were unconstitutional and the state had to release up to 40,000 inmates or, alternatively, spend a great deal more money to bring the conditions up to a standard that met basic human needs for medical care and protection from violence. This decision may be an anomaly because the California system was so extreme, or it may be a harbinger of a new era of prisoners' rights.

CAUSES OF ACTION AND SOURCES OF RIGHTS

In every case involving prisoners' rights, there is a decision to be made between the alleged right of the prisoner and the state's interest to run a safe, secure, and orderly prison. Issues such as the prisoner's right to practice his or her religious beliefs, the right to correspond without censorship, the right to adequate medical care, and the right to have some type of hearing before being punished are only some of the issues that have been litigated. Prisoners' rights come from, in most cases, either the federal or state constitutions. For instance, the right to practice one's religion freely comes from the First Amendment; the right to be free from excessive brutality comes from the Eighth Amendment; and so on. In some cases, specific state legislation or interpretations of the state constitution may give to prisoners rights beyond those recognized as coming from the federal Constitution.

In many cases, the test used by the court will determine whether the state wins or the inmate wins. In general, if the court uses a strict scrutiny test, the state must prove an overriding state interest, a close relationship between the rule or procedure at issue and the safety or security of the institution, and prove that no less intrusive means are available to reach the goal of safety and security. If, on the other hand, the court applies a rational relationship test, then prison administrators must simply prove a state interest and some relationship between that interest and the rule or procedure in question.

One of the more frequently used legal mechanisms for suing is found under Title 42 U.S.C. Sec. 1983. This section strips officials of immunities enjoyed by governmental entities if they violate an individual's constitutional rights. This is the reason that many prisoners' rights suits are filed against the director of corrections or the warden. In effect, the suit is against the official in his or her individual capacity. The prisoner must show that there has been a constitutional deprivation or violation by the governmental official acting under color of law. Under Section 1983, the prisoner is entitled to actual and punitive damages and injunctive relief if successful.

> Every person who, under color of any statute, ordinance, regulation, custom, or usage, of any State or Territory, subjects or causes to be subjected, any citizens of the United States or other persons within the jurisdiction thereof to the deprivation of any rights, privileges, or immunities secured by the Constitution and laws, shall be liable to the party injured in an action at law, suit in equity, or other proper proceeding for redress. (Title 42 U.S.C., Sec. 1983)

Most often, prisoners look to the Bill of Rights and the Fourteenth Amendment for the source of the right at issue. It should be understood that the protections enumerated in the Bill of Rights applied only to individuals as citizens of the United States. They protect us from intrusive actions by the federal government. Before any of the protections could be applied against actions by state officials (i.e., prison administrators of state prisons), that right had to be "incorporated" into one's rights as a state citizen. This is done by case law through an application of the Due Process Clause of the Fourteenth Amendment. For any particular prisoner's case that utilized a right specified in the Bill of Rights, the Supreme Court must determine, first, whether the right was important enough that a violation of it by a state actor would violate "fundamental fairness." If it did, then the right was incorporated to state citizens.

In addition to the federal Bill of Rights, prisoners might also have rights recognized under their own state constitution. Rights might also be created by state statute. For instance, if a state statute specifies that each prisoner "must" have a parole hearing every year, then the statute has created that right. It does not exist in either a state or federal constitution. Of course, what is created by statute can be taken away by rewriting the statute. In this chapter, we cover only those cases based on the First, Fourth, Eighth, or Fourteenth Amendments of the Constitution of the United States.

THE FIRST AMENDMENT

> **The First Amendment:** Congress shall make no law respecting an establishment of religion, or prohibiting the free exercise thereof; or abridging the freedom of speech, or of the press; or the right of the people peaceably to assemble, and to petition the government for a redress of grievances.

The First Amendment covers such areas as religious practices (diet, hair, clothing, rituals), censorship (both incoming and outgoing and prison newspapers), association (visiting, labor unions), and media access to prisoners. It is a mistake to believe that anyone's First Amendment rights are absolute. Although we have a great deal of freedom to say what we want, some types of speech are restricted and can be punished. Examples include speech defined as obscenity and speech that poses an immediate threat (yelling "fire" in a crowded theater). Nor does one have complete freedom to practice religion in any way one sees fit. If one's religious practices violate some law, then the behavior will be punished. Our freedom to associate is similarly circumscribed. The state can regulate associations (i.e., demonstrations) that pose a clear and present danger to the public. Thus, even free people do not have completely untrammeled rights under the First Amendment. The strict scrutiny test is the test used to determine if any governmental regulation or practice can infringe on these rights. In this test, the governmental interest must be extremely important and there must be no other way to accomplish the objective. The first prisoner rights' cases heard under the First Amendment were decided under strict scrutiny, but in later years, the "rational relationship" test was used. As we will see, the test used has everything to do with who is likely to win the case.

Freedom of Religion

The first point to note is that these cases concern religious practices as opposed to beliefs. It is only when the prisoner desires to undertake some practice to further their beliefs that controversy arises. Some of the practices that have been litigated include wearing religious jewelry, i.e., a crucifix (Christian); wearing hair in dreadlocks (Rastafarian); refusing to take a shower in front of others (Islam); demanding the prison allow a sweat lodge to be built (Native American); wearing a head-covering (Islam and Judaism); demanding the prison provide a pork-free diet (Islam and Judaism); and demanding the space and time for religious ceremonies (all religions).

The arguments for restricting religious practices in prison usually involve security. If the government makes a good case that the practice interferes with the security of the institution, then the courts always decide in their favor. If the practice has no security implications, and the state's only concern is convenience, then the courts have sometimes upheld the prisoners' rights to practice.

Another question, however, is whether the prisoner's religion is a religion at all. This question has forced the courts to deal with some very fundamental issues, such as "What is a religion?" Obviously, when the prisoner practices an established, recognized religion such as Islam, Christianity, or Judaism, this is not an issue. However, some prisoners' rights cases dealt with unrecognized and/or newer religions (arguably cults or made-up religions). For instance, several cases concerned a group of inmates who had created the "Church of the New Song" (CONS). They argued that in order to practice this religion, they must eat steak and drink cream sherry. In *Theriault v. A Religious Office* (1990), it was clear that the court was not amused. Eventually this so-called religion was practiced in several different states and spawned a number of court cases. Interestingly, some courts did recognize it as a religion, but they could not convince any court of their need to drink Harvey's Bristol Cream as part of their religious doctrine (see also *Theriault v. Silber* 1977).

> . . . a religion addresses fundamental and ultimate questions having to do with deep and imponderable matters . . . a religion is comprehensive in nature, [consisting] of a belief system as opposed to an isolated teaching . . . religion can often be recognized by the presence of certain formal and external signs. . . .
> (*Africa v. Commonwealth of Pennsylvania* 1981: 1032)

Another issue that has arisen is the inmate's sincerity in practicing the religion. Courts have routinely refused to consider this issue with the reasonable argument that no one can stand in judgment of another in this regard.

The early cases balancing religious rights against institutional security tended to be brought by Black Muslims who were denied the opportunity to meet for religious purposes, access religious leaders, wear religious emblems, and so on. Prison officials in the 1960s and 1970s believed that the Muslim faith included beliefs that were contrary and threatening to the security of the institution, so Muslims were usually treated differently from those who practiced other faiths. For instance, religious leaders were barred from the prison and the Muslim prisoners were not allowed to gather for religious ceremonies. Although some lower courts agreed at times that there was a compelling security interest, many more cases were decided in favor of the inmates' rights, especially when their argument also included an equal protection challenge. In *Cruz v. Beto* (1972), for instance, the Supreme Court held that inmates cannot be denied the opportunity to practice an unconventional

American religion (Buddhism) when other inmates are given the chance to pursue conventional faiths.

When the state's argument is merely convenience or economic considerations, courts are sometimes more protective of religious freedoms. However, courts have been willing to accept economic rationales. For instance, in *Gittlemacker v. Prasse* (1970), a Jewish prisoner wanted the prison to provide him with a rabbi at state expense. Because of the small number of Jewish prisoners in the prison, the Third Circuit did not require the state to provide one. In *Walker v. Blackwell* (1969), the Fifth Circuit upheld the state's right to deny Muslims special meals during Ramadan, a religious holiday, because they asked for the meals at special times, with special foods, for 30 days. The Second Circuit decided much the same thing when they determined that the prison was not obligated to provide Jewish prisoners with kosher foods in *Kahane v. Carlson* (1975).

In the myriad of federal appellate court cases, confusion reigned. Some circuit courts used a fairly stringent test to determine whether or not prison regulations passed constitutional muster; others used the rational relationship test, which was more likely to result in the upholding of prison regulations. Some courts held that prison officials could not deny entry to Muslim religious leaders (due to their criminal records); some courts held that such prohibitions were justified by security concerns. Most courts held that the state did not need to provide a pork-free diet or pork alternative for Muslims, but a few courts said that the state could provide a pork substitute with low-cost protein, such as peanut butter. While some courts held that prison officials could not prohibit religious publications or materials, other courts held that as long as there was some opportunity to practice religion, those materials that might be misconstrued or inflammatory could be denied.

The Supreme Court finally accepted another religious freedom case in 1987. By this time, the "activist era" had given way to the "due deference era," with greater weight given to prison authorities' arguments that the practice in question compromised the safe, secure, and orderly running of the prison. In *O'Lone v. Shabazz* (1987), Muslim prisoners in New Jersey on an outside work squad argued that their religious freedom was being compromised by not being allowed back in the facility during the day to worship. The Supreme Court, using the rational relationship test, determined that prison authorities showed a legitimate governmental interest (security) and the regulation or restriction in question bore some rational or reasonable relationship to security; therefore, the prisoners lost. After *O'Lone v. Shabazz,* lower courts have typically followed the Supreme Court's lead and deferred to prison officials' arguments in conflicts between prison policies and inmates' rights to exercise their religion.

In 1993, Congress passed the Religious Freedom Restoration Act [42 U.S.C. Sec. 2000b(b)(1)]. Congress was attempting to bolster protection for religious convictions against governmental actions because the Supreme Court had begun to use the rational relationship test in all controversies when religious practices conflicted with state laws, which meant, of course, that individuals almost always lost. Prisons and jails were not expressly excluded from the protection of the Act;

thus, it appeared that the act would drastically limit the state's ability to restrict or prohibit religious practices even in prison.

Under the Religious Freedom Restoration Act (RFRA), if the state restriction constituted a "substantial burden" on one's ability to practice his or her religion, then the government must show that the restriction "is in furtherance of a compelling governmental interest" and that it is the "least restrictive means" of furthering that interest (in effect, Congress was forcing the courts to use strict scrutiny). The Supreme Court in *City of Boerne v. Flores* (1997) declared that Congress did not have the power to pass the RFRA and ruled it unconstitutional, at least as applied to the states. With a presidential executive order, the law was still valid against federal actions that impinged upon citizens' religious practices. Then, in 2000, Congress passed the Religious Land Use and Institutionalized Persons Act (RLUIPA). This Act reinstated the strict scrutiny test when government actions presented a substantial burden to the practice of religion, in cases of land use (zoning) and, surprisingly, to prisoners. The RLUIPA was used in *Cutter v. Wilkinson* (2005), when a Wiccan, a Satanist, and a member of a racist Christian cult challenged the Ohio prison's restrictions against their religions. Although the state argued the RLUIPA violated the establishment clause because it led to more favorable policies for those who followed a religion over those prisoners who followed no religion, the Supreme Court disagreed, upheld the RLUIPA, and remanded the case to the lower court to determine if the state met the strict scrutiny test for restricting those religions.

Religion has been present in prisons for a long time and early court cases approved of the practice of the state paying for chaplains for prisoners. However, some states have recently been experimenting with faith-based rehabilitative programming, and this raises some concerns.

There have been a few cases concerning prisoners' challenges to requirements that they attend Alcoholic Anonymous (AA) meetings. Since AA refers to a higher power and does have religion as one of its core values, some courts have forbidden states to require AA attendance. The Court of Appeals of New York in *Griffin v. Coughlin* (1996) and the Seventh Circuit Court of Appeals in *Kerr v. Farrey* (1996) held that privileges given to those inmates involved in Alcoholics Anonymous and Narcotics Anonymous violated the First Amendment. In *Americans United for Separation of Church and State v. Prison Fellowship Ministries* (2007), the Eighth Circuit agreed with the federal district court that Iowa had violated the establishment clause of the First Amendment when it provided part of the funds to run the InnerChange religious program in an Iowa prison. Even though the program was voluntary, prisoners received special privileges and the program was paid for out of the fund generated by phone calls paid for by the general population. The Eighth Circuit held that this was an unconstitutional promotion of one religion over others. At this point we know that states must show a compelling interest before impinging upon a prisoner's religion; however, the state cannot favor one religion over any other in terms of resources or special privileges.

Freedom of Speech and Press

Freedom of speech, as applied to prisoners, has typically dealt with censorship of both incoming and outgoing mail and publications. The prisoner's right to receive mail and publications is balanced against the prison's right to protect safety and security. So, for instance, a prisoner has no right to a publication that describes, in detail, how to make a bomb out of kitchen ingredients, nor does he have a right to receive a letter detailing an escape attempt, nor a publication that advocates the overthrow of all prison regimes. The prison also has a right to address "order" concerns, so that they are usually free to restrict the number of pieces of outgoing and incoming mail in order to manage it.

Some of the issues that are raised concerning the First Amendment and prison regulations include the following:

- communication with the news media (generally courts have upheld prisoners' right to contact the media through letters, although they have rejected the media's right to interview or visit inmates);
- communicating with public officials (this type of mail is generally considered to be legal mail and deserving of legal mail privileges);
- communicating with other inmates (prison officials have the right to ban this communication);
- receipt of inflammatory or pornographic material (prisons have the right to ban this material);
- use of mail lists that restrict inmates to "approved" individuals (these are upheld but there must be a valid reason for denying a request);
- receipt of books and packages (usually these are allowed, but prisons may prohibit items and may have a "publisher only" rule that limits books only to those sent directly from publishers).

One of the early cases concerning censorship of mail was *Procunier v. Martinez* (1974). This Supreme Court case dealt with a challenge to California prison rules regarding outgoing mail. Not unlike other states at this time, prison officials in California routinely read outgoing mail and censored or refused to mail letters that were critical of the prison administration or made political statements. The regulations at issue in *Procunier* prohibited inmates from "unduly complaining" or "magnifying grievances," or "expressing inflammatory political, racial, religious or other views or beliefs." Another regulation prohibited letters that were lewd, obscene, defamatory, or contained foreign matter or were "otherwise inappropriate."

In the case holding, the Supreme Court switched the analysis from a consideration of prisoner rights to one where the First Amendment rights of the free person receiving the letter were considered. In *Procunier*, the Court seemed to use the highest level of scrutiny to judge whether the prison regulation was acceptable. In the strict scrutiny test, the state must show a "compelling" governmental interest, the regulation must be strictly tailored to that interest, and the regulation must be the "least restrictive alternative." Furthermore, the suppression must be unrelated to the expression—meaning that prison officials could not suppress inmates' views because of their content (unless such content was directly related to a security threat).

After *Procunier,* state officials had to show that there was a legitimate governmental interest at stake, and that they were using the least restrictive means necessary to meet that interest. Ordinarily, this meant that inmates' letters were read but only at random, unless there was some reason for suspicion: for example, the inmate was suspected of being engaged in escape plans or contraband smuggling.

In 1987, the Supreme Court decided *Turner v. Safley* (1987), the case where they explicitly describe the rational relationship test as it applies to prisoners. The Court upheld a ban on mail between inmates in two different prisons because it could be justified by "legitimate penological interests." Missouri prison officials argued that such mail might be used for such things as communicating about escapes, fostering gang activity, and arranging to assault other inmates. Rather than employ a strict scrutiny test which would require the state to use the least restrictive alternative, a prison official must show only that: (1) There is a rational connection between the prison regulation and the legitimate governmental interest put forward to justify it; (2) there are alternative means of exercising the right in spite of the regulation; (3) accommodating the asserted right would be burdensome and affect guards, other inmates, and prison resources; and (4) there are no ready alternatives to the prison regulation available and the regulation is not an "exaggerated response" to the problem. The state won, although the Supreme Court left open the question of mail to and from those outside prison.

Two years later, in *Thornburgh v. Abbott* (1989), the Court dealt with regulations in federal prisons regarding what type of outside publications prisoners could receive. Not surprisingly, the Court explicitly rejected the more stringent requirements of *Procunier* in favor of allowing broad deference to prison administrators' judgments. Prison administrators merely needed to have a "reasonable" relationship between the ban or rejection of a publication and institutional security. Nor did they require prison administrators to search for the "least restrictive" alternative: for instance, banning only certain issues of a publication rather than a blanket prohibition. The court did not overturn *Procunier v. Martinez,* but it limited the more stringent test to the inmates' outgoing mail, arguing that incoming materials posed more of a security threat. Thus, it seems that the Court is saying that prison administrators can reject inmates' incoming publications if, in their judgment, the publications are detrimental to the order, discipline, and security of the institution; and it can also reject incoming correspondence from private parties, even nonprisoners, for the same reasons.

In *Beard v. Banks* (2006), the Supreme Court upheld the right of the prison to withhold all incoming materials, such as newspapers, magazines, and other forms of communication, at least for some categories of prisoners. In Pennsylvania, inmates at the highest classification level were barred from receiving any outside materials. The Third Circuit held that, even under the rational relationship test, this violated the First Amendment rights of the prisoners, but the Supreme Court disagreed and held that it was not unconstitutional because the inmate might be able to transfer out of the highest classification level.

A special case of First Amendment rights concerns the media's right of access. In early and more recent cases, media representatives and prisoners have argued that the First Amendment guarantees the media's right to access prisons, specifically to interview certain inmates and "tell their story" to the world. In *Pell v. Procunier* (1974), *Saxbe v. Washington Post Co.* (1974), and *Houchins v. KQED* (1978), the Court made it clear that news people enjoyed no special rights of access over and above the general public and accepted the governmental objective of preventing the creation of celebrity inmates. They noted that there were alternative ways the inmate could reach the public, including writing letters and having visits with a family member who, in turn, could be interviewed by the media. The media could participate in public tours and speak to inmates during these tours, so there was no absolute ban on media access.

Rights of Association

The First Amendment has also been used to address prisoners' rights to associate and assemble. In *Jones v. North Carolina Prisoners' Union* (1977), the Court dealt with North Carolina's restrictions of the activities of a growing prisoner union. This case was argued under both the First Amendment rights of speech as well as the right to associate. The prisoner's union, modeled after such prisoner unions in some Scandinavian countries, had reached a membership of 2,000 by 1975. The state, in an effort to restrict and discourage membership, did not prohibit individuals to join but did prohibit solicitation, meetings, and bulk mailings. The Supreme Court upheld these regulations, despite inmates' allegations that the regulations violated their First and Fourteenth Amendment rights (they argued that barring them from soliciting members violated equal protection, since other groups could do so freely). The state won.

Maintaining contact with family has long been held to be an important part of reintegration for inmates. In *Kentucky v. Thompson* (1989), the Supreme Court held that the prison was not required to provide due process protections before denying an individual inmate visits with certain individuals on his visiting list. Inmates were not prevented from seeing other visitors. In both cases, and in other situations, the duty officer and/or a higher official made the decision without any hearing or other due process protection. The Supreme Court held there was no liberty interest in "unfettered visitation." In *Overton v. Bazzetta* (2003), the Supreme Court, using the rational relationship test, held there was no constitutional violation in Michigan's stringent visitation rules that limited the number of visitors on an approved list, barred all non-first-degree relative children and enforced a two-year ban of all visitation for those found guilty of a drug infraction.

Conjugal visitation allows "marital relations" between inmates and their spouses. Although a few states allow conjugal visits, or "family" visits, no court has ruled that inmates have a right to them. Contact visitation is that in which the visitor and inmate are not separated by a glass or mesh screen. There may still be rules regarding touching: for instance, inmates in some states are allowed only one kiss and/or hug at the beginning of the visit. Again, no court has ruled that inmates have a right to contact visits. In *Block v. Rutherford* (1984), for instance, the Court held that pretrial detainees can be denied contact visits due to security concerns. Obviously, if pretrial detainees can be denied contact visits, it is certain that the Court would not extend such a right to convicted felons.

Interestingly, in *Turner v. Safley* (1987), the same case in which the Court upheld an absolute ban on inmate-to-inmate correspondence, the majority rejected a prison ban on marriages between inmates. The majority recognized the essential right of a prisoner to marry whomever he or she chooses, even if that happens to be another prisoner. The state regulation in question denied the right to marry, unless it was approved by the warden, and even then approval could only be given for "compelling reasons." The state's argument was that prisoners did not have the same rights as free people, and that the ban was "rationally related" to security and rehabilitation concerns. The Court disagreed. The *Turner v. Safley* holding has been criticized as being logically inconsistent. It certainly does seem strange that the Court upheld a restriction on inmate-to-inmate correspondence but rejected the regulation banning inmate-to-inmate marriage. This means that inmates may marry, but after the marriage, they may not be able to write to each other.

The Court seemingly used the rational or reasonable relationship test to arrive at both parts of the holding, but this illustrates the somewhat arbitrary nature of how the test might be applied. Obviously, both sections of Missouri's regulations were related to the stated objectives of security and rehabilitation. It is hard to see why one was considered "reasonable" and the other not.

THE FOURTH AMENDMENT

The Fourth Amendment: . . . the right of the people to be secure in their persons, houses, papers, and effects, against unreasonable searches and seizures, shall not be violated, and no warrants shall issue but upon probable cause, supported by oath or affirmation, and particularly describing the place to be searched, and the persons or things to be seized.

The Fourth Amendment protects our right to be free from unreasonable search and seizure by governmental officials. Inmates basically have no Fourth Amendment rights in prison. There is simply no such thing as an "unreasonable" search of a prisoner, up to and including full body cavity searches.

Two cases illustrate the U.S. Supreme Court's views on this issue. In *Bell v. Wolfish* (1979), the Court ruled that inmates had no right to be present during searches of their cells and also ruled that strip searches (including body cavity searches) are reasonable for purposes of contraband control and do not require probable cause. In *Hudson v. Palmer* (1984), a Virginia inmate sued for violation of his Fourth Amendment rights after prison officials conducted what the inmate saw as an unreasonable search of his cell. The Supreme Court declared that since prison officials must look for contraband and maintain sanitary conditions, the Fourth Amendment has no applicability to a prison cell. In effect, they said that the Fourth Amendment was "fundamentally incompatible" with prison security and order. The only time a court might reject a search as unreasonable or unconstitutional is when it is done conclusively for purposes of harassment, in which case the source of the right comes from the Eighth Amendment's protections against cruel and unusual punishment, not the Fourth Amendment.

There have been cases of prisoners protesting strip searches and/or pat downs by opposite sex guards. Interestingly, most of these cases have been filed by male inmates. In some lower court opinions, privacy rights have been recognized, especially for female inmates who protest searches by male officers, although there is no consistency in these opinions and there are conflicting decisions among the lower courts (see Bennett 1995; Pollock 2002: 166–167;).

After 1987, courts used the *Turner v. Safley* rational relationship test to evaluate claims that searches by guards of the opposite sex violated the Fourth Amendment or prisoners' privacy rights. In cases involving male prisoners through the 1990s courts basically asserted that male inmates did have a privacy interest, but as long as the female officers were not routinely observing showers and did not conduct strip searches except in emergencies, then their rights were fairly balanced against state interests. In *Jordan v. Gardner* (1993), previously discussed in chapter 7, female inmates won a court ruling that held that the practice of male officers' patting down female inmates violated the Eighth Amendment (cruel and unusual punishment). This holding was based on the finding that a large majority of female inmates were victims of sexual abuse and experienced post-traumatic stress syndrome symptoms when patted down by a male guard. This holding by the Ninth Circuit seems not to have established any persuasive authority since subsequent cases in other circuits did not follow the same line of reasoning.

THE EIGHTH AMENDMENT

The Eighth Amendment: . . . excessive bail shall not be required, nor excessive fines imposed, nor cruel and unusual punishments inflicted.

The Eighth Amendment protects us from cruel and unusual punishment. It has been used in the past to invalidate corporal punishment (i.e., whipping) (*Jackson v. Bishop* 1968). It has also been used to challenge inadequate medical care. It has been used to challenge inadequate or nonexistent rehabilitative treatment, but, also, to challenge forced or coerced rehabilitative treatment. Finally, the more recent approach under the Eighth Amendment has been called "the totality of circumstances" approach. In these cases, an argument is made that the combination of conditions creates a total experience that is unconstitutional.

Medical Care and Rehabilitation

In *Estelle v. Gamble* (1976), the Supreme Court held that to be "deliberately indifferent" to the medical needs of an inmate would cause needless pain, unrelated to the goals of incarceration. As such, it would constitute cruel and unusual punishment and violate the individual's constitutional rights. The standard to be met, however, is "deliberate indifference," which is harder to prove than simple or even gross negligence. *Madrid v. Gomez* (1999) is probably the best-known case where allegations of neglect and malfeasance were substantiated and became the basis for a court order and consent decree. In this case, inmates proved that the California Department of Correction was deliberately indifferent to the medical needs of prisoners in its staffing patterns and in having nonmedical staff members make decisions about who could see the doctor. Further, the practice of transferring inmates without their charts or prescription drugs and the delay in providing medical care for sick or injured inmates was found to be undue interference in the right of the inmate to have reasonable medical care. The case resulted in a consent decree whereby the state of California agreed to pay millions of dollars in improvements in its medical care delivery system.

Although prisoners may deserve medical attention for injuries or illnesses, no such right exists for rehabilitative treatment: namely, for drug abuse. For instance, in *Marshall v. U.S.* (1974), the Supreme Court held that a prisoner did not have a constitutional right to drug treatment. No court has held that lack of rehabilitative programs constitutes a violation of the Eighth Amendment, except perhaps as part of a "totality of the circumstances" case.

Mental health treatment is more akin to medical treatment than "rehabilitative" treatment; thus, the absence of any psychiatric or psychological treatment has been ruled unconstitutional (*Bowring v. Godwin* 1977). The only other way a "right to rehabilitation" might exist is if there is a sentencing statute that increases or changes the sentencing of an individual for the purpose of treatment (e.g., special sex offender sentencing).

The Eighth Amendment has also been used to challenge being required to participate in treatment programs and/or be subjected to involuntary injection of psychotropic drugs. In *Knecht v. Gillman* (1973), it was decided that prisoners could not be forced to stay in a behavior modification program that was defined as experimental. However, in *Washington v. Harper* (1990), the Supreme Court held that prisoners could be injected with antipsychotic drugs against their will if prison and medical staff felt the inmate posed a continuing danger to self or others.

In an unusual use of the Eighth Amendment, a prisoner in a Nevada prison filed a petition arguing that prison authorities were deliberately indifferent to his health by forcing him to cell with a prisoner who smoked. The Supreme Court in *Helling v. McKinney* (1993) agreed and held that exposing inmates to cigarette smoking did endanger their health and authorities were deliberately indifferent if they did not accommodate requests to be housed away from cigarette smoke. This case decision eventually led to the majority of states banning tobacco entirely.

Finally, in *Farmer v. Brennan* (1994) a transgender inmate (who was transitioning from being a man to a woman) was placed in general population despite the obvious risk of rape. She was raped repeatedly and beaten, and acquired HIV through the sexual assaults. The Supreme Court held that correctional officers were deliberately indifferent to the risk of sexual assault and violated the Eighth Amendment by not placing this inmate in protective housing.

Excessive Use of Force/Other Punishments

> They would make you lie down on your stomach and whip you with a bull hide. I got whipped the first day I was on the hoe squad. . . . It was like being backed up against a heating stove all day long. At night, you couldn't pull your shorts off. You had to take a shower and shake them loose. (an inmate describing the Cummins Prison Farm before prison reform, quoted in Nelson 2002: 2)

In *Jackson v. Bishop* (1968), a lower federal court held that whipping was cruel and unusual punishment. Since the Supreme Court denied certiorari, and has subsequently cited the case with approval, it has become accepted law that physical punishment—beatings, whippings, and so on—are unconstitutional. More recent cases concern incidents of alleged "excessive force." Two cases illustrate the Supreme Court's view on what is permissible under the Constitution.

In *Whitley v. Albers* (1986), the Supreme Court held that an Oregon inmate who had been shot in the leg during a prison hostage situation needed to prove an "unnecessary and wanton infliction of pain" to constitute an Eighth Amendment violation. The Court concluded that the shooting took place in a good-faith effort to restore prison order rather than for malicious or sadistic purposes. It was clear from the Court's holding that they were willing to grant state officials great latitude in determining the proper course of action in collective violence situations. The Supreme Court offered four factors to consider in a balancing test to determine if state actions are malicious and sadistic: (1) the need to apply force; (2) the relationship between that need and the amount of force actually used; (3) the threat to staff and other inmates' safety as reasonably perceived by prison officials; and (4) efforts made to temper the severity of officials' forceful response.

In *Hudson v. McMillian* (1992), a prisoner had been hit in the face after being handcuffed and shackled. The state attorneys deemed his injury "minor" and undeserving of Eighth Amendment protection. The Supreme Court ruled that an excessive use of force against an inmate need not cause a significant degree of injury to constitute cruel and unusual punishment. Even relatively mild injury might offend standards of decency if imposed in a manner that was unnecessary and wanton, and in this case, since the inmate was already subdued, the injury was deemed wanton and in violation of the Eighth Amendment.

In a more recent case, the Supreme Court decided in favor of an Alabama prisoner who sued correctional officers for handcuffing him to a "hitching post" for seven hours with no water or bathroom breaks. The inmate had refused to work and scuffled with correctional officers. He was taken back to the prison and handcuffed to a bar that kept his arms at shoulder height causing extreme discomfort after several hours. He was also shirtless and left in the hot sun for the seven hours, causing severe sunburn. The Court said that because any reasonable person should know that the practice was a violation of the Eighth Amendment, the officers did not have qualified immunity for their actions (*Hope v. Pelzer* 2002).

Totality of Circumstances

The more recent cases involving the Eighth Amendment propose that a combination of living conditions in a prison could constitute a "totality of the circumstances" that create cruel and unusual punishment. Factors, including violence, lack of staffing, sanitation deficiencies, and/or lack of rehabilitative programs, may create living conditions that constitute cruel and unusual punishment. The remedy in many of these cases has been to appoint prison monitors to track the progress of prison systems in meeting many court-ordered conditions; sometimes these monitors oversee prison systems for years.

One of the most notorious cases of this type was *Holt v. Sarver* (1971). In this case, described also in chapter 1, Arkansas prisoners won their class action lawsuit against the state for inhumane conditions in the prison, including the use of inmates to guard other inmates, extreme levels of violence in open barracks with no guard supervision, overcrowded and unsanitary cells, lack of rehabilitative programming, and lack of medical care.

In *Ruiz v. Estelle* (1980), a federal district judge in Texas held that many conditions in the Texas prison system, including the use of building tenders, formed the totality of circumstances that created unconstitutional conditions. This case concluded over 20 years later in 2002 when Judge Justice finally released Texas from mandatory monitoring (*Austin American Statesman* 2002).

The Supreme Court has made it much more difficult for an inmate to win a "totality of circumstance" case. In *Wilson v. Seiter* (1991), an inmate alleged a totality of circumstance argument whereby the total conditions of the prison, including overcrowding, sanitation, programs, and violence, created conditions that violated the Eighth Amendment. In a reversal of past analyses, the Court held that the inmate had to prove "deliberate indifference," not just a pattern of deficits. Thus, inmates would have to prove that the prison administration knew and deliberately disregarded all the elements that constituted the claim of unconstitutional conditions.

This requirement evidently was met in *Madrid v. Gomez* (1995), the case concerning Pelican Island, California's super-max facility. Inmates alleged constitutional violations in the lack of medical care, excessive use of force, and the presence of mentally ill inmates in the super-max prison with no access to treatment. The federal district court agreed with the inmates and the state entered into a consent decree that involved a special monitor. In 2011, the state was finally released from the monitor's oversight, but its troubles were not over.

In 2011, the most important prisoner rights case to occur in years was decided. In *Brown v. Plata* (2011), the Supreme Court finally ended years of conflict between the federal courts and California over prison medical care, or, more specifically, the lack of it due to overcrowding. For years, in several class action suits, courts had found deficiencies, including inadequate medical screening of incoming prisoners; delays in or failure to provide access to medical care; untimely responses to medical emergencies; the interference of custodial staff with the provision of medical care; the failure to recruit and retain sufficient numbers of competent medical staff; disorganized and incomplete medical records; a lack of quality control procedures; and a lack of protocols to deal with chronic illnesses, including diabetes, heart disease, hepatitis, and HIV. After giving the state years to address these problems with no progress made, the Circuit Court ordered the release of 40,000 prisoners. The state appealed the decision to the Supreme Court and, in a surprising 5 to 4 decision, the majority agreed. The Supreme Court held that the overcrowded conditions of California prisons created conditions that violated the Eighth Amendment and the state must release prisoners if it cannot run its prison system in a manner consistent with the Eighth Amendment.

THE FOURTEENTH AMENDMENT

The Fourteenth Amendment: Section 1: All persons born or naturalized in the United States, and subject to the jurisdiction thereof, are citizens of the United States and of the State wherein they reside. No State shall make or enforce any law which shall abridge the privileges or immunities of the citizens of the United States; nor shall any State deprive any person of life, liberty, or property, without due process of law, nor deny to any person within its jurisdiction the equal protection of the laws.

The Fourteenth Amendment includes both the Equal Protection Clause and the Due Process Clause. Both have been utilized in prisoners' rights suits. The Due Process Clause dictates that every individual facing a possible deprivation of a "liberty interest" by a governmental entity be entitled to certain due process procedures designed to prevent or minimize error in the decision. So, for instance, when the government seeks to take away one's life, liberty, or property, or any other liberty interest, it must first allow certain fact-finding procedures: namely, notice, a neutral hearing, the right to be present and present evidence, the right to cross-examine, counsel, and the right of appeal. Not all elements are deemed to be necessary for all deprivations. Generally, the greater the deprivation, the more extensive are the due process elements. Note that the Due Process Clause does not protect individuals against these deprivations by the state; the purpose is only to prevent arbitrary and capricious state action or deprivations through error.

The Fourteenth Amendment is the source of prisoners' rights either directly (if the right is determined to be of a fundamental nature) or indirectly (if it is a state-created right, because then procedural protections attach). The Fourteenth Amendment covers issues such as access to courts, prison discipline, parole and probation revocation hearings, mental health/transfer hearings, and perhaps protections for such things as visitation, a healthy environment, treatment, and so on.

Access to Courts

It is not an overstatement to propose that access to courts is the sword that protects all other rights. Access cases involve allegations that the prisoner is blocked from communicating with the courts. If communication is blocked, then recognized rights are worthless because there is no way to protect them when they are denied. If courts do not hear the cases, no one can protect the inmate against illegal deprivations. Even during the so-called hands-off era, the Supreme Court made it clear that state officials could not interfere with access to courts.

In *Ex parte Hull* (1941), a Michigan prison regulation required inmates to submit all legal documents (briefs, petitions, motions, habeas corpus proceedings, and appeals) to the institutional welfare official and the legal adviser for the Parole Board. Only if these officials believed that the legal documents were valid and properly written would they be forwarded to the court. The Supreme Court found this regulation invalid. In *Johnson v. Avery* (1969), the Supreme Court held that a state could not punish a jailhouse lawyer for helping inmates with their cases if the state provided no alternative means for inmates to receive legal assistance.

Early cases merely removed barriers to court access, such as regulations that stopped a petitioner's claims from going forward. Once these barriers were removed, later challenges took up issues of "real" access as opposed to simply removing barriers. For instance, illiterate and unschooled inmates must have help if they are to have "real" access to the courts, and indigents must receive free of charge things like transcripts, postage, and photocopying. Inmates also received expanded visitation rights with attorneys or attorney-representatives to assist in case preparation. "Legal mail" can be sealed going out of prison and incoming legal mail can't be read by prison officials.

After *Johnson v. Avery*, the most common method of meeting the Court's demand for real access was the creation of law libraries and some version of inmate or officer clerks to help inmates research legal questions. In *Bounds v. Smith* (1977), the Supreme Court decided that having to travel to a law library at another prison was not unduly burdensome. They evidently were not concerned that in order to access a library, the prisoner might have to be transferred for a temporary period, thereby having to give up his cell, his place on any waiting list for programs, or his place in a coveted program.

Now there have been limits placed on the right of the individual to access the court. In *Murray v. Giarratano* (1989), the Supreme Court majority held that indigent death row inmates did not have a right to counsel in collateral appeals of their sentence (collateral appeals are those that come after the first, direct appeal process). This followed *Pennsylvania v. Finley* (1987), an earlier case that denied such a right to inmates seeking collateral appeals of sentences other than the death penalty.

Some believe that prisoner rights to law libraries or other assistance in filing legal claims has been more or less eviscerated by *Lewis v. Casey* (1996). In this case, the Supreme Court held that a prisoner must demonstrate that alleged shortcomings of the prison's library (or other type of legal assistance program) caused actual injury and hindered the prisoner's efforts to build a case in order to win. According to the Court's ruling, if the prisoner cannot show actual injury, then evidently the program, however superficial or inadequate, will be deemed sufficient, but they did not explain how an inmate was supposed to prove that the lack of legal materials or assistance was the reason why his petition was denied or otherwise was injured by the deficient legal resources.

Disciplinary Proceedings

In *Wolff v. McDonnell* (1974), an "adjustment committee" in a Nebraska prison found an inmate guilty of a prison infraction and took away good time. The inmate argued he should have had the same due process safeguards given to parolees facing revocation. These rights include advance notice, an impartial hearing body, the conditional right to present witnesses and evidence, the conditional right to confront and cross-examine, the right to a statement of fact-finding, the right to appeal, and a conditional right to counsel. The Supreme Court majority found that although there was no "right" to good time inherent in the Due Process Clause, such a right had been state-created (by statutory language) and, therefore, required due process protections. The Court held that at a minimum the procedural protections necessary included a disciplinary proceeding by an impartial body, 24 hours advance written notice of the claimed violation, a written statement from the fact-finders as to the evidence relied upon and the reasons for the disciplinary action, and an opportunity for the inmate to call witnesses and to present documentary evidence (provided this is not hazardous to institutional safety or correctional goals). The Court held that the prison setting may restrict the right to call witnesses and cross-examine, and so these rights would be conditional. Prisoners were not awarded the right to counsel except those who were illiterate or otherwise unable to defend their claims themselves. In *Wolff v. McDonnell* (1974), the Court also extended due process protections to solitary confinement. Evidently, the Court grouped the two together because both affected the length and nature of confinement. Solitary confinement was described as a "major change" and the Court also discussed the possibility that a sanction of punitive segregation could later ruin the prisoner's chance for an early parole.

After *Wolff*, states were required to hold some form of disciplinary hearings. Most adopted the two-tier procedure suggested in Wolff whereby minor infractions that might be punished by less severe sanctions were separated from major infractions with potential loss of good time and/or segregation. Only the latter charges were processed through the disciplinary hearing procedures. Disciplinary hearings are often conducted by "adjustment committees," with both classification and treatment represented. Some states employ outside hearing officers.

One should also note that most inmates describe such proceedings as little more than kangaroo courts, where their guilt is decided ahead of time. With rare opportunity to present witnesses or evidence or have outside counsel, and with the hearing officer usually a superior of the officer who filed the original "ticket," there is often the merest patina of due process in such proceedings. "Counsel substitutes" are often either correctional officers or other inmates; their ability to provide an aggressive defense is questionable. Further, according to *Superintendent v. Hill* (1985), the level of proof necessary to determine guilt in a prison disciplinary case is merely "some evidence."

Later cases have further eroded the reach of the *Wolff* decision. Prisons ordinarily have two types of segregation. In addition to punitive segregation (or solitary confinement), there is also administrative segregation. It operates in much the same way as punitive segregation but is reserved for those awaiting transfer, newly transferred prisoners, those seeking protective custody, and others for a variety of reasons. It is virtually indistinguishable from punitive segregation. Prisoners are locked in their cells for 23 hours a day, they have no access to programs or yard recreation, they have isolated visitation schedules, and they cannot visit the law library, although they can request law books be brought to them in their cells.

In *Hewitt v. Helms* (1983), an inmate who was sent to administrative segregation challenged the transfer, arguing that he deserved the same due process protections as those awarded in *Wolff v. McDonnell*. Aaron Helms was accused of assaulting prison officers and of conspiracy to disrupt the institution. After a number of hearings, officials charged him with assault and ordered him to disciplinary segregation for six months. Helms sued, claiming that his confinement in administrative segregation prior to his sentencing violated his due process rights. In this prison, administrative segregation was used for those inmates who posed a threat to security, when disciplinary charges were pending, or when an inmate required protective custody.

The Supreme Court, in a holding written by Justice Rehnquist, illustrated the shift to a deference approach in their identification of the source of rights and their decision as to what process was due. They did find that prisoners in this state had a protected liberty interest in the transfer to administrative segregation, but only because it was created by state statute and prison regulations. According to the Court, when states explicitly mandate administrative segregation for certain violations, some due process was required. Note the importance of this shift in rights. The Court did not say that the move from general population freedoms to extremely restricted living conditions, by itself, was a grievous loss, only that the state may create a right to due process by statute or procedural rules.

Justice Rehnquist held that a "liberty interest arises when the action taken by the prison is not 'within the terms of confinement ordinarily contemplated by a prison sentence'" (*Hewitt v. Helms* 1983: 869). However, according to Justice Rehnquist, the transfer of an inmate to more restrictive quarters for nonpunitive reasons was well within the terms of confinement ordinarily contemplated by a prison sentence. Thus, the majority opinion in this case concluded that the inmate possessed due process protections when being transferred to administrative segregation only when it was created by statutory language. In this case, the prison regulations required only an informal, non-adversary review of information with the inmate's statement of events. This review was to be done within a "reasonable time" after confinement to administrative segregation. The Court agreed that these minimal due process protections were sufficient to protect the liberty interest created; therefore, the state won.

In *Sandin v. Conner* (1995), the Supreme Court overruled their *Hewitt* decision and completed its evisceration of the *Wolff v. McDonnell* holding, at least as it regarded transfer to segregation. Demont Conner, a Hawaiian prisoner, complained that prior to his disciplinary hearing he wasn't given a summary of facts relevant to the charge, he was not permitted to question the guard who charged him with the offense, he was not allowed to call witnesses at the hearing, and prison officials "doctored his testimony" and used it against him. According to Hawaii's regulations, an adjustment committee could only find guilt when the inmate admitted the violation or upon "substantial evidence."

The Court of Appeals applied the *Hewitt v. Helms* "source of rights" rationale and concluded that Hawaii's regulations created a liberty interest in remaining free from disciplinary segregation and these same regulations mandated the specific due process elements that must be met before transfer to punitive segregation could occur. The Supreme Court overturned the Court of Appeals ruling. Justice Rehnquist wrote the opinion for the 5 to 4 decision, rejecting the statutory source of right argument and instructing lower courts to look only at the nature of the deprivation. The Court argued that the practice of searching for statutory rights "encouraged prisoners to comb regulations in search of mandatory language on which to base entitlements to various state-conferred privileges," created disincentives for states to codify prison management procedures, involved the courts in day-to-day management of prisons, and did not allow "appropriate deference and flexibility to state officials trying to manage a volatile environment" (*Sandin v. Conner* 1995: 2299).

The majority were no doubt responding to the explosion in prisoners' rights litigation and perhaps also to the public's increasing impatience with "frivolous" due process complaints. Certainly, after the *Hewitt* decision, a rash of cases emerged in which prisoners sought to find liberty interests in mandatory language of prison rules and regulations. Another issue that evidently was on the justices' minds was that the states that had attempted to provide guidance and develop some restrictions on unrestrained discretion of prison officers found themselves in litigation more often than those states that did not provide extensive guidance through policies and procedures. The Court noted that this was an unfortunate side effect of the state-created right analysis and discouraged greater codification of procedures.

The *Sandin* majority held that the source of the liberty interest, if there is one, should be found in the nature of the deprivation. Now, only when the deprivation constitutes an "atypical, significant deprivation" and is not "within the range of confinement to be normally expected" does a liberty interest exist, thus triggering due process requirements.

In *Hewitt v. Helms,* the Court, in dictum, opined that the nature of the deprivation (in that case administrative segregation) was not atypical or outside the scope or range of the original sentence because it was similar to disciplinary segregation. Now, in *Sandin,* dealing with disciplinary segregation, the Court utilized that same argument to dismiss the deprivations of disciplinary segregation as well, arguing that it is similar to administrative segregation and thus not atypical. The Court also noted that the general inmate population often spent many hours in their cells because of lockdowns in the prison; thus, the longer period of time in disciplinary segregation was not relatively more burdensome.

Although the Court argued that it was merely reverting back to the analysis first proposed in *Wolff,* in truth, this decision overturns *Wolff* as well because in that earlier case the majority did believe that being locked in one's cell for 23 hours a day and having no opportunity to take part in any programs or education was "atypical" and implicated a significant liberty interest. Evidently, the only liberty interest left to inmates that deserves due process protection is any deprivation that fundamentally alters the length of the original prison sentence (such as taking away one's good time).

Thus, prisoners who face administrative segregation or punitive segregation today arguably have no rights of due process protections stemming from the Fourteenth Amendment. States could evidently abandon the disciplinary proceedings that were instituted after *Wolff* for every sanction except, perhaps, the loss of good time with no argument from the Court. The widespread use of administrative segregation is a direct result of this line of cases. In "ad seg" units, inmates are locked in their cells for 23 hours a day without access to programming or social contact. Sometimes the only reason for the transfer is a suspicion that the inmate is a gang member. Recall that the super-max prison is used to isolate suspected gang members and some individuals may spend most of their prison sentence in the super-max. In *Wilkinson v. Austin* (2005), Ohio's practice of sending prisoners to the super-max prison was challenged. The Supreme Court surprisingly held that there was a liberty interest in this type of transfer, specifically, that the super-max constituted an appreciably harsher and more punitive environment. Thus, due process was required; however, according to the Supreme Court, Ohio met due process requirements by its procedures whereby a classification committee made the decision, which was reviewed by the warden and a central classification bureau.

Other Deprivations
The above discussion concerned transfers to administrative or punitive segregation. Other cases have dealt with other types of transfers. In *Meachum v. Fano*

(1976), the Court held that inmates had no due process rights when being trans-ferred to a prison where conditions were harsher. This case has had far-reaching effects, even beyond correctional law, because of its "source of rights" analysis. In this case, officials removed Arthur Fano and five other prisoners from Norfolk to Walpole prisons in Massachusetts. Living conditions were substantially less favor-able in Walpole because it is a maximum-security prison. Fano and others were suspected of setting nine serious fires. The prison classification board held indi-vidual classification hearings, and inmates were represented by counsel. Each pris-oner was allowed to present evidence but was not given transcripts or summaries of the testimony. Fano alleged violation of due process.

The Court held that there was no liberty interest at stake. According to Justice White, there was no right to be in any particular prison; therefore, transfers deserved no due process. The case became important because of Justice White's discussion regarding the source of rights. In *Meachum*, the Court held that liberty interests came from the Constitution or through some statute or state regulation. They had no existence apart from these sources. Justice Stevens and other dis-senters argued passionately that rights were not merely man-made. They argued, utilizing natural law concepts, that such sources were not the sole sources of rights; rather, they were only man-made notations of rights that existed independent of judicial or statutory recognition of them. Each individual is endowed with certain "inalienable" rights by virtue of being. Laws and statutes merely recognize such rights. Justice Stevens, in his dissent, joined by Justices Brennan and Marshall, argued that even inmates retained fundamental liberty interests or, at a minimum, the right to be treated with dignity—which the Constitution may never ignore.

> If a man were a creature of the State, the analysis [regarding source of rights] would be correct. But neither the Bill of Rights nor the laws of sovereign States create the liberty which the Due Process Clause protects. The relevant consti-tutional provisions are limitations on the power of the sovereign to infringe on the liberty of the citizen. . . . I had thought it self-evident that all men were endowed by their Creator with liberty as one of the cardinal unalienable rights. It is that basic freedom which the Due Process Clause protects, rather than the particular rights or privileges conferred by specific laws or regulations . . . the inmate retains an unalienable interest in liberty—at the very minimum the right to be treated with dignity—which the Constitution may never ignore.
> (Justice Stevens in *Meachum v. Fano* 1976: 233)

The *Meachum* analysis that prisoners had no rights regarding transfer was applied to a challenge of a state prisoner being transferred to a federal prison in *Howe v. Smith* (1981) and to a state prisoner being transferred to another state prison in *Olim v. Wakinekona* (1983). Evidently, prisoners have no due process protections, even when such transfers involve being transferred to worse living conditions or cause great hardship to the prisoner and/or his or her family because he or she is transferred across the country to another state.

The only transfer case that has turned out differently involved a transfer to a mental hospital. As of now, it is still good law. In *Vitek v. Jones* (1980), the Court ruled that involuntary transfer from a prison to a mental hospital setting did involve a liberty interest and necessitated a due process hearing. This was because a mental hospital was qualitatively different from a prison, residents had greater limitations on their freedom, there is stigma attached to a stay in a mental hospital (evidently worse than or at least different from a prison sentence), and there was a mandatory behavior modification program in operation. These elements created a "major change in the conditions of confinement" amounting to a "grievous loss."

The Supreme Court held that before an inmate can be transferred to a mental hospital, the same due process protections that are required before civilians can be committed must be in place. This meant that inmates deserved all of the *Wolff* protections plus cross-examination. Specifically, they deserve written notice, a hearing, disclosure of evidence relied upon, an opportunity to be heard in person and present documentary evidence, an opportunity to present testimony and to confront and cross-examine witnesses (except upon a finding, not arbitrarily made, of good cause for not permitting such presentation, confrontation, or cross-examination), an independent decision maker, a written statement by a fact-finder as to evidence relied upon and reasons for transferring the inmate, legal counsel (furnished by state if indigent), and effective and timely notice of all foregoing rights.

CONCLUSION

This chapter started with a review of "access" cases, those cases that have created the right of inmates to have their grievances heard by a court. We have seen that the early sensitivity to the importance of access has dissipated. In a number of decisions, the Supreme Court has closed doors to prisoner writ writers and made their entry more difficult. The final and most troubling blow was the *Lewis v. Casey* decision, which held that only if the inmate could show specific injury or harm, could the actions of prison officials in hampering his access to the court be considered a constitutional violation. If there are situations that block or impair access to the court (such as inadequate law libraries or legal assistance), then it is hard to see how the prisoner is going to be able to get his grievance to court in the first place, much less be able to show specific harm.

In disciplinary and transfer proceedings, the Supreme Court has overturned prior decisions that recognized liberty interests could be created by statutory language. The Court has returned to the "grievous loss" analysis, as first presented in *Wolff*: however, today the Court majority seems to believe that almost any deprivation endured by prisoners should be considered "typical" and characteristic of imprisonment. Being pulled from the general population and spending 23 hours in a cell—removed from programs, educational opportunities, and certain visitation opportunities—is considered "typical," as is being sent thousands of miles away from one's family and legal counselors in the ever-increasing interstate transfers.

Today, in the Supreme Court's current "due deference" approach, prison administrators have been given broad latitude to run their prisons in the way they see fit. Although prisoners still possess certain fundamental rights (of minimal medical care, sanitation, and safety), there are few other recognized rights. Inmates may be transferred at will, sometimes across the country or to a private prison with no notice or reason. They may correspond or visit with their family, marry, practice their religion, and write or speak freely only when it has been approved by prison officials. It is obviously an overstatement to say that we have returned to a "hands off" era; however, the rational relationship test, as it is used by the courts today, rarely finds that prisoners' interests outweigh prison administrators' arguments of security or order. Perhaps that is as it should be, but observers have complained that because the courts have deferred to prison administrators, conditions have become worse. Recently, in *Brown v. Plata* (2011), the majority on the Supreme Court has evidently agreed.

WEBSITES

For more information on the ACLU Prison project, visit:
   http://www.aclu.org/prisoners-rights
For more information on the Prisoner Litigation Reform Act, visit:
   http://www.aclu.org/images/asset_upload_file79_25805.pdf
For more information on the Religious Freedom Restoration Act, visit:
   http://religiousfreedom.lib.virginia.edu/sacred/RFRA1993.html

STUDY QUESTIONS

1. Describe the hands-off era, the activist era, and the due deference era of prisoners' rights litigation.
2. Describe the source(s) of prisoners' rights.
3. Describe the Prisoners Litigation Reform Act.
4. What prisoners' rights might be recognized as coming from the First Amendment?
5. What is the test used to determine whether or not a particular religious practice must be allowed?
6. Do prisoners have any Fourth Amendment rights? Explain.
7. What prisoners' rights might be recognized as coming from the Eighth Amendment?
8. What are totality of circumstances cases?
9. What prisoners' rights might be recognized as coming from the Fourteenth Amendment?
10. Identify and describe at least five important prisoner rights cases.

❧

CHAPTER 9

Correctional Staff
and Administration

> Out in the free world, people have only two notions of how prisons are run. Some believe prisons are staffed by sadistic guards, and others believe social-worker types are in control. Both kinds can be found working in prisons, but neither has any say at all about how a prison is operated. Bureaucrats run prisons. Sadists and social workers come and go but the paper-shuffling bureaucrats endure forever. (an ex-prisoner, Martin and Sussman 1993: 101)

Up to this point, the discussion has focused on prisoners. However, three distinct groups exist in prison—the inmates, the correctional officers, and the administration. There is conflict between the "keepers" and the "kept." There is also conflict between correctional officers and the administration. In fact, as will be discussed, correctional officers report feeling more stress stemming from administration policies than they do from inmate behavior. Officers are both workers and supervisors. They are the lowest level of line staff, taking orders from everyone above them, but they are also supervisors of all inmates.

CORRECTIONAL OFFICERS

There is an inherent conflict between inmates and officers. At times, the power and authority all officers possess by virtue of their uniform is abused. Other officers, however, go out of their way to instill a bit of humanity in the prison world of violence and depersonalization. Stereotypes of correctional officers as sadistic brutes are present in books and movies and are reinforced by some works written by inmates. But the reality is, of course, much more complex.

The Changing Role of the Guard

Crouch (1995: 184), in a discussion of the changes throughout the 1970s and 1980s that affected the guard force, noted that three factors combined to change the prison world for inmates and officers alike. First, there was a new emphasis on rehabilitation that led to a loosening of the tight controls that characterized prisons in early years, as well as an expectation that officers would do more than just "lock and unlock" doors. The second factor was a change in the size and composition of the inmate population. There were more inmates entering the system and more of them had serious drug problems. Finally, judicial intervention eventually affected every policy and procedure, leading to a belief that the courts ruled the prison.

> It [legal reform] has resulted in the absolute abdication of control by the people of Texas, handing what was once their prison system to the federal courts. The civilian Board of Criminal Justice has been reduced to a political correctness monitor for a legislature that runs for cover every time a federal judge even hints that some convict may not be receiving his court-mandated gym class. (a retired and disgruntled Texas warden, Glenn 2001: 76)

These three events created role conflict and ambiguity, danger, loss of control, stress, racial and sexual integration, and deviant behavior among officers. Other factors that have changed the role of the guard include unionization, professionalism, and bureaucratization (Crouch 1995; Crouch and Marquart 1989; Johnson 1997; Irwin 1980; Silberman 1995).

It wasn't until the 1960s that there was any thought that the guard could assist in rehabilitation. With an expanded role came a different title—correctional officer. Some old-timers refused the offer, preferring to continue calling themselves guards. Even today, one hears correctional officers use the term guard as often as correctional officer. There is a definite split between the custody-oriented officer and the "professional" officer who welcomes a more diverse agenda and role.

In the 1960s and 1970s, treatment supplanted custody as the theme in many prisons and older methods of control were challenged and abandoned. Court holdings requiring due process protections for prisoners eliminated the unquestioned authority of correctional officers. Other prisoners' rights, such as to send and receive legal mail, to practice their religion, and to receive medical care, were recognized. Prison administrators rescinded strict rules of inmate movement. Ironically, curtailing "official oppression" opened the door to gangs and inmate cliques that filled the power vacuum and used violence to get what they wanted. Inmates in the 1980s had less to fear from guards but more to fear from each other as racial gangs and other powerful cliques or individuals solidified their control over prison black markets.

Mississippi, for instance, notorious for its brutality, slowly and reluctantly accommodated court orders to integrate, got rid of the trustee system, and improved physical conditions. Mississippi officers, feeling powerless and vulnerable, expressed their alienation:

> Nobody knows what to do. They [middle managers] tell you one thing one day, something else the next, and all the while you know they'll cut your balls off and save their own asses if someone in Jackson gets embarrassed or pissed off by something you do or don't do. (Taylor 1993: 217)

Correctional officers adapted to the new legal and social landscape. In the intervening years, it could be argued that the prison world changed again and some argue that the pendulum has now swung back to a time when correctional officers have very little oversight in how they control inmates.

Correctional Officers Today

There were approximately 518,000 correctional officers working in state, federal, and county facilities in 2008 (Occupational Outlook Handbook 2010-2011). In 1988, 14 percent of the guard force was women, but this percentage increased to almost 21 percent by 1997. Minority representation grew from 30.4 percent to 32.2 percent in the same years (Carlson 1999b: 186). In 2000, 33 percent of all correctional staff were women; blacks made up 19 percent, and all minorities comprised 29 percent of the correctional staff (Sourcebook of Criminal Justice Statistics 2003: 96).

The salary of correctional officers varies quite a bit from state to state. The median salary in 2008 was $38,380. The middle 50 percent earned between $29,000 and $51,000, but the lowest 10 percent of officers earned less than $23,500. Federal correctional officers earned a median of $53,459 (Occupational Outlook Handbook 2010-2011).

Officers usually also have the opportunity to make substantial overtime, sometimes up to double their salary. For instance, in the California prison system, reports indicate that some officers make over $100,000 because of overtime (Gladstone and Arax 2000; Morain 2002b). Texas officers, on the other hand, are woefully underpaid. In the early 2000s, Texas ranked 46th in pay for prison guards (Associated Press 2000a, B3; Fikae 2000; Hendricks 2000).

Qualifications for correctional officers are usually merely good health and a high-school diploma or a GED. About 24 percent of states use psychological testing to screen out inappropriate job candidates (Josi and Sechrest 1998: 7, 24). About 80 percent of states use a written civil service exam to hire correctional officers. Training of new officers ranges from a low of 17 days to a high of 16 weeks (Michigan), but the average number of training hours for new hires is about 221 hours. In these academies, officers experience training somewhat similar to law enforcement, a combination of practical how-to courses, and a sampling of sociological and psychological offerings such as communication, cultural sensitivity, criminology, and legal rights of prisoners. One training curriculum included: relevant legal knowledge, rules of the institution, administrative policies and procedures, elementary personality development, methods of counseling, self-defense tactics and use of firearms, report writing, inmate rules and regulations, inmates' rights and responsibilities, race relations, basic first aid and CPR techniques, radio communication, substance abuse awareness, and how to deal with special inmate populations like the mentally ill (Josi and Sechrest 1998: 37). About 75 percent of the states also require about 40 hours of annual in-service training for all officers (Josi and Sechrest 1998: 28).

There is about 15–25 percent turnover every year (Freeman 1999: 59; Lambert and Hogan 2009). The reasons include low pay, the nature of the job, long hours, stress, and a poor fit between person and job. Studies indicate that over two-thirds of correctional officers wished they were in a different job and their satisfaction level was lower than that of most other occupations measured (cited in Johnson 2002: 207). Burn out can lead to decreased work performance, increased absenteeism, turnover, and other negative behaviors. It is linked to job stress, which will be discussed below. Job satisfaction has been linked to support for rehabilitation, reduced absenteeism, and better performance (Cullen, et al. 1989; Lambert, Hogan, & Barton 2002).

Officers often say they are "doing time" in 8- or 10-hour installments. There is some truth to the idea that officers are the "other inmates." They spend a great deal of time inside the prison walls and must adapt to the prison world just as surely as do the inmates who live there (Lombardo 1989). What makes the analogy even more salient is the prevalence of overtime, sometimes forced or coerced overtime, so the officer may spend up to 18 hours in the prison without going home. Some prisons even have (or have had) officers' quarters that don't look all that much different from prisoners' living quarters, where officers live part time or full time if the prison is far away from their home.

"Structured Conflict"

The relationship between officers and inmates is one of structured conflict (Jacobs and Kraft 1978). This term refers to the inherent tension between the two groups arising from the role conflict of the keepers and the kept. This "structured conflict" permeates the prison and the relationship between officers and inmates. It is present in even the most cordial of relationships and influences every interaction between the two groups. It is why officers say "you can be friendly with an inmate, but you can't trust them," and why inmates, despite their surface friendliness, could never look upon an officer as a friend (Carroll 1974).

Of course, this situation varies tremendously from institution to institution, especially between institutions of different custody levels. Whereas minimum-security work camps are fairly calm, with generally non-antagonistic relationships between officers and inmates, maximum-security institutions often seethe with a high level of tension and frequent altercations between inmates and staff. Lin (2000) describes several institutions, and the general atmosphere, inmate-officer relationships, and central values of the institutions were quite strikingly different.

A so-called treatment institution had an atmosphere in which both inmates and officers felt more relaxed and trusting of each other. Of course, part of the dynamics might have been the custody level of the inmates, but part of the difference was no doubt the leadership and general culture, which did not discourage interaction. One thing is clear: prisons, even at the same custody level, can be very different institutions because of the "social climate" that is created and nurtured by a clear vision, strong leadership, and competent management.

> [at other prisons] you always had to have a mask on—you show no emotions, you be a hard convict. Antelope Valley[pseudonym]…it's the first place I've laughed or smiled since I've been in….(an inmate describing the atmosphere of a treatment-oriented prison, quoted in Lin 2000: 100)

Only a small fraction of inmates are so hostile and antagonistic to guards that they erupt in frequent outbursts and/or assaults. Likewise, only a small percentage of officers are actively abusive—either physically or psychologically—to inmates. The majority of both guards and inmates prefer to live in peace and understand that they need to treat each other with some modicum of respect to get along. Unfortunately, both feel they must take sides when conflict occurs. Inmates must support their fellow inmates and guards must support their fellow guards, regardless of how little support the individual deserves. Thus, a brutal guard may be protected by his fellows and a racist guard will not be informally or formally sanctioned. Likewise, an assaultive inmate will not be kept in check by his peer group unless his actions are perceived to hurt their interests.

> Seventy to seventy-five percent there's no problems with. Tell them to do things and they do it. They look at the CO as doing a job. But fifteen to thirty percent you have problems with regardless. They hate the world and the CO's because they deal with the CO's most frequently and the CO's represent the state. Those guys give you lots of problems with drugs, extortion and verbal abuse. They're constantly into something. (an officer quoted by Lombardo 1989: 115)

Many guards believe that other guards think all inmates are dishonest, lazy, and manipulative. This constructed reality that all inmates are scum is part of the guard subculture. Riley (2000) discusses how officers construct a reality of who they think prisoners are. This "sense-making" links belief with action and attaches meaning to ambiguous situations. Officers very quickly develop a working understanding of inmates as "untrustworthy, manipulative, and dangerous" (2000: 363). Further characteristics include immature, unpredictable, weak, perverse, and trouble for staff (2000: 371). If newcomers or others challenge this stereotype, then certain activities will be engaged in to enlighten the naïve. "Reading the record" is where the officer will provide the criminal offense sheet to prove what a "bad character" the inmate is. Yet despite this tendency to place all inmates into a category of inmate rather than treat him or her as an individual, many officers will point to one inmate and say "he's different" or "he may be like that, but he's alright because...," and the "because" may be: he's a veteran, or he comes from the same city, or he's worked with him for years.

The most productive relationships between COs and inmates are when each treats the other as an individual and understands the person, or tries to. The most unproductive, but all too common, relationship is when all officers see inmates as a group—where individual differences are not recognized. Officers are outnumbered and unarmed, and live with the constant knowledge that they may be assaulted, taken hostage, and/or killed. Because of this, inmates are perceived with suspicion, distrust, cynicism, and bitterness, especially by those officers who have been tricked and/or threatened.

As early as the 1950s, Sykes discusses the concept of reciprocity, which he used to describe the reliance officers have on inmates to help them do their job (Sykes 1956). The experts in prison operations are sometimes the inmates themselves. Some new officers learning their jobs find themselves slowly and insidiously dependent on inmates to help them learn the tasks and get things done. Before long, the inmate has become indispensable and the officer may find himself allowing special favors and rewards to the inmates who help them (Crouch 1995; Lombardo 1989). They, in effect, give up a certain amount of their power to the inmates. Reciprocity also occurs when officers accept goods and gifts from an inmate. The gift-giving may be innocuous at first. For instance, officers on a duty station may accept a cold soda on a hot day from an inmate. However, such small gifts may result in the officer doing favors for the inmate. Relationships also develop when officers come to rely on inmates to control or "keep the lid on." These relationships eventually become corrupting when inmates expect the officer to overlook their own transgressions in return for controlling others (Stojkovic 1990). Over time, the power balance shifts between officer and inmate because the officer knows the inmate could report him for numerous rule violations. Although officers are trained to avoid this type of manipulation in the training academy, the process is so slow and insidious that many officers still get trapped by the process.

Despite the inherent "structured conflict" between inmates and officers, and despite the presence of some officers who abuse their power, there is a good deal of positive interaction that occurs between officers and inmates. Because officers spend the most time with inmates, some inmates report that it is an officer who has helped them by acting as a role model or informally advised them regarding personal problems. Silberman (1995) reported in his study that inmate respondents described surprisingly positive interactions with correctional officers. Good officers are obviously invaluable in running a safe and secure facility. Their careful observations of inmates can avert riots, suicides, and assaults. Vuolo and Kruttschnitt (2008) found objective evidence that female inmates' relationships with officers was correlated with their adjustment to prison; that is, those inmates' who reported positive interactions with officers also experienced a better adjustment to prison.

> We can't solve much, but we can communicate with the inmates. I get along with them pretty well....I can get the job done....When you start out, they'll test you. I let them think they're fooling me; then I turn the tables on them to let them see where the line is. It's entertainment to them, and that's how I look at it too....(an officer, quoted from Lin 2000: 50)

The officers' interactions with inmates will depend on what type of job assignment he or she has. Some assignments have direct, all-day contact with inmates. Some have almost none at all (such as the tower officer). Job assignments may include block officer, work detail officer, transportation officer, industrial shop and school officer, yard officer, administration building officer, hospital/infirmary officer, wall post officer, and relief officer (Freeman 1997a).

Hepburn's (1985) typology of power is useful for understanding the interactions between inmates and officers. In this typology, there are several kinds of power an officer might employ to perform the functions of the role. *Legal authority* is what comes with the uniform. In other words, every officer, just by wearing his uniform, has this type of authority. *Coercive power* is the implicit power behind the uniform. If an inmate does not follow orders because the officer says so, then coercive power is always the next potential alternative. It includes taking away privileges and segregation or loss of good time, as well as the power to use brute force to move the inmate or compel him to comply. *Reward power* is the ability of officers to provide inmates with things in order to gain compliance. *Expert power* is the officer's ability to depend on some special skill, ability, or expertise. For instance, an officer supervising a work detail might possess this power because of his superior knowledge of carpentry or some other skill. Finally, *referent power* is personal authority that comes from the officer's individual personality, especially his ability to deal with inmates fairly and with respect. An officer with referent power will be able to elicit inmate compliance because of respect for that individual.

> You do have some officers that because they have a badge they're...they have the attitude...they don't treat [you] as human, you know? You're just another inmate. You're a piece of dirt. Then you have those that....give you respect if.... It's given to them. They don't...push the power of authority on you. (an inmate, reported in Vuolo and Kruttschnitt 2008: 325)

In the famous Stanford experiment young male college students were randomly assigned the role of guards or inmates. The experiment was abandoned after only six days because of the transformation of the students into brutal, sadistic "guards" who took pleasure in cruelty. About one-third of the guards became "tyrannical in their arbitrary use of power" (Zimbardo 1982: 196). The experiment illustrates the potential of the "power corrupts" truism. Although many argue that the experiment was very different from real prison in that prisons today are governed by a panoply of laws, regulations, policies, and procedures, the specter of students turning into the worst stereotypes of brutal guards is a cautionary lesson in the danger of power and how easy it is for some people to abuse that power when they receive messages from the institutional culture that it is acceptable.

The Officer Subculture

Just as one can observe a prisoner subculture consisting of values that are sometimes anti-ethical to dominant society, there is also an observable correctional officer subculture. As with the prisoner subculture, the officer subculture is formed by the needs and realities of the officers. The norms or values of the officer culture include the following:

- Always go to the aid of an officer in distress
- Never make a fellow officer look bad in front of inmates
- Always support an officer in a dispute with an inmate
- Always support another officer's sanctions against an inmate
- Show concern for fellow officers
- Don't lug drugs
- Don't be a "white hat." (sympathetic to inmates). (Kauffman 1988)

These norms promote safety and a unified front, but they also encourage a curtain of secrecy that protects those officers who exceed their authority.

Farkas (1997) found officers adhered to these important principles:

- Always go to the aid of an officer in real or perceived physical danger
- Do not get too friendly with inmates
- Do not abuse your authority with inmates
- Keep your cool
- Back your fellow officers in decisions and actions
- Do not stab a coworker in the back
- Do not admit to mistakes
- Carry your own weight
- Defer to the experience and wisdom of veteran officers
- Mind your own business.

According to Farkas, the code engenders solidarity among officers, provides meanings for their actions, and supports the officer through relationships and shared values.

Some argue that the officer culture is not monolithic. Klofas and Toch (1982; also see Toch 1981) propose that only some officers uphold those values of the officer subculture that are representative of pure custody and anti-inmate. In their view, officers are divided into the "subculture custodians," who are anti-treatment and place high value on security and control; the "supported majority," who are pro-treatment and professional; and the "lonely braves," who are pro-treatment but feel custodians overwhelm institutions and have trouble expressing support for pro-treatment initiatives. Additional evidence indicates that Klofas and Toch may be right. Officers do hold fairly supportive attitudes toward treatment. Variables that affect attitudes toward treatment in a positive direction included age, the size of town an officer came from, and race. Younger officers, officers from larger cities, and African-American and Hispanic officers are more positively oriented toward treatment. Gender, interestingly, is not found to be significant in views toward treatment in many studies (Paboojian and Teske 1997). Other studies find that correctional administrators express a fairly high degree of support for treatment as well, and perhaps higher than officers (Cullen, et al. 1993).

Farkas (1999), in a study of 125 county correctional officers, found that many officers expressed support for rehabilitation. For instance, over 70 percent disagreed with the statement "rehabilitative programs are a waste of time and money." These officers also overwhelmingly agreed that you could not trust an inmate (84 percent) and that a personal relationship with an inmate invites corruption (95 percent). Further, she found that older officers expressed greater support for a counseling orientation. This finding is inconsistent with the findings of Paboojian and Teske (1997) but consistent with those of Toch and Klofas (1982).

Britton (1997) reviewed a number of studies of correctional officers, including their adherence to the correctional officer subculture and their views toward rehabilitation and inmates. She found that most studies reported there were differences in how minority and female officers responded, although female officers were not substantively more likely to express support for rehabilitation or have higher positive regard for inmates. In Britton's own study, she found that women reported higher levels of job satisfaction than white men and that African-American men reported feeling greater efficacy in handling inmates. Further, she found that officers with more experience reported more satisfaction but also higher stress in working with inmates.

Tewksbury and Mustaine (2008) reviewed prior research, noting that there have been mixed findings regarding whether or not the factors of correctional officer gender, age, and race affect support for rehabilitation. The majority of studies do support the finding that black officers are more likely to hold favorable views of rehabilitation as are female officers (when compared to white male COs). In their study, they find that women, those with college, those who hold administrative positions, and those who have more experience are more likely to hold favorable views. These authors offer an interesting perspective on why age may show mixed results (sometimes showing a positive correlation and sometimes a negative one to support for rehabilitation). They suggest that it is not the age of the officer that is important, but, rather, the age at which he or she entered corrections. They note that officers who entered corrections in the 1970s when rehabilitation was strongly emphasized show stronger support for this ideology of corrections than those officers who were hired in the 1980s or more recently, regardless of how old they were when hired.

Interestingly, another study showed that COs' attitudes toward treatment could change after going through a training session designed to illustrate the benefits of treatment. In this study, while attitudes of treatment staff did not significantly change (because they were fairly high before the training session), custodial staff members' attitudes toward treatment changed significantly (Antonio, Young, and Wingeard 2009). This study suggests that training and management leadership can affect the level of support for programming in an institution.

The role of discretion is particularly troublesome for officers who feel "damned if they do and damned if they don't." The myriad of rules present in the prison makes it virtually impossible to enforce all of them. The officers must learn which rules are sacrosanct, which are overlooked, and which are overlooked only in some situations or by some inmates. If they make a mistake in either direction, they are vilified—by the inmates if they enforce too stringently rules that are usually ignored and by the administration if they do not enforce a rule that is viewed as more important. Sometimes, they receive informal training by officers, more often by inmates, but they also learn by trial and error. The result, of course, is a pervasive defensiveness that officers live with and learn to deal with (Conover 2000).

Stress

Prison officers have high levels of medical and social problems related to stress (Cheek and Miller 1983; Kauffman 1988; Williamson 1990). Heart disease, smoking, alcoholism, and divorce are high among officer groups. One of the major reasons for disability leave is stress-related alcoholism, cardiac problems, and emotional disorders (Gross, et al. 1994). Kamerman (1995) notes that correctional officer suicides may be at least as great a problem as law enforcement officer suicides.

Freeman (1999) reviewed the literature on correctional officer stress. He found that some reports showed higher than normal levels of stress, while others indicated that stress may be related to the period of time on the job. What possibly occurs is that some individuals are not suited for a corrections job and leave, since older officers report lower levels of stress. However, other reports indicate divorce, hypertension, and alcoholism are all elevated in correctional officer populations.

Stress is caused by the pervasive sense of danger in the prison; the lack of predictability; feeling trapped in the job; low salaries; inadequate training; an absence of standardized policies, procedures, and rules; lack of communication with management; and little participation in decision making. What is clear from the above list is that management can alleviate or exacerbate a good many of these elements. Research indicates that role conflict (conflicting orders), role overload (unreasonable expectations), and role ambiguity (lack of clear mission) lead to job stress and reduced job satisfaction (Lambert, et al. 2005). Also, other research indicates that lack of input into decision making, supervision, feedback, instrumental communication, and other factors were more predictive of role stress than individual attributes (Lambert, Hogan, and Tucker 2009).

Stohr, Lovrich, Menke, and Zupan (1994), in a survey analysis of management approach and social climate in jails, inadvertently found that jail officers reported higher levels of stress-related symptomology than did the psychiatric patient group the instrument was designed for. Personnel investment strategies (for instance, training) were related to higher job satisfaction and officers reported fewer psychosomatic stress symptoms. There was also more organizational identification and a reduction in turnover. Lambert and Paoline (2005) also reported that training was inversely linked with job stress and positively associated with job satisfaction.

Another study conducted in the federal prison system studied the effects of job autonomy and participation on job satisfaction, commitment, stress, and efficacy in working with inmates (Wright, et al. 1997). These authors found that, contrary to Diulio's (1987) argument that the best management approach for a prison was a bureaucracy with little input from staff, indexes of job satisfaction and commitment were positively correlated with a feeling of autonomy and participation in management decisions. Thus, in many surveys, it is found that officers identify stress as arising not from inmates but from management. The lack of control over rules and procedures, shift work, and a feeling of lack of support create the negative feelings officers have for prison management (Freeman 1997a).

In one study there were similar levels of stress between female and male correctional officers when using such measures as number of absences from work, number of demotions, amount of sick leave used, health outcomes (blood pressure), subjective workplace outcomes (emotional exhaustion, depersonalization, personal accomplishments), perceptions of emotional distress, and life satisfaction (Gross, et al. 1994). Other studies, however, report that female COs experience and report higher levels of stress (Dial, Downey, and Goodlin 2010; Lambert, et al. 2010).

Stress is negatively correlated with "organizational citizenship behavior (OCB)." Lambert, Hogan, and Griffin (2008) defined OCB as those behaviors performed by some employees that are above and beyond minimal job duties. It is a positive characteristic for an employee and improves the organization to have high levels of OCB. A positive correlation exists between organizational commitment and OCB. Stress, however, was negatively associated with OCB. No other individual characteristic seemed to influence the level of OCB once other factors were controlled.

The Human Service Officer

Johnson (2002) has long been an advocate of an expanded role for the correctional officer. He urges recognition of the fact that some officers are and many other officers should be encouraged to play a very positive role in the lives of inmates. The "human service" officer may be at his or her most effective simply by being honest, straightforward, and caring. Many inmates, at least in private, admit that an officer has helped them by listening, giving advice, or helping them get a phone call or a doctor's appointment.

> Here was a guy…who saw gallery work as an art, something you could per-
> form creatively. Interpersonal skills were a big part of it…[he] melded tough-
> ness with an attitude of respect for the inmates. In turn, he was respected back.
> (Conover 2000: 91)

Research shows that those guards who take on a more enriched role have greater job satisfaction (Hepburn and Knepper 1993). Further, human service orientations may come with seniority; older officers expressed more positive views toward an enriched role and more positive attitudes toward inmates in some studies (Toch and Grant 1982; Jurik 1985).

One of the changes in prison that has perhaps changed the role of the guard is that increased liberties for inmates made the guards' role less salient. Grievance counselors, ombudsmen, and other job titles usurp informal roles held by guards. This point should not be overstated, however, since there are still many ways in which the officer can help inmates.

> They get bad news letters, they stay in and brood about it. I call the service unit
> and get a "it's none of your business." We took care of all these things before the
> service unit was set up. (an officer, quoted in Lombardo 1989: 68)

Toch (1981) was one of the earliest to describe how some officers were able to utilize their position to help inmates adjust to prison and even, perhaps, move toward being a better person. These officers influenced inmates by personality and role modeling.

> He said "what about this peer pressure thing, explain that to me." So I tried to sit
> down and tell him the term and just what it meant to him and everybody else and
> he said "gee, that's very interesting, I never looked at it that way." So then we got
> talking, and we'd sit down and talk about marriage and the problems he had with
> his children and that type of thing. (an officer describing a relationship with an
> inmate, Toch 1981: 96).
>
> …since then he's been a personal friend and not a guard to me…I talk to him
> about every problem. I go to him before I'll come to a chaplain or to a sergeant or
> something. (an inmate talking about an officer, Toch 1981: 98).
>
> And it [an officer giving him advice on personal problems] bring [sic] you back
> closer to the world mentally. And when you're close to the world it makes you want

to get back there because you remember the good things that happened.... when somebody's concerned about you, you've got the natural instinct to give them something back, whether it's affection or concern. (an inmate describing how he feels about an officer who shows an interest in him and gives him advice about problems, Toch 1981: 100).

The job of the correctional officer is not an easy one. Supervising inmates, who are held in captivity against their will, requires a good deal of human relations skill. If one also aspires to help in the process of reformation, or even make the experience less debilitating, it is an even harder task. In the past several decades, officers have seen their role responsibilities change and change again. Their world was virtually turned upside down by court orders, inmate population changes, and the pressures of overcrowding. They continue to struggle to control an increasingly frustrated inmate population with inadequate programming and little innovation, and do so in some states with abysmal salaries or expectations for advancement.

VIOLENCE

Prison is a world where violence and the threat of violence are more the norm than the aberration, and officers are affected by the reality of this world just as surely as inmates. Thus, we need to revisit two forms of violence—that of inmates assaulting officers and the reverse situation, where officers assault inmates.

> I gave up trying to figure out if the inmates arrived on the row behaving like animals or if the unit made them that way. Just working in the place was degrading. The environment was charged with anger and open hatred between convicts and guards. Inmates routinely threw feces and urine at us, flooded their cells, and stopped up toilets. Officers and trusty workers—patience depleted and nerves frayed—responded with brute force. (a former officer, Cabana 1996: 81)

It appears that the high rate of inmate-on-officer assaults has decreased from the 1980s (Silberman 1995); however, the rates of inmate assaults on staff increased 27 percent from 1995 to 2000 (reported in Lahm 2009). There is an interesting difference in perspective one discovers when reading inmate authors and comparing them to penologists like Silberman (1995). As mentioned above, many prisons went through periods of excessive violence either in the late 1970s or 1980s. By the end of the 1990s, most observers noted a dramatic lessening of violence (similar to the rise and fall of criminal violence on the outside). Analysts propose that the prisons were brought under control by able administrators and good management skills (Wright 1994; Lin 2000). According to inmate authors, however, the violence was partially caused by officers and administrators who pitted races against each other and managed the prison poorly either by favoring inmate-informants or allowing incompetent and brutal guards to operate. They argue that the prisoners themselves "sorted it out" when they got tired of the violence. As in primitive societies, prisoners learned they had to control each other in order for all to live more comfortably. In this view, regardless of what administrators do, inmates still run the prison (Hassine 1999; Rolland 1997). Of course, the truth, as always, is probably a complicated shade of gray.

Light (1999) conducted an analysis of 694 incidents of assaults on guards in New York State. Findings indicated that much of violence directed toward officers was unplanned and unpredictable. Fully 25 percent of the incidents fell into the category of "unexplained." The next most frequent category was violent retaliation in response to an officer's command (13 percent). In an earlier project, Light (1991) pointed out that the deprivations of imprisonment compel inmates to resist attempts to deprive them of perceived "rights."

In one study of inmate attacks, it was found that there was an association between inmate alienation and expressions of hostility toward the staff. Those who expressed hostility toward the staff (and engaged in actual incidents of assault against officers) were also more likely to assault other inmates (Silberman 1995: 85). Another study found a correlation between a number of variables and the frequency of assaults on the staff. Prisons that reported higher numbers of staff assaults were more likely to be those with open designs; those that had a high percentage of black prisoners and young, inexperienced staff; and those with a high percentage of sex offenders. It should be noted that this was a study of the British prison system (Ditchfield and Harries 1996).

An American study collected information on 604 assault incidents in 21 state and federal prisons. After analyzing the incidents, the authors concluded that the typical assaulter was 26 years old and was 10 years younger than the victimized officer. The prisoner was almost as likely to be African-American as white and was likely to have had prior incarcerations, to be incarcerated for a violent crime, and to be serving a long sentence. The assault took place during the course of basic job tasks, such as enforcing institutional rules, giving orders, conducting searches, and supervising. Officers were likely to be assaulted with hands and feet (i.e., punch, slap, kick) and the most common injury was a back injury or a fracture. The most frequent victims of inmate assaults are officers with five to eight years of experience and between the ages of 30 and 45 (Ross 1996). In another study, inmate age (younger), security level, and aggression were the strongest predictors of assaults. Reviewing prior research, the authors noted that other factors associated with a high rate of assaults may include age of officer (younger), age of inmate (younger), experience of officer (less), ratio of white officers to inmates, crowding, level of program involvement of inmates, and security level of institution (Lahm 2009).

Officers also assault inmates. Obviously all officers may at times have to use force to subdue a violent inmate, separate two fighting inmates, or move a recalcitrant prisoner by legitimate force. It becomes assault and unlawful when the officer uses violence beyond what is necessary to accomplish the legitimate goal. In the prison world, officers have historically used physical coercion against those inmates who disrespected or assaulted officers. Crouch and Marquart (1989) described Texas "tune-ups"—abuse administered to those inmates who did not show proper respect. These incidents involved profanity, shoving, kicks, and slaps. Inmates who attacked officers were severely beaten. There is evidence to indicate that these "lessons" continue to occur in today's prisons, albeit less frequently.

In a 1994 study, 424 use-of-force reports were examined from 27 Florida prisons. The authors of this study found that most use-of-force incidents were in response to inmate fights (36 percent) or inmate disobedience (35 percent). Inmates physically resisted the guards in 42 percent of the cases. The authors then undertook a national survey and found that 60 percent of use-of-force incidents were in response to inmates fighting or disobeying orders. Note that these use-of-force incidents were almost always determined to be legitimate use of force (Henry and Senese 1994). Information on those incidents where guards' use of force was illegitimate and illegal is harder to come by.

Silberman (1995) reported that officers respect those who could dish it out to inmates and were not afraid to use violence. The use of violence has been seen as a rite of passage for officers (Marquart and Crouch 1985). "War stories" indoctrinate new officers and include stories of officers who were murdered by inmates, as well as incidents of officers beating inmates (Silberman 1995). State-sanctioned violence violates the Eighth Amendment protection against cruel and unusual punishment. There is no question that officer-on-inmate violence, undertaken to teach a lesson to a disrespectful inmate, is not only unethical but also illegal.

> The Christian in me says it's wrong, but the corrections officer in me says, "I love to make a grown man piss himself." (Charles Graner, ex-CO in Pennsylvania and military reservist, convicted in Abu Ghraib of abusing detainees. Reported in Higham and Stephens 2004: A24)

Silberman (1995) surveyed 96 inmates and none reported being abused by officers, although they did report threats and believed that such beatings occurred in segregation. These results led Silberman to conclude that officer-to-inmate violence occurs much less often today than in years past. However, Hamm, Coupez, Hoze, and Weinstein (1994) in a non-random study using inmate-surveys collected evidence of abuse across the country. Despite many prisons not allowing the surveys and others in which officers read the surveys before they were mailed, they received 605 surveys from 41 different states (for a return rate of 10 percent) (1994: 181). About 62 percent of the sample had observed physical beatings (almost 50 percent said they occurred routinely). Inmates reported that the two most frequently mentioned reasons for the abuse were being verbally abusive to guards and not following orders. The survey respondents also indicated that "jailhouse lawyers" were beaten (Hamm, et al. 1994). Although some may argue that inmates may not be the most accurate and unbiased source for such information, the trends and patterns that seemed to exist, as well as the reinforcing information from other sources (such as officers), lends credibility to the proposition that officer-on-inmate violence is neither rare nor unsupported by the officer subculture.

Special response teams or disturbance teams are the prison world's version of law enforcement SWAT teams. The stated advantages of such teams are that they result in reduced injury to officers. The action is videotaped for the protection of both inmates and officers, and highly trained officers are less likely to hurt inmates. However, others allege that abuses continue to occur. The training, uniforms, and practices of the team create a mystique among officers and inmates. In some prisons, inmates have such antipathy for team members that their identities are kept secret. This safeguard may be necessary since it has been noted that in some hostage-taking situations officers on such squads are often on "hit lists" of inmates. In actuality, when professionally run, this approach probably reduces injury for both inmate and officer. However, as stated before, we have very little information on incidents of abuse—either from a special response team or an individual officer.

MANAGING THE PRISON

Wardens used to rule their prisons out of the sight of public scrutiny. They were promoted from the guard ranks and, typically, the toughest guards became tough wardens. Today, prisons are just as likely to be administered by professionally trained managers as those who have been promoted from the ranks of officers. Administrators must now respond to a multitude of legal, political, social, and economic pressures (Carroll 1998; Freeman 1997b). Correctional administrators face a variety of pressures from the courts, officers' unions, the media, ex-prisoner and family groups, and legislators. Centralization is the trend, and the needs or unique characteristics of each prison are becoming less important in a policy of homogenization.

A well-run prison is one where inmates and officers are safe. There are productive activities for inmates, with a balance of self-improvement programs and work. There is little or no corruption on the part of officers or inmates. How close prisons come to these ideals depends, to a great extent, on the expertise and skill of the managers and the managers' ability to hire and retain good people. Carlson (1999a: 43) identifies some elements necessary to reach these goals: well-articulated policies, adequate training, compliance audits, "benchmarking" (comparing the institution to others), accreditation, identification of corruption, and strategic planning.

Wright (1994) describes how leadership can dramatically affect the management of a prison. Effective leaders are those who demonstrate their commitment, provide training and education, create a climate of change, trust staff to take responsibility, listen, share management tasks, and institutionalize feedback (Wright 1994). Further, he argues that an important aspect of management and leadership is integrity. If leaders do not provide a moral example, then they will not be effective in other areas either. Good leaders in corrections provide an institutional culture for staff through their actions and words that convey important values and missions. Staff who don't have a clear sense of where they are going and what they are doing have low morale. Wright (1994) promotes the four "c's" of management—candor, caring, commitment, and confidence.

The challenges for correctional administrators have been described as including the impact of the rehabilitative model, increasing accountability, civil service, unions, judicial intervention, legislative action and prison overcrowding, workforce diversity, the media, special needs inmates, and improving the quality of staff (Freeman 1997b: 285–294).

Unionization

Where they exist, correctional officers' unions have developed into powerful political bodies that can affect policy as management struggles to accommodate union demands for pay, benefits, and the bidding system. Correctional officers' unions tend to act as a resistant force to treatment initiatives. For instance, unions fight vigorously to defend the "bidding" system whereby senior officers get first choice over assignments. Because many, if not most, officers prefer posts away from inmates, what occurs is that officers with the least experience are left in the undesirable posts with the most inmate-officer interaction. Thus, those with the least experience are given the most difficult positions.

In the 1980s, unions became increasingly powerful in the Northeast and California. Carroll (1998) notes their power in Rhode Island. In California, the correctional officers' union has become so powerful that it is a real political force in gubernatorial races and other political contests. In the 1994 political race, the union contributed more than any other donor to Governor Wilson's campaign (Josi and Sechrest 1998). The California Correctional Peace Officers Association (CCPOA) represents over 29,000 officers and has a budget of over $17 million. In 1999, it employed 22 in-house lawyers and distributed millions in political contributions (Parenti 1999).

In other states, correctional officers often belong to the American Federation of State, County, and Municipal Employees (AFSCME). The political power of guards' unions is important because, unlike unions in the private sector, the power of guards' unions to call for a strike is limited by legislative or executive action that makes strikes by public employees illegal. The unions that can dispense large monetary contributions to members of the legislature do not need the power of the strike to affect raises and other benefits, since a legislative vote is what determines these benefits for its members.

Unions have so far been seen by researchers as a force resistant to rehabilitation and concerned only with individual benefits for members rather than the mission or goal of corrections. Unions provide legal assistance to officers in personnel and legal attacks and often support officers who, many would argue, have no business working in corrections. It should also be noted that where there are strong unions, correctional officers' pay is much higher and there is a better CO-to-inmate ratio.

Civil Service and Workforce Diversity

In the past, wardens and superintendents had absolute authority over whom they would hire and fire. Not any longer. Civil service eliminates political patronage and protects individual workers against arbitrary and biased hiring, promotion, and firing decisions. It also makes it more difficult to fire employees and tends to make it difficult to promote promising staff quickly. Although it does tend to be a barrier to quickly firing errant officers, civil service has done a great deal to protect workers from arbitrary decision making. Two groups that have benefited include minorities and women. Since the 1960s, ethnic minorities and women have entered corrections in increasing numbers. Whereas women have always worked in facilities for juveniles and women, they began to work in prisons for men starting in the 1980s.

Female Officers. Women enter corrections largely for the same reasons that men do—security and pay. Women report that they "drifted" into corrections after exploring other jobs. Female officers are in virtually all maximum-security institutions for men and in every part of those prisons. Because they are still fewer in number than male guards, women still experience some features of tokenism. Criticism of female officers in prisons for men has centered on the fact that they tend to be weaker and less able to protect themselves, that they may be subject to intimidation or seduction from inmates, and that they create sexual tension in the prison.

Evaluations of female officers in prisons for men have found that they perform their duties as well as men. Management and male officers feared that women would not be able to handle aggressive inmates, would be subject to harassment and assault, and would be co-opted by inmates (Freeman 1999). Evaluations indicated, however, that by most measuring sticks, there were few differences between male and female officers. Freeman (1997a) reports there is no statistical evidence to indicate they are more subject to assault and they write approximately the same number of misconduct reports. Some studies report that women experience more stress although others show the opposite (Zupan 1992). They exhibit significantly less intense feelings of cynical attitudes that depersonalize inmates (Gross, et al. 1994).

Some authors report that women may perform their job functions in a manner different from their male colleagues. For instance, one hypothesis is that women employ a more nurturing, "listening" style of supervision, while male staff members are more likely to employ an authoritarian, formal mode of interaction (Pollock 1995). Evidence to support such an assertion tends to be anecdotal and phenomenological, since paper-and-pencil tests of attitudes toward inmates fails to uncover any differences between male and female correctional staff. Jenne and Kersting (1996), for instance, used hypothetical situations and asked male and female officers to respond. They discovered few differences between the sexes in the use of aggression in resolving hypothetical situations. When differences were observed, they were in the opposite direction from that predicted; that is, it was female officers who were more likely to use aggressive responses.

Zimmer (1986) observed three role types emerge among female officers. The institutional role (rule-oriented, professional stance), the modified role (feared inmates, avoided contact, relied heavily on male workers for backup), and the inventive role (looked to inmates for support, expressed little fear, preferred work that involved direct inmate contact). Later observations indicated that these adaptations were not necessarily unique to women. Male officers also have a variety of adaptations to the role and some avoided inmates, while others sought them out and participated fully in the more complex nature of the treatment role offered (Johnson 1981).

Attitudinal surveys among male coworkers and inmates show that male coworkers have more resistance to female officers than male inmates do. Also, male inmates rate female officers more highly on "listening" capability but feel that female officers are less able to protect them against physical threats (Pollock 1995). Inmates indicate a generally positive regard for the entry of women as officers although not necessarily for the right reasons. Evidently female officers are perceived as "sexual objects" and make life more interesting; not all inmates appreciate them, however.

> Personally, I came to regret the existence of female guards. Being a prisoner in a world devoid of sex I would rather not even see them, because it was frustrating to be around women who were off-limits and untouchable.... For the most part, they were a reminder of what was missing, and in that regard, their mere presence was painful. (Terry in Richards, Terry, and Murphy 2002: 212)

In one study in a midwestern prison, researchers discovered that there is still a degree of male resistance to the presence of women officers. Male officers were less likely than their female counterparts to agree with a statement that "male staff accepted women as corrections officers" (47 percent to 67 percent) and also less likely to agree with the statement "most inmates accept women as corrections officers" (44 percent to 74 percent). Interestingly, however, 80 percent agreed that women "should be hired as corrections officers." Male officers were more likely than female officers to believe that female officers were in more danger than male officers (61 percent to 32 percent) and that male officers' safety is endangered when working with a female officer (37 percent to 16 percent). Only 44 percent of the male officers believed that women could control a fight between inmates (compared to 96 percent of the responding female officers), and only 52 percent of the male officers agreed that the presence of women officers improved the prison environment (compared to 89 percent of the women) (Lawrence and Mahan 1998).

Objections to female officers in prisons for men also included the fact that inmates would lose a certain amount of privacy by having opposite sex guards watching them shower and perform other private bodily functions. In most court cases, there was little sympathy for this challenge, at least when presented by male inmates arguing against the entry of female officers (see *Johnson v. Phelan* [1995]; *Timm v. Gunter* [1990]). As was discussed in a previous chapter, courts have been more sympathetic to female prisoners who argued against the entry of male corrections officers. Cross-sex supervision is evidently here to stay, but it is also a management issue that creates problems for officers and inmates alike.

Black officers. The entry of black and other minority officers into the ranks of corrections officers in large rural prisons occurred in the 1970s, when prison administrators actively sought to dispel the image that prisons were places with mostly black inmates being guarded by mostly white guards. The first minority officers were subjected to racial slurs from their white colleagues and other forms of discrimination. Initially, white officers mistrusted minority officers, believing them to be sympathetic to inmates and therefore not to be trusted. Black officers felt completely unprotected by white colleagues and depended on inmates to keep them safe (Owen 1985).

Some research indicates that neither race nor ethnicity is related to job satisfaction, although minority officers report more feelings of effectiveness in working with inmates (Wright and Saylor 1992). In another study of 2,979 correctional officers, using the Prison Social Climate Survey, it was found that race and sex did influence the officers' perception of their work environment (Britton 1997). In an interesting study on officers' perceptions of job opportunities, it was discovered there was a wide gap between black and white officers in their perceptions of the available opportunities for advancement for minority officers. The white officers perceived greater advancement opportunities for minority officers than did minority officers themselves (Camp, et al. 1997).

It is probably true that the blatant racism that correctional officers experienced in the 1960s and 1970s has been eliminated; however, more subtle evidence of discrimination may still be present in corrections. There is no indication that minority officers perform their jobs differently from white officers, but it would be helpful to have more information on how they perceive their jobs, their advancement, and their interactions with inmates.

Cross-Sex Supervision and Sexual Misconduct
In the 17th and 18th centuries female prisoners were housed together with men in jails, with predictable results. Women were raped and sexually exploited, and sold themselves for food and other goods. With the development of the Walnut Street Jail and penitentiaries, women were separated from male inmates but still guarded by men, and sexual exploitation continued. Various scandals and exposés of prostitution rings led to women's reform groups pressuring legislatures to build completely separate institutions for women in the late 1800s and early 1900s. Finally, women were guarded by women, although men often held the highest administrative positions in these institutions.

This pattern continued until the mid-1970s, when female officers challenged the hiring patterns of state prison systems that barred them from working in institutions for men. Female officers had a very constricted career path in corrections when they were only allowed in institutions for women—few could get promoted, and they often had to move great distances to the only facility in the state for women even if one for men was located in their hometown. States resisted assigning women to prisons for men because of a fear that they would be victimized, that they would have less control over the inmates, and that they would "sexually excite" the inmates, leading to disruption in the institution.

In *Dothard v. Rawlinson* (1977), the Supreme Court agreed with these fears, but only because the Alabama prison where Diane Rawlinson wanted to work had such high levels of violence that it was already under a federal monitor. The dictum of this case convinced many state systems that, despite the holding that Rawlinson could be prohibited from the Alabama prison, in most states female COs would have to be allowed in to men's prisons. And so they were, and early evaluations showed that they did their jobs about as well as male officers (Pollock 1995; Zimmer 1986; Zupan 1992). Inmates tended to appreciate the presence of women, although evaluations indicated inmates had concerns over privacy and the ability of female officers to protect them. Male officers were much more antagonistic toward their presence.

By the mid-1980s, female correctional officers could be found in most prisons for men. The ironic effect of these court cases and the entry of women into prisons for men was that male officers were no longer barred from working in prisons for women. In the early 1980s, fairly small percentages of male officers could be found in prisons for women and they were restricted to public places. Now, male officers are assigned to all posts inside prisons for women, including sleeping and shower areas. Thus, male officers again are in positions of power over women; and again, abuses are occurring, as was discussed in chapter 7.

Some estimate that as much as 19 to 45 percent of all sexual interactions in the prison involve officers (Struckman-Johnson, et al. 1996). Of course, not all instances of sexual contact between a guard and an inmate involve a male guard and a female inmate. It appears that a large portion of the staff sexual misconduct that occurs across the country involves female correctional officers and male inmates (Marquart, Barnhill, and Balshaw-Biddle 2001). Recall that in the national survey of sexual victimization, 2.8 percent of prison inmates said they had sexual contact with staff members. Half of the inmates said that the contact was consensual. Sexual activity with staff was reported by 2.9 percent of male inmates and 2.1 percent of female inmates.

Surprisingly, most victims of staff sexual misconduct were male inmates and most perpetrators were female staff members. One needs to be careful about these statistics however. In this survey, there were 39,121 male victims and 2,123 female victims of staff sexual misconduct, and 69 percent of male victims reported a female staff member perpetrator and 72 percent of women reported a male staff member perpetrator (Beck, et al. 2010: 24). Thus, while it is true that the majority of staff member perpetrators were female, one should have expected this since 97 percent of prisoners are men and most sexual activity is heterosexual. Male inmates were

twice as likely as female inmates to report no pressure or force was used (64 percent versus 30 percent). Men were also less likely to report injury (9 percent versus
19 percent), and they were less likely to report the sexual activity to authorities
(21 percent versus 35 percent) (Beck, et al. 2010: 2, 23).

> The defendant had the authority and power to write false disciplinary reports
> against [me]...without any problems and get away with it if I refused her sex-
> ual advances....(an inmate in a lawsuit complaining of sexual harassment by a
> female officer, reported in Teichner 2008: 260)

Generally, prison staff members who engage in sexual misconduct are not
prosecuted even though it is a crime in all states and there is a federal crime that
covers the Federal Bureau of Prisons. The most common punishment is firing;
followed by a forced resignation. It is important to recognize and respond to the
problem of sexual misconduct in prison and also recognize that the issue does
not only involve male correctional officers and female victims. However, it would
also be a mistake to consider the sexual victimization that takes place in men's and
women's prisons to be exactly the same, since, evidently, a much larger portion of
the sexual misconduct in men's institutions is consensual. Of course, because of
the power differential between correctional officers and inmates, consent is not
a legal defense in at least half of all states (Teichner 2008), and certainly it is not a
defense to the ethical transgression.

Corruption and Unethical Practices

Pollock (2010), McCarthy (1991), Souryal (2011), and Braswell, McCarthy, and
McCarthy (2010) provide descriptions of some ethical issues of correctional officers relating to their use of discretion and authority. Unfortunately, one does not
need to look very hard to find examples of unethical and illegal behavior on the
part of correctional workers. Trafficking in contraband, theft, warehouse sabotage,
sexual relations with inmates, bartering with inmates, assisting in escape, theft of
weapons, and brutality are a partial list of the types of unethical behaviors that
occur (McCarthy 1991). Corruption falls into abuse of power and abusing authority for personal gain (extortion, smuggling, theft).

Periodically, news stories will describe officers who committed illegal and/
or unethical acts. For instance, state prison guards have been found to "laun-
der" money for inmates, smuggle drugs into the facility, and commit other acts
(Associated Press 2000b). On Youtube.com one can find videos of officers beating inmates, caught by surveillance cameras. As mentioned in an earlier chapter,
Corcoran guards in California were accused of setting up "gladiator"-type fights
between inmates and encouraging or allowing prisoner rapes (Arax 1999a & b).
Several guards received federal indictments and were tried for the killing, as well as
the other acts of oppression. They were acquitted even though former guards and

other experts supported the inmate's allegations ("Guards Acquitted" [*New York Times*] 2000). Some argue that the officers' union "tainted" the jury pool by running television ads before the jury selection that showed officers as tough, brave, and underappreciated. The television ads, with the tagline of "Corcoran officers: they walk the toughest beat in the state," aired only in the Fresno area, where the trial was held (Lewis 1999).

Nine Florida guards were indicted in 1999 for the murder of an inmate. The inmate died from injuries, including broken ribs, swollen testicles, and innumerable cuts and bruises. He was on death row for killing a prison guard in a botched escape attempt in 1983. Prosecutors alleged he was killed because he was planning to go to the media with allegations of widespread abuse in the prison. Accused guards insisted he killed himself by flinging himself against the concrete wall of his cell. They were acquitted (Cox 2000; "Three Guards Acquitted" [*New York Times*] 2002).

It should be noted that corrupt practices are not limited to the ranks. The highest management levels have also been implicated. For instance, two high-level correctional administrators are serving time in a Florida prison after being found guilty of accepting kickbacks (over $100,000) from businessmen in return for awarding them contracts related to the prison canteen (Morgan 2010). Pollock (2010) and Carroll (1998) present other examples where investigations uncovered abuses, including sexual abuse of inmates, brutality, and bribery at the highest levels of corrections departments.

Officers have extreme difficulty when they testify against each other or in any way break the code of silence. This is very similar to the police subculture. Thus in corrections, as in law enforcement, even if only a small number of officers are engaged in illegal or unethical practices, they are protected by the large silent majority, who are afraid to come forward because of the powerful subcultural prohibitions against exposing fellow officers.

> If an incident went down, there was no one to cover my back. That's a very important lesson to learn. You need your back covered and my back wasn't covered there at all. And at one point I was in fear of being set up by guards. I was put in dangerous situations purposely. That really happened to me. (an officer, Houston 1999: 365)

To reduce corruption in corrections, there must be a concerted effort to improve hiring practices (background checks and psychological testing), institute training, and employ supervisory devices to reduce temptation and punish wrongdoers. By most accounts, law enforcement seems to be ahead of corrections in ethics training for its officers. The trickle-down theory of ethical management predicts that officers will treat inmates the way they perceive they are being treated. If they feel they are being treated with fairness, compassion, and respect, they will treat inmates in a like manner. If they feel they are being exploited, treated unfairly, and with disrespect, some will treat inmates that way. It becomes easier to justify unethical actions if one feels victimized. Furthermore, staff who are coerced into unethical or illegal actions by management are more likely to behave in unethical and illegal ways on their own initiative.

CONCLUSION

In this chapter we have shifted the focus from the inmates to those who guard them. It bears repeating that most officers are professional, effective, and even compassionate in their treatment of inmates. The problem may be that the subculture requires a closing of the ranks to protect those officers who behave corruptly and/or with brutality. There is a "structured conflict" between officers and inmates whereby there will always be inherent antagonisms between the two groups. This is moderated by characteristics of the institution, however, and management practices. Women and minority officers have entered the correctional officer force in large numbers and, similar to law enforcement, this has changed the subculture somewhat.

Management challenges include unionization, corruption, and the sexual misconduct that arises with cross-sex supervision. Management challenges also include how to house, feed, and provide adequate services to 1.6 million prisoners with a correctional guard force that is underpaid for the most part, and with issues of stress and low morale. The biggest challenge of correctional management is to create a social climate within an institution where officers feel valued and trusted. Once that is achieved, then the trickle-down effect will be that officers will treat inmates with respect. Only in this atmosphere can anything positive come out of the prison experience. It bears repeating that prisons differ. In some institutions, enthusiastic staff members are given the support necessary to create an environment where change can occur. Unfortunately, all too many institutions are simply warehouses, where disgruntled staff and bitter inmates consider it a good day when there are no serious assaults on either side.

WEBSITES

For more information on the Occupational Outlook Handbook, visit:
    http://www.bls.gov/OCO/
For information on the Stanford Prison Experiment, visit:
    http://www.prisonexp.org/
    http://www.youtube.com/watch?v=FkmQZjZSjk4
For more information on the American Correctional Association, visit:
    http://www.aca.org/
For more information on the California Correctional Peace Officers Association, visit:
    http://www.ccpoa.org/

STUDY QUESTIONS

1. In the 1970s and 1980s, what three factors combined to change the prison world for both inmates and officers?
2. Describe the concept of "structured conflict." Describe "reciprocity."
3. Describe the typology of power used in officer-inmate interactions.
4. Describe the officer subculture.
5. What are some causes of officer stress?
6. Briefly describe the "human service officer."
7. What do we know about officer-on-inmate and inmate-on-officer violence?
8. Describe the major challenges to correctional management.
9. Describe what we know about cross-sex supervision. What did evaluations show about the effectiveness of female correctional officers? How extensive is the problem of sexual misconduct?
10. What types of unethical behavior do some officers engage in?

CHAPTER 10

✦

Release, Reentry, and the Future of Prisons

> …the fight to keep my freedom had only begun. There were many reasons, but the main one was the uncertainty I had about being able to stay out of trouble and away from all those old friends and places that got me in trouble in the first place. Most of the public doesn't understand that after five and a half years in prison, those old friends and old places are the only things we remember; therefore, they are likely to call us back to them. (an inmate, in Johnson and Toch 2000: 199)

One of the most obvious facts about incarceration is that almost everyone serving a prison sentence will be released—eventually. Except for the few who will die in prison, these individuals will be released to live among us. Even those who do not favor rehabilitation should pause and reflect on the reality of this fact. An individual will exit prison either better able to face the rigors and temptations of life or less able to because of the prison sentence.

Prison does change a person. Of that there is no doubt. Whether it is positive or negative change depends on the individual's willingness and readiness to take advantage of vocational training, education, drug treatment programs, and other opportunities in prison; but partly it depends on whether or not those opportunities exist and how deeply prison has ravaged the individual's personality, self-esteem, and capacity to live with "straights".

> Getting out is a weird and alien experience.... Prison has a way of eating at your self-esteem. Upon release into the "normal" world, you find yourself feeling less and less normal every day. (an ex-prisoner, Martin and Sussman 1993: 301)

REENTRY AND RECIDIVISM

Close to 700,000 inmates are reentering communities each year. Most of them have the same low levels of education and vocational skills that they had going into prison. Many ex-offenders who have no help on the outside are released with from $20 to $200 from the state to help them get started. With that money, they are supposed to buy clothes, get a place to live, and eat while they look for work. It is no wonder that some use the money to get drunk or buy drugs. The anxiety of release is sometimes overwhelming to an individual who has, for perhaps years, been woken up, told where and when to work, and been fed and clothed by the state.

It is estimated that about 40 percent of those who are released from prison will return. Usually recidivism occurs within three years. It is reported that half of all parolees who fail do so within the first eight months of release (Clement, Schwarzfeld, and Thompson 2011: 20). In a Justice Department study, 67 percent of released inmates were charged with at least one serious crime within three years, 47 percent were reconvicted of a new crime, 25 percent were returned to prison for a new crime, and 52 percent were sent back to prison for either a new crime or technical violation. The study tracked 272,111 released inmates in 15 states. Other study findings indicated that the recidivism rate of offenders was worse than 20 years ago, not better, despite longer sentences imposed. Men were more likely to recidivate than women (68 percent compared to 57 percent), blacks were more likely to recidivate than whites (73 percent compared to 63 percent), and young people under 18 were more likely to recidivate than older offenders 45 and over (80 percent compared to 45 percent). Offenders with the highest recidivism rates included car thieves, those convicted of receipt of stolen property, burglars, and those convicted of robbery (Langan and Levin 2002). In a secondary analysis of this same data set, researchers found that the factors associated with recidivism for female offenders included number of prior arrests, age at release, and being black (Deschenes, Owen, and Crow 2007).

The Pew Center on the States released a more recent recidivism study that reported 43 percent of inmates released in 2004 and 45 percent released in 1999 were returned to prison within three years. In this study, 33 states provided recidivism information for the 1999 cohort of releasees and 41 states provided data on the 2004 releasees. There was an increase (11 percent) in the number of offenders returned to prison for new crime convictions and a 17 percent decrease in the number returned for technical violations. The Pew Center study showed that there were large differences between states in levels of recidivism, for instance 61 percent of Minnesota prisoners recidivated, but only 24 percent in Wyoming. What the numbers cannot tell us is whether the difference is due to stricter revocation policies or whether the states differ in their likelihood of releasing high-risk offenders in the first place. States varied in the percentage of those who were revoked for technical violations. For instance, about 40 percent of California's prisoners were revoked for technical violations compared to four percent in Connecticut. Changes in recidivism rates over the two study periods also differed between states. Some states increased their return-to-prison rates while other states showed a decrease (Pew Center on the States 2011).

In a recidivism study by the California Department of Corrections, it is reported that the three-year recidivism rates of California prisoners is 61 percent for first releases and 78 percent for re-releases. Women had lower recidivism rates than men and younger offenders were more likely to recidivate (CDC 2010). In this report, recidivism was measured as return to prison. Unfortunately, the research did not separate out returns for technical violations versus new convictions; however, one-year recidivism rates were displayed which showed that 47 percent of the cohort were returned to prison but only 20 percent had new convictions, so it seems that, in the year displayed, more than half were returned for technical violations (CDC 2010: iv).

In a study of women released from prison, 47 percent recidivated (however, less than half were returned to prison for new crimes, the remainder were revoked for technical violations of their parole) (Huebner, DeJong, and Cobbina 2009: 232). Forty percent of those who failed on parole did so within the first year. Similar to other research, predictors of recidivism included age, race, and education. Women with stable work histories before incarceration, those with a high school education, and those who had no indication of mental health issues were less likely to fail. Most women (81 percent) reported dependent children, and mothers were significantly less likely to fail on parole, as were those who lived with an intimate partner upon release. Women with prior convictions were more likely to fail, but type of crime was not a significant predictor, although drug use was significantly associated with failure. Institutional misconduct, length of time served, and prison program completion were not significant predictors of recidivism in this study. It should be noted that when these factors were subjected to multivariate analysis, some did not achieve statistical significance (e.g., race, having dependent children, marital status, employment, and age) (Huebner, DeJong, and Cobbina 2009).

Risk factors that have been associated with failure on community supervision include: antisocial personality patterns, pro-criminal attitudes, antisocial associates, poor use of leisure/recreation time, substance abuse, problematic home life (e.g., homelessness), and problematic work life (e.g., unemployment) (Bonta and Andrews 2010). Factors such as employment, housing, and criminal associates play a large role in recidivism.

PAROLE

There are over eight million people on parole in this country so it may be surprising to find that the use of parole has declined over the last 25 years. Prisoners do not have a right to parole unless the state creates a right to it. In *Greenholtz v. Nebraska* (1979), the U.S. Supreme Court held that inmates had no inherent liberty interest in parole. The state could create the right to parole through the language of a statute, and, if such a right is created, then there must be due process in the decision to award or not award parole. Due process is satisfied by some type of hearing; generally, this is some panel of the parole board or parole examiners. If the state does not create the right, then parole is considered a privilege, which is why states can eliminate it. Fifteen states have abolished parole and five additional states have eliminated parole for some categories of offenders (Greene and Schiraldi 2002: 19). Other states have informally cut their use of parole drastically through parole release decisions. In Texas, for instance, about 80 percent of prisoners eligible for parole received it in 1991, but by 1999, only about 20 percent of eligible prisoners received parole. Political pressure finally shifted strict parole policies so that the decision rate rose to close to 30 percent in 2000 (Fabelo 2001: 3). In 2011 it was still about 30 percent and, just as important, it appeared that the rate of revocations had declined. About 24 percent of parolees returned to prison in 2009, which is much lower than the 33 percent back in 1999 (Levin and Reddy 2011: 6).

Reduced use of parole means that prison populations back up and become bloated by the closing of the "back door". It also means that those who are released are more likely to be "maxed out," having served their full sentence. Once released, they are under no supervision or oversight at all. In fact, they may be maxed out from the super-max prisons where they have not had much of any human interaction for years, or from solitary confinement for being unable to live within the general population of the prison. They may be released from prison while under the effects of Thorazine or other anti-psychotic drugs with the admonition to seek medical assistance from a community mental health center to receive their "meds," but with no supervision to see that they do.

Many parolees go back to the same communities. These communities are characterized by high rates of joblessness, inadequate housing, chronic illness, homelessness, drug dependence, and a host of other social problems, including high rates of crime. These "million dollar blocks" (because they absorb a huge proportion of social resources) are the worst places to try to maintain a crime-free lifestyle, but they are home to many parolees. It is reported that when offenders return to these neighborhoods they have a higher re-arrest rate than those who do not, even after controlling for individual factors associated with recidivism (reported in Clement, Schwarzfeld and Thompson 2011: 49).

Inmates who are released to parole are expected to be employed, have a stable living arrangement, pay any fees or court costs associated with their conviction, and meet regularly with their parole officer. Technical violations can occur when they break any of the conditions (rules) of their parole. They can face a revocation hearing where hearing examiners (with the approval of the parole board) can revoke their parole and send them back to prison. Even though parole is considered a privilege and no inmate has a right to parole, once given it becomes a liberty interest and due process is required before it can be taken away. In *Morrissey v. Brewer* (1972), the Supreme Court held that a parolee deserved a two-stage hearing process, the first preliminary hearing should take place at the location where he lives to determine if there is enough evidence to justify a full hearing. At the full hearing, the parolee has a right to be present, to present evidence, and a qualified right to present and cross-examine witnesses (the right can be overcome by a showing of unreasonableness). Today, many parolees waive the preliminary hearing and the full hearing sometimes takes place once they are already back in prison.

One important, but overlooked, contribution to the rise of this nation's prison population has been increased parole violations and returns to prison. From 1990 to 1998, new commitments rose by 7.5 percent, but parole violation returns rose 54 percent (Butterfield 2000). The percent of new admissions to prison that are parole violators increased from 17 percent in the mid-1980s to over a third of admissions in more recent years. This is a national average and some states are much higher (Wodahl, Ogle, and Heck 2011). It is reported that successful discharges from parole rapidly declined in the middle to late 1980s, and then stabilized for a period of years and stands now at less than 50 percent (Glaze and Bonczar 2009). Completion rates (the number of parolees who complete their term of parole and regain full liberty) vary between states. Massachusetts successfully discharges about 81 percent of its parolees, but in New Hampshire only 14 percent are successfully discharged (Glaze and Bonczar 2008). Only about a quarter of parolees are sent back to prison for a new crime, the remainder have been revoked and returned to prison for technical violations (Glaze and Bonczar 2009; Wodahl, Ogle, and Heck 2011).

Graduated sanctions, rather than a return to prison, make sense despite being politically unpopular. For instance, a failed drug test could result in a mandated residential drug program; absconding could result in some type of curfew or expanded monitoring; and technical violations could require stricter monitoring. Oregon, for instance, reduced recidivism by 31 percent between 1999 and 2004 by responding to violations quickly and using graduated sanctions rather than returning parolees to prison. In Missouri, parole officers can utilize electronic monitoring, residential drug treatment, or even "shock time" in jail instead of revocation. Missouri's recidivism rate dropped from 46 percent to 36.4 percent between 2004 and 2009 (Pew Center on the States 2011).

The Urban Institute published a report on parole that offered a number of suggested strategies and policies that would reduce recidivism. They are as follows:

- Define success as recidivism reduction (not revocation).
- Tailor the conditions of supervision to the offender and make them realistic, relevant, and research based.

- Focus resources on moderate and high-risk parolees.
- Front load supervision resources (since most parolees fail in the first eight months).
- Implement earned discharge.
- Promote place-based supervision (organize caseloads by neighborhoods).
- Engage partners to expand intervention capacities.
- Assess criminogenic risk and need factors.
- Develop and implement supervision case plans that balance surveillance and treatment.
- Involve parolees to enhance their engagement in assessment, case planning, and supervision.
- Engage informal social controls to facilitate community reintegration.
Incorporate incentives and rewards into the supervision process.
- Employ graduated, problem-solving responses to violations of parole conditions in a swift and certain manner (Solomon, et al. 2008).

CIVIL LIBERTIES

One should remember that for offenders, their punishment often does not end when they leave prison. Many states suspend civil rights, such as voting—either permanently, during the course of their sentence and parole supervision, for some legislated period of time after correctional supervision has ceased, or to be granted only after the individual petitions for reinstatement.

A Harris Poll indicated that 80 percent of Americans feel ex-felons that have served their time should be allowed to vote (Richey 2002). In the last several years, several states have changed their laws to allow ex-felons to vote after completing their period of supervision, even though most still have to petition for restoration. Now 12 states bar voting by those in prison, on parole, or on probation, and some categories of offenders lose their right permanently. In other states (18) those in prison, on parole, or on probation lose their right; and, another five states restrict voting only for those in prison or on parole. Finally, in 13 states, only those in prison lose their rights and in two states (Maine and Vermont), there are no restrictions on voting (ProCon.org 2011). Observers have noted that a state like Florida, which has a very high population of blacks, can actually have elections determined by removing a large percentage of the minority population from voter eligibility. In fact, roughly a quarter of the state's black men were not allowed to vote in the Bush-Gore election, Florida's popular vote was determined by fewer than 600 votes and there were 400,000 Floridians unable to vote because of their criminal history (Cernetig 2002, A9; Richey 2002). Washington's voting restrictions on ex-felons were the subject of *Farrakhan v. Gregoire* (2010). Although a three-judge panel of the Ninth Circuit agreed that the voting restrictions placed on ex-felons violated the Voting Rights Act, upon rehearing, the full panel disagreed. Still, this case illustrates the concern that some have regarding the large numbers of minorities disenfranchised due to state laws barring voting.

Ex-felons have other civil disabilities. For instance, many states bar ex-felons from obtaining professional licenses or running certain businesses. The federal government and states bar ex-felons from possessing firearms. In some states, conviction can be grounds for termination of parental rights. Ex-felons are required to register with authorities in some states and this requirement is not just limited to sex offenders (Belbot and Hemmens 2010).

Critics argue that such civil disabilities are a clear message to ex-felons that even though they are released from prison, they are still not fully accepted back into society. What effect these restrictions have on recidivism is unknown.

BARRIERS TO SUCCESS

Why do ex-inmates recidivate? Some prisoners have the best of intentions. Yet despite exhortations that they will never come back, that they are going to stop using drugs and get a job and stay out of trouble, they end up coming back to prison. The main barriers for them in their journey out of prison are employment, housing, family adjustments, and the lure of old friends combined with the difficulties and loneliness of the outside. It has been said that the three basic needs of ex-prisoners are a place to stay, employment, and someone to believe in them (which also gives them something to lose) (Ross and Richards 2003: 3).

The National Reentry Council identified the following challenges facing those who are released from prison:

- 3 out of 4 have a substance abuse problem, but only 10 percent have received formal treatment;
- 55 percent have children under 18;
- 40 percent lack a high school diploma or GED;
- Only about 1 in 3 has received vocational training in prison;
- About 1 out of 3 has some type of physical or mental disability;
- In most states, needs outweigh available resources, for example, in California there were 10,000 homeless parolees but only 200 beds and 85,000 substance abusers and only 750 treatment beds (Reentry Policy Council 2004: 1).

Obtaining gainful, interesting employment is difficult for most of us. Having the millstone of being an ex-offender is a weight that is almost insurmountable. It should be noted that many offenders have had gainful employment before prison. Having the ex-felon status, however, makes a return to the old employment or finding new employment almost impossible, even if the ex-offender is willing to settle for less.

Inmates often have no families to return to. They may find that missions or halfway houses are the only homes they can arrange on the outside. Sometimes release plans, including housing promised by relatives, is just a sham for the paroling authorities and there is no such arrangement offered, or if it is, the ex-inmate feels compelled to leave quickly so as not to be a burden to a parent, sibling, or other relative. Federal laws have mandated that those with felony drug convictions be permanently barred from public housing. What this means is that if a man is released from prison and his wife and children are living in a low-income housing project, he cannot live with them. If he does, they will all be evicted. A released woman, attempting to regain custody of her children from foster care, may have a job but still need public housing in order to make ends meet. Because she is barred from low-income housing eligibility due to a drug conviction, she may never get her children back.

Besides employment and housing, there are very real adjustment problems facing releasees. Stresses that do not exist in prison suddenly confront them. Women can't get their children back but feel they cannot live without them. Men either can't return to their families because their wives have divorced them, or they return and find that they are unneeded, and wives and children are resentful and angry at them for being away. Parents and relatives, at first jubilant and grateful for the releasee's return, quickly move on and may vent years of stored up frustration and disappointment. The releasee's first thoughts may be to relax and "party" a little —alcohol, sex, and fun are natural and predictable as the releasee's agenda. Parole officers obviously have a different viewpoint. Single parolees are often told to have no relationships for a year, or to inform their parole officer when they begin "seeing" someone.

Female offenders have special challenges in returning to the community even though they are less likely to recidivate than men. Women form about 12 percent of all parolees. Recall that female prisoners were more likely than male prisoners to have substance abuse problems. They are also more likely to be victims of abuse. Drug programs often are not developed or adapted to their specific problems. Once released, women sometimes find themselves in community drug treatment programs or halfway houses where they are outnumbered by male offenders in ratios as high as 10 to 1. There are some reports that these environments are not conducive to treatment. Women sometimes become sexually involved with other residents, a distraction that subverts treatment goals. Some report feeling afraid of and intimidated by the surrounding men similar to their previous lives of abuse (Robbins, Martin, and Surratt 2007). Few programs have the capacity to allow children to live with female residents even though the residents are more likely to stay in a drug treatment program when they can live with their minor children (Robbins, Martin, and Surratt 2007). One research study shows that female offenders who completed a drug treatment program that included a community component (a work release therapeutic community) were more successful than those who left the program before the completion of the community phase (Robbins, Martin, and Surratt 2007).

If the preceding are barriers to success, what elements seem to be correlated with a crime-free lifestyle for ex-offenders? One of the strongest correlates is just getting older. Offenders past the age of 35 are much less likely to re-offend. Other correlates include marriage with children, job stability, and being drug free (Maruna and Toch 2002). Participating in community-based, post-release programs is associated with reduced recidivism. It is reported that community programs reduce recidivism by five to 10 percent and intensive supervision with community-based services can reduce recidivism by up to 18 percent (reported in Clement, Schwarzfeld, and Thompson 2011: 26). However, some research has indicated that while placing high-risk offenders in community corrections programs reduces their rate of recidivism, placing low-risk offenders in such placements actually increases their recidivism (Latessa, Lovins, and Smith 2010). Why this is so is puzzling, but it may be that low-risk offenders would not have associated with those who were more prone to commit future crimes except that they were living with them in halfway houses. Also, the program may have disrupted more law-abiding activities such as maintaining employment or strengthening family ties.

In the last five years the federal government has supported and encouraged programs designed to help ex-prisoners reintegrate into the community. Murphy (2002) reported that 49 states shared $100 million in federal aid for programs as part of the Serious and Violent Offender Reentry Initiative (SVORI). In a national, multi-site evaluation with a sample size of 2,391, researchers found that states provided more pre-release services to SVORI participants, and they received moderately more services than the control group after release; however, the level of services did not match offenders' self-reported needs. Despite receiving more services than non-SVORI releasees, there was no difference in the level of recidivism at 24 months; both groups had recidivism rates around 40 percent. Female SVORI participants were even more likely to be returned to prison than nonparticipants (Lattimore and Visher 2009). This unfortunate finding illustrates the difficulties of developing and implementing programs that significantly affect recidivism for serious and violent offenders.

In 2008, Congress passed the Second Chance Act (Public Law 110-199) which authorized federal grants to provide services to parolees and other releasees. Grants funded employment assistance, substance abuse and mental health treatment, housing support, family programming, mentoring, and other services. The Act also established the National Reentry Resource Center. The Bureau of Justice Assistance received about $25 million in FY2009 and $100 million in FY2010 to allocate for Reentry grants (Clement, Schwarzfeld, and Thompson 2011). In October of 2011 the House of Representatives voted to zero out the budget for the Reentry Act. The Senate has yet to make a decision and supporters are hopeful that at least some of the funds can be restored.

ENVISIONING THE PERFECT PRISON

There will always be the need for prisons. Some individuals must be kept incapacitated for the safety of the rest of us, and some individuals deserve some deprivation of liberty. Given that reality, what would a perfect prison look like? Obviously, it would be a place in which individuals maintained their humanity and, hopefully, exited better people than when they entered. At least they should be no worse. Research on staff and inmate adjustment suggest some intriguing findings that help us begin the process of envisioning the perfect prison.

The Importance of Justice

Liebling (2004) discusses the "moral performance" of a prison. This concept includes such things as safety, dignity, humanity, respect, and opportunities for personal development for staff. There is increasing evidence that indicates such concerns are not only important for staff; they also affect outcomes for prisoners. Tyler (2006, 2010) has developed the concept of justice as it impacts those in the criminal justice system. He identifies the concept of procedural justice which includes "voice" (providing opportunities to be a part of decision making), neutrality (consistent application of rules), treatment with respect and dignity, and trust in authorities. If legal authorities are seen as legitimate, and processes are considered fair, this leads to people following the law and/or rules, even without monitoring. Interestingly, this research seems to support similar findings whether one is examining citizens' probability of following the law, staff members' organizational commitment and willingness to abide by organizational rules, or inmates' willingness to follow policies and procedures in prison. Perceptions of justice may even affect success after prison.

There is research to indicate that officers who experience "organizational fairness" have higher job satisfaction and lower stress. Organizational fairness is said to include distributive justice (fair allocation of resources) and procedural justice (Lambert 2003; Lambert, Hogan, and Griffin 2007). Several studies indicate that inmates' views of procedural justice lead to feelings of legitimacy of correctional authorities, while feelings of injustice seem to affect recidivism (Jackson, et al. 2010; Rottman 2007). Inmates who believed in a "just world" expressed less anger, reported greater well-being, and were less likely to manifest problem behaviors even after controlling for criminal and personal backgrounds (Dalbert and Filke, 2007).

> Security and control—given necessities in a prison environment—only become a reality when dignity and respect are inherent in the process. (Warden James Bruton, reported in Corrections Forum 2006: 60)

In 2005, after the debacle of Abu Ghraib and the knowledge that several of the soldiers who were responsible for the abuses were prison guards in civilian life, Congress formed the Commission on Safety and Abuse in America's Prisons. This 21 member bipartisan panel explored the problems of America's prisons and issued a report after a year-long study. In Box 10.1 the final recommendations of this panel are presented. Many of the issues and suggested solutions are based on the quite simple proposition that inmates, despite their crimes, deserve to be

---

BOX 10-1

Recommendations of the Commission on Safety and Abuse in America's Prisons

Prevent Violence

1. Reduce crowding.
2. Promote productivity and rehabilitation.
3. Use objective classification and direct supervision.
4. Use force and non-lethal weaponry only as a last resort.
5. Employ surveillance technology.
6. Support community and family bonds.

Health Care

1. Partner with health providers from the community.
2. Build real partnerships within facilities.
3. Commit to caring for prisoners with mental illness.
4. Screen, test, and treat for infectious diseases.
5. End co-payments for medical care.
6. Extend Medicaid and Medicare to eligible prisoners.

Segregation

1. Make segregation a last resort and more productive form of confinement and stop releasing people directly from segregation to the streets.
2. End conditions of isolation.
3. Protect mentally ill prisoners.

Change the Culture and Enhance the Profession

1. Promote a culture of mutual respect.
2. Recruit and Retain a qualified corpus of officers.
3. Support today's leaders and cultivate the next generation.

Increase Oversight and Accountability

1. Demand independent oversight.
2. Build national non-governmental oversight.
3. Reinvigorate investigation and enforcement.
4. Increase access to the courts by reforming the PLRA.
5. Monitor practice not just policy.
6. Strengthen professional standards.
7. Develop meaningful internal complaint systems.
8. Encourage visits to facilities.
9. Strive for transparency.

Improve Knowledge and Data

1. Develop nationwide reporting.
2. Fund a national effort to learn how prisons and jails can make a larger contribution to public safety.
3. Require correctional impact statements.

SOURCE: Commission on Safety and Abuse in America's Prisons. Available from http://www. prisoncommission.org/.

treated humanely and always with the expectation that they will be returning to our communities.

Perhaps the most important element of the perfect prison, however, is that it be used rarely. We will conclude our examination of prisons by revisiting the issues brought up in chapter 2 and discuss the possibility of reducing our dependence on prisons.

CUTTING BACK ON PRISON

One of the most effective solutions to the problems of reentry is not to imprison in the first place. If an offender is punished in the community, there is no reentry issue. If prison sentences are shortened, at least the adjustment problems are minimized. It is truly a disturbing statistic that one in every 31 Americans are in prison or on probation or parole (Pew Center on the States 2011: 1). The seemingly unstoppable trend of ever-increasing numbers of people in U.S. prisons has now slowed and even been reversed in some states. Thus, it is possible to choose a different future than the path we have been on for over 20 years.

There is increasing evidence that our practice of incarceration is devastating communities. Whole neighborhoods are affected when a large percentage of their population is sent away for years at a time. Wacquant (2001) discusses the situation wherein children raised in public housing communities with razor wire and armed guards view prison as an almost inevitable part of their future. Generational effects are obvious; we know that children of inmates are six times as likely to be delinquent. More subtle effects exist as well. The economy and social fabric of a community are also affected when large numbers of young people are removed (Mauer and Chesney-Lind 2002).

> Like an overused antibiotic, it [the use of prison] has left the prisoner untreated and unchastened, the community unprotected and the whole society demonstrably worse off. (columnist William Raspberry 2002: A13)

The Prison Industrial Complex

The "prison industrial complex" refers to the massive buildup of prisons in this country and the incestuous relationship between politicians who approve the budget and those who reap the profits, similar to the military industrial complex in the Vietnam and post–Vietnam War years (Dyer 2000). The fact of the matter is that crime does pay, not necessarily for criminals, but it has been profitable for those who build and maintain prison facilities. When the stock profits of private corrections companies surge, someone is getting rich. The economic rewards of prison building act as a barrier to deinstitutionalization. Small towns will not give up their prison "factories" without a fight. Private prison profiteers, who have been contributing huge amounts of money to politicians, do not want to see crime rate decreases translate into declining incarceration rates—why would they? Politicians benefit because they are able to convince the public that they are doing something about crime. The media contributes by creating the climate of fear. The emphasis on violent crime misleads the public as to the true risk of crime in society and promotes the idea that prison is the best solution to the problem. The vast array of prison profiteers, either those in the private prison industry or the vendors who contract with prisons, certainly have everything to gain by rising prison rates.

The economics of private prisons is that desperately poor towns look at the promise of a private prison as an economic boon. They are promised jobs and contracts for everything from food to mattresses. In return, the towns and counties vying for these institutions are willing to offer free land, tax rebates, and other incentives so that they are chosen over other contenders for the right to have the prison. Many of these areas surround military bases that were closed in the federal downsizing of the 1980s and 1990s. Some towns cut out the middleman and build their own institutions. Observers note that the small rural communities that experienced an economic boost with the arrival of state or private prisons are going to fight to keep their "prison factories", even if there are fewer inmates to be housed (Rohde 2001).

A huge network of profitable enterprises has sprung up because of the "corrections industry." At the American Correctional Association, twice a year delegates are enticed to a huge ballroom or conference hall filled from front to back with vendors selling their wares. Participants pick up "freebies" of pens, water bottles, candy, and other items while they stroll the aisles and look at prison wares— everything from riot batons to stainless steel stools are displayed. High tech is represented, too. Corrections is big business and it supports an incredibly large number of ancillary businesses that provide products to state and private prisons. Even prison beds themselves are products to be sold: "prisoner brokers" are the middlemen between states or private agencies who are seeking to fill beds and states with more prisoners than beds. Evidently the profits involved in making the deals are quite substantial (Dyer 2000).

Profits seem to be even more important than security in some situations. Thirty years ago, prisoners could not use the telephone except as a very limited privilege (i.e., once a month) or because of an emergency and with a counselor's approval. Today, some prisons allow virtually unlimited calling and phones are placed in dayrooms or in the yard. Officers grumble about this and mutter darkly about courts giving inmates more rights than guards, but it isn't the courts that spur the widespread availability of telephones—it is telephone companies offering high incentives to states to allow them to provide the service, at an exorbitant cost. Prisoners must call collect and families end up paying several times more for the call than free world collect calls would be. In effect, telephone companies are gouging prisoners' families and acquiring huge profits, which they then split with the states and counties (in jails).

We are only now beginning to glimpse the social and financial costs of this institution in terms of: reduced state budgets for other spending; the alienation of whole sectors of the population; the normalization of the prison experience and the transfer of prison culture into the community; the criminogenic consequences of custody for inmates and their families and their children; and the disenfranchisement of whole sectors of the community (Garland 2001a: 2). It costs an average of $78 a day to keep someone in prison, which is 20 times what it would cost to supervise them on parole (Pew Center on the States 2011: 6). Worse, there is some evidence that imprisonment itself contributes to crime. Those states that incarcerate and then release more individuals may see the effect on levels of crime (Vieraitis, Kovandzic, and Marvell 2007).

There are good examples across the country of states that are reducing their prison populations through an array of options, including drug courts, sentencing guidelines, repealing mandatory sentencing laws, reducing security classifications, increasing the use of parole and early release options, restitution programs, and compassionate release programs for elderly prisoners (Greene and Schiraldi 2002; King and Mauer 2002a: 3). It is important to note that in the last 10 years, the 19 states that reduced the number of people in prison also experienced declines in crime (Pew Center on the States 2011: 5).

There was a flurry of such activity in the early 2000s during an economic recession when states needed to find money and bloated corrections budgets were targeted. In the last few years, because of the latest economic crisis, such alternatives to prison have also received support from the most conservative legislators looking to save money. However, as states' deficits become even more crushing, many rehabilitative programs have faced cutbacks. For instance, about 40 percent of Texas prisoners released in 2004 returned to prison, but only 24 percent of those released in 2007 recidivated. Observers noted that the reason for the decline was that Texas was heavily involved in the Justice Reinvestment Initiative supported by the National Institute of Justice, which encouraged funds to be directed to reentry programs such as intermediate sanction facilities, diversion programs for the mentally ill, and drug treatment programs. Unfortunately, such programs may be on the chopping block for the 2012–2014 budget though critics argue that the short-term savings will lead to increased numbers in prison and greater costs down the road (Clement, Schwarzfeld, and Thompson 2011; Turner 2011). Unfortunately, when states must cut spending, programs are easier to cut than the personnel or maintenance costs of prisons.

CONCLUSION

Recidivism ranges from 40 to 67 percent. There is no way one can say that prison is an effective deterrent. The challenges and barriers to success on parole are many, including employment, housing, and adjusting back into a society that may be very different from the one the ex-inmate left. For some offenders, prison, even with the violence, dehumanization, and meaninglessness, is more comfortable than life on the outside. No wonder so many find their way back.

In recent years we have seen a slight decline in the use of imprisonment. This may be the beginning of a downward trend, a plateau that will be stable for many years, or it may be a momentary blip and the incarceration rate will begin to climb again. The decision to incarcerate seems to be driven largely by politics and public support. In recent years, there has been federal support, public support, and political investment in some alternatives to prison and reentry programs to reduce recidivism. Reducing the number of people sent to prison or sent back to prison on parole revocations can free up money for other social programs.

The resistance to such a change in policy is very strong. It comes from correctional officer unions that don't want to see jobs disappear, private prison companies that don't want to see their profits decline, the thousands of companies that build facilities and/or provide goods and services to the prison industry, the public that has been indoctrinated to believe that prison will reduce crime, and politicians who don't want to seem soft on crime. "Follow the money," is an old piece of advice on how to solve a crime. It applies here, too, on the mystery of why this country seems so intent on spending more and more money to incarcerate people who are not dangerous—sacrificing education, healthcare, and other governmental services in the process.

Prison is banishment. Prison is a place from which few come out better people than when they went in. Some people belong in prison, but it should be used sparingly, with gravity, and with full knowledge that we are altering that person's life in fundamental ways. It should not be an industry because people are not products. Finally, attributed to Fyodor Dostoyevsky (1821–1881) is the saying, "The degree of civilization in a society can be judged by entering its prisons." We should question what our prisons say about us.

WEBSITES

For more information about the Justice Reinvestment Project, visit:
    www.justicereinvestment.org
For more information about the National Parole Resource Center, visit:
    http://www.nationalparoleresourcecenter.org
For more information about the National Reentry Resource Center, visit:
    http://www.nationalreentryresourcecenter.org
For more information about the National Institute of Corrections, visit:
    http://www.nicic.gov
For more information about Pew Center on the States, visit:
    http://www.pewcenteronthestates.org
For more information about the American Probation and Parole Association,
    visit:
    http://www.appa-net.org/eweb/
For more information about the Urban Institute, visit:
    http://www.urban.org.

STUDY QUESTIONS

1. When does recidivism usually occur? What are the rates of recidivism (distinguish new crimes versus technical violations)?
2. How has the use of parole changed over time?
3. What difficulties/challenges do parolees face?
4. What are some rights felons lose even after serving their sentence?
5. What are some alternatives to parole revocation?
6. What are the factors associated with recidivism? What are the factors associated with success?
7. In what ways has the federal government tried to help ex-prisoners?
8. What were the findings of the Commission on Safety and Abuse in America's Prisons?
9. What is the importance of perceptions of justice in prisons?
10. What is the prison industrial complex?

Table of Cases

Bibliography

Abbott, J. 1981. *In the Belly of the Beast*. New York: Vintage Books.

Abramsky, S. 2002. *Hard Time Blues: How Politics Built a Prison Nation*. Boston: St. Martins Press.

Adams, K. & J. Ferrandino. 2007. Managing Mentally Ill Inmates in Prisons. *Criminal Justice and Behavior*, 35, 8: 913–927.

Akers, R., N. Hayner, & W. Grunninger. 1977. "Prisonization in Five Countries." *Criminology* 14: 527–554.

Alexander, M. 2010. *The New Jim Crow: Mass Incarceration in the Age of Colorblindness*. New York: New Press.

Altman, L. 1999. "Much More AIDS in Prisons Than in General Population." *New York Times*. url: nytimes.com/library/national/science/aids/090199hth-aids-prison.html.

Amnesty International. 1999. *"Not Part of My Sentence": Violations of the Human Rights of Women in Custody*. London, England: Amnesty International.

Andrews, D., I. Zinger, R. Hoge, J. Bonta, P. Gendreau, & F. Cullen. 1990. "Does Correctional Treatment Work? A Clinically Relevant and Psychologically Informal Meta-Analysis." *Criminology* 28, 3: 369–404.

Annin, P. 1998. "Inside the New Alcatraz," *Newsweek*, July 13, 1998: 13–15.

Antonio, M., J. Young, & L. Wingeard. 2009. "When Actions and Attitude Count Most: Assessing Perceived Level of Responsibility and Support for Inmate Treatment and Rehabilitation Programs Among Correctional Employees." *The Prison Journal*, 89: 363–382.

Arax, M. 1999a. "Ex-Guard Says 4 Men Set Up Rape of Inmate." *Los Angeles Times*, October 14, 1999, A6.

Arax, M. 1999b. "Ex Guard Tells of Brutality, Code of Silence at Corcoran." *Los Angeles Times,* July 6, 1999, B4.

Archambeault, W. 2003. "Soar Like an Eagle, Dive Like a Loon," in J. Ross & S. Richards, *Convict Criminology*, pp. 287–308. Belmont, CA: Wadsworth, ITP.

Arriens, J. 1991. *Welcome to Hell*. Boston, MA: Northeastern University Press.

Associated Press. 2000a. "Prison Guards Send Plea to Bush." *Austin American Statesman*. January 11, 2000, B3.

Associated Press. 2000b. "Prison Guards Suspected of Money Laundering." *Austin American Statesman*. January 27, 2000, B3.

Associated Press. 2001. "Record Number Held in Prison. State Rise Slows." *New York Times*. Retrieved March 26, 2001 from www.nytimes.com/2001/03/26/national/26PRIS.html.

Associated Press. 2001. "New Jersey Prison Population Declined 5.4% in 2000." *New Jersey News*, August 14, 2001, A12.

Associated Press. 2011. "Man Burns House to Return to Prison Life." *Austin American Statesman*, September 26, 2011, B1.

Austin American Statesman. 2002. "Protect Prison Reforms Along with Inmates." *Austin American Statesman*, June 19, 2002, A12.

Austin, J. 1999. "Rehabilitation: Reality or Myth.". In P. Carlson and J. Garrett (eds.), *Prison and Jail Administration*, pp. 287–294. Gaithersburg, MD: Aspen Publishing Company.

Austin, J., B. Bloom & T. Donahue. 1992. *Female Offenders in the Community. An Analysis of Innovative Strategies and Programs*. Report prepared by the National Council on Crime and Delinquency. Washington, DC: National Institute of Corrections.

Austin, J., M. Bruce, L. Carroll, P. McCaul, & S. Richards. 2000. The Use of Incarceration in the U.S. National Policy White Paper. American Society of Criminology. Retrieved 9/17/2011 from http://www.acontrario.org/files/ascincarcerationdraft.pdf.

Austin, J. & J. Irwin. 2001. *It's About Time: America's Imprisonment Binge*. Belmont, CA: Wadsworth.

Bales, D. 1997. *Correctional Officer Resource Guide*. Lanham, MD: American Correctional Association.

Bales, W., L. Bedard, S. Quinn, D. Ensley, & G. Holley. 2005. "Recidivism of Public and Private State Prison Inmates in Florida." *Criminology and Public Policy* 4, 1: 57–92.

Barnes, H.E. 1987. "The Historical Origin of the Prison System in America." In K. Hall (ed.), *Police, Prison and Punishment: Major Historical Interpretations*. New York, NY: Garland Press.

Batchelor, S. 2005. "'Prove me the bam!': Victimization and Agency in the Lives of Young Women Who Commit Violent Offenses." *The Journal of Community and Criminal Justice*, 52, 4: 358–375.

Battle, C., C. Zlotnick, L. Najavits, M. Guttierrez, and C. Winsor. 2003. "Post-traumatic Stress Disorder and Substance Use Disorder Among Incarcerated Women." In P. Ouimette & P. Brown (eds.), *Trauma and Substance Abuse: Causes, Consequences, and Treatment of Co-morbid Disorders*, pp. 209–225. Washington, D.C.: American Psychological Association.

Baunach, P. 1984. *Mothers in Prison*. New Brunswick, NJ: Rutgers/Transaction Press.

Beaumont, G. & A. de Tocqueville. 1833/1964. *On the Penitentiary System in the United States and Its Application to France*. Carbondale, IL: Southern Illinois University.

Beck, A. 1995. *Profile of Jail Inmates, 1989*. Washington, D.C.: U.S. Dept. of Justice.

Beck, A. 1998. *Profile of Jail Inmates, 1996*. Washington, D.C.: U.S. Dept. of Justice.

Beck, A., P. Harrison, M. Berzofsky, R. Caspar, & C. Krebs. *Sexual Victimization in Prisons and Jails, Reported by Inmates, 2008–2009*. Washington, D.C.: Bureau of Justice Statistics, U.S. Dept. of Justice.

Beck, A. & J. Karberg. 2001. *Bureau of Justice Statistics Bulletin: Prison and Jail Inmates at Midyear 2000*. Washington D.C.: U.S. Dept. of Justice.

Beck, A., J. Karberg, & P. Harrison. 2002. *Prison and Jail Inmates at Midyear 2001*. Washington D.C.: U.S. Dept. of Justice.

Beck, A. & C. Mumola. 1999. *Bureau of Justice Statistics Bulletin: Prisoners in 1998* Washington, D.C.: U.S. Dept of Justice.

Becker, R. 1997. "The Privatization of Prisons." In J. Pollock (ed.) *Prisons: Today and Tomorrow*, pp. 382–413 . Gaithersburg, MD: Aspen Publishing Company.

Beckerman, A. 1994. "Mothers in Prison: Meeting the Prerequisite Conditions for Permanency Planning." *Social Work*, 39, 1: 9–14.

Beckett, K. & B. Western. 2001. "Governing Social Marginality," in D. Garland (ed.), *Mass Imprisonment: Social Causes and Consequences*, pp. 35–48. Thousand Oaks, CA: Sage Publishing.

Bedell, P. 1997. *Resilient Women*. Master's Thesis. Unpublished. Vermont College of Norwich University.

Belbot, B. & R. del Carmen. 1991. "AIDS in Prison: Legal Issues." *Crime & Delinquency*, 37, 1: 137.

Belbot, B. & C. Hemmens. 2010. *The Legal Rights of the Convicted*. El Paso, TX: LFB Scholarly Publishing.

Belknap, J. 2000. *The Invisible Woman*. Albany, NY: SUNY Press.

Belknap, J. 2003, "Responding to the Needs of Women Prisoners," in S. Sharp, *The Incarcerated Woman*, pp. 93–106. Upper Saddle River, NJ: Prentice-Hall.

Bennett, K. 1995. "Constitutional Issues in Cross-Gender Searches and Visual Observations of Nude Inmates by Opposite-Sex Officers: A Battle Between and Within the Sexes." *Prison Journal* 75 (1): 90–112.

Bergner, D. 1998. *God of the Rodeo: The Quest for Redemption in Louisiana's Angola Prison*. New York City: Ballantine Books.

Berk, R., H. Ladd, H. Graziano, & J. Baek. 2003. "A Randomized Experiment Testing Inmate Classification Systems." *Criminology & Public Policy* 2, 2: 215–242.

Bernstein, N. 2001. "Out of the Big House." *Salon Magazine*. Retrieved August 30, 2001 from http//www.salon.com/mwt/feature/2001/08/30/clemency_women/index.html.

Bianculli, L. 1997. "The War on Drugs: Fact, Fiction and Controversy." *Seton Hall Legislative Journal* 21: 169–200.

Blackburn, A., J. Mullings, & J. Marquart. 2008. "Sexual Assault in Prison and Beyond." *The Prison Journal*, 88, 3: 351–377.

Blakely, S. 1995. "California Program to Focus on New Mothers." *Corrections Today*. December: 128–130.

Block, K. & M. Potthast. 1997. "Living Apart and Getting Together: Inmate Mothers and Enhanced Visitation through Girl Scouts." Paper presented at Academy of Criminal Justice Sciences, March 1997.

Bloom, B. 1995. "Imprisoned Mothers." In K. Gabel and D. Johnston (eds.), *Children of Incarcerated Parents*, pp. 21–30. New York: Lexington Books.

Bloom, B., B. Owen, & S. Covington. 2003. *Gender-responsive strategies: Research, practice, and guiding principles for women offenders*. Washington D.C.: National Institute of Corrections.

Bloom, B., B. Owen, & S. Covington. 2004. "Women Offenders and the Gendered Effects of Public Policy." *Review of Policy Research*, 21: 31–48.

Bloom, B. & D. Steinhart. 1993. *Why Punish the Children? A Reappraisal of the Children of Incarcerated Mothers in America*. San Francisco: National Council on Crime and Delinquency.

Blumstein, A. & J. Wallman. 2000. *The Crime Drop in America*. New York: University Press.

Bonner, R. & A. Rich. 1990. "Psychosocial Vulnerability, Life Stress, and Suicide Ideation in a Jail Population." *Suicide and Life-Threatening Behavior* 20, 3: 213–224.

Bonta, D. & J. Andrews. 2010. *The Psychology of Criminal Conduct*, 5th Ed. Cincinnati, OH: Anderson Publishing.

Boudouris, J. 1996/1998. *Prisons and Kids*. College Park, MD: American Correctional Association.

Bourge, C. 2002. "Sparks Fly Over Private v. Public Prisons." United Press International. Retrieved February 21, 2002 from www.upi./com/view.cfm?storyID=20022002-0648 51-41221. Reprinted by Prison Policy Initiative. Retrieved 3/1/2012 from http://www.prisonpolicy.org/scans/sparksfly.shtml.

Braswell, M., B. McCarthy, & B. McCarthy. 2010. *Justice, Crime and Ethics*. Cincinnati, OH: Anderson .

Braswell, M., R. Montgomery & L. Lombardo. 1994. *Prison Violence in America*. Cincinnati, OH: Anderson.

Brennan, P. 1999. "Male and Female Prison Populations: Differential Effects of Technical Violations of Probation and Parole." Paper presented at the American Society of Criminology meeting, Toronto, Ontario, November 1999.

Breitenbecher, K. 2001. "Sexual Revictimization Among Women: A Review of the Literature Focusing on Empirical Investigations." *Aggression and Violent Behavior*, 6: 415–432.

Brewster, D. 2003. "Does Rehabilitative Justice Decrease Recidivism for Women Prisoners in Oklahoma?" in S. Sharp, *The Incarcerated Woman*, pp. 29–45. Upper Saddle River, NJ: Prentice-Hall.

Brewster, D. & S. Sharp. 2002. "Educational Programs and Recidivism in Oklahoma: Another Look." *The Prison Journal* 82, 3: 314–334.

Briggs, C., J. Sundt, & T. Castellano. 2003. "The Effect of Supermaximum Security Prisons on Aggregate Levels of Institutional Violence." *Criminology* 41, 4: 1341–1376.

Britton, D. 1997. "Perceptions of the Work Environment Among Correctional Officers: Do Race and Sex Matter?" *Criminology* 35, 1: 85–105.

Brown, J. 2002. "Aging Prison Populations Drive Up State Costs." *Stateline.org*. Retrieved 3/1/2012 from http://www.stateline.org/live/ViewPage.action?siteNodeId=136&languageId=1&contentId=14851.

Browne, A. 1987. *When Battered Women Kill*. New York: Free Press.

Browne, A., B. Miller, & E. Maguin. 1999. "Prevalence and Severity of Lifetime Physical and Sexual Victimization Among Incarcerated Women." *International Journal of Law and Psychiatry* 22, 3-4: 301–322.

Browne, D. 1989. "Incarcerated Mothers and Parenting." *Journal of Family Violence* 4, 2: 211–221.

Bryce, R. 1999. "Louder Than Words." *Salon Magazine*. Retrieved August 24, 1999 from http//www.salonmagazine.com/newsfeature/1999/08/24/texas/html.

Bureau of Prisons. 2010. *State of the Bureau* (Annual Report 2009). Washington, D.C.: U.S. Dept. of Justice. Retrieved 9/30/2011 from http://www.bop.gov/news/PDFs/sob09.pdf.

Bureau of Justice Statistics (BJS). 2000. *Correctional Populations in the U.S., 1997*. Washington, D.C.: U.S. Dept. of Justice.

Bureau of Justice Statistics. 2011. *Felony Sentences in State Courts, 2006*—Statistical Tables. Washington, D.C.: U.S. Dept. of Justice.

Bureau of Justice Statistics (BJS). 2011. Key Facts website. Retrieved various dates from http://bjs.ojp.usdoj.gov/index.cfm?ty=kftp&tid=1.

Butterfield, F. 1996. "Tough Law on Sentences is Criminal," *New York Times*, March 8, A14.

Butterfield, F. 1999. "Report Shows Jump in Number of Inmates." *San Antonio Express*, A2.

Butterfield, F. 2000. "Getting Out: A Special Report." *New York Times*, November 29, 2000.

Butterfield, F. 2001. "U.S. State Prison Population Declining in Last Half of 2000." *New York Times*, Monday, August 13, 2001, A7.

Butterfield, F. 2002a. "States Ease Sentencing Laws as Prison Numbers Rise." *Austin American Statesman*, September 2, 2001, A15.

Butterfield, F. 2002b. "Father Steals Best: Crime in an American Family." *New York Times*, Retrieved 8/15/2002 from www.nytimes.com/2002/08/21/national/21FAMI.html.

Byrne, J., & F. Taxman. 2005. "Crime (Control) is a Choice: Divergent Perspectives on the Role of Treatment in the Adult Corrections System." *Criminology and Public Policy 4*, 2: 291–310.

Cabana, D. 1996. *Death at Midnight*. Boston, MA: Northeastern Press.

California Department of Corrections and Rehabilitation. 2010. *2010 Adult Institutions Outcome Evaluation Report*. Sacramento: California Department of Corrections and Rehabilitation. Available from http://www.cdcr.ca.gov.

C.A.S.A. (Center on Addiction and Substance Abuse). 2001. *Shoveling Up: The Impact of Substance Abuse on State Budgets*. Retrieved August 14, 2002 from casacolumbia.org/publications1456/publications_show.htm?doc_id=47299.

Camp, G. & G. Camp. 1997. *The Corrections Yearbook, 1997*. South Salem, NY: Criminal Justice Institute.

Camp, S., G. Gaes, N. Langan, & W. Saylor. 2003. "The Influence of Prisons on Inmate Misconduct: A Multilevel Investigation." *Justice Quarterly 20*, 3: 501–533.

Camp, S., T. Steiger, K. Wright, W. Saylor, & E. Gilman. 1997. "Affirmative Action and the 'Level Playing Field': Comparing Perceptions of Own and Minority Job Advancement Opportunities." *Prison Journal 77*, 3: 313–334.

Carceral, K. 2005. *Prison, Inc.: A Convict Exposes Life Inside a Private Prison*. New York, NY: NYU Press.

Carlson, P. 1999a. "Management and Accountability." In P. Carlson and J. Garrett (eds.), *Prison and Jail Administration*, pp. 41–46. Gaithersburg, MD: Aspen Publishing.

Carlson, P. 1999b. "Correctional Officers Today: The Changing Face of the Workforce." In P. Carlson and J. Garrett (eds.), *Prison and Jail Administration: Practice and Theory*, pp. 183–188. Gaithersburg, MD: Aspen Publishing.

Carroll L. 1974. *Hacks, Blacks, and Cons*. Lexington, KY: Lexington Books.

Carroll, L. 1998. *Lawful Order: A Case Study of Correctional Crisis and Reform*. New York: Garland Press.

Cernetig, M. 2002. "U.S. Solidifies its Rankings as the World's Biggest Jailer." *Globe and Mail*. August 27, 2002.

Chang, T. & D. Thompkins. 2002. "Corporations Go to Prisons: The Expansion of Corporate Power in the Correctional Industry." *Labor Studies Journal*, 27, 1: 45–69.

Cheek, F. & M. Miller. 1983. "The Experience of Stress for Correction Officers: A Double-Bind Theory of Correctional Stress." *Journal of Criminal Justice* 11: 105–120.

Chen, D. 2000. "Ex-Attica Inmates Recount Shattered Lives and Dreams." *New York Times* On the Web. Retrieved 3/1/2012 from http://www.nytimes.com/2000/02/15/nyregion/ex-attica-inmates-recount-shattered-lives-and-dreams.html?pagewanted=all&src=pm.

Chesney-Lind, M. 1997. *The Female Offender: Girls, Women and Crime*. Thousand Oaks, CA: Sage.

Chesney-Lind, M. & J. Pollock. 1994. "Women's Prisons: Equality with a Vengeance." In A. Merlo and J. Pollock (eds.), *Women, Law and Social Control*, pp. 155–177. Boston, MA: Allyn and Bacon.

Chiricos, T. & C. Crawford. 1995. "Race and Imprisonment: A Contextual Assessment of the Evidence." In Darnell F. Hawkins (ed.), *Ethnicity, Race and Crime: Perspectives Across Time and Place*, pp. 281–309. Albany, NY: SUNY Press.

Clark, J., J. Austin & D. Henry. 1997. "Three Strikes and You're Out: A Review of State Legislation." Washington D.C.: National Institute of Justice. U.S. Department of Justice.

Clement, M. 1993. "Parenting in Prisons: A National Survey of Programs for Incarcerated Women." *Journal of Offender Rehabilitation* 19, 1: 89–100.

Clement, M., M. Schwarzfeld, & M. Thompson. 2011. *The National Summit on Justice Reinvestment and Public Safety*. New York: Council of State Governments Justice Center.

Clemmer, D. 1940. *The Prison Community*. Boston: Christopher Publishing.

Cole, D. 1999. *No Equal Justice: Race and Class in the American Criminal Justice System*. New York: The New Press.

Collins, M. 2002. "Prison Spending Outpaces Higher Education." *The Cincinnati Post Online*, August 28, 2002. Reprinted in Policy Matters Ohio. Retrieved 3/1/2012 from http://www.policymattersohio.org/prison-spending-outpaces-higher-ed.

Colvin, M. 1992. *The Penitentiary in Crisis: From Accommodation to Riot in New Mexico*. Albany, NY: SUNY Press.

Commission on Safety & Abuse in America's Prisons. 2006. *Confronting Confinement* Washington, DC: Commission on Safety & Abuse in America's Prisons. Retrieved 9/17/2011 from http://www.prisoncommission.org.

Common Sense for Drug Policy. 2003. CSDP Research Report: Revising the Federal Drug Control Budget Report: Changing the Methodology to Hide the Cost of the Drug War. Retrieved on 5/30/03 from www.csdp.org.

Conley, J. 1992. "The Historical Relationship Among Punishment, Incarceration and Corrections." In S. Stojkovic and R. Lovell (eds.), *Corrections: An Introduction*, pp. 33–65. Cincinnati, OH: Anderson publishing.

Conover, T. 2000. *Guarding Sing Sing*. New York: Random House.

Conrad, J. 1981. "Where There's Hope, There's Life," in D. Fogel and J. Hudson (eds.) , *Justice as Fairness: Perspectives on the Justice Model*, pp. 17–23. Cincinnati, OH: Anderson Publishing.

Corrections Alert. 1997. *Corrections Alert* 4, 25: 8.

Corrections Compendium. 2002. Prison Industries: Survey Summary. Retrieved 10/6/2011 from http://www.highbeam.com/doc/1G1-92403708.html.

Corrections Digest. 2002. "Prisons Operate Above Capacity Despite Slowest Growth in 28 Years." *Corrections Digest* 33, 15: 1–3.

Corrections Forum. 2006. Commission on Safety and Abuse in America's Prisons. Summary and Recommendations, Part 2. *Corrections Forum* 15, 5: 60–63.

Couturier, L. 1995. "Inmates Benefit from Family Services Program." *Corrections Today*, December: 100–107.

Covington, S. 2001. "Creating Gender-Responsive Programs: The Next Step for Women's Services." *Corrections Today*, 61: 85–87.

Cox, D. 2000. "Grand Jury Inquiry Into Death of Inmate Extended." *Sun-Sentinel,* January 5, 2000.

Cox, V., P. Paulus, & G. McCain. 1984. "Prison Crowding Research." *American Psychologist* 39, 10: 1148–1160.

Crouch, B. 1995. "Guard Work in Transition." In K. Haas and G. Alpert (eds.), *The Dilemmas of Corrections, Third Edition,* pp. 183–203. Prospect Heights, IL: Waveland Press.

Crouch, B. & J. Marquart. 1989. *An Appeal to Justice: Litigated Reform of Texas Prisons.* Austin, TX: University of Texas Press.

Crouch, B. & J. Marquart. 1990. "Resolving the Paradox of Reform: Litigation, Prisoners' Violence and Perceptions of Risk." *Justice Quarterly* 7: 103–122.

Crow, I. 2001. *The Treatment and Rehabilitation of Offenders.* Thousand Oaks, CA: Sage Publishing.

Cullen, F. 1982 . *Reaffirming Rehabilitation.* Cincinnati, OH: Anderson.

Cullen, F., E. Latessa, V. Burton, & L. Lombardo. 1993. "The Correctional Orientation of Prison Wardens: Is the Rehabilitative Ideal Supported?" *Criminology* 31, 1: 69–92.

Cullen, F., B. Link, J. Cullen, & N. Wolfe. 1989. "How Satisfying is Prison Work? A Comparative Occupational Approach." *Journal of Offender Counseling, Services and Rehabilitation* 14: 89–108.

Cullen, F. & C. Jonson. 2011. "Rehabilitation and Treatment Programs." In J. Wilson & J. Petersilia, *Crime and Public Policy,* pp. 293–344. New York, NY: Oxford University Press.

Cunningham, M., & J. Sorenson, J. 2006. "Actuarial Models for Assessing Prison Violence Risk: Revisions and Extensions of the Risk Assessment Scale for Prison (RASP)." *Assessment,* 13, 3: 253–265.

Dalbert, C. & E. Filke. 2007. "Belief in a Personal Just World, Justice Judgments, and Their Functions for Prisoners." *Criminal Justice and Behavior,* 34, 1516–1527.

Datesman, S. & G. Cales. 1983. "I'm Still the Same Mommy: Maintaining the Mother/Child Relationship in Prison." *Prison Journal* 63, 2: 142–154.

Davidson, R. 1974. *Chicano Prisoners: The Key to San Quentin.* Thousand Oaks, CA: Sage Publishing.

Daly, K. 1992. "Women's Pathways to Felony Court: Feminist Theories of Lawbreaking and Problems of Representation." *Southern California Review of Law and Women's Studies,* 2: 11–52.

Daly, K. 1994. *Gender, Crime, and Punishment.* New Haven, CT: Yale University Press.

Deschenes, E. & D. Anglin 1992. "Effects of Legal Supervision on Narcotic Addict Behavior: Ethnic and Gender Influences." In T. Mieczkowski (ed.) , *Drugs, Crime and Social Policy,* pp. 167–196. Needham, MA: Allyn and Bacon.

Deschenes, E., B. Owen, & J. Crow. 2007. *Recidivism Among Female Prisoners: Secondary Analysis of the 1994 BJS Recidivism Data Set.* Long Beach: California State University. Cited in: Huebner, B., C. DeJong, & J. Cobbina 2009.

Dial, K., R. Downey, & W. Goodlin. 2010. "The Job in the Joint: The Impact of Generation and Gender on Work Stress in Prison." *Journal of Criminal Justice* 38: 609–615.

DiIulio, J., Jr. 1987. *Governing Prisons: A Comparative Study of Correctional Management.* New York: Free Press.

Ditchfield, J. & R. Harries. 1996. Assaults on Staff in Male Local Prisons and Remand Centres. *Home Office Research and Statistics Directorate Research Bulletin Issue* 38: 15–20.

Ditton, P. 1999. *Mental Health and Treatment of Inmates and Probationers*. Washington, D.C.: Bureau of Justice Statistics, Dept. of Justice.

Domanick, J. 2010. "Anatomy of a Prison Crisis." *The Crime Report*. Retrieved 10/28/2010 from http://thecrimereport.org/2010/10/13/anatomy-of-a-prison-crisis/

Donaldson, S. 2001. "A Million Jockers, Punks, and Queens." In D. Sabo, T. Kupers, and W. London, *Prison Masculinities*, pp. 118–126. Philadelphia: Temple University Press.

Dorsey, T., M. Zawitz, & P. Middleton. 2002. *Bureau of Justice Statistics Bulletin: Drug and Crime Facts*. Washington, D.C.: U.S. Dept. of Justice.

Dressel, P. & S. Barnhill 1994. "Reframing Gerontological Thought and Practice: The Case of Grandmothers with Daughters in Prison." *The Gerontologist* 34, 5: 685–691.

Driscoll, D. 1985. "Mother's Day Once a Month." *Corrections Today*, August: 18–24.

Drury, A. & M. DeLisi. 2010. "The Past is Prologue: Prior Adjustment to Prison and Institutional Misconduct." *The Prison Journal*. 90, 3: 331–352.

Dumond, A. 2000. "Inmate Sexual Assault." *The Prison Journal* 80, 4: 407–414.

Durlauf, S. & D. Nagin. 2011. "Imprisonment and Crime: Can Both be Reduced?" *Criminology and Public Policy* 10, 1: 13–54.

Dyer, J. 2000. *The Perpetual Prison Machine*. Boulder, OH: Westview Press.

Early, D. 1992. *The Hot House: Life Inside Leavenworth*. New York: Bantam Books.

Eigenberg, H. 2000. "Correctional Officers' Definitions of Rape in Male Prisons." *Journal of Criminal Justice* 28, 5: 435–449.

Einat, T., & H. Einat. 2000. "Inmate Argot as an Expression of Prison Subculture: The Israeli Case." *The Prison Journal*, 80, 3, 309–325.

Eisenberg, M. 2001. *Evaluation of the Performance of the Texas Department of Criminal Justice Rehabilitation Tier Programs*. Austin, TX: Criminal Justice Policy Council. Available through website.

Ekland-Olson, S. 1986. "Crowding, Social Control and Prison Violence: Evidence from the Post-Ruiz years in Texas." *Law and Society Review* 20, 3: 389–421.

Enos, S. 2001. *Mothering From the Inside*. Albany, NY: SUNY Press.

Ewing. C., 1987. *Battered Women Who Kill*. Lexington, MA: Lexington Books.

Fabelo, T. 2001. *Texas Correctional Population Changes in Historical Perspective*. Austin, TX: Criminal Justice Policy Council.

Faith, K. 1993. *Unruly Women: The Politics of Confinement and Resistance*. Vancouver, British Columbia: Press Gang Publishing.

Farkas, M. 1997. "Normative Code Among Correctional Officers: An Exploration of Components and Functions." *Journal of Crime and Justice* 20, 1: 23–36.

Farkas, M. 1999. "Correctional Officer Attitudes Toward Inmates and Working with Inmates in a 'Get Tough' Era." *Journal of Criminal Justice* 27, 6: 495–506.

Farrabee, D. 2002. "Reexamining Martinson's Critique: A Cautionary Note for Evaluators. " *Crime & Delinquency* 48, 1: 189–192.

Fecteau, L. 1999. "Private Prisons Warned." *Albuquerque Journal*, August 27, 1999.

Feucht, T. & A. Keyser 1999. "Reducing Drug Use in Prisons: Pennsylvania's Approach." *National Institute of Justice Journal* (October) : 11–15.

Fields, G. 2001. "Mandatory Prison Time is Being Rethought." *Wall Street Journal*. August 9, 2001.

Fikae, P. 2000. "Guards Petition for Pay Increase." *San Antonio Express News*, Tuesday, Jan. 4, 2000, B1.

Flanagan, T. 1995. *Long Term Imprisonment: Policy, Science, and Correctional Practice*. Thousand Oaks, CA: Sage Publishing.

Fleisher, M. 1989. *Warehousing Violence*. Beverly Hills, CA: Sage Publishing.

Fleisher, M. & R. Rison. 1999. "Gang Management in Corrections." In P. Carlson and J. Garrett (eds.), *Prison and Jail Administration*, pp. 232–238. Gaithersburg, MD: Aspen Publishing.

Fleisher, M. & J. Krienert. 2006. *The Culture of Prison Sexual Violence*. Washington, D.C: National Institute of Justice, U.S. Dept. of Justice.

Flesher, F. 2007. "Cross Gender Supervision in Prisons and the Constitutional Right of Prisoners to Remain Free from Rape." *William and Mary Journal of Women and the Law* (Spring): 841–867.

Fletcher, B. & R. Chandler. 2007. *Principles of Drug Abuse Treatment for Criminal Justice Populations*. Washington, D.C.: National Institute on Drug Abuse, U.S. Dept. of Health and Human Services.

Fletcher, B., L. Shaver, & D. Moon. 1993. *Women Prisoners: A Forgotten Population*. Westport, CT: Praeger.

Flower, S. 2010. *Gender-Responsive Strategies for Women Offenders*. Boulder, CO: National Institute of Corrections.

Foucoult, M. 1977. *Discipline and Punish: The Birth of the Prison*. New York: Pantheon.

Fox, J. 1982. *Organizational and Racial Conflict in Maximum Security Prisons*. Lexington, MA: Lexington Books.

Fox, J. 1990. "Women in Prison: A Case Study in the Social Reality of Stress." In R. Johnson and H. Toch, *The Pains of Imprisonment*, pp. 205–220. Newbury Park, CA: Sage.

Freeman, R. 1997a. "Correctional Officers: Understudied and Misunderstood." In J. Pollock (ed.), *Prisons: Today and Tomorrow*, pp. 306–337. Gaithersburg, MD: Aspen Publishing.

Freeman, R. 1997b. "Management and Administrative Issues." In J. Pollock (ed.), *Prisons: Today and Tomorrow*, pp. 270–299. Gaithersburg, MD: Aspen Publishing.

Freeman, R. 1999. *Correctional Organization and Management: Public Policy Challenges, Behavior, and Structure*. Boston, MA: Butterworth/Heinemann Publishing Co.

Freedman, E. 1981/1986. *Their Sisters' Keepers: Women's Prison Reform in America, 1830–1930*. Ann Arbor: University of Michigan Press.

Gabel, K. & D. Johnston 1995. *Children of Incarcerated Parents*. New York: Lexington Books.

Gabrielson, R. 2011. "Voters Want Three Strikes Reform." *California Watch*, June 20, 2011. Retrieved 9/20/2011 from http://californiawatch.org/dailyreport/voters-want-3-strikes-reform-fate-ballot-initiative-unclear-10874.

Gaes, G. 2010. Cost, "Performance Studies Look at Prison Privatization." *NIJ Journal*, 259, March 2008. Retrieved 9/14/2010 from http://www.ojp.usdoj.gov/nij/journals/259/prison-privatization.htm.

Garland, D. 1990. *Punishment and Modern Society: A Study in Social Theory*. Chicago: University of Chicago Press.

Garland, D. 2001a. *Mass Imprisonment: Social Causes and Consequences*. Thousand Oaks, CA: Sage Publishing.

Garland, D. 2001b. *The Culture of Control: Crime and Social Order in Contemporary Society*. Chicago: University of Chicago Press.

Gaudin, J. 1984. "Social Work Roles and Tasks With Incarcerated Mothers." *Social Casework* 53: 279–285.

Geis, G., A. Mobley, & D. Shichor. 1999. "Private Prisons, Criminological Research and Conflict of Interest." *Crime and Delinquency* 45, 3: 372–388.

Gendreau, P. 1996. "The Principles of Effective Intervention with Offenders" in A. Harland (ed.), *Choosing Correctional Interventions that Work*, pp. 117–130. Beverly Hills, CA: Sage Publishing.

Gendreau, P. & R. Ross. 1979. "Effective Correctional Treatment: Bibliotherapy for Cynics." *Crime and Delinquency* 25: 463–489.

Gendreau, P. & R. Ross. 1980. *Effective Correctional Treatment*. Toronto: Butterworth Publishing.

Gendreau, P. & R. Ross 1989. "Revivication of Rehabilitation: Evidence from the 1980s," *Justice Quarterly* 4, 3: 349–407.

Gerber, J. & E. Fritsch. 1995. "Adult Academic and Vocational Correctional Education Programs: A Review of Recent Research," *Journal of Offender Rehabilitation* 22, 1/ 2: 119–142.

Gilbert, M. 1997. "The Illusion of Structure: A Critique of the Classical Model of Organization and the Discretionary Power of Correctional Officers." *Criminal Justice Review* 22, 1: 49–64.

Gilbreath, A. & J. Rogers 2000. "A Deadly Game," in R. Johnson and H. Toch (eds.), *Crime and Punishment: Inside Views*, pp. 183–193. Los Angeles, CA: Roxbury Press.

Gilliard, D. & A. Beck. 1994. *Prisoners in 1993*. Washington, D.C.: U.S. Dept. of Justice.

Gilliard, D. & A. Beck. 1996. *Jail Inmates in 1993*. Washington, D.C.: U.S. Dept. of Justice.

Gilliard, D. & A. Beck. 1998. *Prisoners in 1997*. Washington, D.C.: U.S. Dept. of Justice.

Gilligan, C. 1982. *In a Different Voice: Psychological Theory and Women's Development*. Cambridge, MA: Harvard University Press.

Gilligan, J. 2002. "How to Increase the Rate of Violence and Why," in T. Gray (ed.), *Exploring Corrections*, pp. 200–214. Boston: Allyn & Bacon.

Girshick, L. 1999. *No Safe Haven: Stories of Women in Prison*. Boston: Northeastern University Press.

Gladstone, M. & M. Arax. 2000. "Prisons Audit Cites Excessive Overtime Pay." *Los Angeles Times*, Thursday, January 27, 2000.

Glaser, D. 1994. "What Works and Why it is Important: A Response to Logan and Gaes." *Justice Quarterly* 11, 4: 711–723.

Glaze, L. 2010. *Correctional Populations in the United States, 2009*. Washington, D.C.: Bureau of Justice Statistics, U.S. Dept. of Justice (Retrieved 9/17/2011).

Glaze, L. & T. Bonzcar. 2007. *Probation and Parole in the United States, 2006*. Washington, D.C.: Bureau of Justice Statistics. U.S. Department of Justice.

Glaze, L. & T. Bonczar. 2008. *Probation and Parole in the United States, 2007, Statistical Tables*. Washington, D.C.: Bureau of Justice Statistics. U.S. Department of Justice.

Glaze, L. & A. Bonczar. 2009. *Probation and Parole in the United States, 2008*. Washington, D.C.: Bureau of Justice Statistics, U.S. Dept. of Justice.

Glaze, L. & L. Maruschak. 2008. *Parents in Prison and Their Minor Children*. Washington, D.C.: Bureau of Justice Statistics, U.S. Dept. of Justice.

Glenn, L. 2001. *Texas Prisons: The Largest Hotel Chain in Texas*. Austin, TX: Eakin Press.

Goldstone, J. & B. Useem. 1999. "Prison Riots as Microrevolutions: An Extension of State-Centered Theories of Revolution." *American Journal of Sociology*, 104, 4: 985–1029.

Gottschalk, M. 2006. *The Prison and the Gallows: The Politics of Mass Incarceration in America*. Cambridge: Cambridge University Press.

Gottschalk, M. 2009. "Money and Mass Incarceration: The Bad, the Mad, and Penal Reform." *Criminology & Public Policy* 8: 97–109.

Gottschalk, M. 2011. "The Great Recession and the Great Confinement: The Economic Crisis and the Future of Penal Reform." In R. Rosenfeld, K. Quinent, and C. Garcia, *Contemporary Issues in Criminological Theory and Research*, pp. 343–371. Belmont, CA: Wadsworth Publishing.

Government Accounting Office (G.A.O.). 1996. *Private and Public Prisons—Studies Comparing Operational Costs and/or Quality of Service.* Washington D.C.: U.S. Government Printing Office.

Graves, R. 2002. "War on Drugs Nets Small Time Offenders." *Houston Chronicle*, December 15, 2002, B1.

Gray, F. 1847. *Prison Discipline in America.* Boston: Little & Brown.

Greene, J. 2001. "Bailing Out Private Jails." *American Prospect* 12, 16: 23–27.

Greene, J. & V. Schiraldi. 2002. *Cutting Correctly: New State Policies for Times of Austerity.* Washington D.C.: Justice Policy Institute.

Greenfield, L. & T. Snell. 1999. *Women Offenders.* Washington, D.C.: U.S. Dept. of Justice.

Greer, K. 2000. "The Changing Nature of Interpersonal Relationships in a Women's Prison." *The Prison Journal* 80, 4: 442–468.

Grissom, B. 2011. "Budget Cuts Would Undo Prison Re-entry Reforms." Texas Tribune. com, 3/13/2011. Retrieved 9/30/2011 from http://www.texastribune.org/texas-dept-criminal-justice/texas-department-of-criminal-justice/budget-cuts-would-undo-prison-re-entry-reforms/.

Gross, G., S. Larson, G. Urban, & L. Zupan. 1994. "Gender Differences in Occupational Stress Among Correctional Officers." *American Journal of Criminal Justice* 18, 2: 219–234.

"Guards Acquitted of Staging Gladiator Fights." 2002. *New York Times*, June 10, 2000, A16.

Guerino, P., P. Harrison, & W. Sabol. 2011. *Prisoners in 2010.* Washington D.C.: Bureau of Justice Statistics, U.S. Dept. of Justice.

Guy, E., J. Platt, I. Zwerling, & S. Bullock. 1985. "Mental Health Status of Prisoners in an Urban Jail," *Criminal Justice and Behavior* 12, 1: 29–53.

Hairgrove, D. 2000. "A Single Unheard Voice." In R. Johnson and H. Toch, *Crime and Punishment: Inside Views*, pp. 147–149. Los Angeles, CA: Roxbury.

Hairston, C. 1991. "Family Ties During Imprisonment: Important to Whom and For What?" *Journal of Sociology and Welfare* 18, 1: 87–104.

Hamm, M., T. Coupez, F. Hoze, & C. Weinstein. 1994. "The Myth of Humane Imprisonment: A Critical Analysis of Severe Discipline in U.S. Maximum Security Prisons, 1945–1990." In M. Braswell, R. Montgomery, Jr., L. Lombardo (eds.), *Prison Violence in America*, pp. 167–200. Cincinnati, OH: Anderson Publishing.

Hammack, L. 2000. "Lawmakers Say Investigation of Supermax Prisons Needed." *The Roanoke Times.* February 1, 2000.

Haney, C. 2002. "Infamous Punishment: The Psychological Consequences of Isolation," in L. Alarid and P. Cromwell (eds.), *Correctional Perspectives*, pp. 101–170. Los Angeles, CA: Roxbury Press.

Haney, C. 2003. "Mental Health Issues in Long-Term Solitary and "Supermax" Confinement." *Crime & Delinquency* 49, 1: 124–156.

Haney, C. 2008. "A Culture of Harm: Taming the Dynamics of Cruelty in Supermax Prisons." *Criminal Justice And Behavior* 35, 8: 956–984.

Harding, R. 1998. "In the Belly of the Beast: A Comparison of the Evolution and Status of Prisoners' Rights in the United States and Europe." *The Georgia Journal of International and Comparative Law.* Retrieved 7/2/02 from http://web.lexisnexis.com/universe/document?_m=45fbb5ec0315e188cb3baabef7e3a9f8&.

Hardyman, P., & P. Van Voorhis. 2004. *Developing gender-specific classification systems for women offenders.* Washington, D.C.: National Institute of Corrections.

Harer, M. & D. Steffensmeier 1996. "Race and Prison Violence." *Criminology* 34, 3: 323–355.

Harland, A. 1996 . *Choosing Correctional Interventions That Work.* Beverly Hills, CA: Sage.

Harlow, C. 1999. *Selected Findings: Prior Abuse Reported by Inmates and Probationers.* Washington, D.C.: Bureau of Justice Statistics, U.S. Dept. of Justice.

Harlow, C. 2003. *Education and Correctional Populations.* Washington, D.C.: Bureau of Justice Statistics, U.S. Dept. of Justice.

Harrison, P. 1999. *Bureau of Justice Statistics: Correctional Populations in the U.S. 1998.* Washington, D.C.: U.S. Dept. of Justice.

Harrison, P. & A. Beck. 2002. *Prisoners in 2001.* Washington, D.C.: Bureau of Justice Statistics, U.S. Dept. of Justice.

Harrison, P., & J. Karberg. 2003. *Prison and Jail Inmates at Midyear 2002.* Washington D.C.: Bureau of Justice Statistics, U.S. Dept. of Justice.

Hartstone, E., H. Steadman, P. Robbins, & J. Monahan. 1999. "Identifying and Treating the Mentally Disordered Prison Inmate." In E. Hartstone, H. Steadman, and L. Teplin (eds.), *Mental Health and Criminal Justice,* pp. 279–296. Thousand Oaks, CA: Sage Publishing.

Hassine, V. 1999 (2004). *Life Without Parole: Living in Prison Today.* Los Angeles: Roxbury Publishing Company. Reprint, New York: Oxford University Press, 2010.

Haycock, J. 1991. "Capital Crimes: Suicides in Jails." *Death Studies* 15: 417–433.

Hayes, L. 1996. "Prison Suicide." *Corrections Today* 58, 1: 88–94.

Hayner, N. & E. Ash. 1940. "The Prison as a Community," *American Sociological Review* 5: 577–583.

Hemmons, C. and J. Marquart. 1998. "Fear and Loathing in the Joint: The Impact of Race and Age on Inmate Support for Prison AIDS Policies." *The Prison Journal* 78, 2: 133–151.

Hench, D. 2002. "Report Demands Prisons Change to Help Mentally Ill." *Kennebuc Journal Online,* September 25, 2002.

Hendricks, B. 1999. "Prison-Building Tied to Decade's Drop in Crime." *San Antonio Express,* Friday, February 4, 2000.

Hendricks, B. 2000. "Prisons Chief Faces Woes." *San Antonio Express News,* Wednesday, January 19, 2000.

Henriques, Z. 1996. "Imprisoned Mothers and Their Children: Separation-Reunion Syndrome Dual Impact." *Women and Criminal Justice* 8, 1: 77–97.

Henry, P. & J. Senese. 1994. "Use of Force in America's Prisons: An Overview of Current Research. *Corrections Today* 56, 4: 108–112.

Hensley, C. (ed.) 2002. *Prison Sex: Practice and Policy.* Boulder, CO: Lynne Rienner Publishers.

Hensley, C., T. Castle, & R. Tewksbury. 2003. "Inmate-to-inmate Sexual Coercion in a Prison for Women." *Journal of Offender Rehabilitation, 37,* 2: 77–87.

Hensley, C., C. Struckman-Johnson, & H. Eigenberg. 2000. "Introduction: The History of Prison Sex Research." *The Prison Journal* 80, 4: 360–367.

Hensley, C., K. Wright, R. Tewksbury, & T. Castle. 2003. "The Evolving Nature of Prison Argot and Sexual Hierarchies." *The Prison Journal* 83, 3, 289–300.

Hepburn, J. 1985. "The Exercise of Power in Coercive Organizations: A Study of Prison Guards." *Criminology* 23, 1: 146–164.

Hepburn, J. & P. Knepper. 1993. "Correctional Officers as Human Service Workers: The Effects of Job Satisfaction." *Justice Quarterly* 10, 2: 315–337.

Herivel, T. & P. Wright. 2007. *Prison profiteers: Who Makes Money from Mass Incarceration?* New York: The New Press.

Higham, S. & J. Stephens. 2004. "Punishment and Amusement." WashingtonPost.com, May 22, 2004. Retrieved 10/20/2011 from http://www.washingtonpost.com/wp-dyn/articles/A46523-2004May21.html.

Hirsch, A.J. 1992. *The Rise of the Penitentiary: Prisons and Punishment in Early America.* New Haven, CT: Yale University Press.

Hochstetler, A., D. Murphy, & R. Simons. 2004. "Damaged Goods: Exploring Predictors of Distress in Prison Inmates." *Crime & Delinquency* 50, 3: 436–457.

Hocker, C. 2002. "More Brothers in Prison Than in College?" *Blackenterprise.com*. Retrieved on 10/10/02 from http://www.blackenterprise.com/ExclusivesOpen.asp?Source=Articles/10082002ch.html.

Holman, B. 2001. *Masking the Divide: How Officially Reported Prison Statistics Distort the Racial and Ethnic Reality of Prison Growth.* Washington, D.C: National Center on Institutions and Alternatives. Retrieved 9/20/2011 from www.ncianet.org/ncia.

Holsinger, K. & A. Holsinger. 2005. "Differential pathways to violence and self-injurious behavior: African American and white girls in the juvenile justice system." *Journal of Research in Crime and Delinquency, 42*, 2: 211–242.

Houston, J. 1999. *Correctional Management: Functions, Skills, and Systems.* Chicago: Nelson-Hall Publishers.

Huebner, B., C. DeJong, & J. Cobbina. 2009. "Women Coming Home: Long-Term Patterns of Recidivism." *Justice Quarterly*, 27, 2: 225–254.

Human Rights Watch. 2000. *Punishment and Prejudice: Racial Disparities in the War on Drugs.* Available through website: www.hrw.org/reports/2000/usa/.

Human Rights Watch. 2001. *No Escape: Male Rape in U.S. Prisons.* Available through website: www.hrw.org/reports/2000/usa/.

Human Rights Watch. 2003. Ill-Equipped: U.S. Prisons and Offenders with Mental Illness. Available through website: http://www.hrw.org/en/reports/2003/10/21/ill-equipped.

Hungerford, G. 1993. *The Children of Incarcerated Mothers: An Exploratory Study of Children, Caretakers and Inmate Mothers in Ohio.* Ph.D. dissertation, Ohio State University.

Hunt, G., S. Riegel, T. Morales, & D. Waldorf. 1993. "Changes in Prison Culture: Prison Gangs and the Case of the 'Pepsi Generation.'" *Social Problems* 40, 3: 398–409.

Hunter, M. 2000. "The Sixth Commandment." In R. Johnson and H. Toch, *Crime and Punishment: Inside Views*, pp. 193–196. Los Angeles, CA: Roxbury Press.

Immarigeon, R. 1994. "When Parents Are Sent to Prison." *National Prison Project Journal* 9, 4: 5 & 14.

Inciardi, J. 1999. "Drug Treatment Behind Bars." In P. Carlson and J. Garrett (eds.). *Prison and Jail Administration,* pp. 312–320. Gaithersburg, MD: Aspen Publishing.

Inciardi, J. 2002 . *The War on Drugs, Part III.* Boston: Allyn and Bacon.

Irwin, J. 1970. *The Felon.* Englewood Cliffs, NJ: Prentice-Hall.

Irwin, J. 1980. *Prisons in Turmoil.* Boston: Little, Brown & Co.

Irwin, J. & J. Austin. 1994. *It's About Time: America's Imprisonment Binge.* Belmont, CA: Wadsworth.

Irwin, J. & D. Cressey. 1962. "Thieves, Convicts, and the Social Inmate Culture." *Social Problems* 10: 142–155.

Jackson, J., T. Tyler, B. Bradford, D. Taylor, & M. Shiner. 2010. "Legitimacy and Procedural Justice in Prisons." *Prison Service Journal*, 191, 4–6.

Jacobs, J. 1977. *Statesville: The Penitentiary in Mass Society*. Chicago: University of Chicago Press.

Jacobs, J. 1980. *Crime and Justice*. Chicago: University of Chicago Press.

Jacobs, J. & L. Kraft. 1978. "Integrating the Keepers: A Comparison of Black and White Prison Guards in Illinois." *Social Problems* 25: 304–318.

Jacobsen, M. 2005. *Downsizing Prisons*. New York: New York University Press.

James, D. & L. Glaze. 2006. *Mental Health Problems of Prison and Jail Inmates*. Washington, D.C.: Bureau of Justice Statistics, U.S. Dept. of Justice.

Jenkins, H. 1999. "Education and Vocational Training." In P. Carlson and J. Garrett. *Prison and Jail Administration,* pp. 87–93. Gaithersburg, MD: Aspen Publishing.

Jenne, D. & R. Kersting. 1996. "Aggression and Women Correctional Officers in Male Prisons." *Prison Journal* 76, 4: 442–460.

Johnson, C., C. Bina, T. Cornelius, B. Holder, T. Kennerer, & L. Larson. 2010. *From the Big House to Your House*. Charleston, SC: CreateSpace (an Amazon Affiliate).

Johnson, R. 1981. "The Complete Correctional Officer: Human Service and the Human Environment of Prison." *Criminal Justice and Behavior* 8, 3: 343–373.

Johnson, R. 1997. Race, Gender, and the American Prison: Historical Observations. In J. Pollock (ed.), *Prisons: Today and Tomorrow,* pp. 26–51. Gaithersburg, MD: Aspen Publishing..

Johnson, R. 1996/2002. *Hard Time: Understanding and Reforming the Prison*. Belmont, CA: Wadsworth Publishing.

Johnson, R. & H. Toch. 1982. *The Pains of Imprisonment*. Prospect Heights, IL: Waveland Press.

Johnson, R. & H. Toch. 2000. *Crime and Punishment: Inside Views*. Los Angeles, CA: Roxbury Press.

Johnson, S. 1999. "Mental Health Services in a Correctional Setting." In P. Carlson and J. Garrett (eds.), *Prison and Jail Administration*, pp. 107–116. Gaithersburg, MD: Aspen Publishing.

Johnston, D. 1995a. "Parent-Child Visitation in the Jail or Prison." In K. Gabel and D. Johnston. *Children of Incarcerated Parents*, pp. 135–143. New York: Lexington Books.

Johnston, D. 1995b. "Effects of Parental Incarceration." In K. Gabel and D. Johnston, *Children of Incarcerated Parents*, pp. 259–263. New York: Lexington Books.

Johnston, D. 1995c. "Intervention." In K. Gabel and D. Johnston. *Children of Incarcerated Parents* , pp. 199–232. New York: Lexington Books.

Johnston, N. 2009. "Evolving Function: Early Use of Imprisonment as Punishment." *The Prison Journal* 89, 1: 105–145.

Jones, R. 1999. "High Tech Prison Designed For 'Toughest of the Tough.'" *Milwaukee Journal Sentinel*. August 31, 1999.

Josi, D. & D. Sechrest. 1998. *The Changing Career of the Correctional Officer: Policy Implications for the 21ˢᵗ Century*. Boston: Butterworth-Heinemann.

Jurik, N. 1985. "Individual and Organizational Determinants of Correctional Officer Attitudes Toward Inmates," *Criminology* 23,3: 523–539.

Justice Policy Institute. 2010. *Money Well Spent: How Positive Social Investments Will Reduce Incarceration Rates, Improve Public Safety, and Promote the Well-Being of Communities*. (Executive Summary). Washington, D.C.: Justice Policy Institute.

Justice Policy Institute. 2011. *Gaming the System: How the Political Strategies of Private Prison Companies Promote Ineffective Incarceration Policies.* Washington, D.C.: Justice Policy Institute.

Kamerman, J. 1995. "Correctional Officer Suicide." *The Keepers' Voice* 16, 3: 7–8.

Kaplan, D., V. Schiraldi, & J. Ziedenberg. 2000. *Texas Tough? An Analysis of Incarceration and Crime Trends in the Lone Star State.* Washington D.C.: Justice Policy Institute.

Kaplan, S. 1999. "State Prison Costs Up 83% in Six Years Report Shows." *Stateline.org,* Retrieved on 3/1/2012 from http://www.stateline.org/live/ViewPage.action?siteNode Id=136&languageId=1&contentId=14612.

Kasindorf, M. 2002. "Three Strikes Laws Fall Out of Favor." *USA Today,* February 28, 2002, A1.

Kauffman, K. 1988. *Prison Officers and Their World.* Cambridge, MA: Harvard University Press.

Keeton, K. & C. Swanson. 1998 . "HIV/AIDS Education Needs Assessment." *The Prison Journal* 78, 2.

Kempker, E. 2003. "The Graying of American Prisons: Addressing the Continued Increase in Geriatric Inmates." *Corrections Compendium,* 28, 6, 1–17.

Kenis, P., P. Kruyen, J. Baaijens, & P. Barneveld. 2010. "The Prison of the Future? An Evaluation of an Innovative Prison in the Netherlands." *The Prison Journal,* 90: 313–328.

Kennedy, D. & R. Homant. 1988. "Predicting Custodial Suicides: Problems with the Use of Profiles." *Justice Quarterly* 5, 3: 441–456.

Kerbs, J. & J. Jolley. 2007. "Inmate-on-Inmate Victimization Among Older Male Prisoners." *Crime & Delinquency* 53, 2: 187–218.

Keve, P. 1991. *Prison and the American Conscience: A History of U.S. Federal Corrections.* Carbondale, IL: Southern Illinois University Press.

Keys, D. 2002. "Instrumental Sexual Scripting: An Examination of Gender-Role Fluidity in the Correctional Institution." *Journal of Contemporary Criminal Justice, 18,* 3: 258–278.

King, R. 2005. "The Effects of Supermax Custody." In A. Liebling and S. Maruna, *The Effects of Imprisonments,* pp. 112–154. Devon, UK: Willan.

King, R. & M. Mauer. 2001. *Aging Behind Bars: Three Strikes Seven Years Later.* Washington D.C: Sentencing Project. Retrieved 8/12/02 from http://www.SentencingProject.org.

King, R. & M. Mauer. 2002a. *State Sentencing and Corrections Policy in an Era of Fiscal Restraint.* Washington D.C.: Sentencing Project. Retrieved August 12, 2002 from http://www.SentencingProject.org.

King, R. & M. Mauer. 2002b. *Distorted Priorities: Drug Offenders in State Prisons.* Retrieved 9/21/02 from http://www.SentencingProject.org.

King, R., M. Mauer & T. Huling. 2003. *Big Prisons, Small Towns: Prison Economics in Rural America.* Washington, D.C.: The Sentencing Project.

Kleindienst, L. 1999. "Florida Prison Guards Twice as Likely as Police to Commit Violations." *Sun-Sentinel,* August 25, 1999.

Kleiner, C. 2002. "Breaking the Cycle." *U.S. News and World Report.* April 29: 48–51.

Klofas, J. & H. Toch. 1982. "The Guard Subculture Myth." *Journal of Research in Crime and Delinquency* 19, 2: 238–254.

Knight, K., D. Simpson, L. Chatham, & L. Camacho 1977. "An Assessment of Prison-Based Drug Treatment: Texas In Prison Therapeutic Community Programs," *Journal of Offender Rehabilitation* 2, 3/ 4: 75–100.

Kovandzic, T., J. Sloan, & L. Vieraitis. 2004. "'Striking Out' as Crime Reduction Policy: The Impact of 'Three Strikes' Laws on Crime Rates in U.S. Cities." *Justice Quarterly* 21, 2: 208–239.

Krebs, C. 2002. "High Risk HIV Transmission Behavior in Prison and the Prisoner Subculture." *The Prison Journal* 82, 1: 19–49.

Kupers, T. 1999. *Prison Madness: The Mental Health Crisis Behind Bars and What We Must Do About It.* San Francisco, CA: Jossey-Bass Publishing.

Kupers, T. 2001. "Rape and the Prison Code." In D. Sabo, T. Kupers, and W. London, *Prison Masculinities,* pp. 111–117. Philadelphia, PA: Temple University Press.

Lahm, K. 2008. "Inmate-on-Inmate Assault: A Multilevel Examination of Prison Violence." *Criminal Justice and Behavior* 35, 1: 120–137.

Lahm, K. 2009. Overlooked Form of Prison Violence: Inmate Assaults on Prison Staff: A Multilevel Examination. *The Prison Journal* 89, 2: 139–150.

Lambert, E. 2003. "Justice in Corrections: An Exploratory Study of the Impact of Organizational Justice on Correctional Staff." *Journal of Criminal Justice* 31: 155–168.

Lambert, E. & N. Hogan. 2009. "The Importance of Job Satisfaction and Organizational Commitment in Shaping Turnover Intent: A Test of a Causal Model." *Criminal Justice Review* 34: 96–118.

Lambert, E., N. Hogan, I. Altheimer, & J. Wareham. 2010. "The Effects of Different Aspects of Supervision Among Female and Male Correctional Staff: A Preliminary Study." *Criminal Justice Review,* 35, 4, 492–513.

Lambert, E., N. Hogan, & S. Barton. 2002. "Satisfied Correctional Staff: A Review of the Literature on the Antecedents and Consequences of Correctional Staff Job Satisfaction." *Criminal Justice and Behavior* 29: 115–143.

Lambert, E., N. Hogan, & M. Griffin. 2008. "Being the Good Soldier: Organizational Citizenship Behavior and Commitment Among Correctional Staff." *Criminal Justice and Behavior* 35, 1: 56–68.

Lambert, E. N. Hogan, & M. Griffin. 2007. "The Impact of Distributive and Procedural Justice on Correctional Staff Job Stress, Job Satisfaction, and Organizational Commitment." *Journal of Criminal Justice* 35: 644–656.

Lambert, E., N. Hogan, E. Paoline, & A. Clarke. 2005. "The Impact of Role Stressors on Job Stress, Job Satisfaction, and Organizational Commitment Among Private Prison Staff." *Security Journal* 18: 33–50.

Lambert, E., N. Hogan, & K. Tucker. 2009. "Problems at Work: Exploring the Correlates of Role Stress Among Correctional Staff." *The Prison Journal,* 89, 4: 460–481.

Lambert, E. & E. Paoline. 2005. "The Impact of Jail Medical Issues on the Job Stress and Job Satisfaction of Jail Staff: An Exploratory Study." *Punishment and Society: The International Journal of Penology* 7: 259–275.

Langan, P. & D. Levin. 2002. *Recidivism of Prisoners Released in 1994.* Washington D.C.: Bureau of Justice Statistics, U.S. Dept. of Justice.

Lanza-Kaduce, L., K. Parker, & C. Thomas. 1999. "A Comparative Recidivism Analysis of Releasees From Private and Public Prisons." *Crime and Delinquency* 45, 1: 28–47.

Latessa, E. & H. Allen. 1999. *Corrections in the Community.* Cincinnati, OH: Anderson.

Latessa, E., F. Cullen, & P. Gendreau. 2002. "Beyond Correctional Quakery-Professionalism and the Possibility of Effective Treatment." *Federal Probation* 66, 2: 43–39.

Latessa, E., A. Holsinger, J. Marquart, & J. Sorenson 2001. *Correctional Contexts: Contemporary and Classical Readings.* Los Angeles, CA: Roxbury Press.

Latessa, E., L. Lovins, & P. Smith. 2010. *Follow-up Evaluation of Ohio's Community Based Correctional Facility and Halfway House Programs-Outcome Study*. Cincinnati, OH: University of Cincinnati Center for Criminal Justice Research. Cited in, Clement, Schwarzfelt, and Thompson, 2011.

Lattimore, P. & C. Visher. 2009. *The Multi-site Evaluation of SVORI: Summary and Synthesis*. Washington D.C: National Institute of Justice. Retrieved 10/21/2011 from https://www.ncjrs.gov/pdffiles1/nij/grants/230421.pdf.

Lawrence, R. & S. Mahan. 1998. "Women Corrections Officers in Men's Prisons: Acceptance and Perceived Job Performance." *Women & Criminal Justice* 9, 3: 63–86.

Lawrence, S., D. Mears, G. Dubin, & J. Travis. 2002. *The Practice and Promise of Prison Programming*. Washington, D.C.: Urban Institute.

Lawrence, S. & J. Travis. 2004. *The New Landscape of Imprisonment: Mapping America's Prison Expansion*. Washington, D.C.: Justice Policy Center, Urban Institute.

Leary, W. 2000. "Violent Crime Continues to Decline." *New York Times*. Retrieved August 28, 2000 from www.nytimes.com/library/national/082800crime-rate.html.

Leduff, C. & A. Liptak 2002. "Defiant California City Hands Out Marijuana. *New York Times*. September 18, 2002 Retrieved 3/1/2012 from http://www.nytimes.com/2002/09/18/us/defiant-california-city-hands-out-marijuana.html?pagewanted=all&src=pm.

Lerner, J. 2002. *You've Got Nothing Coming: Notes From a Prison Fish*. New York City: Broadway Books.

Levin, M. & V. Reddy. 2011. *The Role of Parole in Texas*. Austin, TX: Texas Public Policy Foundation, Center for Effective Justice.

Lewis, M. 1999. "Corcoran Guards Launch Ads." *Fresno Bee*. September 17, 1999, A1.

Liebling, A. (2004). *Prisons and their Moral Performance: A Study of Values, Quality and Prison Life*. Oxford, England: Oxford University Press.

Light, S. 1991. "Assaults on Prison Officers: Interactional Themes." *Justice Quarterly* 8, 2: 242–261.

Light, S. 1999. "Assaults on Prison Officers: Interactional Themes." In M. Braswell, R. Montgomery, Jr., L. Lombardo (eds.), *Prison Violence in America*, pp. 207–223. Cincinnati, OH: Anderson.

Lin, A. 2000. *Reform in the Making: The Implementation of Social Policy in Prison*. Princeton, NJ: Princeton University Press.

Lock, E., J. Timberlake, & K. Rasinki. 2002. "Battle Fatigue: Is Public Support Waning for War-Centered Drug Control Strategies?" *Crime and Delinquency* 48, 3: 380–398.

Logan, C. 1987. "The Propriety of Proprietary Prisons," *Federal Probation* 53, 3: 35–40.

Lombardo, L. 1989. *Guards Imprisoned: Correctional Officers at Work*. Cincinnati, OH: Anderson Press.

Lord, E. 2008. "The Challenges of Mentally Ill Female Offenders in Prison." *Criminal Justice and Behavior*, 35, 8: 928–942.

Lovall, D., L.C. Johnson, & K. Cain. 2007. "Recidivism of Supermax Prisoners in Washington State." *Crime & Delinquency* 53, 4: 633–656.

Maeve, M. 2000. "Speaking Unavoidable Truths: Understanding Early Childhood Sexual and Physical Violence among Women in Prison." *Issues in Mental Health Nursing* 21: 473–498.

Mallaby, S. 2001. "Addicted to a Failing War on Drugs." *Washington Post*, January 8, 2001, A19.

Man, C. & J. Cronan. 2001. "Forecasting Sexual Abuse in Prison." *Journal of Criminal Law and Criminology* 92: 127–185.

Manchak, S., J. Skeem, K. Douglas. 2008. "Utility of the Revised Level of Service Inventory (LSI-R) in Predicting Recidivism After Long-Term Incarceration." *Law & Human Behavior* 32: 477–488.

Manocchio, A. & J. Dunn. 1982. *The Time Game: Two Views of a Prison*. Beverly Hills, CA: Sage Publications.

Mariner, J. 2001. "Body and Soul: The Trauma of Prison Rape." In J. May and K. Pitts (eds.), *Building Violence*, pp. 125–131. Thousand Oaks, CA: Sage Publishing.

Marks, A. 2001. "A Spiritual Approach to Time Behind Bars," *Christian Science Monitor*. April 16, 2001. Retrieved on 3/1/2012 from http://www.highbeam.com/doc/1G1-73220542.html.

Marquart, J., M. Barnhill, & K. Balshaw-Biddle, (2001). "Fatal Attraction": An Analysis of Employee Boundary Violations in a Southern Prison System, 1995–1998." *Justice Quarterly* 18,4: 877–911.

Marquart, J. & B. Crouch. 1985. "Judicial Reform and Prisoner Control." *Law and Society Review* 16: 557–586.

Martin, D. & P. Sussman. 1993. *Committing Journalism: The Prison Writings of Red Hog*. New York: W.W. Norton and Company.

Martin, M. 1997. "Connected Mothers: A Follow–Up Study of Incarcerated Women and Their Children." *Women and Criminal Justice* 8, 4:1–23.

Martin, M. 2001. "Pot Clubs Bracing for DEA Crackdowns." *San Francisco Chronicle*, November 13, 2001.

Martin, S. 2000. "Texans Have a Passion for Punishment." *Austin American Statesman*, August 28, 2000, A9.

Martin, S. & S. Eckland-Olson. 1987. *Texas Prisons: The Walls Came Tumbling Down*. Austin, TX: Texas Monthly Press.

Martinson, R. 1974. "What Works? Questions and Answers About Prison Reform." *Public Interest* (Spring): 22–54.

Maruna, S. & H. Toch. 2001. *Making Good: How Ex-Convicts Reform and Rebuild Their Lives*. Washington, D.C: American Psychological Association.

Marushak, L. 2007. *HIV in Prisons, 2005*. Washington, D.C.: Bureau of Justice Statistics, U.S. Dept. of Justice

Maruschak, L. & A. Beck. 2001. *Medical Problems of Inmates, 1997*. Washington D.C.: Bureau of Justice Statistics, U.S. Dept. of Justice.

Masters, J. 2001. "Scars." In D. Sabo, T. Kupers, W. London, *Prison Masculinities*, pp. 201–206. Philadelphia, PA: Temple University Press.

Mauer, M. 1999. *Race to Incarcerate*. New York: The Free Press.

Mauer, M. 2001. "The Causes and Consequences of Prison Growth," in D. Garland , (ed.), *Mass Imprisonment: Social Causes and Consequences*, pp. 4–14 Thousand Oaks, CA: Sage Publications.

Mauer, M. & M. Chesney-Lind. 2003. *Invisible Punishment: The Collateral Consequences of Mass Imprisonment*. New York: New Press.

Mauer, M. & R. King. 2007. *Uneven Justice: State Rates of Incarceration by Race and Ethnicity*. Washington D.C.: Sentencing Policy Institute. Retrieved 9/17/2011 from http://www.sentencingproject.org.

May, J. 2001. "Feeding a Public Health Epidemic." In J. May and K. Pitts (eds.) , *Building Violence* , pp. 133–137. Thousand Oaks, CA: Sage Publishing.

Mayhew, J. 2002. "Corrections is a Male Enterprise." In B. Gaucher (ed.) Writing as Resistance: The Journal of Prisoners on Prisons Anthology, 1988-2002, pp. 151–159. Toronto: Canadian Scholars Press.

McCarthy, B. 1991. "Keeping an Eye on the Keeper: Prison Corruption and Its Control. "In M. Braswell, B. McCarthy, and B. McCarthy (eds.), Justice, Crime, and Ethics, pp. 239–253. Cincinnati: Anderson.

McCorkle, R., T. Miethe, & K. Drass. 1995. "The Roots of Prison Violence." Crime and Delinquency 41, 3: 317–327.

McGowan, B. & K. Blumenthal . 1978. Why Punish the Children? A Study of Children of Women Prisoners. Hackensack, NJ: National Council on Crime and Delinquency.

McLaren, J. 1997. "Prisoner Rights: The Pendulum Swings." In J. Pollock (ed.), Prisons: Today and Tomorrow, pp. 338–377. Gaithersburg, MD: Aspen Publishing.

Mears, B. 2011. "High Court Orders Drastic Prison Population Reduction in California. "CNN. Retrieved 5/23/2011 from http://www.cnn.com/2011/CRIME/05/23/scotus. california.prisons/index.html .

Mears, D. 2008. "An Assessment of Supermax Prisons Using an Evaluation Research Framework." The Prison Journal, 88, 1: 43–68.

Mears, D. & W. Bales. 2010. "Supermax Housing: Placement, Duration, and Time to Reentry." Journal of Criminal Justice 38: 545–554.

Mears, D. & W. Bales. 2009. "Supermax Incarceration and Recidivism." Criminology 47, 4: 1131–1166.

Merlo, A. 1997. "The Crisis and Consequences of Prison Overcrowding." In J. Pollock (ed.), Prisons: Today and Tomorrow, pp. 52–83. Gaithersburg, MD: Aspen Publishing.

Messemer, J. 2003. "College Programs for Inmates: The Post-Pell Grant Era," Journal of Correctional Education 54, 1: 32–39.

Miron, Jeffey A., 2010. The Budgetary Implications of Drug Prohibition, (February, 2010), p.1. Retrieved 9/17/2011 from http://www.economics.harvard.edu/faculty/miron/ files/budget%202010%20Final.pdf.

Montgomery, R. & G. Crews. 1998. A History of Correctional Violence: An Examination of Reported Causes of Riots and Disturbances. Lanham, MD: ACA.

Morain, D. 2002a. "State Prison Guards Union Endorses Davis." LATimes.com. August 28, 2002.

Morain, D. 2002b. "Overtime Pays Off At Prison." LATimes.com. February 10, 2003.

Morash, M. & T. Bynum. 1995. Findings from the National Study of Innovative and Promising Programs for Women Offenders. Washington D.C.: U.S. Dept. of Justice.

Morash, M., D. Har, & L. Rucker. 1994. "A Comparison of Programming for Women and Men in U.S. Prisons in the 1980s," Crime and Delinquency 40, 2: 197–221.

Morash, M., S. Jeong, & N. Zang. 2010. "An Exploratory Study of the Characteristics of Men Known to Commit Prisoner-on-Prisoner Sexual Violence." The Prison Journal, 90, 2: 161–178.

Morash, M. & P. Schram. 2002. The Prison Experience: Special Issues of Women in Prison. Prospect Heights, IL: Waveland.

Morgan, L. 2010. Two Florida businessmen indicted in prison kickback case. Tampa Bay News, July 16, 2010. Accessed July 26, 2010 from http://www.tampabay.com/news/ politics/two-florida-businessmen-indicted-in-prison-kickback-case/1109244.

Morris, J. 2002. "It's a Form of Warfare: A Description of Pelican Bay Prison." In L. Alarid and P. Cromwell, Correctional Perspectives, pp. 181–183. Los Angeles, CA: Roxbury Press.

Morris, R. 1995. *Penal Abolition*. Toronto: Canadian Scholar Press.

Muir, W. 1977. *Street Corner Politicians*. Chicago, IL: University of Chicago Press.

Mullen, J., et al. 1980. *American Prisons and Jails, Vol. 1*. Washington D.C.: National Institute of Justice.

Mullings, J., J. Marquart, & V. Brewer. 2000. "Assessing the Relationship between Child Sexual Abuse and Marginal Living Conditions on HIV/AIDS-Related Risk Behavior Among Women Prisoners." *Child Abuse and Neglect, 24*, 5: 677–688.

Mullings, J., J. Marquart, & D. Hartley. 2003. "Exploring the Effects of Childhood Sexual Abuse and its Impact on HIV/AIDS Risk-taking Behavior Among Women Prisoners." *The Prison Journal* 83, 4: 442–463.

Mullings, J., J. Pollock, & B. Crouch. 2002. "Drugs and Criminality: Results from the Texas Women Inmates Study." *Women & Criminal Justice* 13, 4: 69–97.

Mumola, C. 1999. *Substance Abuse and Treatment*. Washington, D.C.: Bureau of Justice Statistics, U.S. Dept. of Justice.

Mumola, C. 2000. *Incarcerated Children and Their Parents*. Washington, D.C.: Bureau of Justice Statistics, U.S. Dept. of Justice.

Mumola, C. & J. Karberg. 2006. *Drug Use and Dependence, State and Federal Prisoners, 2004*. Washington, D.C.: Bureau of Justice Statistics, U.S. Dept. of Justice.

Murphy, K. 2002. "State Prisoners Often Return, Report Shows." *Stateline.org*. June 3, 2002. Retrieved 3/1/2012 from http://www.stateline.org/live/ViewPage.action?siteNodeId=136&languageId=1&contentId=14835.

Murphy, K. 2002. "States Get Grants to Help Ex-Offenders." *Stateline.org*. July 17, 2002. Retrieved 3/1/2012 from http://www.stateline.org/live/ViewPage.action?siteNodeId=136&languageId=1&contentId=14894.

Muse, D. 1994. "Parenting From Prison." *Mothering*, 72: 99–105.

Naday, A., J. Freilich, & J. Mellow. 2008. "The Elusive Data on Supermax Confinement." *The Prison Journal* 88, 1: 69–93.

Nagy, J. 2001. "State Budgets Battered by Substance Abuse." *Stateline.org*. Retrieved January 29, 2001 from stateline.org/story.do?storyID=111585.

National Center on Addiction and Substance Abuse. 2010. *Behind Bars II: Substance Abuse and America's Prison Population*. New York, NY: National Center on Addiction and Substance Abuse (Columbia University). Available at http://www.casacolumbia.org/articlefiles/575-report2010behind bars2.pdf.

National Center on Institutions and Alternatives (NCIA). 1998. *Imprisoning Elderly Offenders: Public Safety or Maximum Security Nursing Homes*. Alexandria, VA: NCIA.

National Institute of Justice. 1993. *Sourcebook of Criminal Justice Statistics*. Washington D.C.: GPO.

Nelson, M. 2002. "Arkansas Prison Still Shackled to Dark Past." *LA Times*. January 6, 2002, A1.

New York State, Department of Correctional Services. 2001. *Female Offenders 1999–2000*. Albany, NY: DOCS, Division of Program Planning, Research and Evaluation.

New York Times. 2011. Stock Analysis Table. Retrieved 9/30/2011 from http://markets.on.nytimes.com/research/stocks/tools/analysis_tools.asp?symbol=CXW.

Occupational Outlook Handbook. 2010–2011. Retrieved online from http://www.bls.gov/oco/ocos156.htm.

Office of National Drug Control Policy. 2004. *Drug Use Trends: October 2002*. Retrieved 8/31/2004 from http://www.whitehousedrugpolicy.gov/publications/factsht/druguse/index.html.

Office of National Drug Control Policy. 2010. *National Drug Control Strategy: FY2010 Budget Summary*, 2009. Retrieved 9/17/2011 from http://www.whitehousedrugpolicy. gov/publications/policy/11budget/fy11budget.pdf.

Ogle, R. 1999. "Prison Privatization: An Environmental Catch 22." *Justice Quarterly* 14, 3: 579–600.

Olson, D., A. Lurigio, & M. Seng 2000. "A Comparison of Female and Male Probationers: Characteristics and Case Outcomes." *Women & Criminal Justice* 11, 4: 65–79.

Open Society Institute. 2002. News Release: Majority of Americans Think U.S. Criminal Justice System is Broken. Retrieved 8/14/02 from http://www.soros.org/crime/CJI%20 Poll-PR.htm.

Owen, B. 1985. "Race and Gender Relations Among Prison Workers." *Crime and Delinquency* 31 January: 147–159.

Owen, B. 1988. *The Reproduction of Social Control: A Study of Prison Workers at San Quentin*. New York: Praeger.

Owen, B. 1998. *"In the Mix": Struggle and Survival in a Women's Prison*. Albany, NY: State University of Albany Press.

Owen, B. & B. Bloom. 1994. "Profiling the Needs of California's Female Prisoners: A Study in Progress." Paper presented at the meeting of the Western Society of Criminology.

Owen, B. & B. Bloom. 1995. "Profiling Women Prisoners: Findings From National Surveys and a California Sample." *The Prison Journal*, 75, 2: 165–185.

Owen, B., J. Wells, J. Pollock, B. Muscat, & S. Torres. 2008. *Gendered Violence and Safety: A Contextual Approach to Improving Security in Women's Facilities*. Washington, D.C.: National Institute of Justice.

Paboojian, A. & R. Teske. 1997. "Pre-Service Correctional Officers: What Do They Think About Treatment?" *Journal of Criminal Justice* 25, 5: 425–433.

Padron, E. 2000. "The Long Awaited Day of Freedom." In R. Johnson and H. Toch, *Crime and Punishment: Inside Views*, pp. 196–220. Los Angeles, CA: Roxbury Press.

Palmer, T. 1994. A Profile of Correctional Effectiveness and New Directions for Research. Albany, NY: SUNY Press.

Parenti, C. 1999. *Lockdown America: Police and Prisons in the Age of Crisis*. New York: Verso New Left Books.

Parker, K. 2002. "Female Inmates Living in Fear: Sexual Abuse by Correctional Officers in the District of Columbia." *American University Journal of Gender, Social Policy and the Law*. Retrieved July 2, 2002. from http://web.lexis-nexis.com/universe/document?_M =294eb9c811969dbd76bf1cb0b76f7473&.

Patrick, E. 2000. "Meaning of 'Life' in Prison." In R. Johnson and H. Toch, *Crime and Punishment: Inside Views*, pp. 141–143. Los Angeles, CA: Roxbury Press.

Pearson, F. & D. Lipton. 1999. "A Meta-Analytic Review of the Effectiveness of Corrections-Based Treatments for Drug Abuse." *The Prison Journal* 79, 4: 384–410.

Pearson, F., D. Lipton, C. Cleland, & D. Yee. 2002. "The Effects of Behavioral and Cognitive-Behavioral Programs on Recidivism." *Crime and Delinquency* 48, 3: 476–496.

Pelz, M.E., J. Marquart, & C. Terry Pelz. 1991. "Right Wing Extremism in Texas Prisons: The Rise and Fall of the Aryan Brotherhood of Texas." *Prison Journal* 71, 2: 38–49.

Perez, E. 2001. "For Profit Prison Firm Wackenhut Tries to Break Shackles to Growth." *Wall Street Journal*, May 15, 2001.

Perez, D., A. Gover, K. Tennyson, & S. Santos. 2010. "Individual and Institutional Characteristics Related to Inmate Victimization. "*International Journal of Offender Therapy and Comparative Criminology*. 54, 3: 378–394.

Perkins, C. 1994. *National Corrections Reporting Program: Bureau of Justice Statistics Bulletin*. Washington D.C.: U.S. Dept. of Justice.

Peters, R. & M. Steinberg. 2000. "Substance Abuse Treatment in U.S. Prisons." In D. Shewan and J. Davies (eds.), *Drugs and Prison*, pp. 89–116. London: Harwood Academic Press.

Petersilia, J. 1997. "Justice For All? Offenders with Mental Retardation and the California Corrections System." *The Prison Journal*, 77, 4: 358–380.

Petersilia, J. 1999. "Parole and Prisoner Reentry." In M. Tonry and J. Petersilia (eds.) *Crime and Justice: A Review of Research*, Vol. 26., pp. 34–57. Chicago, IL: University of Chicago Press.

Pew Center on the States. 2011. *Prison Count 2010: State Population Declines for the First Time in 38 Years*. Washington D.C.: Pew Center on the States. Retrieved 9/21/2011 from http://www.pewcenteronthestates.org/uploadedFiles/Prison_Count_2010.pdf.

Pew Center on the States. 2011. *State of Recidivism: The Revolving Door of America's Prisons*. Washington, D.C.: The Pew Charitable Trusts.

Pizarro, J. & R. Narag. 2008. "Supermax Prisons: What We Know, What We Do Not Know, and Where We Are Going." *The Prison Journal*, 88, 1: 23–42.

Pollock, J. 1986. *Sex and Supervision: Guarding Male and Female Inmates*. Westport, CT: Greenwood Press.

Pollock, J. 1995. "Women in Corrections: Custody and the 'Caring Ethic.'" In A. Merlo and J. Pollock (eds.), *Women, Law and Social Control*, pp. 97–116. Needham Heights, MA: Allyn and Bacon.

Pollock, J. 1997. *Prison: Today and Tomorrow*. Gaithersburg, MD: Aspen Publishing.

Pollock, J. 1997. "The Social World of the Prisoner." In J. Pollock (ed.), *Prison: Today and Tomorrow*, pp. 218–258. Gaithersburg, MD: Aspen Publishing.

Pollock, J. 1997. "Rehabilitation Revisited." In J. Pollock (ed.), *Prison: Today and Tomorrow*, pp. 158–208.. Gaithersburg, MD: Aspen Publishing.

Pollock, J. 1998. *Counseling Women in Prison*. Beverly Hills, CA: Sage.

Pollock, J. 1999. *Criminal Women*. Cincinnati, OH: Anderson.

Pollock, J. 2000. *A National Survey of Parenting Programs in Women's Prisons*. Privately published monograph available from the author.

Pollock, J. 2002. *Women, Prison and Crime*, 2d ed. Belmont, CA: Wadsworth Publishing.

Pollock, J. 2010. *Dilemmas and Decisions: Ethics in Criminal Justice,* 7th ed. Belmont, CA: Wadsworth.

Pollock, J., & S. Davis. 2005. "The Continuing Myth of the Violent Female Offender." *Criminal Justice Review,* 30, 1: 5–29.

Pollock, J., J. Mullings, & B. Crouch. 2006. "Violent Women: Findings from the Texas Women Inmates' Study. *Journal of Interpersonal Violence,*" 21, 4: 485–502.

Pranis, K. 2001. "Sodexho to End Support for Right Wing Lobby." News Release. Retrieved April 20, 2001 from www.nomoreprisons.org.

Pratt, T. 2009. *Addicted to Incarceration: Corrections Policy and the Politics of Misinformation in the United States*. Los Angeles, CA: Sage.

Pratt, T. & J. Maahs. 1999. "Are Private Prisons More Cost-Effective Than Public Prisons? A Meta-Analysis of Evaluation Research Studies." *Crime and Delinquency* 45, 3: 358–371.

Prendergast, M., J. Wellisch, & G. Falkin 1995. "Assessment of and Services for Substance Abusing Women Offenders in Community and Correctional Settings." *The Prison Journal* 75, 2: 240–256.

Pro-Con.org. 2011. State Felon Voting Laws. Pro-Con.org website. Retrieved on 10/21/2011 from http://felonvoting.procon.org/view.resource.php?resourceID=286.

Rafter, N. 1985/1990. *Partial Justice: Women in State Prisons, 1800–1935*. Boston: New England University Press.

Raeder, M. 1993. "Gender Issues in the Federal Sentencing Guidelines." *Journal of Criminal Justice* 8, 3: 20–25.

Ralph, P. & J. Marquart. 1991. "Gang Violence in Texas Prisons." *The Prison Journal*, 71, 2: 38–49.

Raphael, S. 2009. "Explaining the Rise in U.S. Incarceration Rates." *Criminology & Public Policy* 8: 87–95.

Raphael, S. & M. Stoll. 2008. *Do Prisons Make Us Safer? The Benefits and Costs of the Prison Boom*. New York: Russell Sage Foundation.

Raspberry, W. 2002. "Prison Sentences Devastate a Community." *Austin American Statesman*, October 14, 2002, A13.

Redifer, K. 2000. "Big Trouble in 'Li'l Chilli.'" In R. Johnson and H. Toch (eds.), *Crime and Punishment: Inside Views*, pp. 143–146. Los Angeles, CA: Roxbury Press.

Reed, B. 1987. "Developing Women-Sensitive Drug Dependence Treatment Services: Why So Difficult?" *Journal of Psychoactive Drugs* 19, 2: 151–164.

Reentry Policy Council. 2004. *Report of the Reentry Policy Council*. Washington, D.C.: Reentry Policy Council. Available from www.reentrypolicy.org.

Reichel, P. 1997. *Corrections*. Minneapolis, MN: West Publishing.

Reimer, H. 1937. "Socialization in the Prison Community." *Proceedings of the 67th Annual Conference of the American Prison Association* 1: 151–155.

Reisig, M., K. Holtfreter, & M. Morash. 2006. "Assessing Recidivism Risk Across Female Pathways to Crime." *Justice Quarterly* 23, 3: 384–405.

Reisig, M. & T. Pratt. 2000. "The Ethics of Correctional Privatization: A Critical Examination of the Delegation of Coercive Authority." *Prison Journal* 80, 2: 210–222.

Reeves, J. 2011. "Buddhist Meditation Calms Alabama Prison." *Austin American Statesman*, Tuesday, February 8, 2011: A3.

Rich, W. 2002. "Prison Conditions and Criminal Sentencing in Kansas." *Kansas Journal of Law and Public Policy*. Retrieved July 2, 2002 from http://web.lexisnexis.com/universe/document?_m=294eb9c811969dbd76bf1cb0b76f7473&.

Richards, S. 2003. "My Journey Through the Federal Bureau of Prisons." In J. Ross and S. Richards (eds.), *Convict Criminology*, pp. 120–149. Belmont, CA: Wadsworth, ITP.

Richards, S., C. Terry, & D. Murphy. 2002. "Lady Hacks and Gentleman Convicts." In L. Alarid and P. Cromwell, *Correctional Perspectives*, pp. 207–216. Los Angeles, CA: Roxbury Press.

Richey, W. 2002. "Bans on Ex-Con Voting Reviewed." *Christian Science Monitor*. October 1, 2002. Retrieved 10/1/02 from http://www.csmonitor.com/2002/1001/p02s01-usju.html.

Rideau, W. & R. Wikberg. 1992. *Life Sentences: Rage and Survival Behind Bars*. New York: Times Books.

Riley, J. 2000. "Sensemaking in Prison: Inmate Identity as a Working Understanding." *Justice Quarterly* 17, 2: 359–376.

Robbins, C., S. Martin, & H. Surratt. 2007. "Substance Abuse Treatment, Anticipated Maternal Roles, and Reentry Success of Drug-Involved Women Prisoners." *Crime & Delinquency* 55: 388–411.

Robinson, C. 2000. "Disenfranchisement of Blacks Hurt Gore." Dawn: The Internet Edition. Retrieved May 30, 2003 from http://dawn.com/2000/11/13/int11.htm.

Robinson, R.A. 1992. "Intermediate Sanctions and the Female Offender." In J. Byrne, A. Lurigio, and J. Petersilia (eds.), *Smart Sentencing: the Emergence of Intermediate Sanctions,* pp. 245–260. Newbury Park, CA: Sage.

Rogers, K. 2000. "A True Story." In R. Johnson and H. Toch (eds.), *Crime and Punishment: Inside Views,* pp. 67–69. Los Angeles, CA: Roxbury Press.

Rohde, D. 2001. "A Growth Industry Cools." *New York Times,* August 21, 2001.

Rolland, M. 1997. *Descent into Madness: An Inmate's Experience of the New Mexico State Prison Riot.* Cincinnati, OH: Anderson Publishing.

Roots, R. 2002. "Of Prisoners and Plantiffs' Lawyers: A Tale of Two Litigation Reform Efforts." *Willamette Law Review.* Retrieved July 2, 2002 from http://web.lexisnexis.com/universe/document?_m=294eb9c811969dbd76bf1cb0b76f7473&.

Ross, D. 1996. "Assessment of Prisoner Assaults on Corrections Officers." *Corrections Compendium* 21, 8: 6–10.

Ross, J.I., & S. Richards. 2002. *Behind Bars: Surviving Prison.* Indianapolis, IN: Alpha Books.

Ross, J.I. & S. Richards. 2003. *Convict Criminology.* Belmont, CA: Wadsworth, ITP

Rothman, D. 1971/1990. *The Discovery of the Asylum: Social Order and Disorder in the New Republic.* Boston: Little, Brown.

Rottman, D. 2007. "Adhere to Procedural Fairness in the Justice System." *Criminology & Public Policy,* 6, 835–842.

Rouse, J. 1991. "Evaluation Research on Prison-Based Drug Treatment Programs and Some Policy Implications." *International Journal of the Addictions* 26, 1: 29–44.

Rusche, G. & O. Kirchheimer. 1939. *Punishment and Social Structure.* New York: Russell and Russell.

Rydell, C., J. Caulkins, & S. Everingham. 1996. *Enforcement or Treatment? Modeling the Relative Efficiency of Alternatives for Controlling Cocaine.* Santa Monica, CA: The RAND Corporation.

Rynne, J., R. Harding, & R. Wortley. 2008. "Market Testing and Prison Riots: How Public-Sector Commercialization Contributed to a Prison Riot." *Criminology & Public Policy,* 7, 1: 117–142.

Sabo, D., T. Kupers, & W. London. 2001. "Gender and the Politics of Punishment," in D. Sabo, T. Kupers, and W. London, *Prison Masculinities,* pp. 3–20. Philadelphia: Temple University Press.

Sabol, W., H. West, & M. Cooper. 2009. *Prisoners in 2008.* Washington, D.C.: Bureau of Justice Statistics, U.S. Dept. of Justice.

Salant, J. 2002. "More Americans on Parole in Jail by the End of 2001." *Austin American Statesman,.* August 26, 2002, A5.

Salisbury, E., P. Van Voorhis, & G. Spiropoulos. 2008. "The Predictive Validity of a Gender Responsive Needs Assessment: An Exploratory Study." *Crime and Delinquency,* 54, 4: 225–258.

Salladay, R. 1999. "Prison Guard Union, Davis Cozy Pairing," *San Francisco Examiner,* September 14, 1999, B3.

Samaha, J. 1997. *Criminal Justice.* Minneapolis, St. Paul: West Publishing Company.

Sampson, R. & J. Lauritsen 1997. "Racial and Ethnic Disparities in Crime and Criminal Justice in the U.S." In M. Tonry (ed.), *Ethnicity, Crime and Immigration: Comparative and Cross-National Perspectives,* pp. 311–374. Chicago: University of Chicago Press.

Sandifer, J. & S. Kurth. 2000. "The Invisible Children of Incarcerated Mothers," *Families, Crime and Criminal Justice* 2: 361–279.

Sanger, B. 2001. "Bush Names a Drug Czar and Addresses Criticism." *New York Times*. May 11, 2001. Retrieved May 11, 2001 from www.nytimes.com/2001/05/11/politics/11DRUG.html.

Sapp, A. & M. Vaughn 1990. "The Social Status of Adult and Juvenile Sex Offenders in Prison," *Journal of Police and Criminal Psychology* 6: 2–6.

Saylor, W. & G. Gates. 1994. "The Post Release Employment Project: Prison Work has Measurable Effects in Post Release." In P. Kratcoski (ed.), *Correctional Counseling and Treatment*, pp. 535–542. Prospect Heights, IL: Waveland Press.

Schemo, D. 2001. "Students Find Drug Law Has Big Price: College Aid." *New York Times*. May 3, 2001. Retrieved May 3, 2001 from www.nytimes.com/2001/05/03/politics/03DRUGhtml.

Schiraldi, V. 2002. "Tough on Crime, But Hardly Smart." *Albany Times Union*, April 17, 2002, A1.

Schiraldi, V. 2002. *Cellblocks or Classrooms?: The Funding of Higher Education and Corrections and Its Impact on African American Men*. Washington, D.C.: Justice Policy Institute.

Schiraldi, V. & J. Greene. 2002. "Ripe for Cutting: Prison Budgets". *LA Times*, February 10, A2.

Schiraldi, V. & V. Jones. 2001. "New Youth Movement Organizing to Fight Consequences of their Parents Mistakes." *Pacific News*. August 24, 2001..

Schneider, A. 1999. "Public-Private Partnerships in the U.S. Prison System." *American Behavioral Scientist*, 43, 1: 192–208.

Schoen K. 1982. *Overcrowded Time: Why Prisons Are So Crowded and What Can Be Done*. New York: Edna McConnell Clark Foundation.

Schrag, C. 1961. "Leadership Among Prison Inmates." *American Sociological Review* 19: 37–42.

Sentencing Project. 2011. *On the Chopping Block: State Prison Closings*. Washington D.C.: The Sentencing Project. Retrieved 9/10/2011 from http://www.sentencingproject.org.

Sentencing Project. 2001. *U.S. Surpasses Russia As World Leader in Rate of Incarceration*. Washington D.C.: The Sentencing Project. Retrieved 1/10/2002 from http://www.sentencingproject.org.

Sharp, S. 2003. *The Incarcerated Woman*. Upper Saddle River, NJ: Prentice-Hall.

Sheehan, S. 1978. *A Prison and a Prisoner*. Boston: Houghton-Mifflin.

Sherman, M. 2001. *California's Three Strikes Law Fails to Reduce Crime*. Washington D.C.: The Sentencing Project.

Shichor, D. & D. Sechrest. 2002. "Privatization and Flexibility: Legal and Practical Aspects of Interjurisdictional Transfer of Prisoners." *The Prison Journal* 82, 3: 386–407.

Shuler, M. 2001. "Senators Vote to Relax Prison Terms." *The Advocate Online*, May 3, 2001.

Siegel, N. 2002. "Stopping Abuse in Prison." In T. Gray (ed.), *Exploring Corrections*, pp. 135–139. Boston: Allyn & Bacon.

Sieh, E. 1989. "Less Eligibility: The Upper Limits of Penal Policy. *Criminal Justice Policy Review*, 3: 159–183.

Silberman, M. 1995. *A World of Violence: Corrections in America*. Belmont, CA: Wadsworth, ITP.

Singer, S. 1996. "Essential Element of the Effective Therapeutic Community in the Correctional Institution." In K. Early (ed.), *Drug Treatment Behind Bars: Prison Based Strategies for Change*, pp. 75–88. Chicago: Praeger Publishing.

Sloan, B. 2011. "The Prison Industries Enhancement Certification Program: Why Everyone Should Be Concerned." *Prison Legal News*, October 4, 2011. Retrieved 10/4/2011 from https://www.prisonlegalnews.org/(S(ecx1bqfnc5bdvwudrukj3zip))/displayArticle. aspx?articleid=22190&.

Snell T. 1994. *Women in Prison. Survey of State Prison Inmates, 1991*. Bureau of Justice Statistics Special Report. Washington D.C.: U.S. Dept. of Justice.

Snell, T. 1992. *Women in Jail: 1989*. Bureau of Justice Statistics Special Report. Washington, D.C.: U.S. Dept. of Justice.

Snell, T. 1995. *Correctional Populations in the United States. 1992*. Bureau of Justice Statistics Special Report. Washington, D.C.: Bureau of Justice Statistics.

Snell, T. & D. Morton. 1992. *Prisoners in 1991*. Washington, D.C.: Bureau of Justice Statistics, U.S. Dept. of Justice.

Solomon, A. 1999. "Wackenhut Detention Ordeal." *Village Voice*. Retrieved March 5, 1999 from villagevoice.com/features/9935/solomon.shtml.

Solomon, A., J. Osborne, L. Winterfield, B. Elderbroom, & P. Burke. 2008. *Putting Public Safety First: 13 Parole Supervision Strategies to Enhance Reentry Outcomes*. Washington, D.C.: The Urban Institute.

Sorensen, J. & M. Cunningham. 2010. "Conviction Offense and Prison Violence." *Crime & Delinquency* 56, 1: 103–125.

Sorensen, J. & D. Stemen. 2002. "The Effect of State Sentencing Policies on Incarceration Rates." *Crime and Delinquency* 48, 3: 456–475.

Sourcebook of Criminal Justice Statistics. 2003. *Employees of Private, State, and Federal Correctional Facilities*. Retrieved 10/15/2011 from http://www.albany.edu/source-book/pdf/t1104.pdf.

Souryal, S. 1999. "Corruption of Prison Personnel." In P. Carlson and J. Garrett (eds.) *Prison and Jail Administration: Practice and Theory,* pp. 171–177. Gaithersburg, MD: Aspen Publishing.

Souryal, S. 2011. *Ethics in Criminal Justice: In Search of the Truth*. Cincinnati, OH: Anderson/LexisNexis.

Spelman, W. 2009. "Crime, Cash, and Limited Options: Explaining the Prison Boom." *Criminology & Public Policy* 8: 87–95.

Spencer, D. 1997. "The Classification of Inmates." In J. Pollock (ed.), *Prison: Today and Tomorrow,* pp. 84–115. Gaithersburg, MD: Aspen Publishing.

Spohn C. & D. Holleran. 2000. "The Imprisonment Penalty Paid by Young, Unemployed Black and Hispanic Male Offenders." *Criminology* 38, 1: 281–306.

Stanton, A.M. 1980. *When Mothers Go To Jail*. Lexington, MA: Lexington.

Star Tribune. 2011. "Sober Path Out of Prison in Jeopardy." StarTribune.online. May 25, 2011. Retrieved 10/4/2011 from http://www.startribune.com/local/122632424.html.

Steffensmeier, D. and E. Allan. 1996. "Gender and Crime: Toward a Gendered Theory of Female Offending." *Annual Review of Sociology* 22: 459–487.

Steffensmeier, D., H. Zhong, J. Ackerman, J. Schwartz, & S. Agha. 2006. "Gender Gap Trends for Violent Crimes, 1980 to 2003: A UCR-NCVS Comparison." *Feminist Criminology* 1, 1: 72–98.

Steiner, B. 2009. "Assessing Static and Dynamic Influences on Inmate Violence Levels." *Crime & Delinquency* 55, 1: 134–161.

Steiner, B. & J. Wooldredge. 2009a. "Rethinking the Link Between Institutional Crowding and Inmate Misconduct." *The Prison Journal* 89, 2: 205–233.

Steiner, B. & J. Wooldredge. 2009b. "Individual and Environmental Effects on Assaults and Nonviolent Rule Breaking by Women in Prison." *Journal of Research in Crime and Delinquency* 46: 437–467.

Stephan, J. 1997. *Census of State and Federal Correctional Institutions, 1995.* Bureau of Justice Statistics Reports. Washington, D.C.: Dept. of Justice.

Stohr, M., N. Lovrich, B. Menke & L. Zupan. 1994. "Staff Management in Correctional Institutions: Comparing DiIulio's 'Control Model' and 'Employee Investment Model' Outcomes in Five Jails." *Justice Quarterly* 11, 3, 471–497.

Stojkovic, S. 1990. "Accounts of Prison Work: Corrections Officers Portrayals of the Work Worlds." *Perspectives on Social Problems* 2: 211–230.

Stone, W. 1997. "Industry, Agriculture and Education." In J. Pollock (ed.), *Prison: Today and Tomorrow,* pp. 116–157. Gaithersburg, MD: Aspen Publishing.

Stratton, R. 1999. "Skyline Turkey." In B. Chevigny (ed.) *Doing Time: 25 Years of Prison Writing.* New York: Arcade Publishing.

Struckman-Johnson, C., L. Rucker, K. Bumby & S. Donaldson. 1996. "Sexual Coercion Reported by Men and Women in Prison." *Journal of Sex Research* 33, 1: 67–76.

Struckman-Johnson, C. & D. Struckman-Johnson. 2006. "A Comparison of Sexual Coercion Experiences Reported by Men and Women in Prison." *Journal of Interpersonal Violence* 21, 12: 1591–1615.

Substance Abuse & Mental Health Services Administration. 2010. *Results from the 2009 National Survey in Drug Use & Health.* Rockville, MD: SAMHSA, U.S. Dept. of Health and Human Services.

Sullivan, L. 1990. *The Prison Reform Movement: Forlorn Hope.* Boston: Twayne Publishing.

Sundt, J., T. Castellano & Ch. Briggs. 2008. "The Sociopolitical Context of Prison Violence and its Control: A Case Study of Supermax and its Effect in Illinois." *The Prison Journal* 88: 94–122.

Sung, H. 2001. "Rehabilitating Felony Drug Offenders Through Job Development." *Prison Journal* 81, 2: 271–286.

Susswein, G. 2000. "Report: Reading Class Aids Inmates." *Austin American Statesman,* August 30, 2000, B1, B6.

Sutner, S. 2002. "Glodi's Bill Would Charge Prisoners for Keep." *Telegram News.Com,* July 12, 2002.

Sykes, G. 1956. "The Corruption of Authority and Rehabilitation." *Social Forces* 34: 257–265.

Sykes, G. 1958/1966. *The Society of Captives.* Princeton: Princeton University Press.

Sykes G. & S. Messinger. 1960. "The Inmate Social System." In R. Cloward, D. Cressey, G. Grosser, R. McCleery, L. Ohlin, G. Sykes, and S. Messinger (eds.) *Theoretical Studies in the Social Organization of the Prison,* pp. 5–19. New York: Social Science Research Council.

Taylor, W. 1993. *Brokered Justice: Race, Politics, and Mississippi Prisons, 1798–1992.* Columbus, OH: Ohio State University Press.

Teepin, T. 1996. "For Private Prisons, Crime Does Pay." *Austin American Statesman.* December 12, 1996, A15.

Teichner, L. 2008. L. Teplin, K. Abrams, & G. McClelland 1996. "Prevalence of Psychiatric Disorders Among Incarcerated Women." *Archives of General Psychiatry* 53, 2: 505–512.

Terry, C. 2003. *The Fellas: Overcoming Prison and Addiction.* Belmont, CA: Wadsworth, ITP.

Tewksbury, R. & E. Mustaine. 2008. Correctional Orientations of Prison Staff. *The Prison Journal,* 28, 2: 207–233.

Texas Department of Criminal Justice 2001. Statistical Summary: Fiscal Year 2000. Austin, TX: Texas Department of Criminal Justice.

Theis, S. 2002. "New Tact Pushed in War on Drugs." *Plain Dealer-Columbus, Ohio*, August 8, 2002, A1.

"Three Guards Acquitted." 2002. *New York Times*, February 16, 2002; A13.

Timms, E. 2001. "Judge to Lessen Oversight of Texas Prisons." *Dallas News*. June 20, 2001.

Toch, H. 1975. *Men in Crisis: Human Breakdowns in Prison*. Chicago: Aldine.

Toch, H. 1977. *Living in Prison: The Ecology of Survival*. New York: Free Press.

Toch, H. 1980a. *Violent Men*. Cambridge, MA: Schenkman Publishing.

Toch, H. 1980b. *Therapeutic Communities in Corrections*. New York: Praeger.

Toch, H. 1981. "Is a 'Correctional Officer,' By Any Other Name, a 'Screw?'" In R. Ross. *Prison Guard/Correctional Officer*, pp. 87–103. Toronto: Butterworth Publishing.

Toch, H. 1982. *Mosaic of Despair: Human Breakdowns in Prison*. Washington D.C.: American Psychological Association.

Toch, H. 2001. "The Future of Supermax Confinement." *The Prison Journal* 81: 376–388.

Toch, H. & K. Adams. 1989. *Coping and Maladaption in Prison*. New Brunswick: Transaction Press.

Toch, H. & J. Grant. 1982. *Reforming Human Services: Change Through Participation*. Beverly Hills, CA: Sage.

Toch, H. & J. Klofas. 1982. "Alienation and Desire for Job Enrichment Among C.O.'s," *Federal Probation* 46: 35–47.

Trammell, R. 2006. *Accounts of Violence and Social Control: Organized Violence and Negotiated Order in California Prisons*. Dissertation: University of California, Irvine.

Trammell, R. 2009. "Relational Violence in Women's Prison: How Women Describe Interpersonal Violence and Gender." *Women & Criminal Justice* 19: 267–285.

Treaga, W. 2003. "Twenty Years Teaching College in Prison." In J. Ross and S. Richards (eds.), *Convict Criminology*, pp. 309–324. Belmont, CA: Wadsworth, ITP.

Trout, C.H. 1992. "Taking a New Look at an Old Problem." *Corrections Today* (July): 62, 64, 66.

Trulson, C. & J. Marquart. 2002a. "Inmate Racial Integration: Achieving Racial Integration in the Texas Prison System." *The Prison Journal* 82, 4: 498–525.

Trulson, C. & J. Marquart. 2002b. "Racial Desegregation and Violence in the Texas Prison System." *Criminal Justice Review* 27, 2: 233–255.

Trulson, C. & J. Marquart. 2002c. "The Caged Melting Pot: Toward an Understanding of the Consequences of Desegregation in Prisons." *Law & Society Review* 36, 4: 743–782.

Turner, A. 2011. "Study Praises Texas for Prison Reforms, but Comes With Warning." Houston Chronicle.com, April 13, 2011. Retrieved 4/13/2011 from http://www.chron.com/disp/story.mpl/metropolitan/7519063.html.

Turner, A. 2011. "Texas Inmates Turn to Meditation as a Way to Tame Mind, Build Awareness." *Austin American Statesman*, Friday, September 23, 2011: B5.

Tyler, T. 2006. *Why People Obey the Law*. Princeton, NJ: Princeton University Press.

Tyler, T. 2010. "Legitimacy in Corrections." *Criminology & Public Policy*, 9, 1, 127–134.

Uggen, C. 2000. "Work as a Turning Point in the Life Course of Criminals: A Duration Model of Age, Employment, and Recidivism." *American Sociological Review* 65: 529–546.

Uniform Crime Reports. 1995. Washington D.C.: Federal Bureau of Investigation.

Uniform Crime Reports. 2001. Washington D.C.: Federal Bureau of Investigation.

United States Substance Abuse and Mental Health Services Administration. 2002. 2001 National Household Survey on Drug Abuse. Available through website: www.samhsa.gov/oas/nhsda.htm.

United States Substance Abuse and Mental Health Services Administration. 2001. *2000 National Household Survey on Drug Abuse*. Available through website: www.samhsa. gov/oas/nhsda.htm.

Useem, B. & P. Kimball. 1989. *States of Siege: U.S. Prison Riots: 1971–1986*. New York: Oxford University Press.

Useem, B. & M. Reisig. 1999. "Collective Action in Prisons." *Criminology* 37: 735–759.

Van Voorhis, P. 2004. "An Overview of Offender Classification Systems. In P. Van Voorhis, M. Braswell, and D. Lester (Eds.), *Correctional Counseling and Rehabilitation*, 5th Ed., pp. 133–160. Cincinnati, OH: Anderson Publishing.

Van Voorhis, P. 2005. "Classification of Women Offenders: Gender-Responsive Approaches to Risk/needs Assessment." *Community Corrections Report* 12, 2: 19–20.

Vaughn, M. 1993. "Listening to the Experts: A National Study of Correctional Administrators' Responses to Prison Overcrowding." *Criminal Justice Review* 18: 12–25.

Vaughn, M. & L. Smith. 1999. "Practicing Penal Harm Medicine in the U.S. Prisoners Voices from Jail." *Justice Quarterly* 16, 1: 175–231.

Verhovek, S. 1996. "Texas Caters to a Demand Around U.S. for Jail Cells." *New York Times*, February 9, A1, A10.

Vieraitis, L., T. Kovandzic, & T. Marvell. 2007. "The Criminogenic Effects of Imprisonment: Evidence From State Panel Data, 1974–2002." *Criminology & Public Policy* 6, 3: 589–622.

Virella, K. 2003. "Trapped by the System." In T. Herivel and P. Wright (eds), *Prison Nation: The Warehousing of America's Poor*, pp. 100–110. New York: Routledge.

Von Hirsch, A. 1976. *Doing Justice*. New York: Hill and Wang.

Vuolo, M. & C. Kruttschnitt. 2008. "Prisoners' Adjustment, Correctional Officers, and Context." *Law and Society Review* 42: 307–335.

Wacquant, L. 2001. "Deadly Symbiosis: When Ghetto and Prison Meet and Mesh." In D. Garland, *Mass Imprisonment*, pp. 82–120. Thousand Oaks, CA: Sage.

Walker, S. 1980. *Popular Justice: A History of American Criminal Justice*. New York: Oxford University Press.

Wall Street Journal. 2001. "Prisons as Profit Centers." *Wall Street Journal*. March 15, 2001, A17.

Wallace, D. 2001. "Prisoner Rights: Historical Views." in E. Latessa, A. Holsinger, J. Marquart, and J. Sorenson. *Correctional Contexts: Contemporary and Classical Readings*, pp. 229–238. Los Angeles, CA: Roxbury Press.

Walters, G., M. Mann, M. Miller, L. Hemphill, & M. Chlumsky 1988. "Emotional Disorder Among Offenders: Inter- and Intrasetting Comparisons," *Criminal Justice and Behavior* 15: 433–453.

Ward, D. 1999. "Super-Maximum Facilities." In P. Carlson and J. Garrett (eds.), *Prison and Jail Administration*, pp. 252–259. Gaithersburg, MD: Aspen Publishing.

Ward, G. 2001. "CCA Majority Shareholder to Sell Stocks." The *Tennessean*, May 23, 2001.

Ward, M. 2002a. "State's Prison Vacancies May be Costly to Counties." *Austin American Statesman*. March 22, 2002, A1, A22.

Ward, M. 2002b. "UT Calls for Independent Review of Prison Medical Care." *Austin American Statesman*. October 12, 2002.

Ward, P. 2002. "Do the Crime, Do the Time…And Lose the Right to Vote, Too." *Savannah Morning News*. August 19, 2002.

Warren, J. 2000. "When He Speaks, They Listen." *Los Angeles Times*. August 21, 2000.

Warren, J. 2001. "Inmates Health Care Focus of Suit." *Los Angeles Times*. April 6, 2001.

Warren, J. 2002 . "State to Spend Millions on Better Inmate Care." *Los Angeles Times*. January 30, 2002.

Washington State Institute for Public Policy. 2011. *Return on Investment: Evidence Based Options to Improve State-wide Outcomes*. Available through website: http://www. wsipp.wa.gov/rptfiles/11-07-1201.pdf.

Webb, G. & D. Morris. 2002. "Working as a Prison Guard," in T. Gray (ed.), *Exploring Corrections*, pp. 69–83. Boston: Allyn & Bacon.

Webb, V., C. Katz, & T. Klosky. 1995. "Drug Use Among Traditional Versus Non-Traditional Female Offenders: Findings From the National DUF Project." Paper presented at the American Society of Criminology Meeting. Boston, 1995.

Weinstein, C. 2002. "Even Dogs Confined to Cages for Long Periods of Time Go Berserk." In J. May and K. Pitts (eds.) , *Building Violence*, pp. 119–124. Thousand Oaks, CA: Sage Publishing.

Welch, M. 2000. "The Correctional Response to Prisoners with HIV/AIDS." *Social Pathology* 6, 2: 121–142.

Welch, M. 2002. *Detained: Immigration Laws and the Expanding I.N.S. Jail Complex*. Philadelphia, PA: Temple University Press.

Wellisch, J. 1994. Bureau of Justice Statistics Report: Drug Abusing Women Offenders: Results of a National Survey. Washington D.C.: U.S. Dept. of Justice.

Welsh, M. 2002. "The Effects of the Elimination of Pell Grant Eligibility for State Prison Inmates," *Journal of Correctional Education* 53, 4: 154–158.

West, W. & R. Morris. 2000. *The Case for Penal Abolition*. Toronto: Canadian Scholars Press.

West, H., W. Sabol, & S. Greenman. 2010. *Prisoners in 2009*. Washington D.C.: Bureau of Justice Statistics, U.S. Dept. of Justice.

Western, B. 2006. *Punishment and Inequality in America*. New York, NY: Russell Sage Foundation.

Whitehead, T. 2001. "The 'Epidemic' and 'Cultural Legend' of Black Male Incarceration." In J. May, K. Pitts (eds.), *Building Violence*. Thousand Oaks, CA: Sage Publishing.

Widom, C. 1989a. "Child Abuse, Neglect, and Violent Criminal Behavior." *Criminology* 27, 2: 251–366.

Widom, C. 1989b. The cycle of violence. *Science*, 244: 160–166.

Widom, C. 1996. "Childhood Sexual Abuse and Criminal Consequences." *Society* 33, 4: 47–53.

Wilkie, D. 2002. "Three Strikes No Deterrent to Drug Crimes," *San Diego Union-Tribune*, August 11, 2002, B1.

Williamson, H. 1990. *The Corrections Profession*. Newbury Park, CA: Sage.

Wilson, P., C. Gallagher, M. Coggeshall, & D. MacKenzie. 1999. "A Quantitative Review and Description of Corrections Based Educational, Vocational, and Work Programs." *Corrections Management Quarterly* 3, 4: 8–18.

Winfree, T., G. Newbold, & S. Tubb. 2002. "Prisoner Perspectives on Inmate Culture in New Mexico and New Zealand: A Descriptive Case Study," *The Prison Journal* 82, 2: 213–233.

Winterdyk, J. & R. Ruddell. 2010. "Managing Prison Gangs: Results from a Survey of U.S. Prison Systems." *Journal of Criminal Justice* 38: 730–736.

Wodahl, E., R. Ogle, & C. Heck, C. 2011. "Revocation Trends: A Threat to the Legitimacy of Community-Based Corrections." *The Prison Journal*, 91, 2: 207–226

Wolff, N., D. Blitz, J. Shi, R. Bachman, & J. Siegel. 2006. "Sexual Violence Inside Prisons: Rates of Victimization." *Journal of Urban Health: Bulletin of the New York Academy of Medicine* 83, 5: 835–848.

Wolff, N., C. Blitz, J. Shi, J. Siegel, & R. Bachman. 2007. "Physical Violence Inside Prisons: Rates of Victimization." *Criminal Justice & Behavior* 34, 5: 588–599.

Wolff, N. & J. Shi. 2009. "Type, Source, and Patterns of Physical Victimization: A Comparison of Male and Female Inmates." *The Prison Journal* 89, 2: 172–191.

Wolff, N., J. Shi, C. Blitz, & J. Siegel. 2007. "Understanding Sexual Victimization Inside Prisons: Factors that Predict Victimization." *Criminology & Public Policy* 6, 3: 535–564.

Woolredge, J. 1998. "Inmate Lifestyles and Opportunities for Victimization." *Journal of Research in Crime & Delinquency* 35: 480–502.

Woolredge, J. & K. Masters 1993. "Confronting Problems Faced by Pregnant Inmates in State Prisons." *Crime and Delinquency* 39, 2: 195–203.

Wright, E., E. Salisbury, & P. Van Voorhis 2007. "Predicting the Prison Misconducts of Women Offenders." *Journal of Contemporary Criminal Justice* 23, 4: 310–340.

Wright, K. 1994. *Effective Prison Leadership*. Binghamton, NY: William Neil Publishing.

Wright, K., W. Saylor, E. Gilman, & S. Camp. 1997. "Job Control and Occupational Outcomes Among Prison Workers." *Justice Quarterly* 14, 3: 525–546.

Wright, R. 1999. "Governing—The Human Side of Personnel Management." In P. Carlson and J. Garrett (eds.), *Prison and Jail Administration: Practice and Theory*, pp. 151–157. Gaithersburg, MD: Aspen Publishing.

Wright, R. & W. Saylor. 1992. "Comparison of Perceptions of the Work Environment Between Minority and Non-Minority Employees of the Federal Prison System." *Journal of Criminal Justice* 20, 1: 63–71.

Young, D. & R. Mattuci. 2006. "Enhancing the Vocational Skills of Incarcerated Women Through a Plumbing Maintenance Program." *The Journal of Correctional Education* 57, 2: 126–140.

Zamble, E. & F. Porporino. 1988. *Coping Behavior and Adaption in Prison Inmates*. New York: Springer-Vertag.

Zimbardo, P. 1982. "The Prison Game." In N. Johnston and L.D. Savitz (eds.), *Legal Process and Corrections*, pp. 195–198. New York: Wiley and Sons.

Zimmer, L. 1986. *Women Guarding Men*. Chicago: University of Chicago Press.

Zimmerman, J. 1987. "The Penal Reform Movement in the South During the Progressive Era, 1890–1917." In K. Hall (ed.) *Police, Prison and Punishment*, pp. 462–492. New York: Garland Press.

Zimring, F. & G. Hawkins. 1995. *Incapacitation: Penal Confinement and the Restraint of Crime*. New York: Oxford University Press.

Zimring, F., G. Hawkins, & S. Kamin. 2001. *Punishment and Democracy: Three Strikes and You're Out in California*. Oxford: Oxford University Press.

Zupan, L. 1992. "The Progress of Women Correctional Officers in All-Male Prisons." In I. Moyer (ed.) *The Changing Roles of Women in the Criminal Justice System*, pp. 323–343. Prospect Heights, IL: Waveland.

Index